T0397463

Rethinking American Music

MUSIC IN AMERICAN LIFE

*A list of books in the series appears
at the end of this book.*

Rethinking American Music

*Edited by Tara Browner
and Thomas L. Riis*

**UNIVERSITY OF
ILLINOIS PRESS**
Urbana, Chicago, and Springfield

Publication of this book is supported by the Lloyd
Hibberd Endowment of the American Musicological
Society, funded in part by the National Endowment for
the Humanities and the Andrew W. Mellon Foundation.

Library of Congress Cataloging-in-Publication Data
Names: Browner, Tara, 1960– | Riis, Thomas Laurence.
Title: Rethinking American music / edited by Tara
    Browner and Thomas L. Riis.
Description: Urbana : University of Illinois Press, 2019. |
    Includes bibliographical references and index.
Identifiers: LCCN 2018039541| ISBN 9780252042324
    (hardcover : alk. paper) | ISBN 9780252084102 (pbk. :
    alk. paper)
Subjects: LCSH: Music—United States—History and
    criticism. | Music—Social aspects—United States—
    History.
Classification: LCC ML200 .R46 2019 | DDC 780.973—dc23
    LC record available at https://lccn.loc.gov/2018039541

E-book ISBN 978-0-252-05115-9

For Richard Crawford and Judith McCulloh,
best of mentors and friends

Contents

Acknowledgments

No book with as many contributors as this one could have been made without the help and good will of dozens of people behind the scenes, many of whom are unknown even to the editors over the last decade. So the least we can do is thank those whose names are most immediately before us. We are deeply grateful for the assistance provided by Laurie Matheson, Julie Laut, Thomas Ringo, and Julie Gay of the University of Illinois Press, as well as the editorial board of UIP, whose support has been essential; Sam Arnold-Boyd, our scrupulous indexer; Jordan Watson, whose elegant musical typesetting greatly enhanced a number of chapters; and to the anonymous readers whose positive reactions have cheered us and whose helpful critiques we have endeavored to implement. We are also grateful for the subvention provided by the Lloyd Hibberd Endowment of the American Musicological Society, funded in part by the National Endowment for the Humanities and the Andrew W. Mellon Foundation.

Although this book began as a tribute volume to an inspiring mentor for all of the contributors at one time or another—University of Michigan professor emeritus Richard Crawford—the writers and editors finally wished to produce something greater than the sum of its parts in order to celebrate not only the personal achievement of an individual but also the network of collaborative scholarship that Crawford has always fostered among us. Scholarly teamwork, the standard operating procedure of most contemporary scientific research, seems to have considerably less appeal among working humanists nowadays. This situation is limiting, to say the least. To modestly underline the importance of creative collaboration moving forward, this volume, despite its traditional form and format, has morphed into a more focused yet still diverse set of essays. By exploring a variety of subjects in what we hope are fresh, insightful, and occasionally interconnected ways and by including contributions composed by individuals representing several generations of scholars, we mean to suggest that there are many paths and approaches yet to be found and followed in the fascinating field we all occupy.

Introduction

The study of American music by serious scholars who were willing to consider the producers, products, and consumers of music without hierarchical bias, snobbish condescension, or fealty to the canons of nineteenth-century concert-hall culture is a relatively recent development in the United States. Over twenty years ago Richard Crawford traced the historiography of American music in the hands of such writers as William Hubbard, Louis T. Elson, and John Tasker Howard in *The American Musical Landscape: The Business of Musicianship from Billings to Gershwin* (1993, 2000). And it is in the analyses of Crawford himself, anticipated in a few essential ways by the work of Gilbert Chase, Charles Hamm, and H. Wiley Hitchcock, that we might say American styles and sounds have been allowed to stand on their own two feet in the academic world, as has long been the case among popular audiences. Scholarship since Crawford's comprehensive history, represented by, but not limited to, such works as *The Queer Composition of America's Sound* (2004), by Nadine Hubbs, and *Struggling to Define a Nation* (2008), by Charles Hiroshi Garrett, exemplify contemporary efforts to place American music making within new or heretofore neglected contexts, cognizant of how gender presentation, sexual affinity, coded bias, and racial and ethnic considerations beyond the familiar black-white dichotomy inevitably shift our consciousness about music's meaning and impact in culture.

This volume is conceived as a series of commentaries or glosses about American music broadly understood and defined by Crawford, Chase, Hamm, Hitchcock, Hubbs, Garrett, and others. *Rethinking American Music* presents not a comprehensive story but rather a varied set of chapters that consciously seek to explore *four critical factors* when it comes to the making of music but which are not about either repertory or biography alone. Those factors are the impact of performance, broadly defined; the role of economics, commerce, and patronage—both personal and collective—in the creation of musical objects and events; the importance of personal identity; and how the larger cultural context—community values, ethnic markers, and social relations—determine certain musical results. These factors should not be equated with hermetically sealed boxes, of course, nor are they argued to be procrustean beds. What these chapters seek to illustrate is the network or matrix into which all music is born and within which all music making takes place.

Though far from exhaustive, these collected contributions, it is hoped, will shed light by both their data and their arguments on the expanding scope of American music scholarship as a discipline over the last generation as well as hint at the apparently limitless array of styles or modes claiming American roots and inspiration. A concomitant concern in many of the chapters is the manner by which music is *passed on* and disseminated within listening communities—by individual players, singers, and composers, by teachers, publishers, and social activists, and by recorded and digital media in its various forms, including films. This collection is an overt homage to scholars who have come before the present writers, but it is not meant to suggest that we, or any scholars doing research on American subject matter, see our work as the end of a trend. No one can reliably predict the future, but it seems fair to suggest that American popular music—by whatever means it has been presented and made "popular"—over the course of the last century continues to exert an extraordinary influence across the rest of the globe. That it seems fated to do so for at least a few more generations is reason enough to pursue the lines of research that each of these chapters advances.

Organized within four themes noted above, the chapters within each area are placed in loose chronological order. While written by experts in the field of musicology broadly defined, this collection should appeal to both general and academic audiences with an interest in any sphere of American music. Its various parts will discuss figures in hymnody, concert music, jazz, country music, hip-hop, Tin Pan Alley, and Broadway song and dance, among other types— and American culture in general. Readers coming from the fields of American history, ethnic studies, popular culture, Africana studies, theater, dance, and anthropology, as well as Euro-American musical interactions in the nineteenth century, should also be attracted to this volume. The topics to be found here include many genres and perspectives, but each chapter is focused on specific performers, patrons, works, conditions, or institutions within its cultural context. Each contribution will be discussed in more detail in its individual section introduction.

PART I

Performance

In *The American Musical Landscape*, Richard Crawford examines in a variety of contexts the unique economic and artistic matrix that informs most music-making in the United States, outlining the intertwined roles of composers, performers, teachers, distributors, manufacturers, and writers, as well as the roles of the managers and impresarios and the audiences and consumers who supported them.[1] Performers represent a central point in this web of influences, for (in most instances) it is they who create the sound, whether or not it is mediated by other means. In fact, the role of performers in American music and its evolution from the practices of First Nations and the performances of the earliest colonists to the digital age of the twenty-first century remains an important thread through much of Crawford's scholarship. Emphasis on *performers* is a primary way in which his scholarship is set apart from that of most earlier chroniclers of American music.

If performances of the early settlers filled a mainly private, utilitarian role, with religious texts sung during worship to melodies carried by oral tradition from Europe, the advent of music printing in the 1780s and the establishment of singing schools began to build a unique phenomenon that would have a far-reaching effect on music in the United States: the American audience. As Crawford and other historians have frequently pointed out, the lack of an established tradition of institutional support fostered a unique relationship between the performance and those who consumed it. As Crawford writes, "Without opportunities to sing and play for pay, there can be no career for a performer. The creation of such opportunities is itself an occupation—the arm of musical distribution that brings performers together with audiences."[2] Enter the American musical impresario, an entrepreneur with quite different goals and methods than his European counterpart. Especially after the 1830s and '40s, with the creation of black-face minstrelsy, the rise in popularity of Italian opera, and the foundation of American orchestras, choral societies, and relevant institutions, performers, audiences, and entrepreneurs (or their later incarnations, theatrical managers, booking agents, talent scouts, and the like) remained inextricably linked. Sometimes integrated into this trio and sometimes orbiting about it was the composer, who could be the creator of an inviolable work of art, a completely unknown source (as in oral traditions), the inspiration for a casual musical interpretation, or (as in the case of some improvised traditions) one with the performer.

In some cases, entrepreneurs and audiences demanded from performers little more than light entertainment, sometimes providing (for minstrel shows, especially) music and routines that were already so well-known that audiences could sing along. In other cases, both managers and performers themselves sought to foster spiritual uplift and to educate their audience in what they considered the height of (Western) musical creativity. Whatever the case, the machinery of the music business worked tirelessly to expand performers' audiences and, concurrently, their pocketbooks (as well as those of their supporters).

And machinery it was, indeed. For more than two hundred years technology and performance have remained close partners in American music, from the founding of a domestic sheet-music business in the eighteenth century to the latest digital means of musical delivery. In the nineteenth century, new developments in music printing, transportation, and the telegraph all affected performer's musical lives and touring careers. But it was after 1900 that technology truly became embedded in the experience of performers and those who promoted them and experienced their art. With the advent of the phonograph, radio, film, television, and ultimately electronics, performers could create music that might reach their audiences at a considerable distance. No longer was a performer's career based solely on a particular event at a particular time and location, with established promotional tools in place, as well as a specific audience and venue. As Crawford writes:

To survey such [technological] developments with performers, audiences, and entrepreneurs in mind is to glimpse the shifting ground of their interaction. It is also to recognize that changes in their roles are interrelated: for performers, the evolving function of the public appearance; for audiences, the division into more and more specialized segments; for entrepreneurs, the rise of collective and corporate sponsorship. These changes all involve technology's impact upon communication—its power to capture performances and to circulate them more and more swiftly and widely.[3]

Therefore, after the turn of the twentieth century, a quite different set of scholarly tools need to be brought to bear on the role of performance in American life. The introduction of high-speed digital technology and the creation of whole new categories of laptop-wielding performers in virtual orchestras around the world has created yet another branch of performance art in the twenty-first century, about which new critical perspectives have only begun to take shape.

The chapters in this section cover over a century of American musical history. Not only does the context of each piece differ substantially, but so does the definition and role of the performer. The performer lies at the center of Karen Ahlquist's new investigation (in chapter 1) of a long-standing debate about American music since the early 1800s: the so-called divide between "highbrow" and "lowbrow" culture. American performers—and their constant companions of promoters and audiences—have traditionally been judged not just by critics but also by larger issues of economics and social class, which may hinder a nuanced view of musical art (whether or not it has been described with that phrase) in the United States. Jeffrey Magee's theory (in chapter 2) of a popular trope in musical theater depends on a unique relationship between composers, performers, and audiences, where the artists who create and present a production rely on the attentive listening of theater-goers who will recognize—consciously or not—the subtle evolution of a simple idea into a multilayered concept. For Warren Steel, in chapter 3, the performer and audience are one; singers gather in "convivial" settings such as the home or the lodge hall, with secular repertory suitable for performance outside the worship service. The repertory and accompanying instruction also serve as an educational tool. This is not music for public choral performances, events that would become so widely popular later in the century.

So, the word *performer* and the idea and realization of performance finally embraces a range of participants and perspectives, in public and private spaces. Performance, broadly defined, implies a deed done, an accomplishment, an enactment. It may even imply the fulfillment of an obligation to oneself or one's community. Our common human experience with musical performance can be a powerful unifying force in a divided world.

Notes

1. Richard Crawford, *The American Musical Landscape: The Business of Musicianship from Billings to Gershwin* (Berkeley: University of California Press, 2000). See especially 43–46 and 70–71.

2. Ibid., 71.

3. Ibid., 90–91.

1 Balance of Power

*Music as Art and Social Class
in the Late Nineteenth Century*

KAREN AHLQUIST

I first encountered Lawrence Levine's *Highbrow/Lowbrow: The Emergence of Cultural Hierarchy in America* when it came out in 1988 as I was working on my dissertation.[1] Borders Books in Ann Arbor rushed my order, and I have that hardbound copy still today. It is littered with marginalia and holds pages of notes marked "Levine 6/95" and, another, "5/05." Over twenty-five years, I have been far from alone. Dozens of reviews and hundreds of citations show Levine's wide-ranging and effective presentation of late-nineteenth-century "sacralized culture" resonating with scholars across a broad expanse of fields. *Highbrow/Lowbrow* argues that after the Civil War, elites took control of what had been shared public cultural expression to distinguish and separate themselves from the broader population. This idea brought both approbation and counterarguments. Nonetheless, it has had admirable staying power and still has an affinity with social-class debates prominent in American political life in the twenty-first century.

Levine focuses attention on the complex period between the Civil War and World War I. Economic boom-and-bust cycles that brought poverty and labor violence, westward expansion and the so-called Indian Wars, industrialization, urbanization, massive immigration, racial tension and violence, corporate consolidation, and the growth of a consumer society are among the contemporaneous changes that affected the life of every resident of the United States and many beyond its borders. The period also brought ambitious new institutions, including some of today's most prominent arts organizations. Art museums, art schools and conservatories, performance venues, and orchestras allowed burgeoning cities to offer their publics opportunities for cultural growth and served as sources of civic pride. They are, however, also the organizations seen as instruments of a linked aesthetic and social hierarchy. This idea—that elite-created institutions aimed either to exclude a broader audience or invite it only on its own stuffy terms—grew to mainstream proportions over the course of the twentieth century. Furthermore, in a circular argument, scholars (Levine not among them) have sometimes designated European art music as inherently elite culture in order to use it as evidence of elite preoccupation with social distinction.[2]

It is important here to acknowledge that hierarchies exist, class exists, and power imbalances exist. Nor have questions of power relations played themselves out in musicology. Yet exploring the differences among the aesthetic, ideological, and socioeconomic strands of change uncovers a more comprehensive understanding of music in this troubling period in American history. Pursuing that possibility is my aim in this chapter.

I do so in two ways. First, I use empirical studies to assess assertions of elite motivation in the development of music as art in the late nineteenth century. This approach is not new. At a time when *Highbrow/Lowbrow* could still be called "recent," Ralph Locke described some portrayals of concert life by Levine and others as "bordering on caricature" and issued a call for "a more accurate, multifaceted, and appreciative view of America's music patrons and concertgoers."[3] This call continues to be made (as I have done directly here) and inspire research. Thus, I summarize scholarship that either refutes Levine's contention directly or supplies knowledge that undermines it. At some point, one can imagine research and reassessment attenuating, if not eliminating, its explanatory power.

Second, proceeding chronologically, I examine the influence of foundational theories on assertions about social class and art music in this era. Musicologists in recent years have explored a growing and changing body of cultural theory that has opened new questions and sources for music study. Many of these approaches address music's role in relations of power, which makes them attractive for studying this period in American history. I contend, however, that some of the theorizing has gone beyond provoking new questions to the point of creating a priori answers to them. Assessing the balance between theory and historical knowledge in a piece of scholarship helps us assess a theory's importance to a study's historical conclusions and ultimately to the conclusions themselves. For example, critiquing Levine's discussion of the Germania Orchestra, Nancy Newman comments, "The premises of *Highbrow/Lowbrow* are not particularly advanced in terms of post–World War II cultural theory."[4] I agree: Levine's minimal discussion of his theoretical underpinnings tips the balance in the book toward historical research, thereby facilitating comparison with subsequent research on the question of art music and social class.

Much of the discussion that follows centers on orchestras as purveyors of music presented as art from the end of the Civil War to World War I. Along with opera, orchestras have been widely presented as the linchpins of "classical" music in historical studies, thereby offering a body of scholarly work on which to draw.[5] Interest in the orchestra stimulated a rash of new organizations and venues throughout this period. Although orchestra concerts and repertoire are not meant here to stand in for music as art in general, their public prominence as objects of engagement and commentary brings out many of the interpretative complexities and issues that developed over so-called classical works.

It bears mentioning that the connection between music as art and social hierarchy speaks to only a part of the musical change in the United States in the late nineteenth century. The period also saw the rise of popular music styles and genres that were disseminated commercially. This music only slowly became considered worthy of scholarly attention in its own right and on its own terms. Now, however, comprehensive interpretations of musical change through the nineteenth and twentieth centuries give popular music ample space, reminding us that popular culture in the United Sates was a separate movement of individuals and groups unconcerned with (and in some cases disdainful of) music as art.

Finally, although I critique several scholarly arguments over the course of this chapter, I consider all of the work cited worthy of attention. It all contains the proverbial "grain of truth" and, in most cases, more than that. It meets important standards of serious engagement and influence and therefore belongs in ongoing debates.

American Music History and Theories of Social Class

Scholars of social distinction and social class do not necessarily write about music. Nonetheless, the sociology and social history of music beginning in the 1970s and 1980s have contributed much to relativizing musical values and opening new topics for study. Although sociologists do not necessarily claim to supply a comprehensive understanding of an issue or topic, aspects of musical content, music-making, organization, and reception have been included in music sociology in ways that have affected understandings of music's meaning and use.

Influential contributors to this movement have been British scholars concerned with musical meaning as socially constructed and in particular with theorizing homology between musical and sociopolitical structures. In 1981, for example, John Shepherd summarized universalistic beliefs about music aesthetics that precluded acceptance of this idea. He then argued:

> It is more than possible that the lack of a disposition on the part of musicians and aestheticians to accept the significance of 'serious' music as socially located

is due to the fact that such acceptance would implicitly require a questioning of the social and political structure within which we all live. Not only would it mean accepting that the various forms of jazz, rock, and 'pop' music are equally 'good' as serious forms, but it would also mean accepting the social and moral relativity of the deviant realities they have come to represent and articulate.[6]

Since 1981, when Shepherd wrote this, jazz, rock, and other popular genres have, of course, been widely accepted as worthy of serious consideration, and the field of popular music studies has undermined (one might say *destroyed*) claims about the Western canon as expressing musically the essence or core of the human condition. His project, especially an early, co-authored book, *Whose Music?*, helped open the door for interpretations of music in terms of class distinctions and relations of power among groups.[7]

Among Shepherd's early American critics was the sociologist Paul DiMaggio, whose work is significant here on at least three accounts: he writes about music, about the United States, and on historical topics. Reviewing *Whose Music?*, DiMaggio critiques what he sees as an insufficiency of specifics in its claims of the social basis of musical meaning. He writes, "Responsibility for tonal hegemony is attributed to a murky elite whose interest in the matter is unclear if one does not buy the assertion that an unresolved seventh or a legitimated slurred fifth could shake capitalism to its foundations."[8] Similarly, DiMaggio criticized the work of French sociologist Pierre Bourdieu, whose studies were becoming increasingly available in English around the time Shepherd's appeared, for a lack of specific actors needed to adequately account for social systems or power inequities:

> Since Bourdieu takes as the fundamental problem of sociology the means by which systems of domination persist and reproduce themselves without conscious recognition by a society's members, it follows that any social science based on the subjective perceptions of participants, or on commonsense classifications of social groups or social problems, can only reinforce and confirm the very domination he regards as problematic. Yet explanations of social phenomena that posit the existence of unseen structures are by themselves merely *models* of reality and little more than attractive metaphors, unless one can explain how purposeful, reasoning, self-interested actors contribute, in pursuing their own subjective ends, to the maintenance of these structures.[9]

In other words, a foundation for understanding centered on abstract relationships between, for example, tonality and a system of domination lacks validity unless derived from motivated activity of human beings.

DiMaggio's call for empiricism resonates with historians concerned with drawing conclusions and formulating questions from an ever-growing body of evidence. Recognizing the legitimacy and use-value of historical actors in maintaining or undermining social structures opens space for independent understandings of those structures and music's possible influence on them. However, DiMaggio's call for more concrete evidence than Shepherd or Bourdieu seem to provide calls into question some of his own conclusions about the development of arts organizations in late-nineteenth-century Boston.

Focused on institution-building, DiMaggio marries sociological theory and historical research to analyze interrelationships among members of Brahmin elite groups that created and supported the Boston Symphony Orchestra and the Museum of Fine Arts. It is such relationships, he argues, that determine an individual's motivation for action. For example, he lists the many friends, relatives, and organizational connections between the symphony's founder, Henry Lee Higginson, and other Brahmin families. Then, he asks why Higginson loaned the Museum of Fine Arts $17,000 with no hope of repayment: "Was this because he was on the Board; was it a consequence of Higginson's kinship ties with the Cabots, Perkinses or Lowells; his business alliances with Kidder or Endicott; his club friendship with Norton; Harvard ties to the Eliots? The range of possibilities renders the question trivial and illustrates how closely knit was Higginson's world."[10]

DiMaggio makes little reference to the artistic content presented at either the museum or the orchestra's performances. That is, he makes no claim that there is anything specifically elite in the art itself. Instead, he focuses on the Brahmins' position in Boston's social fabric and addresses competing interpretations of their motivation for founding high-art institutions:

> The Brahmins were a status group, and as such they strove towards exclusivity, towards the definition of a prestigious culture that they could monopolize as their own. Yet they were also a social class, and they were concerned, as is any dominant social class, with establishing hegemony over those they dominated. . . . Certainly, the cultural capitalists . . . were wise enough to understand the impossibility of socializing the masses in institutions from which they effectively were barred.

The Brahmins, having created and therefore owning the museum and the orchestra, were better served, as DiMaggio puts it, by using them to legitimate their status by sharing the culture "at least partially. The tension between monopolization and hegemony, between exclusivity and legitimation, was a constant counterpoint to the efforts at classification of American urban elites."[11] Even as he answers the criticism he levels against Shepherd's homology between tonality and social domination by studying the Brahmins, DiMaggio uses theoretical categories from his own field to explain the motivation of Higginson and his associates.

Levine took DiMaggio's Boston argument nationwide: Types of creative expression (such as Shakespeare's plays and opera) had been part of a national common culture for much of the nineteenth century, he asserts, only to be usurped after the Civil War by elites eager to display their (and their country's) cultural maturity while creating high-art institutions to control and remake the broader public in their image. In DiMaggio's formulation, Levine emphasizes hegemony over exclusivity. He also cites and quotes DiMaggio with approbation, calling his account of the founding of the Boston Museum of Fine Arts "a fine example of the process by which art museums in America became sacralized."[12] Levine presents "sacralization" quite literally by emphasizing connections Protestant clergymen made between art and religion.[13] He also extends the model of art as an object of worship briefly into the twentieth century, noting that the idea of sacralized culture allows artists themselves to claim legitimation on grounds of merit. He specifies photographers and film directors, but he might have included musicians as well.[14]

DiMaggio gave *Highbrow/Lowbrow* a glowing review.[15] The book also resonated with scholars who took popular culture seriously and with the tradition of rich contextual studies of American music from Oscar Sonneck to Richard Crawford.[16] It put a dent in the romantic notion of "classical" music as inherently superior to other styles and genres and worthy of worship. It spread the term "sacralization" of culture far into the academic vocabulary. Most important, perhaps, for this essay, it presented relatively little explicit dependence on theoretical formulations to undergird the author's points but instead uses his own and others' research to amass evidence. Such an approach facilitates comparison between *Highbrow/Lowbrow* and studies that may support, supplement, temper, or undermine its claims. By putting theoretical underpinnings at arm's length, Levine helps us more easily assess his arguments from a perspective that takes additional historical knowledge into account.

The influence of DiMaggio's and Levine's work, which emphasizes the essential class character of music as art in the late nineteenth century, has been ongoing for a generation. DiMaggio's Boston essay has been republished at least seven times and as recently as 2003.[17] Scholars of class and class formation in the field of history draw on their work. But how and to what extent does research since their time lead to questions about their conclusions? Answering that question has occupied scholars of music.

Research and Critique

Since Locke's 1993 salvo, other music scholars have joined the critique of Levine's and DiMaggio's assertions. They address additional contributing factors in the emergence of music as art in the late nineteenth century, a needed discussion because (as will be noted herewith) elite funding was essential to many of the arts institutions developing at this time. They show nonfinancial forms of participation undermining the notion that funding in and of itself establishes ownership of the cultural work produced. They temper the idea that artistic complexity and social position can simply be mapped onto each other—that is, the idea that "classical" music and elitism are necessarily intertwined. Dislodging that interconnection as an absolute is, however, not difficult, and critics of (especially) Levine have done so. The result allows for an understanding that does justice to complex interactions within a rapidly changing society, hinders reductionism, and helps convey the role of the music itself in its own perpetuation. It also reinforces the value of empirical research that can confirm or weaken a theoretically based assertion.

First, then, who is elite and who is not? It depends on who asks the question and the city under discussion. DiMaggio equates the Brahmins with the Boston's elite; on New York, Michael McGerr uses well-publicized parties of the late-century socialite Cornelia Bradley Martin to exemplify the conspicuous consumption of the city's "Upper Ten Thousand"—a term that extends back to the Jacksonian era. Similarly, Julia Rosenbaum and Sven Beckert open *The American Bourgeoisie* with a depiction of summer homes in Newport, Rhode Island. The New York elites, many of them celebrities in all but the name, received serious criticism in the early years of sociology as Thorstein Veblen's "leisure class." They also received mockery in the press similar to that heaped on the wealthy beginning in Jackson's day.[18]

These characterizations make it harder to delimit a middle class whose values define the term "Victorian" but whose lives had traits in common with those of the wealthy. In a comprehensive account of the urban American middle class from 1760 to 1900, Stuart Blumin takes note of education, white-collar employment, associations, and department-store shopping, among other indicators of "middling" status.[19] Levine himself draws on Walt Whitman to acknowledge this social group: "Whitman . . . placed his hopes for the creation of a classless, democratic culture in the leadership of the new 'middling' groups—'men and women with occupations, well-off owners of houses and acres, and with cash in the bank.'"[20] Characteristics commonly described as Victorian included hard work, thrift, self-help, personal discipline, modesty, propriety, and dedication to family life. While maintaining and demonstrating such values required a certain level of income, ostentation was not encouraged, and even many wealthy Americans chose to live within their means. In Europe such people would often be called bourgeois.

Derek Scott reminds us that in Europe the term *bourgeoisie* referred to non-aristocrats—that is, people without inherited titles. He also notes that the power of the aristocracy was on the wane. In London, Paris, and Vienna, he says, cultural power was increasingly wielded from below the equivalent of the American "Upper Ten."[21] That difference undoubtedly makes it harder in the United States to focus attention on a broad middle of society separate from an upper class whose members cannot be readily identified. Thus the social position of critics, educators, journalists, professionals in music and other fields, religious leaders, and other educated Americans who supported music as art can be harder to make clear than that of their European counterparts.

Focused attention on "middling classes" helps highlight circumstances in which they initiated change and elites followed. Such an assertion may in fact be more plausible than its opposite. For example, social historian Sven Beckert's study *The Monied Metropolis* (2001) uses the term *bourgeoisie* to denote New York City's upper class and explicitly excludes "the professionals, experts, and intellectuals" with whom the bourgeoisie had a "complex relationship." Beckert then draws on DiMaggio and Levine (and no other sources) to argue that the bourgeoisie used cultural institutions "to distinguish the city's economic elite from the lower classes [and] exert cultural hegemony over middle-class New Yorkers who strove to live up to the cultural standards of their betters."[22] If, however, the bourgeoisie is defined in economic terms only, without education or cultural interests taken into account, it is hard to conclude that the middle class, to which professionals and intellectuals belonged, aped rather than created these standards.

Including social aspiration *among other reasons* for the growth of formal, sacralized musical culture in the United States requires incorporating a broader range of current knowledge of the process. Some of these reasons have had ample research devoted to them and will be familiar to students of American musical life in this period. I mention briefly a few of them here.

Germans and Germanophile Romanticism

While not qualifying as bourgeois on Beckert's terms, many nineteenth-century Americans received a musical education. Some of them chose to promote music as art and/or earn a living by performing or teaching it. The most important ideas that supported music as art drew on German romantic attitudes and thought. Holders of this form of cultural capital (as Pierre Bourdieu has put it) were immigrants from German-speaking Europe—few, if any, of whom belonged to elite groups. Michael Broyles reminds us, however, that Germanocentric romanticism came to Boston well before the waves of German immigration. Either directly from German literary sources or through transcendentalism, Boston writers such as Margaret Fuller and John Sullivan Dwight took on and espoused an idealistic attitude toward music, one consistent with that city's Puritan tradition.[23] In a similar vein, Nancy Newman emphasizes Dwight's writing as imbued with a social utopianism that linked music's power with unity and order in a democratic society.[24] In New York, early meeting minutes of the cooperative New York Philharmonic (1842) show idealism in the practical terms of what the members wanted to play and bring to the public. To offer intellectual enjoyment, they espoused music in the larger forms for orchestra alone, with Beethoven's works at the center.[25] As the century progressed, these musicians and their successors learned new music by composers such as Wagner and (later) Brahms along with their audience, exactly as in Europe. In so doing, they offered opportunities to hear instrumental music sacralized—at the center of a secular religion.

Many of the Germans also taught. By the early twentieth century, they had established conservatories and given non-German Americans skills needed to enter the musical profession. They also earned the respect of nonmusician organizers who needed high quality musical leadership for new institutions and concert halls. Many examples demonstrate these musicians' success. In 1884 conductor Leopold Damrosch enabled the new Metropolitan Opera to produce a second season by successfully proposing performances in German to the board of directors.[26] In spite of financial and aesthetic controversies, the patrons of the Cincinnati May Festival and the Chicago [now Symphony] Orchestra stuck with their founder-conductor, Theodore Thomas, until his death in 1905. That year, Frank Damrosch (Leopold's son) enlisted Princeton University president Woodrow Wilson to speak at the opening of the new Institute of Musical Art, today's Juilliard School. For many years, Fanny Bloomfield-Zeisler performed solo recitals and concertos with major orchestras in the United States and Europe. There are dozens more.

These musicians from German-speaking Europe taught Americans who supported them that their leadership in the service of music was essential to its success and that they were therefore entitled to the respect due artists of distinction. Diplomatic historian Jessica Gienow-Hecht calls these musicians "cultural agents" and "envoys." She writes, "Foreign artists and administrators played a central role in the United States' quest for high culture, artists whose lives for the most part defied any notion of elitism."[27] The legacy of these musicians (Gienow-Hecht discusses mainly Germans) is apparent in much of the country in the twenty-first century. If there is a single group of original "owners" of the music and thereby holders of cultural capital to spend, it is they.

Civic Competition, Events, and Performance Spaces

With Germans as artistic guides, members of elite groups after the Civil War began to invest in venues and institutions for concert performance. And indeed, from this point on elites participated in the institutional establishment of music as art. Many of them were on the receiving end of the idealistic art rhetoric common at the time. George Templeton Strong (1820–75), president of the New York Philharmonic, was a serious listener and critic, as his voluminous diary attests. Henry Lee Higginson, who founded the Boston Symphony Orchestra and funded it until 1918, the year before his death, had studied music in Vienna. Charles Fay, who led the effort to establish the Chicago Symphony Orchestra, was the sister of pianist Amy Fay, whose book, *Music Study in Germany*, recounted her European musical education. Both Higginson and Fay (less so Strong) developed relationships with conductors who could provide the musical substance and guide the nonmusicians as needed.

The belief in the value of art fostered its use as a marker of local and national progress. Sources show intercity competition for reputation nationwide in artistic and non-artistic endeavors alike. A prominent example of the latter was baseball. The first professional team, the Cincinnati Red Stockings, was successful enough to encourage professional teams in other cities and, in 1876, the National League. Although privately owned, the teams were named for their home cities, and Americans followed the sport in the press and attended games in large numbers.[28] Published accounts from travelers and journalists, along with the growth of tourism, served as sources of a city's reputation and beliefs about its character.[29] Even as some popular writers exposed local political corruption, crime, poverty, and public-health challenges, others focused on local resources and offered evidence of prosperity and well-being among the population. The latter evidence included public access to, and participation in, "respectable" amenities such as parks and gardens, theaters, musical performances, and museums. Establishing more and better amenities was central to reputation enhancement and outdoing the competition.

Exhibitions, festivals, and fairs on a large scale, locally produced and funded, served the competitive imperative and brought music and art to a broad audience. Among them were the Civil War sanitary fairs, which raised funds for Union troops; the 1864 fair in Philadelphia, for example, introduced that city to Theodore Thomas as a conductor and premiered Philadelphia composer William Henry Fry's opera *Notre Dame de Paris*.[30] Dozens of such fairs exposed Union supporters to music as an art created for focused listening. In the same vein, from their inception, mechanics' and industrial exhibitions had art departments and musical accompaniment. These events developed into the early American world's fairs in Philadelphia (1876) and Chicago (1893). It was festivals, however, that brought large-scale music-making to broad publics nationwide. The triennial festival of Boston's Handel and Haydn Society was the first to celebrate music and the composers who created it. Initiated on short notice in 1857, it produced *Messiah*, *Elijah*, and *Creation* over two days with an orchestra of seventy-eight players.[31] Patrick Gilmore, who led the Massachusetts 24th Infantry regiment band in the Civil War, organized and conducted a gargantuan festival in New

Orleans to celebrate Louisiana's return to the Union in 1864. He followed up with the National Peace Jubilee in 1869 in Boston and another in 1872. The largest of these events took place in barnlike halls built specifically for them, enlisted thousands of participants, and—perhaps most important—focused national attention on music in a particular city.

The Boston jubilees were not universally praised, and other cities looked to create festivals (and eventually civic organizations) on a more refined model. The Cincinnati May Festival, first held in 1873 with Theodore Thomas as music director, received considerable praise for the quality and scale of its performances. By May 1882, Thomas was able to run successive festivals in Chicago, Cincinnati, and New York with his orchestra and many of the same soloists, supplementary players, and compositions. Only the choruses were local.[32] This model served Thomas and his orchestra for similar events over the many years they traveled.

Festival and exhibition venues were not always permanent. Because of their temporary construction and large size, they sometimes concerned listeners for their safety. At the first Peace Jubilee, for example, one noted "a tempestuous storm of stamping, cheering, waving hats and handkerchiefs, . . . so overwhelming in its demonstration that timid souls have said their prayers and trusted blindly in the stability of wooden rafters."[33] Similarly, other concert settings—many of them new—received reviews from both ordinary listeners and the press. Even a well-constructed building could be problematic. The first Cincinnati May Festival, in 1873, took place over a rainy week that brought delays and interruptions in performances drowned out by water hitting the Saengerhalle's tin roof. The hall, replaced after only six years, had quickly proved unsuitable for close listening.[34]

Dedicated space honored the music to be performed in it, and building was something one could do or support even without appreciating a Beethoven symphony. Halls from the nineteenth century still in operation include the Philadelphia Academy of Music and Mechanics' Hall in Worcester, Massachusetts (both 1857); Troy, New York, Savings Bank Music Hall (1875); Cincinnati Music Hall (1878); Chicago Auditorium (1889); and Carnegie Hall (1891). Most of these halls are large by today's standards. Expectations of large attendance— build it and they will come—seems to have blended with the belief that a broad public could, and would, recognize the value of the music to be experienced and the importance of showing a city's cultural acumen. Having the means to build designated spaces ultimately meant that elite Americans controlled the physical surroundings of a performance. What they did not control, however, was either a performance's artistic or financial success or the event itself. And in no case could they control the effect on audience members individually or collectively.

Experiencing Performance

New venues brought new ways to experience performance,[35] including the tighter standards of decorum often associated with elite control. Taking note of power imbalances between the top and bottom of society, scholars have sometimes linked arts organizations, poor relief, education, and religious outreach with controlling activities such as policing and prisons.[36] Most of their accounts criticize attempts to reform or police the behavior of individuals and groups lower on the social scale. John Kasson uses Theodore Thomas's training of his players to disciplined performance and audiences to silent listening as an example.[37] Evidence exists, however, that decorum and elite ownership were not necessarily equated. Kasson notes that in the late century, demands for decorum in popular entertainment also increased. He mentions amusement parks and focuses mainly on early film, arguing that movie houses encouraged the degree of decorum maintained in concert halls but offered entertainment of interest to a broad public.[38] Moreover, regardless of a performance's setting, decorum had an additional motivation: it let people see and hear a performance by minimizing audience distractions.

The halls themselves required attentive listening. Before amplification, hearing depended on the acoustic properties of sometimes large performance spaces, and commentators sometimes noted that hearing could be difficult. Large venues such as exhibition halls and armories, not to mention outdoor areas, were conducive to one's hearing neither the speaking nor the singing voice, nor strings. Comments on a space's ability to project speakers or music runs through remarks on large-scale events such as the Boston Peace Jubilees and the Philadelphia Centennial Exhibition opening ceremony. Advertising for new concert halls touted their acoustic properties, while diary comments noted specific seats the diarists preferred.[39] Expecting those present to sit or stand quietly privileged an interest in attention to the presentation itself.

Audience members could also *see* a performance regardless of their ability to hear or understand the music. For listeners not fully tutored in music presented as art, the idea of the orchestra as a vast machine not only reinforced beliefs about US technological progress but also could bridge the gap between a new musical style and a novice listener's skills. George Frederick Root said as much: listeners could watch "the bows of the violins moving together with automatic precision, the perfect crescendos and diminuendos, the astounding [s]forzandos, the bewitching pianissimos, and all the consummate mechanism of a model orchestra[, . .] the conductor and the working of the machinery."[40] Seeing and hearing the music being manufactured, as it were, Root argued, could help audience members begin to understand an individual work. Walt Whitman agreed. Having marveled at the motion of the famous Corliss steam engine at the 1876 Centennial Exhibition in Philadelphia, he also remarked of the orchestra, "It did me good to watch the violinists drawing their bows so masterly—every motion a study."[41] Audience members who remarked on the visual aspects of a performance help us understand the many ways they could perceive musical content and meaning.

Focused attention with the ear was most important for music designed to challenge the listener's skills—Theodore Thomas performed Bach regularly, for example—but even the most difficult works could usually be understood in terms of emotion. Jessica Gienow-Hecht highlights emotion as the main bridge builder between German repertoire and the audience. In performance, she writes, the musician "combined two characteristics—masculinity and public emotions—that were otherwise incompatible in Victorian America. . . . The German symphony . . . reflected both feelings and military precision." That combination, she concludes, "became socially acceptable to Victorian men."[42] Similarly, Peter Rabinowitz notes that reviews of performances by composer and pianist Louis Moreau Gottschalk often criticized his music for its emotional appeal to women.[43] Taken together, Rabinowitz and Gienow-Hecht suggest that gender was a more important social distinction this music created than class, even though much of the music could in fact be comprehended through its affective content.

Another approach to music and emotion comes from Daniel Cavicchi in *Listening and Longing*. Cavicchi draws on diaries from the northeastern United States to trace an increased interest in listening to music, rather than making it, as a central mode of musical engagement. He finds listening experiences, some of them described in detail, ranging from chance encounters with a band in the street to formal orchestra concerts. Although he asserts that "high" art could serve social ambition, he also shows active participation through emotional involvement in listening across class and gender lines, thereby supporting an assertion about individual agency: "To see participation in a concert as an audience member as merely an example . . . of encroaching passivity egregiously reduces the significance of what was happening."[44] Together, Gienow-Hecht and Cavicchi highlight the capacity of the German-centered art repertoire to reach and communicate to large numbers of Americans and their willingness to embrace it on their own terms.

Theodore Thomas himself contributed to this way of thinking. His quarter-century of touring exposed thousands of people to orchestra performances on train routes that became known as the "Thomas highway." One such person was Whitman: his compliment to the orchestra quoted above was addressed to Thomas's ensemble. The quality and precision of his orchestra and its performances astounded reviewers wherever it traveled. Sublime in scale and finesse, the modern orchestra was a marvelous thing to witness. New ways of experiencing music and the orchestra's wide availability encouraged interest in its "establishment"—an attractive object of civic aspiration and one that listeners could be expected to understand and support.

By including the listener's experience in their arguments, Gienow-Hecht, Cavicchi, and Rabinowitz undermine the belief that late-nineteenth-century listening in formal settings such as concerts was passive and bound by oppressive rules of behavior that imposed elite control.[45] One also remembers that attendance at concerts was voluntary and by the end of the century competed with myriad popular entertainments whose etiquette was as particular as that of a symphony orchestra performance. By then it was understood that music worth hearing intellectually and emotionally was worth conscious and practiced attention.

From this perspective, the terms *high* and *higher*, which were used repeatedly by nineteenth-century advocates of symphonies and other concert pieces, do not necessarily connect music as art (even "sacralized" art) with high social class. Thomas is a prominent example: as Richard Crawford notes, his programs were designed to ease the audience into attentiveness with attractive and accessible pieces and to embed the more difficult works within that framework. This successful approach required a repertory that "aimed to please while also extending the reach of [an audience's] taste." One recalls Mozart remarking that three of his piano concertos had something to offer both the novice and the experienced listener; Thomas's biographer, Ezra Schabas, calls his programming "a mixture of daring and prudence."[46] Crawford also reminds us that this approach was necessary for orchestras dependent on public patronage through the purchase of tickets.[47] As Boston Symphony Orchestra conductor Arthur Nikisch remarked in 1893, "[Art music is] the last material in the world which anybody would use pour passer le temps. . . . You can't get people to sit through it merely that they may elbow some local leader of fashion and be counted 'in the swim.'"[48]

Joseph Horowitz has made this point emphatically and often, especially on New York and Boston. On New York, he details the reception of Wagner's music, showing not only its accessibility to the public but also the ecstatic response from audience members, especially women. As sacralized culture—as art religion whose adherents were impassioned (Horowitz's word)—Wagner's music brought non-elite audience members into the new house at the Metropolitan, in turn enabling it to pay its bills.[49] Of the opera's nine seasons in German, Horowitz writes, "A religious silence was enforced: every noise from the boxes was shushed by less affluent patrons downstairs and up."[50] On the Boston Symphony's founder, Henry Higginson, he addresses Levine by name: "Lawrence Levine and others have depicted [Higginson] and his Symphony patrons as essentially conservative and elitist, staid and authoritarian." He goes on to depict Higginson as steeped in the music of Beethoven and similar composers after the manner of journalist

Margaret Fuller and some of Cavicchi's diarists. He shows Higginson eager to share that music with the public.[51] And finally, he offers an excerpt of an 1889 Higginson address to a Boston Symphony audience:

> Why is the hall so crowded? Why do so many listeners of all ages sit on the steps and stand in the aisles each week and each year? They do not come there to please Mr. Gericke [the conductor] or me; they do not come twenty miles to show their good clothes; they come to hear the music. . . . You and I know that very well. That audience is not from the Back Bay or from any particular set of people. They are town folks and country folks, and they come to hear the music at the hands of Mr. Gericke and his Orchestra.[52]

We can either take Higginson at his word or accept the assertions of his elite motivation, but not both.

Philanthropy and Progressivism

Higginson was not the first American to offer support for public musical performance. Financial backing dates at least from 1869, when the first Boston Peace Jubilee's expenses were underwritten by a guarantee fund. Philanthropy and local fundraising built Cincinnati's Music Hall (1878) and, most famously, created the Boston Symphony Orchestra. By the time Americans had built dedicated performance spaces and established the orchestras intended to exist in perpetuity, music as art had received ample philanthropic support. Higginson's financing of the BSO became the envy of musical interests and musicians in cities nationally.[53] In Chicago, the orchestra's earliest supporters (1891) included meatpacker Philip Armour, retailer Marshall Field, farm equipment manufacturer Cyrus McCormick, and railroad-car builder George Pullman. Historian Peter Gay remarks that these men learned quickly enough that a large orchestra was an expensive operation not likely to produce profits like those of their business enterprises. "Thus onetime contributors became permanent sponsors," Gay writes, "caught in the silken trap of the civic self-esteem they had so actively promoted."[54] In Cincinnati, the symphony's first board consisted entirely of women from the Ladies' Musical Club, which had managed local performances of the Boston Symphony and other prominent artists. Led by Helen Herron Taft (Mrs. William Howard Taft), the women solicited contributions in amounts as small as five dollars to get the orchestra off the ground and contracted with Frank Van der Stucken as music director.[55] Other female patrons of orchestras, organizations, and individuals fill Ralph P. Locke and Cyrilla Barr's *Cultivating Music in America*. Even the New York Philharmonic, founded in 1842 as a musicians' cooperative, was reorganized as a nonprofit corporation with a nonmusician board of directors in 1909.[56] Supported by modern patrons, orchestras offered the public reliable performances of old and new music in respectable settings at moderate cost. Orchestras also served as markers of successful local efforts to offer cultural amenities in national comparison.

Some of the beliefs that inspired musical philanthropy may well be considered musical progressivism avant la lettre. Although an early-twentieth-century movement, progressivism incorporated attitudes and trends that had spanned much of the nineteenth. In her study of musical progressives in Los Angeles, Catherine Parsons Smith finds the rhetoric of secular religion prominent among that city's musicians and especially music teachers. Central to that creed was access: Smith points to the successful but short-lived People's Orchestra, which in 1913 offered thirty concerts at low prices, even as the Los Angeles Philharmonic, managed by an impresario for profit, offered only six.[57] Similarly, Derek Vaillant begins his study of musical progressivism in Chicago with Theodore Thomas's popular Summer Night Concerts in the late 1870s.[58] On these terms, orchestras in Boston and Cincinnati also exemplified progressive attempts to overcome barriers to concert attendance, as did most of Thomas's career.[59]

Musical progressives participated in a social, political, and economic reform movement to mitigate the power of corporate titans such as J. P. Morgan, John D. Rockefeller, Cornelius Vanderbilt, and Andrew Carnegie and the politicians who enabled them to exert extraordinary economic control over American society. Progressivism was also a rejection of the ostentatious lives of such men and their families, whose largesse could even be read as unseemly. In 1896 Philip H. Goepp wrote on Philadelphia's musical life, "In these days we are wont to solve every problem with the cheque of rich individuals."[60] Although Goepp's interest was wide involvement in art music, he also implicitly denies the worth of contributions from those able to offer foundational support. With "rich individuals" widely disparaged, the impetus for musical progressivism came from members of the white, American-born or assimilated middle class, including musicians, members of musical clubs, music teachers, social workers, and journalists who believed in the uplifting, assimilating power of "good" music and the broad population's entitlement to experience it. The activities of musical progressives in schools, settlement houses, and community organizations came with a mass of ideology and advocacy centered on Western art music and American patriotism, which reached from urban immigrant and "ethnic" neighborhoods to the halls of Congress.[61]

If progressives disparaged the mores of the wealthiest Americans, including their purported musical habits, what was the "good" music they wanted to reach "the people"? The most often *excluded* genre was ragtime. Ragtime, of course, originated among African Americans, who were rarely the object of progressives' projects. Instead, they were left in an inferior political and social position, segregated by law or custom from the white "mainstream." Ragtime also exemplified the burgeoning commercial popular-music industry, a frequent object of progressive scorn. Progressives favored music they believed could unify Americans through participation and listening opportunities: classical music, folk music of the United States and Europe, and patriotic songs. They organized concert performances that sometimes included music from opera, but they did not expose their charges to opera itself. Rather, as World War I approached, they redoubled their efforts to assimilate immigrants and members of the working class into what they believed was the American way of life—the melting pot. For all their faults, however, these middle-class progressive leaders carried out the most widespread and clearly articulated use of music for social purposes between the Civil War and World War I.

Familiarizing Americans with the idea of music as art took the entire nineteenth century. Participants in the process included native-born and immigrant citizens, visiting artists and local musicians, advocates (especially writers), teachers and their students, entrepreneurs, philanthropists, and listeners of the upper, middle, and sometimes working classes. Music as art did not interest everyone, and it could be met with disapproval or even disdain. Nor were competent performances always available beyond urban areas. Yet it established a place in the national cultural matrix, expressed American cultural competition with Europe, served an abiding interest in music itself, and provided a source for a variety of social, aesthetic, and moral controversies. Social controversies were prominent in public discourse. Nonetheless, the evidence outlined here establishes that the social issues were not settled in favor of any one class, group, or "set." Instead, the evidence and many questions have allowed scholars to challenge arguments focused on class alone.

Shades of Gray

In his afterword to *American Orchestras in the Nineteenth Century*, Ronald Walters compares the book's individual essays with general histories of the period: "White hats and black hats remain in such [historical] accounts (as here), but gray hats are more common."[62] Historians of musical progressivism Campbell, Smith, and Vaillant, for example, acknowledge the gray hats worn by the individuals and groups in their studies. Like the progressives themselves, these authors distinguish between social and aesthetic-moral meaning, thereby implicitly rejecting the axiom that cultural production at the top of the critic's hierarchy is necessarily owned by those at the top of the socioeconomic one. Paul DiMaggio says as much: his historical sociology of the arts in Boston acknowledges of the late century that "it seems certain from contemporary accounts (and sheer arithmetic) that many of [the audience members] were middle class." He also notes that the Museum of Fine Arts was swamped with visitors on its scheduled free-admission days.[63] Simply put, connections between "high" art and the motivations of black-hatted elitists are best established and contextualized where they are found, rather than merely assumed.

The notion of assumptions takes us back to the early work of John Shepherd, along with scholars whose premises draw on layers of theory. For example, Steven Baur uses the concept of hegemony to imbed nineteenth-century power imbalances more deeply in the realm of cultural theory than does either Levine or DiMaggio.[64] In an article on Felix Mendelssohn's music in the United States, whose main points appear in the *Grove Dictionary of American Music*, he uses hegemony as defined by Italian political and cultural theorist Antonio Gramsci.[65] Hegemony, Baur writes, "is exacted internally through intellectual and moral leadership, which promote subordinate-class consent by molding personal convictions into alignment with prescriptive norms."[66] He continues, "Gramsci's notion of the historical bloc—any group of individuals and institutions that coalesce around commonly held values, which tend to reinforce, whether consciously or not, established economic, social, or cultural hierarchies—provides a mechanism by which to conceptualize the phenomenon of social domination without making claims or assumptions concerning the intentionality of the various participants."[67] These statements distinguish Baur's work from that of DiMaggio, Levine, and the music historians cited here. Baur holds that commonly held values are those of the dominant (in other words, most powerful) group and, perhaps more important, that dominant individuals and groups do not necessarily intend to enforce their domination. The motivations and specific actions of DiMaggio's Brahmins, Levine's elites, and philanthropists such as Higginson are, at a fundamental level, rendered moot.

Baur's argument on music's role in hegemony draws on work by Christopher Small, although it could well have used the early work of John Shepherd to which DiMaggio objected. Baur demonstrates that Mendelssohn's music is as well crafted, effective, and affirmative as any concert music Americans heard in the late nineteenth century. Based on nineteenth-century writing in support of Protestant (or Victorian) values, he argues that the popular oratorio *Elijah* was a call to hard work and submission to "established authorities."[68] He then backs up this assertion with musical description and analysis, calling the contrapuntal style of the overture "labored" and the modulations in the chorus "Yet doth the Lord" "dutiful."[69] These descriptors do support his contention. However, the music does not: both movements benefit from the composer's wide knowledge of Bach and Handel honed over his conducting career. His experience allowed him to use the old techniques in appropriate places, as here in brisk tempos, to high dramatic effect. Moreover, the use of counterpoint in an oratorio chorus commonly presents the singers as a collective voice drawn from the individual vocal parts, in this case crying out, "His wrath will pursue us till they destroy us!" Neither counterpoint nor particular modulations are markers of labor or duty in and of themselves. Further, Baur omits discussion of the six-section sequence in which Elijah alone stands up to the priests of Baal, the golden calf worshiped by the Philistines. Twice the Philistine chorus shouts, "Hear and answer!" to the golden god, and Mendelssohn responds with silence, thereby asserting that their god does not exist. Elijah the prophet and *Elijah* as a whole are at their most powerful when he is presented as bravely resisting imposed power rather than submitting to it.

Baur is on firmer ground analyzing examples of the composer's tonal processes (including the overture to *A Midsummer Night's Dream* in addition to *Elijah*). Nonetheless, he connects "common-practice" tonality with "bourgeois values by virtue of [its] reliance on teleological organizational paradigms that emphasize continuous striving toward specific goals, all within an ordered, hierarchical framework."[70] Anyone with a grasp of tonal idioms can appreciate their teleological features and name pieces (some of Beethoven's come to mind) whose use of tonality sets out to make listeners stand up and cheer. One can analyze these practices and marvel at tonality's power as used in myriad styles. But such analyses are insufficient as statements of the music's meaning in the culture that has created it; if they were, it would be plausible to denounce the oppressiveness immanent in many of tonality's most elaborate examples. It would then hardly matter whether nineteenth-century elites led the middle class to accept their culture or the educated middle-class showed them it was worthy of their support. Or whether the late-century movement toward decorum in performance spaces happened in venues that drew and admitted non-elite audiences. Or who (if anyone) wore a black or a white hat at a given time.

Research on music in the United States is massive and continues to grow. For the nineteenth century, merely incorporating new pieces of evidence into a narrative or an argument can be daunting. And yet, ongoing attention to historiographic issues both serves as a sign of a mature field and puts current interests and narratives into a context of other possibilities.[71] It may also help us identify and choose whether to participate in a paradigm shift and dislodge entrenched narratives that can inhibit research incompatible with them.[72]

On social class, compelling new scholarship in the field of history invites exploration.[73] We can acknowledge the difficulties imposed on many in the United States by members of the top 1 percent at the end of the nineteenth century and still question the idea that formal musical culture and its music served only elite ownership and control of society. Examining that idea is important for the independence of mind of scholars in our field, for our leadership in presenting music and its practices to readers across disciplines and to the public at large, and for the value our knowledge offers toward understanding the American past.

Finally, the more musicologists communicate on the same discursive plane as historians, the more broadly their work may be read. Recent articles by Jane Fulcher and Celia Applegate explore developments in a "new cultural history of music," through which music offers avenues into complex questions that today interest historians and musicologists alike.[74] Included are various theories of culture, most of them lightly worn, thereby making visible—and communicable in both directions—the gray hats worn by denizens of the musical past.

The notion that music, when used as art, is inherently elitist will probably never entirely disappear from American society. No amount of knowledge of the music or its performance settings in the past will counter such thinking. Simply put, too many populists benefit (if only psychologically) from separating themselves from such music and from scholars, whose interests they can paint as outside the mainstream. For that reason, if for no other, it remains vital to remind anyone who will listen that someone else's beliefs about (in this case) music are not necessarily information about it.

Notes

1. Levine, *Highbrow/Lowbrow*.

2. Holbrook, Weiss, Habich, "Class-Related Distinctions"; DiMaggio, "Cultural Entrepreneurship." DiMaggio's article is discussed later in this chapter.

3. Locke, "Music Lovers," 151, 150. Locke expands his ideas in "Paradoxes of the Woman" and *Cultivating Music in America*, chapter 10. For additional commentary on Locke's article, see Ahlquist, "Mrs. Potiphar at the Opera."

4. Newman, *Good Music for a Free People*, 114.

5. Opera demonstrates a range of issues that overlap with the orchestra's but are by no means alike. Opera performances, with their theatrical associations and venues, high-cost singers, and sometimes-controversial plots, took place more often thanks to traveling troupes that presented short seasons in local theaters. See Dizikes, *Opera in America*; Preston, *Opera on the Road*; Horowitz, *Wagner Nights*; Ottenberg, *Opera Odyssey*; Ahlquist, *Democracy at the Opera*; Kirk, *American Opera*; Martin, *Verdi in America*.

6. Shepherd, "Toward a Sociology of Musical Styles," 124.

7. Shepherd, Virden, Vulliamy, and Wishart, *Whose Music?*

8. DiMaggio, review of *Whose Music?* 753.

9. DiMaggio, "On Bourdieu," 1461–62. Bourdieu's influence in historical studies has increased as his work has appeared in English. Musicologists have used aspects of his work to interpret relations in "symbolic power" that allow for nuanced, contextualized interpretations of power relations. See, for example, Fulcher, "Symbolic Domination."

10. DiMaggio, "Cultural Entrepreneurship," 47.

11. Ibid., 48.

12. Levine, *Highbrow/Lowbrow*, 151. On DiMaggio's Boston study, see also 189 and 241.

13. Levine, *Highbrow/Lowbrow*, 150.

14. Ibid., 168.

15. DiMaggio, review of Levine, *Highbrow/Lowbrow*.

16. As late as 1993, Crawford nonetheless suggested that room for historical agents other than composers must be explicitly opened up (*American Musical Landscape*, 85).

17. The essay was cited as recently as the 2012 AMS/AMT/SEM conference program.

18. McGerr, *Fierce Discontent*, 4–6; Rosenbaum and Beckert, *American Bourgeoisie*, 1; Veblen (1857–1929), *Theory of the Leisure Class*. For comments on the term Upper Ten Thousand with regard to opera, see Ahlquist, *Democracy at the Opera*, 133–34, 141.

19. Blumin, *Emergence of the Middle Class*.

20. Quoted from Kaplan, *Democratic Vistas*, 961–62, in Levine, *Highbrow/Lowbrow*, 225.

21. Scott, "Music and Social Class," 544. Scott sometimes uses the terms *bourgeoisie* and *middle class* interchangeably.

22. Beckert, *Monied Metropolis*, 6–7, 268.

23. Broyles, *"Music of the Highest Class,"* 218.

24. Newman, *Good Music for a Free People*, 117, 156–58. Newman also rebuts many of Levine's points about the Germania Musical Society by correcting information and tracing his assumptions to misperceptions in earlier scholarship (113–24 and generally).

25. Block, "Thinking about Serious Music," 435–36.

26. Krehbiel, *Chapters of Opera*, 115. The negotiations were held in August 1884; the first German performance was on November 17.

27. Gienow-Hecht, *Sound Diplomacy*, 3, 5.

28. Chacar and Hesterly, "Innovations and Value Creation"; Moore, "Ideology on the Sports Page." For a chronology, see Cassuto and Partridge, *Cambridge Companion to Baseball*, xv. Cassuto suggests that baseball uses cultural capital to break down, rather than strengthen, social barriers (2).

29. Cocks, *Doing the Town*.

30. Thomas, "Music of the Great Sanitary Fairs," 151–59.

31. Perkins and Dwight, *History of the Handel*, 1:72–78.

32. Ahlquist, "Playing for the Big Time," 26–48.

33. *Boston Advertiser*, clipping in National Peace Jubilee scrapbook, Massachusetts Historical Society, quoted in Cavicchi, *Listening and Longing*, 122.

34. The replacement on the same site, today's Music Hall, was constructed from summer 1876 to May 1878.

35. Listening in the mid- to late nineteenth century precedes the development of "music appreciation" beginning at the turn of the twentieth century. On the latter, see Horowitz, *Understanding Toscannini*, 202–34 and generally; Dale, "Britain's 'Armies of Trained Listeners.'" Dale's article includes discussion of American listening pedagogy as presented in Britain.

36. This line of work draws in part on the work of Michel Foucault, especially *Discipline and Punish* (1975).

37. Kasson also acknowledges *Highbrow/Lowbrow*, which was published after he had drafted his chapter on spectatorship. See *Rudeness and Civility*, 236–42, 281.

38. Ibid., 255. For a useful overview of cultural attitudes exemplified by New York's Central Park and the Chicago World's Columbian Exposition, see Kasson, *Amusing the Million*, 11–28. See also Kathy Peiss, *Cheap Amusements*, 116–17, 129–32, 142–43; Nasaw, *Going Out*, 19–33, 86–88.

39. *New York Tribune*, May 11, 1876; *New York Observer and Chronicle*, May 18, 1876; Cavicchi, *Listening and Longing*, 125–28.

40. "GFR," [Root], "Here and There," 144. On the orchestra as a machine, see also John Spitzer, "Metaphors of the Orchestra," 247–48.

41. Quoted in Cavicchi, *Listening and Longing*, 127.

42. Gienow-Hecht, *Sound Diplomacy*, 68.

43. Rabinowitz, "Gottschalk."

44. Cavicchi, *Listening and Longing*, 190. On listening as a form of engagement, see Locke, "Music Lovers," 159–61.

45. Both Cavicchi and Gienow-Hecht explicitly reject Levine's contention that formal musical culture developed mainly from upper-class interests. See Cavicchi, *Listening and Longing*, 173; Gienow-Hecht, *Sound Diplomacy*, 6.

46. Spaethling, *Mozart's Letters*, 336–37; Schabas, *Theodore Thomas*, 16.

47. Crawford, The *American Musical Landscape*, 82–84.

48. Quoted in Gienow-Hecht, *Sound Diplomacy*, 140.

49. Horowitz, "Sermons in Tones," 334–35.

50. Horowitz, "Music and the Gilded Age," 229.

51. Ibid., 233.

52. Louis Elson, quoted in ibid., 236.

53. Ahlquist, "Performances to 'Permanence.'"

54. Gay, *Pleasure Wars*, 176–77.

55. Ahlquist, "Performances to 'Permanence,'" 170–71; Whitesitt, "Women as 'Keepers of Culture,'" 74–76.

56. Shanet, *Philharmonic*, 207–10, 219–20, 224–26; Mauskapf, "New York Goes Corporate."

57. Smith, *Making Music in Los Angeles*, 96, 117.

58. Vaillant, *Progressivism and Music in Chicago*, 33–38.

59. Horowitz, "Music and the Gilded Age," 234–35; Ahlquist, "Performances to 'Permanence,'" 172–73; Clague, "Industrial Evolution of the Arts," 483–87.

60. Goepp, Preface, 14–15.

61. Campbell, "Higher Mission."

62. Walters, "Afterword," 452, 453.

63. DiMaggio, "Cultural Entrepreneurship," 40, 42.

64. For DiMaggio's use of the term in "Cultural Entrepreneurship," see p. 48.

65. Baur, "Class."

66. Steven Baur, "Music, Morals," 71.

67. Ibid., 77.

68. Ibid., 93, 105, 106.

69. Ibid., 93.

70. Ibid., 106; see also 88.

71. For examples of this work, see Stevenson, *Philosophies of American Music History*; Crawford, "Cosmopolitan and Provincial: American Musical Historiography," in his *American Musical Landscape*; Garrett, introduction to *Struggling to Define a Nation*; Root, "Toward a History," 1–15; Davidson et al., "Disciplining American Music."

72. For discussions of this problem, see Preston, "What Happened?"; Magee, "Rethinking Social Class."

73. In addition to studies previously cited, see the essays in Brown, *Reconstructions*, especially Leslie Butler, "Reconstructions in Intellectual and Cultural Life," 172–205; Bellesiles, *1877*; Hahn, *Nation under Our Feet*; Foner, *Reconstruction*.

74. Fulcher, "Defining"; Applegate, "Music among the Historians."

References

Ahlquist, Karen. *Democracy at the Opera: Music, Theater, and Culture in New York City, 1815–60*. Urbana: University of Illinois Press, 1997.

———. "Mrs. Potiphar at the Opera: Satire, Idealism, and Cultural Authority in Post–Civil War New York." In *Music and Culture in America, 1861–1918*, edited by Michael Saffle, 29–51. New York: Garland, 1998.

———. "Performances to 'Permanence': Orchestra Building in Late Nineteenth-Century Cincinnati." In Spitzer, *American Orchestras*, 156–74.

———. "Playing for the Big Time: Musicians, Concerts, and Reputation-Building in Cincinnati, 1872–82." *Journal of the Gilded Age and Progressive Era* 9, no. 2 (April 2010): 26–48.

Applegate, Celia. "Music among the Historians." *German History* 30, no. 3 (Fall 2012), 329–49.

Baur, Steven. "Class." In the *Grove Dictionary of American Music*, 2nd ed., *Oxford Music Online*, 2013.

———. "Music, Morals, and Social Management: Mendelssohn in Post–Civil War America." *American Music* 19, no. 1 (Spring 2001): 64–130.

Beckert, Sven. *The Monied Metropolis: New York City and the Consolidation of the American Bourgeoisie, 1850–1896*. Cambridge: Cambridge University Press, 2001.

Bellesiles, Michael A. *1877: America's Year of Living Violently*. New York: New Press, 2010.

Block, Adrienne Fried. With John Spitzer. "Thinking about Serious Music in New York, 1842–82." In Spitzer, *American Orchestras*, 435–50.

Blumin, Stuart M. *The Emergence of the Middle Class: Social Experience in the American City, 1760–1900*. Cambridge: Cambridge University Press, 1989.

Brown, Thomas J., ed. *Reconstructions: New Perspectives on the Postbellum United States*. Oxford: Oxford University Press, 2006.

Broyles, Michael. *"Music of the Highest Class": Elitism and Populism in Antebellum Boston*. New Haven, Conn.: Yale University Press, 1992.

Butler, Leslie. "Reconstructions in Intellectual and Cultural Life." In Brown, *Reconstructions*, 172–205.

Campbell, Gavin James. "'A Higher Mission than Merely to Please the Ear': Music and Social Reform in America, 1900–1925." *Musical Quarterly* 84, no. 2 (Summer 2000): 259–86.

Cassuto, Leonard, and Stephen Partridge, eds. *The Cambridge Companion to Baseball.* Cambridge: Cambridge University Press, 2011.

Cavicchi, Daniel. *Listening and Longing: Music Lovers in the Age of Barnum.* Middletown, Conn.: Wesleyan University Press, 2011.

Chacar, Ava S., and William Hesterly, "Innovations and Value Creation in Major League Baseball, 1860–2000." *Business History* 46, no. 3 (July 2004): 407–38.

Clague, Mark. "The Industrial Evolution of the Arts: Chicago's Auditorium Building (1889–) as Cultural Machine." *Opera Quarterly* 22, nos. 3–4 (Summer–Fall 2006): 477–511.

Cocks, Catherine. *Doing the Town: The Rise of Urban Tourism in the United States, 1850–1915.* Berkeley: University of California Press, 2001.

Crawford, Richard. *The American Musical Landscape.* Berkeley: University of California Press, 1993.

Dale, Catherine. "Britain's 'Armies of Trained Listeners': Building a Nation of 'Intelligent Hearers.'" *Nineteenth Century Music Review* 2 (2005): 93–114.

Davidson, Mary Wallace, Dale Cockrell, Guthrie P. Ramsey Jr., Anne K. Rasmussen, and Kay Kaufman Shelemay. "Disciplining American Music." *American Music* 22, no. 2 (Summer 2004): 270–316.

DiMaggio, Paul. "Cultural Entrepreneurship in Nineteenth-Century Boston: The Creation of an Organizational Base for High Culture in America." Part 1. *Media, Culture and Society* 4, no. 1 (1982): 33–50.

———. "On Bourdieu." *American Journal of Sociology* 84, no. 6 (May 1979): 1460–74.

———. Review of Levine, *Highbrow/Lowbrow. Sociological Review* 38, no. 3 (1990): 608–11.

Dizikes, Paul. *Opera in America: A Cultural History.* New Haven, Conn.: Yale University Press, 1993.

———. Review of Shepherd, et al., *Whose Music?* In *American Journal of Sociology* 87, no. 3 (November 1981): 752–54.

Foner, Eric. *Reconstruction: America's Unfinished Revolution, 1863–1877.* 1988. New York: Perennial, 2002.

Fulcher, Jane F. "Defining the New Cultural History of Music, Its Origins, Methodologies, and Lines of Inquiry." In *The Oxford Handbook of the New Cultural History of Music*, edited by Jane F. Fulcher, 1–14. Oxford: Oxford University Press, 2011.

———. "Symbolic Domination and Contestation in French Music: Shifting the Paradigm from Adorno to Bourdieu." In *Opera and Society in Italy and France From Monteverdi to Bourdieu*, edited by Victoria Johnson, Jane F. Fulcher, and Thomas Ertman. Cambridge: Cambridge University Press, 2007, 312–29.

Garrett, Charles Hiroshi. *Struggling to Define a Nation: American Music and the Twentieth Century.* Berkeley: University of California Press, 2008.

Gay, Peter. *Pleasure Wars: The Bourgeois Experience Victoria to Freud.* Vol. 5. London: Fontana, 1998.

Gienow-Hecht, Jessica C. E. *Sound Diplomacy: Music and Emotions in Transatlantic Relations, 1850–1920*. Chicago: University of Chicago Press, 2009.

Goepp, Philip H. Editor's preface. In *Annals of Music in Philadelphia and History of the Musical Fund Society from its Organization in 1820 to the Year 1858*, by Louis Madeira, 11–16. Philadelphia: Lippincott, 1896.

Hahn, Steven. *A Nation under our Feet: Black Political Struggles in the Rural South from Slavery to the Great Migration*. Cambridge, Mass.: Harvard University Press, 2003.

Holbrook, Morris B., Michael J. Weiss, and John Habich. "Class-Related Distinctions in American Cultural Tastes." *Empirical Studies of the Arts* 22, no. 1 (2004): 91–115.

Horowitz, Joseph, "Music and the Gilded Age: Social Control and Sacralization Revisited." *Journal of the Gilded Age and Progressive Era* 3, no. 3 (July 2004): 227–45.

———. "'Sermons in Tones': Sacralization as a Theme in American Classical Music." *American Music* 16, no. 3 (Fall 1998): 311–40.

———. *Understanding Toscanini: How He Became an American Culture-God and Helped Create a New Audience for Old Music*. Minneapolis: University of Minnesota Press, 1987.

———. *Wagner Nights: An American History*. Berkeley: University of California Press, 1994.

Kasson, John F. *Amusing the Million: Coney Island at the Turn of the Century*. New York: Hill and Wang, 1978.

———. *Rudeness and Civility: Manners in Nineteenth-Century Urban America*. New York: Hill and Wang, 1990.

Kirk, Elise K. *American Opera*. Urbana: University of Illinois Press, 2001.

Krehbiel, Henry E. *Chapters of Opera: Being Historical and Critical Observations and Records Concerning the Lyric Drama in New York from Its Earliest Days Down to the Present Time*. New York: Holt, 1908.

Levine, Lawrence W. *Highbrow/Lowbrow: The Emergence of Cultural Hierarchy in America*. Cambridge: Harvard University Press, 1988.

Locke, Ralph P. "Music Lovers, Patrons, and the 'Sacralization' of Culture in America." *Nineteenth-Century Music* 17, no. 2 (autumn 1993): 149–73.

———. "Paradoxes of the Woman Music Patron in America." *Musical Quarterly* 78, no. 4 (Winter 1994): 798–825.

Locke, Ralph P., and Cyrilla Barr, eds. *Cultivating Music in America: Women Patrons and Activists since 1860*. Berkeley: University of California Press, 1997.

Magee, Gayle Sherwood. "Rethinking Social Class and American Music." *Journal of the American Musicological Society* 64, no. 3 (Fall 2011): 696–99.

Martin, George Whitney. *Verdi in America: Oberto through Rigoletto*. Rochester: University of Rochester Press, 2011.

Mauskapf, Michael. "New York Goes Corporate: The Philharmonic's Shift to a Nonprofit Operating Model." Paper given at the American Musicological Society annual conference, San Francisco, November 10, 2011.

McGerr, Michael. *A Fierce Discontent: The Rise and Fall of the Progressive Movement in America, 1870–1920*. New York: Oxford, 2003.

Moore, Glenn. "Ideology on the Sports Page: Newspapers, Baseball, and Ideological Conflict in the Gilded Age." *Journal of Sport History* 23, no. 3 (Fall 1996): 228–55.

Nasaw, David. *Going Out: The Rise and Fall of Public Amusements.* New York: Basic, 1993.

Newman, Nancy. *Good Music for a Free People: The Germania Musical Society in Nineteenth-Century America.* Rochester, N.Y.: University of Rochester Press, 2010.

New York Observer and Chronicle, May 18, 1876.

New York Tribune, May 11, 1876.

Ottenberg, June C. *Opera Odyssey: Toward a History of Opera in Nineteenth-Century America.* Westport, Conn.: Greenwood, 1994.

Peiss, Kathy. *Cheap Amusements: Working Women and Leisure in Turn-of-the-Century New York.* Philadelphia: Temple University Press, 1986.

Perkins, Charles C., and John Sullivan Dwight. *History of the Handel and Haydn Society, of Boston, Massachusetts.* 2 vols. Boston: Mudge, 1893.

Preston, Katherine K. *Opera on the Road: Traveling Opera in the United States, 1825–60.* Urbana: University of Illinois Press, 1993.

———. "What Happened to the Nineteenth Century?" *Bulletin of the Society for American Music* 31, no. 3 (Fall 2005): 41–43.

Rabinowitz, Peter J. "Gottschalk, Gender, and the Power of Listening." *Nineteenth-Century Music* 16, no. 3 (Spring 1993): 242–52.

Root, Deane L. "Toward a History of American Orchestras." In Spitzer, *American Orchestras*, 1–15.

[Root, George Frederick]. "Here and There." *Church's Musical Visitor*, June 1883, 144.

Rosenbaum Julia B., and Sven Beckert, eds. *The American Bourgeoisie: Distinction and Identity in the Nineteenth Century.* Basingstoke: Palgrave Macmillan, 2010.

Schabas, Ezra. *Theodore Thomas: America's Conductor and Builder of Orchestras, 1835–1905.* Urbana: University of Illinois Press, 1989.

Scott, Derek B. "Music and Social Class." In *The Cambridge History of Nineteenth-Century Music*, edited by Jim Samson, 544–67. Cambridge: Cambridge University Press, 2002.

Shanet, Howard. *Philharmonic: A History of New York's Orchestra.* New York: Doubleday, 1975.

Shepherd, John. "Toward a Sociology of Musical Styles." *Canadian University Music Review/Revue de musique des universités canadiennes* 2 (1981): 114–37.

Shepherd, John, Phil Virden, Graham Vulliamy, and Trevor Wishart. *Whose Music? A Sociology of Musical Languages.* London: Latimer, 1977.

Smith, Catherine Parsons. *Making Music in Los Angeles: Transforming the Popular.* Berkeley: University of California Press, 2007.

Spaethling, Robert. *Mozart's Letters, Mozart's Life.* New York: Norton, 2000.

Spitzer, John, ed. *American Orchestras in the Nineteenth Century.* Chicago: University of Chicago Press, 2012.

———. "Metaphors of the Orchestra: The Orchestra as a Metaphor." *Musical Quarterly* 80, no. 2 (1996): 234–64.

Stevenson, Robert. *Philosophies of American Music History*. Washington, DC: Library of Congress, 1970.

Thomas, Jean Waters. "Music of the Great Sanitary Fairs: Culture and Charity in the American Civil War." PhD diss., University of Pittsburgh, 1989.

Vaillant, Derek. *Progressivism and Music in Chicago, 1873–1935*. Chapel Hill: University of North Carolina Press, 2003.

Veblen, Thorstein. *The Theory of the Leisure Class: An Economic Study of Institutions*. London: Macmillan, 1899.

Walters, Ronald. "Afterword: Coming of Age." In Spitzer, *American Orchestras*, 451–58.

Whitesitt, Linda. "Women as 'Keepers of Culture': Music Clubs, Community Concert Series, and Symphony Orchestras." In Locke and Barr, *Cultivating Music in America*, 65–86.

2 From Flatbush to *Fun Home*

The Broadway Musical's "Cozy Cottage" Trope

JEFFREY MAGEE

In the past three decades, scholars in music, theater, dance, film, literature, performance studies, and American culture have converged on the Broadway musical and created a rich and distinctive site of interdisciplinary study. Critical and analytical approaches have shown how musical dramaturgy works in a musical, how archival research illuminates the subject, how individual figures and canonic shows shaped the genre, how stage musicals transfer to film (and vice versa), how Broadway's frankly commercial milieu shapes its creative products, and how musical theater amplifies aspects of individual and collective experience—including national, international, racial, ethnic, gender, and sexual identity. Musical theater has long secured a firm beachhead in university curricula, graduate and undergraduate; university presses are publishing peer-reviewed scholarly studies; and peer-reviewed periodicals are devoted to musical theater in the United States and abroad.

Scholars from all perspectives have recognized that the single most powerful engine driving the traditional musical theater plot is heterosexual romance and marriage. Musicologist Raymond Knapp developed the concept of "the marriage trope" to identify the ways musicals depict "couples whose individual issues mirror or embody larger ones that turn out to be what the musical in question is 'really' about."[1] Film theorist Rick Altman, focusing on Hollywood musicals, has written bluntly that "the genre as a whole is about heterosexual partnerships."[2] And, as theater historian Stacy Wolf has put it, such partnerships form the "narrative spine of most musicals."[3] Yet much remains to be said about how the musical develops that narrative *through song*. In fact, there are archetypal patterns in the ways musicals develop that narrative, which could be dubbed the "marriage plot."

This chapter uses the term *marriage plot* rather than *marriage trope* to serve as a reminder of the musical's links to other literary and dramatic forms, and because the word *trope* here connotes bundles of traits that cohere around individual song types. Literary scholars of the marriage plot have explored the ways in which the novel, from its eighteenth-century inception, helped to define and reinforce values of the rising middle class.[4] Jane Austen's novels comprise a prime example of the most sophisticated exemplars of the marriage plot. In theater and music, comparable precedents include Shakespearean comedy and Mozartian opera buffa. The term has not yet entered the lexicon of musical theater studies. Deploying it for that purpose highlights both the musical's participation in narrative patterns that predate it and the ways in which the musical does it uniquely, by showing how *song* plays a central role in articulating key moments in the plot archetype.

One type of song serves to illuminate the American musical theater's marriage plot through varied inflections and inversions across a century or more. Let us begin with lines from a play co-written by George S. Kaufman, a playwright with a somewhat cynical view of theatrical song who nevertheless wrote numerous musical-comedy scripts in the 1920s and 1930s, including the Pulitzer Prize–winning libretto for George and Ira Gershwin's political operetta *Of Thee I Sing*.

In the final scene of Kaufman and Ring Lardner's 1929 comedy, *June Moon*, two songwriters create a number about an innocent young couple settling "In a bungalow for two, / Where we can bill and coo—." A stage direction follows: "Mercifully, the curtain is down."[5] *June Moon*'s final jab makes it clear that by 1929 such a lyric was already cliché, and its appearance at the end gives it pride of place in the play's send-up of Tin Pan Alley.

Broadway regulars would have recognized the song type. Indeed, no musical comedy marriage plot of the period would have seemed complete without the members of its primary couple envisioning a little bungalow, blue room, cozy flat, cunning cottage, small hotel, hut, hideaway, or two-by-four, in Yonkers, in Flatbush, in Quogue, by the sea, or somewhere in the mountain greenery where they could bill and coo and settle down in domestic bliss. And yet, by condemning the bungalow, Kaufman and Lardner did not bring about its demolition. On the contrary, the architects of American musical theater would go on to build a large subdivision of such little homes, and what may be dubbed Broadway's *cozy-cottage trope* continued to resonate for decades to come. The song type objectifies the marriage plot's benefits in the form of property, and the property it envisions stands in opposition to the theater itself. If we recognize the trope's various inflections, explore the way it constructs an image of the audience and the theater, and consider its possible roots, we have a rich perspective from which to understand what is distinctively American about the American musical.

* * *

Most of the key elements of the cozy-cottage trope appear in a well-known number from *No, No, Nanette* (1925), which begins:

> I'm discontented with homes that are rented
> So I have invented my own.
> Darling, this place is a lover's oasis
> Where life's weary chase is unknown.
> Far from the cry of the city
> Where flowers pretty caress the streams,
> Cozy to hide in, to live side by side in,
> Don't let it abide in my dreams.[6]

The verse alone strikes many of the keynotes. The man sings first. His first line announces the theme in terms of real estate: home ownership trumps renting and offers a symbol of long-term commitment and enduring love. In Irving Caesar's virtuosic triple-double rhyme, the "*place is* a lover's *oasis* / Where life's weary *chase is* unknown." The little house is "cozy," perhaps the single most frequently used word in these numbers. Moreover, it stands far from hustle and bustle of city life, nestled in an idyllic pastoral setting. Location, location, location, as a realtor might say—except that so far it exists only in the character's "dreams."

The refrain strives to convert dreams into reality:

> Picture you upon my knee,
> Just tea for two,
> And two for tea,
> Just me for you,
> And you for me alone.
> Nobody near us to see us or hear us,
> No friends or relations,
> On weekend vacations.
> We won't have it known, dear,
> That we own a telephone, dear.
> Day will break, and you'll awake,
> And start to bake a sugar cake,
> For me to take for all the boys to see.
> We will raise a family,
> A boy for you,

A girl for me,
Can't you see how happy we would be?[7]

That refrain confirms the ideal of romantic solitude: "just you and me alone," out of reach of even friends and relations. The telephone remains the couple's single secret link to the outside world. The song continues with two images of patriarchal domestic bliss: the woman will *bake*—in this case, a "sugar cake" for the man to show off to his friends—and ultimately, the couple will have children, a boy and a girl.

Irving Berlin's song "A Little Bungalow," from the 1925 musical comedy *The Cocoanuts*, begins in a similar way. In the verse, the man lays out his "wonderful plan" for the future—the word *plan* standing in here as a practical synonym for the loftier and more commonly invoked *dream*. The refrain develops the now-familiar imagery: it's a "little" place, far from the urban space implied by the words "all the crowds," in a setting with "shady trees" and a modest plot of land—"just enough . . . to fool around with you." "Fool around" and "birds and bees" are as far as such lyrics are willing to go for sexual provocation.[8]

Cozy-cottage rhetoric appears to have been the common tongue. Rodgers and Hart several such numbers. In "Thou Swell," the singer pictures a "hut for two" with just two rooms, a kitchen, a small plot of land, and the beloved, expressed through Hart's juxtaposition of archaic and colloquial language in the title phrase.[9] For Rodgers and Hart, the cozy cottage appeared in many forms—as a "blue room,"[10] a "small hotel,"[11] and a modest retreat in the "mountain greenery."[12] Whatever Hart calls it, his lyrics tap the same well of sentiment and imagery. Likewise for Ira Gershwin, who rarely writes a complete cozy cottage lyric, but who, often with tongue firmly in cheek, set his brother George's music to words, referring to a "cunning cottage,"[13] a "little cottage,"[14] a "two-by-four,"[15] and a "cottage for two."[16]

Composers reinforced the stable imagery of such numbers with an almost equally stable musical language. Most notable is the regular, even clichéd, use of a dainty, swaying dotted rhythms in the refrain—a melodic style that can be heard in both "Tea for Two" (example 1) and "A Little Bungalow" (example 2), and in at least two other numbers of this type separated by three decades: Jerome Kern and P. G. Wodehouse's "Nesting Time in Flatbush" (example 3), from *Oh, Boy!* of Princess Theatre vintage in 1917, and Kurt Weill and Langston Hughes's "We'll Go Away Together" (example 4), from *Street Scene* (1947). Although Weill dubbed his work an "American opera," both Weill and Hughes here borrowed musical and verbal language from the world of musical comedy.

Several other details in "We'll Go Away Together" reveal the characters Sam and Rose as operatic cousins of their musical comedy forerunners. In the underscored dialogue between statements of the refrain, they envision a place far

Pic - ture you up - on my knee just tea for two and two for tea,

Example 1. "Tea for Two" (Vincent Youmans and Irving Caesar, *No, No, Nanette*, 1925)

A lit - tle bung - a - low, an hour or so, from an - y - where,

Example 2. "A Little Bungalow" (Irving Berlin, *The Cocoanuts*, 1925)

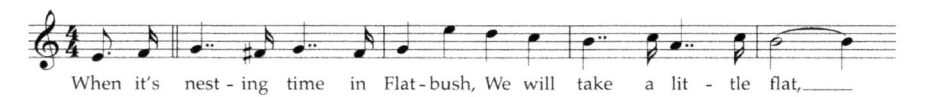

When it's nest - ing time in Flat-bush, We will take a lit - tle flat,_____

Example 3. "Nesting Time in Flatbush" (Jerome Kern and P.G. Wodehouse, *Oh Boy!*, 1917)

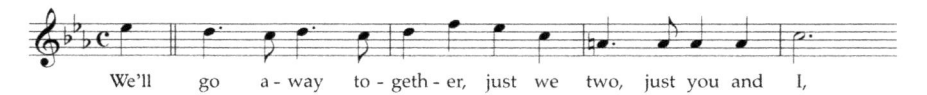

We'll go a - way to - geth - er, just we two, just you and I,

Example 4. "We'll Go Away Together" (Kurt Weill and Langston Hughes, *Street Scene*, 1947)

from the "street scene" where they live. "I've heard that people are nicer and friendlier, when you get away from New York," says Rose, who thus joins her predecessors in rejecting the city as the site for their cozy retreat.[17] Moreover, as the number continues, Sam and Rose, like their Broadway parents in the 1910s and 1920s, make a point of envisioning their future home as a modest one. It "need not be a palace or a golden castle in Spain. . . . just a roof to keep out snow and rain."[18] The difference here is that, in *Street Scene*, the couple never gets close to realizing its dream. That failure becomes increasingly normative in wartime and postwar Broadway musicals, as we'll see.

* * *

Identifying the song model and its proliferation makes it easier to recognize parodies of it. Evidence that the cozy cottage number had by 1947 long been recognized as a cliché—even before Kaufman and Lardner's *June Moon*—comes from one of the songwriters who had regularly invoked it in his shows: Irving Berlin. In his World War I revue *Yip Yip Yaphank* (1918), Berlin wrote a reflexive parody, dubbed "Love Interest," whose verse offers a clinical explanation of its own function and continues by explaining that "It's very necessary / To have a sweet melodious lay / For the boy and girl in the plot; / It always helps a lot / To have them sing / A pretty thing / Of which the chorus goes this way." The refrain that follows is a deliberately inane send-up that imagines "a cozy spot up in Yonkers / For just us two. / All day through / We will bill and coo."[19] That the number was sung in a revue produced by the US Army, by two men, including one in drag, added to this scene's ironic comment on the style. The song type's heteronormative requirements scarcely needed to be stated. (The drag act here is hardly a visionary anticipation of *La Cage aux Folles*; its roots lay in minstrelsy, where female impersonation was commonplace.[20])

More than a decade later, in a musical comedy called *Face the Music* (1932), Berlin again references the cozy-cottage trope but swerves away from it. Written with Moss Hart, *Face the Music* mocks the Depression-era corruption of New York City's police and government even as it celebrates the city itself. So, in keeping with the show's relentless urban focus, the principal couple pointedly rejects clichés of the cozy-cottage number: "A cottage by the sea / Is not for you and me," sings the man, and the woman agrees: "A little bungalow / Would never do I know." Instead, they favor a home on an urban summit: "[A] castle in Spain / On a roof in Manhattan."[21] The song's pulsating habañera rhythm reinforces its urbanity: the rumba craze had just hit New York City with Don Azpiazú's 1930 recording of the popular song "The Peanut Vendor," and, beginning the following year, Xavier Cugat's residency at the Waldorf Astoria.

In *Pal Joey* (1940), Rodgers and Hart created a number that put a new, more urbanized, and now lascivious spin on the cozy-cottage trope in the musical number "Den of Iniquity." In a show where the principal couple is more in lust than in love, and the heroine is married to another man, the lovers enjoy their bliss in a rented space, Joey's apartment, which Vera makes a point of contrasting with her real home. The verse begins in the conventional way, with a picture of "lovebirds all alone" in a "cozy nest" with a "secret telephone," but soon takes off in its own direction by replacing the usual pastoral imagery with "artificial roses" and substituting a "loving room" for the "living room." The second refrain gives more details about the "loving room," with its "canopy bed" and "ceiling made of glass," implying the sexual thrill of an overhead mirror. Later lines refer to the enjoyment the couple gets from listening to music on the radio. In alternate lyrics, Hart specified Ravel's *Bolero* or Tchaikovsky's *1812 Overture* as the music.[22] It hardly matters which title the actors sing: both refer to pieces with a strong, throbbing pulse and an orchestral crescendo to a massive climax. Neither sugar cakes nor children are the goals of *this* "tea for two."

* * *

With *Pal Joey* we stand on the cusp of a new phase in the development of the musical theater's cozy-cottage neighborhood: a period in which the trope's elements begin to disassociate, in which the individual goals of the principal couple often do not coalesce into a single ideal embodied by the modest, stable home. Many numbers and scenes, comedic and dramatic, treat the trope with considerable irony or critique—or allude to it, even obliquely, as an impossible goal.

In *Guys and Dolls*, a comical romance develops between Adelaide and Nathan in terms that regularly invoke cozy-cottage imagery. But the idea never blossoms into song, perhaps because the two do not quite see eye to eye about Adelaide's longing to settle down and raise babies. In her ongoing frustration about Nathan's compulsive gambling, she pleads: "What about you men? Why can't you marry people like other people do, and live normal like people? Have a home, with—wallpaper, and book ends."[23] When Adelaide catches Nathan in the midst of a crap game, he tries to assuage her even as he obviously has no desire to share her cozy-cottage vision: "We'll get married," he pleads. "We'll have a home, a little white house with a green fence."[24] Later, as Adelaide shares her romantic misery with Sarah Brown, she notes that:

> For fourteen years I've tried to change Nathan. I've always thought how wonderful he would be, if he was different. . . . I've sat and pictured him by the hour. Nathan—my Nathan—in a little home in the country—happy—"

As she says this the stage directions read: "*Lights go on behind her R. revealing a NATHAN in overalls and farmer's hat, standing beside a trellis of beautiful roses. With a spray gun he is tenderly treating each bud with loving care.*"[25] The modest but well-kept garden is an obligatory accessory to the cozy cottage.

The image of the "little home" comes back once more in the show's final line, after Adelaide and Nathan have finally been married. She says: "Thank you very much—I know we're going to be happy. We're going to have a little place in the country, and Nathan will be sitting there, beside me, every single night."[26] That the line brings a loud sneeze from Nathan suggests that settling down in the country homestead may not in fact be the happiest ending for this burlesque dancer and her gambler husband, both of whose talents are best nurtured in the city.

Two musical numbers from Leonard Bernstein's operetta *Candide* resonate with cozy-cottage imagery, but again with an important twist. Early in act 1, the naïve and unlikely couple Candide and Cunegonde happily agree to marry, but they sing a duet of contrasting visions of their ideal life together: "Oh Happy We." In Richard Wilbur's lyric, the humble Candide envisions "a little modest farm," while the spoiled Cunegonde imagines living on a yacht, "rolling in luxury and stylish charm."[27] For both characters, the dream in their minds blinds them to the dream of the other. Candide pictures a "sweet Westphalian home," as Cunegonde insists that "we'll live in Paris when we're not in Rome."[28] The music reinforces the separation. Throughout the number they exchange solo phrases, and the only music they actually sing together is the number's last phrase.

At the end of the *Candide*, after enduring a series of traumatic experiences, they come together again in a musical number with a more unified vision, "Make Our Garden Grow," which stands closer to Candide's original plan. Candide, no longer naïve about the world's horrors, realizes he's been a "fool" and vows to "make some sense of life"—to "do the best we know," to "build our house, and chop our wood, and make our garden grow." Cunegonde answers in a way that pointedly harks back to the innocence of "Tea for Two," replacing life's "sugar cake" with the down-to-earth image of baking their "daily bread." Cunegonde sings: "I thought the world / Was *sugar cake* / For so our master said. / But now I'll teach / My hands to bake / Our loaf of *daily bread*."[29]

* * *

In the post–Rodgers and Hammerstein age the musical reveals more self-consciousness about its history and conventions, and plots open up to reveal more of the dark side of human nature.[30] Evidence of both self-consciousness and the emerging "dark side" may be found in the ways in which the cozy-cottage ideal continues to be invoked.

In *Sweet Charity* (1966), for example, Neil Simon's script invokes the cozy cottage explicitly, but here it appears, in quotation marks, as the central image in a joke about a vision that is unlikely to be realized. Charity, who we learn has been serially dumped by a parade of creeps, claims that she has at last met a man who appears to be refreshingly average and normal. And she has been singing his praises to her skeptical co-workers, Helene and Nickie, in the seedy taxi-dance hall where they ply male customers with feigned intimacy. In this scene, however, the allegedly happy couple is not present. Instead, Charity has just exited, and her friends *imagine* a romantic scene between Charity and her new beau, and Nickie guesses cynically that "He probably does all the talking. Handing her those smooth lines like, 'Baby, last night I dreamt you and I were in a cozy little cottage covered with clinging vines—.'"[31]

The word "dream" becomes the keynote of a song called "Baby, Dream Your Dream," which the women deliver in explicit quotation marks. (The cue line is: "Quote.") The refrain presents a kind of list song that drags out the usual props, now expanded by inflation and the possibilities of easy credit: furniture, the fancy bed, in a house with "three and one-half rooms with a walk-in closet," a welcome addition to Rodgers and Hart's two rooms and kitchen. If the first refrain affirms the stereotype, the second refrain develops the plot by describing the long-term effects of domestic stability: the women imagine how the home becomes a prison for Charity and her "three fat, hungry kids" while the obstetrician reaps the financial rewards and Charity's would-be husband seeks pleasure outside the home: "He says he's going bowling / But a bowling ball / Is not what Daddy's rolling." In the number's final section, however, the women still cling to the possibility that the dream could come true in their own lives. The music slows down, indicating a more reflective, less sarcastic tone, as they sing: "But come to think of it, / How happy I would be / If someday I could find / The kind of guy who'd say to me / 'Baby, dream your dream; / Close your eyes and try it.'"[32] In the end, Charity is dumped—actually dumped—into the pit by her dream man.

And yet: more than a decade later, that dream still lives in the mind of Stephen Sondheim and Hugh Wheeler's London pie-shop proprietor named Nellie Lovett, a widow whose fortunes have risen after teaming up with Sweeney Todd, a barber so bent on revenge that he becomes a serial murderer. Todd and Lovett make a perfect couple, but not in the way of traditional musical comedy: they dispose of *his* corpses by using them for meat in *her* pies. When business is booming, Lovett enjoys a respite in which she envisions a place where she can settle down with her business partner and would-be lover, far from the dirty, smelly, murderous city.

In the line leading into the song, Lovett reveals her "dream" about settling down by the sea. In the song itself she mentions "a house wot we'd almost own" and invokes comfortable and conventional imagery of slipping off Todd's slippers. He, however, is preoccupied with his plan of revenge on the judge who banished him to Australia and stole his wife and daughter. So he sings just one recurring line in the song, "anything you say," a verbal signifier of his complete indifference to Lovett's cozy-cottage dream.[33] As the song continues, Lovett conjures more of the conventional domestic imagery with references to baking and knitting, with no impact on Sweeney Todd. And in case any listener had missed the trope that Sondheim has tapped in this song, Lovett even refers to the house as a "cozy retreat."[34]

Of course, the couple never comes close to realizing this vision. In *Sweeney Todd*'s final scene, Todd has just discovered that the beggar woman he stabbed to death moments earlier was none other than his wife, Lucy. He mourns her briefly and passionately and then suddenly turns to Lovett, who revives her hopes for marriage ("Can we still be married?") as Todd pointedly sings, "What's dead is dead." With bodies on the floor around them, they continue the horrifically cheerful waltz duet that reprises fragments of earlier numbers, one of which is a frantic phrase from "By the Sea": "By the sea, Mr. Todd, / We'll be comfy-cozy, / By the sea, Mr. Todd, / Where there's no one nosy."[35] This turns out to be Lovett's last solo line before Todd flings her into the meat oven a few seconds later.

In *Sweeney Todd* we seem to witness a kind of apocalypse of Broadway's cozy-cottage neighborhood. But a last example suggests that a bomb had been detonated two decades earlier by Sondheim himself, along with his collaborator Arthur Laurents, in *Gypsy*. Like many musical theater heroines, Mama Rose must negotiate the powerful and sometimes opposing pulls of her marriage plot and her show-business plot. For Rose, the choice is obvious and simple: having failed three times at marriage, she is above all determined to see her daughter succeed in show business. Throughout the show, the line "I had a dream" becomes her mantra, and that dream is, defiantly, *not* to settle down with a husband in a cozy cottage with a nice garden, away from all the "care and strife" of the big city. On the contrary, the very title of the show signals a woman who is homeless by choice, a wanderer whose dream can only come true *away* from the home. This becomes explicit very early in the show, in act 1, scene 2.

The vaudeville-style placard that identifies the scene in this case reads: "'Home Sweet Home,' Seattle." This is Rose's *childhood* home, which is now just a temporary lodging. Rose argues with her father, and soon after the telling line "Anybody that stays home is dead!" she begins to launch her big "I-am" number, "Some People," in which she contrasts the sedentary home life she despises with the vitality of the theatrical life she yearns for. The song, launched on a jarring tritone (example 5), begins with a complete and conventional AABA-format refrain in which the A sections describe with derision the humble, static home life that

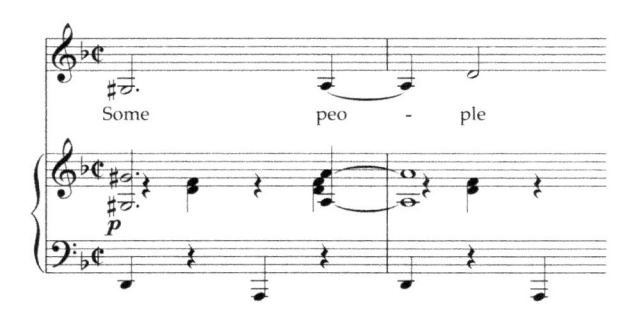

Example 5. Tritone in "Some People," beginning of refrain (Jule Styne and Stephen Sondheim, *Gypsy*, 1959)

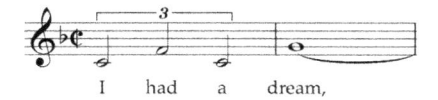

Example 6. "Dream" motif, as sung in "Some People" (Jule Styne, Stephen Sondheim, *Gypsy*, 1959)

"some people" like, and the B section begins to describe Rose's dynamic effort to escape it. It is then telling that the song continues beyond its conventional form to include a new section in which Rose describes her "dream," using the show's principal musical motif (example 6)—a dream about show business that contradicts the one voiced in every other cozy-cottage number before and after.

* * *

The scene's prominently displayed reference to "Home, Sweet Home" brings us full circle to what are surely the American roots of the cozy-cottage song type: the "home song" archetype embodied most famously in the imported British opera song "Home, Sweet Home." One of the most popular songs in nineteenth-century America, "Home, Sweet Home" resonated well into the twentieth, most famously in the last lines of Irving Berlin's "God Bless America" and Dorothy Gale's mantra in *The Wizard of Oz*: "There's no place like home."[36] In the "humble" and "lowly thatched cottage" we can find the prototype of Broadway's cozy cottage:

> 'Mid pleasures and palaces though we may roam,
> Be it ever so humble, there's no place like home!
> . . .
> An exile from home splendor dazzles in vain,
> Give me my lowly thatched cottage again.

All of these examples lead to a reflection on their collective meaning. First, identifying the cozy-cottage trope only serves to highlight one of the features of the traditional Broadway musical that is already obvious: its commitment to constructing its audience, even flattering it, as ethnically blank, white, heterosexual, patriarchal, and middle class. Yet from the late 1950s onward, women take charge of the song and direct it into new territory. As a result, the cozy-cottage trope may be construed as iconic for the changing relationship between the makers of Broadway musicals and their audiences.[37] The early manifestations of the song type, whether straightforward or parodistic, reinforce its visions as stable and normative. The trope is so stable, in fact, that it almost appears as a stereotype of white, middle-class people and values. It's even possible to recognize the stereotype as a *minstrelization* of middle-class, Anglo-Saxon whiteness, a stereotype thrown into relief by the uprooting and migration experienced by the immigrants and first-generation Americans who wrote many of the most notable cozy-cottage numbers.

In contrast, many of the postwar examples destabilize the ideal vision of the modest home and the family romance for which it serves as a staging ground. And yet, conjuring a sense that it may be out of reach may serve to heighten desire for it. The women in *Sweet Charity* and *Sweeney Todd*, for example, still hold out hope for the "dream" reified in cozy-cottage imagery, even if they understand that it remains unlikely to come true. Only *Gypsy* stands out as truly unique among these examples, for its heroine joyously, fiercely, and systematically deconstructs the cozy-cottage ideal as she celebrates its opposite: the theater itself. Ultimately, then, it appears that the cozy-cottage trope serves a meta-theatrical function. Even as it ostensibly, even ostentatiously, points away from the theater and the city that nurtures it, the song type reminds its audience that the cozy-cottage vision is most vividly realized in the theater, in the imaginations of the characters and the spectators.

But not everyone longs to sustain that vision, even in the theater. *Sweeney Todd* came to Broadway twenty years after *Gypsy*, but they share a common sensibility. When Sweeney sings, "What's dead is dead," and when Mama Rose says, "Anybody that stays home is dead," they are channeling two figures, Stephen Sondheim and Arthur Laurents, who steered musical theater in new directions in the post–Rodgers and Hammerstein age and who seem to be telling us that the Broadway musical's conventional marriage plot is dead, and while the longing for a home remains, the cozy cottages that embody it have been, or should be, demolished at last.

*   *   *

This brings us close to the present. The Bechdel family home in *Fun Home* (2015) meets all the crucial specs of the happily-ever-after dwelling imagined in "Tea for Two": owned, not rented; "far from the cry of the city"; beautifully furnished inside, with a carefully tended garden outside; and occupied by a married couple and their children, including at least one of each sex. But these features obscure some disturbing and unstable undercurrents. "Welcome to our house on Maple Avenue," they sing. "See how we polish and we shine. / We rearrange and realign / Everything is balanced and serene / Like chaos never happens if it's never seen."[38]

The "chaos" stems from the problem that the couple is not happily married; Bruce, the husband and father, is a tortured, self-hating, closeted homosexual who ultimately commits suicide; Helen, the wife and mother, regrets a life of self-deception and missed opportunity. More than that, Bruce's avocation as a home renovator and interior designer shapes an extended metaphor of his challenges of self-realization. He relentlessly strives to perfect his cozy cottage and never achieves satisfaction, an impulse that frustrates Helen so much she refers to their home as a "museum."[39] Meanwhile, he begins work on renovating another house that Helen describes as "an old shell of a house out on Route 150."[40] Helen continues to describe the place in language that comes close to describing Bruce himself:

Years ago he talked about buying it and he looked it over and said *it wasn't worth it, it was too far gone* and that was back then so *I don't know why now that it's even more broken down he's decided he can fix it up.* [41]

In Bruce's climactic eleven o'clock number, "Edges of the World," he rhapsodizes about the house from a liminal space between hope and despair, in reflexive language pregnant with personal meaning. On one hand, Bruce sees the place as full of possibility: "But when the sunlight hits the parlor wall / at certain times of day / I see how fine this house could be / I see it so damn clear / What's the matter? Why am I standing here?"[42] On the other hand, there is so much work to do the renovation appears to be impossible. "Bad foundation, twisting floorboards, shoddy pipes, a gaping hole / It's a lot, it's a lot to keep under control. / Something cracking, something rotting, piles of ruin and debris, / Killing me! crushing me! pushing me!"[43] In each stanza, the observations turn reflexively inward, and a line has been planted earlier in the script to hint that the house is a reflection of Bruce himself: "Did I mention I've taken on a new project?" he asks Alison in what turns out to their final conversation. "That old house out on Route 150! You've seen it, Al. It's been sitting empty out there for forty, fifty years at least."[44]

"Old." "Sitting empty." "Forty, fifty years at least." These phrases describe Bruce himself. (We know Bruce's age at the time of his death because in the first scene Alison notes, "Now I'm the one who's forty-three and stuck."[45]) *Fun Home* thus has two cozy cottages: the family home and the fixer-upper. One is a trap, a prison, a "museum," and the other is a sad reflection of the unrealized and unrealizable potential of a strangled soul with an artistic spirit. That Bruce steps in front of a truck and dies on Route 150 provides the final clue to the analogy between him and the empty house he sought to renovate.

Although the small town of Beech Creek, Pennsylvania, where Alison Bechdel grew up and her father died, is less than a four-hour drive from Flatbush, Yonkers, and other cozy-cottage sites of Broadway's past, *Fun Home*'s two houses stand worlds apart from their predecessors, even as they demonstrate the uncanny persistence of the models that Broadway writers have envisioned, designed, built, and renovated for more than a century.

Notes

1. Knapp, *American Musical*, 9.
2. Altman, *American Film Musical*, 20.
3. Wolf, "Gender and Sexuality," 213.
4. See, for example, Boone, *Tradition Counter Tradition*, and White, "Jane Austen."
5. Kaufman and Lardner, *June Moon*, 272.
6. "Tea for Two" (from *No, No, Nanette*). Words by Irving Caesar. Music by Vincent

Youmans. © 1924 (Renewed) WB Music Corp. and Irving Caesar Music Corp. All rights administered by WB Music Corp. All rights reserved.

7. Ibid.

8. Irving Berlin, "A Little Bungalow," in *The Cocoanuts* (1925). Reprinted in Berlin, *Complete Lyrics*, 236.

9. Richard Rodgers and Lorenz Hart, "Thou Swell," in *A Connecticut Yankee* (1927). Reprinted in Rodgers and Hart, *Complete Lyrics of Lorenz Hart*, 107–8.

10. Rodgers and Hart, "The Blue Room," in *The Girl Friend* (1926). Reprinted in ibid., 64.

11. Rodgers and Hart, "There's a Small Hotel," in *On Your Toes* (1936). Reprinted in ibid., 222.

12. Rodgers and Hart, "Mountain Greenery," in *The Garrick Gaieties* (1926). Reprinted in ibid., 71.

13. George Gershwin and Ira Gershwin, "I've Got a Crush on You," in *Treasure Girl* (1928) and *Strike Up the Band* (1930). Reprinted in Gershwin and Gershwin, *Complete Lyrics*, 128–29.

14. George Gershwin and Ira Gershwin, "Soon," *Strike Up the Band* (1930). Reprinted in ibid., 151–52.

15. George Gershwin and Ira Gershwin, "But Not for Me," in *Girl Crazy* (1930). Reprinted in ibid., 166–67. The song represents a rare instance imagining the cottage in a (whimsical) torch song.

16. George Gershwin and Ira Gershwin, "Blah, Blah, Blah," in *Delicious* (1931). Reprinted in ibid., 173.

17. Weill, Hughes, and Rice, *Street Scene*, 217.

18. Ibid., 216.

19. Berlin, "Love Interest," in *Yip Yip Yaphank* (1918). Reprinted in Berlin, *Complete Lyrics*, 168.

20. Toll, *Blacking Up*, 140.

21. Berlin, "On a Roof in Manhattan," in *Face the Music* (1932). Reprinted in Berlin, *Complete Lyrics*, 275.

22. Richard Rodgers and Lorenz Hart, "Den of Iniquity," in *Pal Joey* (1940). Reprinted in Rodgers and Hart, *Complete Lyrics*, 274–75.

23. Loesser, Swerling, and Burrows, *Guys and Dolls*, 91.

24. Ibid. 104.

25. Ibid., 117.

26. Ibid., 124.

27. A lyricist who should know commented: "Wilbur's lyrics for *Candide* are unequaled for their combination of wit and skill," and "Oh Happy We" may serve as an example. See Sondheim, *Look, I Made a Hat*, 303.

28. Bernstein, *Candide*, 42–47.

29. Ibid., 266–75, emphasis added.

30. See, for example, Laird, "Musical Theater," 8.

31. Simon, Coleman, and Fields, *Sweet Charity*, 81.

32. Ibid., 81–83.

33. Sondheim and Wheeler, *Sweeney Todd*, 164.

34. Ibid., 165.

35. Ibid., 199.

36. Sheryl Kaskowitz has explored these dimensions of "God Bless America" in Kaskowitz, *God Bless America*, 5.

37. This notion has its seed in Joseph Kerman's analogous claim about Mozart's piano concertos; see Kerman, "Mozart's Piano Concertos," 151–68.

38. Kron and Tesori, *Fun Home*, 14–15.

39. Ibid., 63. Earlier in the show, Bruce's friend Roy uses the same word, *museum*, to describe the house: "This place is like a museum" (30).

40. Ibid., 63.

41. Ibid., emphasis added.

42. Ibid., 72.

43. Ibid.

44. Ibid., 70.

45. Ibid., 11.

References

Altman, Rick. *The American Film Musical*. Bloomington: Indiana University Press, 1987.

Berlin, Irving. *The Complete Lyrics of Irving Berlin*. Edited by Robert Kimball and Linda Emmet. New York: Knopf, 2001.

Bernstein, Leonard. *Candide*. New York: Boosey and Hawkes, 1994.

Boone, Joseph Allen. *Tradition Counter Tradition: Love and the Form of Fiction*. Chicago: University of Chicago Press, 1987.

Caesar, Irving, and Vincent Youmans. *Tea for Two*. New York: Harms, 1924.

Gershwin, George, and Ira Gershwin. *The Complete Lyrics of Ira Gershwin*. Edited by Robert Kimball. 1993. Reprint, New York: Da Capo, 1998.

Kaskowitz, Sheryl. *God Bless America: The Surprising Story of an Iconic Song*. New York: Oxford University Press, 2013.

Kaufman, George S., and Ring Lardner. *June Moon*. In *Kaufman and Co.: Broadway Comedies*, edited by Laurence Maslon. New York: Library of America, 2004.

Kerman, Joseph. "Mozart's Piano Concertos and Their Audience." In *On Mozart*, edited by James M. Morris. Cambridge: Cambridge University Press, 1994.

Knapp, Raymond. *The American Musical and the Formation of National Identity*. Princeton, N.J.: Princeton University Press, 2005.

Kron, Lisa, and Jeanine Tesori. *Fun Home*. New York: Samuel French, 2015.

Laird, Paul. "Music Theater." In *The Grove Dictionary of American Music*, 2nd ed., edited by Charles Hiroshi Garrett. Grove Music Online.

Loesser, Frank, Joe Swerling, and Abe Burrows. *Guys and Dolls*. In *The Guys and Dolls Book*. London: Methuen, 1982.

Rodgers, Richard, and Lorenz Hart. *The Complete Lyrics of Lorenz Hart*. Edited by Dorothy Hart and Robert Kimball. 1986. Reprint, New York: Da Capo, 1995.

Simon, Neil, Cy Coleman, and Dorothy Fields. *Sweet Charity*. New York: Random House, 1966.

Sondheim, Stephen. *Look, I Made a Hat: Collected Lyrics (1981–2011)*. New York: Knopf, 2011.

Sondheim, Stephen, and Hugh Wheeler. *Sweeney Todd: The Demon Barber of Fleet Street*. New York: Applause, 1991.

Toll, Robert. *Blacking Up: The Minstrel Show in Nineteenth-Century America*. New York: Oxford University Press, 1974.

Weill, Kurt, Langston Hughes, and Elmer Rice. *Street Scene*. New York: Chappell Music, 1948.

White, Laura Mooneyham. "Jane Austen and the Marriage Plot: Questions of Persistence." In *Jane Austen and Discourses of Feminism*, edited by Devoney Looser, 71–86. New York: St. Martin's, 1995.

Wolf, Stacy. "Gender and Sexuality." In *The Oxford Handbook of the American Musical*, edited by Raymond Knapp, Mitchell Morris, and Stacy Wolf, 210–24. New York: Oxford University Press, 2011.

3 Secular Music in Shape Notes

DAVID WARREN STEEL

Students of American sacred music have long acknowledged the role of shape notation in the emergence and dissemination of a native musical idiom. While urban reformers denounced and derided the new notation almost from the beginning,[1] this simple pedagogical innovation soon developed implications of class and regional identity. Richard Crawford observes that "shape-note collections . . . issued not from major cities but from smaller ones in more recently settled regions: upstate New York (Albany), western Pennsylvania (Harrisburg), the Shenandoah Valley of Virginia (Harrisonburg), the Ohio River Valley (Cincinnati), and places farther west and south."[2] In some of these areas, "patent notes," as they came to be known, dominated music publication for decades. Referring to Cincinnati, John Bealle writes, "For the [first] half [of the nineteenth] century, shape notes dominated the music publishing business to the extent that some publishers, fearing a possible loss of sales, would sometimes refuse to print music in any other manner."[3] Even musical reformers like Timothy Flint and Lowell Mason, intent on introducing cultivated or "scientific" music to the frontier, found it necessary to publish in shape notes to reach their intended audience.[4]

It should be understood that the popular shape-note tunebooks of the period contained an almost entirely sacred repertory, at least where the texts are concerned. After all, American Protestants regarded congregational singing as a sacred duty; American composers, singing masters, and music publishers sought to make their living by providing the skills and repertory to fulfill that duty. Shape notes were themselves a pedagogical adjunct to singing schools, whose ostensible purpose was the improvement of congregational singing. The religious connotations of this repertory were readily accepted on the frontier but did not limit it to purely sacred uses such as public worship. The singing school became a social institution as well as a religious and educational one. Diaries and other literature show that young people looked upon singing schools as a valuable opportunity for late-night courting in a relatively unsupervised atmosphere, and several writers noted the apparent discrepancy between the words sung and the deeds done at such gatherings: "Young, gay, and thoughtless persons . . . continually commit the grossest sacrilege, mockery, and falsehood, by singing sacred composition . . . at times, and under circumstances which entirely exclude the possibility of their feeling any part of what they express."[5]

The music in the shape-note tunebooks was not confined to the slow, repetitive strophic hymn settings often associated with congregational singing today. The lively and inventive fuging-tunes, odes, and anthems of the New England tunesmiths could be enjoyed on their musical merits, as they are by Sacred Harp singers today. In addition, the tunebook compilers and composers of the South and West enriched their product by acting as folk song collectors, from about 1810. Notating and harmonizing the songs they heard, these singing masters set ballad tunes, dance tunes, and other melodies to sacred words. George Pullen Jackson, in his pioneering studies of what he called "folk hymns,"[6] noted hundreds of tunes for which he was able either to find secular versions of the same melody or to identify them as folk songs on the basis of supposed melodic characteristics. The richness of the tunebook repertory, together with its general acceptance in convivial as well as solemn occasions and the convenience of its notation, may have enabled the shape-note tunebook to usurp, to some degree, the position of secular sheet music, and, perhaps, to obviate the demand for other forms of notated music.

Of course, Americans sang and played much secular music that found no place in these sacred tunebooks, including songs and tunes of many kinds learned from oral transmission. One form of notated secular music was sheet music, largely consisting of single songs with keyboard accompaniment, printed from engraved metal plates. Immigrant craftsmen and entrepreneurs created a native sheet music industry only in the last two decades of the eighteenth century in the cities of the Eastern Seaboard, where a market existed for imported theater songs, operatic excerpts and keyboard pieces, as well as the productions of American composers. During the period 1801–1826, a single item of sheet music, consisting of two pages laboriously printed from engraved plates, cost an average of twenty-five cents,[7] while a tunebook printed from movable type or from stereotype plates, containing more than two-hundred pages of music, might cost only a dollar or two and could be relied on not to go out of fashion within a year or two of purchase. While shape-note tunebooks were printed in the Ohio Valley and Virginia as early as 1815–1820, the production of sheet music entered the western country much more slowly, as residents gradually acquired pianos and skills in playing them from standard (round) notation.[8]

Secular songs were also available in another form, in printed songsters. Cheaply available in a convenient pocket format, the songster normally contained words only, without musical notation, but often cited the name of a well-known tune to which a given poem could be sung.[9] The songster corresponded to the hymn books used in homes and churches, which likewise provided complete texts that could be sung to tunes learned from tunebooks, manuscripts, or oral tradition.

To summarize, up to 1830, the only printed music widely available and popular in the "western country" consisted of shape-note tunebooks containing a rich musical variety but set almost entirely to sacred texts. Between 1831 and 1853 there appeared a group of publications, scarcely noticed by bibliographers or music scholars, containing tunes in shape notes underlaid with secular texts. At least fourteen titles of this nature, comprising nineteen distinct editions, were printed in Ohio and Pennsylvania. They present a repertory that tends toward the moral and sentimental and often seems behind the times compared with East Coast publications. These books fall into three broad categories: books in standard oblong tunebook format, music typically in three or four parts, with theoretical "rudiments"—that is, typical psalmody books with the substitution of secular texts; books in pocket songster format—that is, songsters with the addition of music for one or more voices notated in shape notes, often for one or two voices; and books designed for children in common and Sunday schools, containing a mixture of sacred, secular, and pedagogical songs.

The first of the secular shape-note collections, and in many ways the most interesting, was *The Western Minstrel, or Ohio Melodist; Containing a Choice Collection of Moral, Patriotic and Sentimental Songs, with the Appropriate Music for Each Piece in Patent Notes, Carefully Selected and Affixed Thereto* (1831), compiled by Joseph Anthony Jr. of Clinton County, Ohio, and published by E. H. Flint in Cincinnati.[10] Anthony's preface reveals a threefold purpose for the collection: to "prevent sacred music from being profaned" by providing tunes for singing on convivial occasions where psalmody would be inappropriate; to provide a standard for regulating the singing of songs, since "persons who are not accustomed to singing together, vary so much as to make it difficult for them to keep in time and tune with each other"; and finally, to provide a means of musical instruction for those who do not care for hymns, since "hymns cannot please all."[11]

The unique features of *The Western Minstrel* may be partly explained on the basis of its compiler's personal background, which is likewise unique among tunebook compilers in the early nineteenth century. Joseph Anthony Jr. (1805–1862) was the son of Joseph Anthony and Rhoda Moorman, both Quakers from Virginia who had settled in Clinton County, Ohio, in 1814, "having left the state of Virginia in consequence of his aversion to educating his family where slavery was tolerated and where the influence of its principles might be installed in the minds of his children."[12] With his Quaker upbringing, Joseph, Jr. would have been familiar with an outlook that did not care for hymns and would not have shrunk from publishing songs that espoused antislavery sentiments (see below).

The lyrics in Anthony's collection are, as the title page states, "moral, patriotic and sentimental" and thus typical of the songster tradition. Love is the most popular subject and appears in several guises: tragic, teasing, unfulfilled, and even fulfilled, as in two texts on domestic bliss. Morally elevating texts demonstrate the joys of "Friendship," the dangers of "Intemperance,"

> O tell me not the burning bowl
> Still sparkles high with joy;
> It is the Scylla of the soul—
> It foams but to destroy.

The obligations of filial loyalty ("Forget not thy mother"), the avoidance of youthful folly ("While beauty and youth are in their full prime"), the just rewards of crime ("Captain Kid"), and pity for the plight of the enslaved African, who, separated from home and beloved, defiantly threatens suicide:

> Tomorrow, the white man in vain
> Shall proudly account me his slave:
> My shackles I plunge in the main,
> And rush to the realms of the brave[13]

Patriotic offerings include "Hail Columbia," "The Star-Spangled Banner," and "Yankee Doodle," the latter in an unusual lyric that extols American hospitality and educational improvements in the following stanzas:

> America's a dandy place,
> The people all are brothers
> And when one's got a pumkin [*sic*] pie
> He shares it with the others.
> > Yankee Doodle, boys, huza
> > Down outside, up the middle,
> > Yankee doodle, fa, sol, la,
> > Trumpet, drum, and fiddle.
> We're happy, free, and well to do
> And cannot want for knowledge,
> For almost every mile or two,
> You find a school or college.
> > Yankee doodle, boys, etc . . . [14]

British patriotism is represented by Bruce's Address and Wellington's March, while Washington, "Columbia's chieftain," is the object of several fulsome paeans. Local color in Anthony's collection is remarkably cosmopolitan, though largely

depending on Irish poet Thomas Moore: "The Song of the Tyrolese Peasants,"
"The Rose of Lucerne," "The Indian Philosopher," "The Blue Bells of Scotland,"
and "Kate Kearney" (from the banks of Killarney). There are examples of Scots
and Irish dialect, and even a phonetic rendering of the Gaelic refrain "mo chailín
deas cruite na mbó."

A cursory examination of the song texts suggests that they represent the
popular song of the Eastern states for the past twenty years or more before 1831,
which remained in circulation in songsters, broadsides, and the poetry corner
of the weekly newspaper. The music for these songs may have come from urban
sheet music and engraved song collections, or from manuscript copies. Keyboard accompaniments are absent, and many songs have only a single melodic
line printed in shape notes. In addition to this repertory, there are two other
genres of composition that make *The Western Minstrel* the most varied and
eclectic music book then available. One is a group of some half-dozen favorite
instrumental dance tunes, including "Fisher's Hornpipe" and "Miss McLeod's
Reel," printed in shape notes without lyrics. These tunes, occasionally printed
and abundant in manuscripts, were usually learned aurally; this may be their
unique printed appearance in shape notes.

The second distinctive group of selections is a substantial repertory of tunes,
many of apparent folk origin, which had already appeared in patent-note sacred
collections, notably the popular *Missouri Harmony* (1820). *The Western Minstrel*
shares forty-three of its 189 tunes with *Missouri Harmony*; of these, however,
only eleven share the same text with *Missouri Harmony*—the common texts were
among the small minority of secular texts in a predominantly sacred tunebook.
Where more than one voice part is printed, the parts usually agree with the version in *Missouri Harmony*; it is safe to say that Anthony knew this collection
and drew upon it in his own work. Evidently, he first canvassed the *Missouri
Harmony* and other sacred tunebooks for settings that already had secular texts,
such as "Liberty" and "Hail, Columbia"; he then added to these by adapting
secular words to many tunes that had been previously printed only as hymns
or spiritual songs. Among these were many "folk hymns," or tunes presumed
by Jackson and others to be traditional airs originally sung to ballads and other
poetry, which had been notated, harmonized, and underlaid with sacred texts
by early American psalmodists. Anthony now "re-secularized" them, not by
collecting traditional texts from oral tradition but by fitting them with literary
texts from various sources. The tune "Leander," for instance, appears as a ballad
called "William and Margaret," yet this is not the traditional ballad (Child 74)
but a literary recasting of it by David Mallet (1705–1765).[15] Another ballad tune,
collected in America with texts such as "Barbara Allen" and "Gypsy Davy," is
known in the sacred tunebooks as "The Church's Desolation." Anthony printed

this air, not with a traditional text but with Thomas Campbell's romantic literary narrative "Lord Ullin's Daughter."

Some of the texts and tunes in *The Western Minstrel* may be original with Anthony, but his skill, like that of most tunebook compilers, consisted in anthologizing and adapting. His views were surprisingly enlightened, but his innovation was doomed to failure. Singing classes still preferred to sing sacred music, singers of secular music scorned his "regulation," and his book failed to set a standard for song singing in the West.

A second attempt to provide secular music in a tunebook format was the work of another Ohioan, twenty-one-year-old Disciples preacher Amos Sutton Hayden (1813–1880). His collection, curiously titled *Introduction to Sacred Music*, was printed in Pittsburgh in 1835. While its title proclaims its sacred purpose, the preface explains the avoidance of overtly sacred texts:

> It has been a uniform practice of authors to set sacred poetry to their tunes. Hence the scholar has often been subjected to the necessity of incurring the displeasure of the Author of his being, by taking his sacred name in vain. The most solemn supplications and invocations are, sometimes, most thoughtlessly repeated, while the mind of the learner is wholly employed upon the sound of a tune! It is as certainly profanity, to utter the name of the Most High in an irreverent manner, while learning to sing, as it is under any other circumstances. Wherefore, to relieve the learner from the necessity of thus profanely desecrating the Holy Name, good moral sentiment, expressed in smooth and easy verse, has, as far as practicable, been substituted.[16]

Although the texts largely avoid addressing or naming the Deity, the tunes are clearly designed for singing in worship, many of them bearing citations such as "Song 134." Hayden explains: "The Songs referred to, will be found in the last publication of 'Psalms, Hymns and Spiritual Songs,'" evidently referring to Alexander Campbell's *Psalms, Hymns, and Spiritual Songs* (1834).[17] Hayden issued a revised edition of *Introduction to Sacred Music* in 1838. Despite this, neither the Restoration movement nor the general populace adopted Hayden's plan for teaching sacred music through secular words. However, in Hayden's final tunebook, *The Sacred Melodeon* (Philadelphia, 1849), printed in Jesse B. Aikin's seven-shape notation, he nevertheless continued his practice of avoiding hymns, writing that "in this work, as in a former one, the author has endeavoured to displace words that are entirely religious, and to supply their place with good moral poetry."[18]

A fourth tunebook containing mainly secular music is *The Vocalist's Pocket Companion* (1839), by Chambersburg, Pennsylvania, singing master Henry Smith and printer Henry Ruby. Printed, like Smith's popular *Church Harmony*

(1831), in somewhat smaller dimensions than the typical oblong tunebook, the *Companion* differs from its predecessors in lacking instructional rudiments, explaining that "such instruction is here deemed superfluous, there being such a variety of musical works that contain the rudiments; nor is there scarcely a family but one or more copies of such works will be found in their libraries."[19]

The repertory of *The Vocalist's Pocket Companion* is distinctive. This collection contains fewer hymn tunes than those of Anthony and Hayden, but these tunes are set to the same largely sacred texts as in the typical tunebooks. On the other hand, the *Companion* includes two types of song rarely found in the sacred or secular tunebooks: the Masonic song and the canon or round (called "catch" in this collection). Convivial songs figured prominently at meetings of Freemasons, and Masonic songs (including those of Robert Burns) were published with and without musical notation.[20] Masonic songs in the collection include "The Mason's Farewell" (Burns), "The Mason's Daughter," the ode "Let There Be Light," and "Hail, Mysterious, Glorious Science," a contrafactum of Giardini's glee "Viva tutte le vezzose." The ten "catches" in Smith and Ruby's collection are similar to the simple canons at the unison occasionally published in other collections and include such favorites as "Scotland's Burning" and "White Sand." Among the patriotic offerings in *The Vocalist's Pocket Companion* is the first appearance of "The Star-Spangled Banner" as a part-song.[21]

Also aimed at convivial gatherings is another collection, *The Aeolian Glee-Book* (Philadelphia, 1853) by Tillinghast King Collins Jr. (1828–1858), which offered "a choice collection of glees, quartetts, trios, rounds, and harmonized songs, arranged for soprano, alto, tenor, and base voices, designed for singing classes, musical societies, and social singing parties."[22] Like Hayden's *Sacred Melodeon*, Collins's sixty-four-page book is printed in the Aikin's seven-character notation. Though not examined for this study, the *Glee-Book*, like the *Vocalist's Pocket Companion*, appears to represent a partial accommodation to another form of printed songbook: the songster with musical notation.

The term *songster* generally refers to a small printed collection of song texts without notation. Irving Lowens noted several hundred of these printed in America before 1821. While many songsters offer suggestions of well-known tunes to which a text may be sung, only a small minority contains one or more tunes in musical notation. A few go so far as to provide a melody for every text in the book. If such songsters with music were to be printed in the "western country," it is not surprising that their notation should be in the form most widely understood in the region—namely, shape notes. Songsters were usually published by printers and booksellers and offered a selection of songs often described as "sentimental, patriotic, and moral." Their compilers frequently attempted to allay widespread distrust of secular music by assuring purchasers that "nothing will be found in this volume which can either directly or indirectly offend even the most fastidious."[23]

Shape-note songsters were issued in Cincinnati and Dayton, Ohio, and Harrisburg, Pennsylvania, from 1832 to 1853; three of them ran through three or more editions or printings, demonstrating their continued popularity and their success in addressing the "want of . . . secular music, as is suited to the capacity of that extensive portion of our community, who use only patent notes."[24] The first of the shape-note songsters was *The Eolian Songster* (1832), published and presumably compiled by Cincinnati bookseller Uriah Pierson James (1811–1889). This 252-page collection remained in print for more than two decades and existed also in an inexpensive forty-two-page edition with paper covers. *The American Minstrel* (1836), issued in Cincinnati by Uriah's brother Joseph A. James (1807–1882), was apparently sold or licensed to Philadelphia printer Henry F. Anners, who issued a revised edition in 1844. *The Rural Songster* (1850), published by Dayton, Ohio, printer Benjamin Franklin Ells (1806–1874) and enlarged in 1853, was advertised as "a collection of national and sentimental songs, for rural life," though the contents do not seem more rustic than those of its competitors. While the James brothers and B. F. Ells were primarily booksellers or printers, John Hoyt Hickok (1792–1841), author of *The Social Lyrist* (Harrisburg, 1840) stands out among this group as the compiler of two sacred tunebooks, *The Sacred Harp* (Lewistown, 1832) and (with George Fleming) *Evangelical Musick* (Carlisle, 1834).

As with Anthony's collection, the shape-note songsters offer an eclectic selection of American and foreign, old and new. Those evoking foreign lands include several Scots and Irish songs, as well as "Canadian Boat Song," "Tyrolese Song of Liberty," "The Bavarian Girl's Song," "The Castilian Maid," "The Neva Boatman's Song," and "Araby's Daughter." Like the ample selection of American patriotic songs, these were typical of the songster repertory, attempting to offer something for everyone.

Among these basically similar songsters, one stands out for its relative disregard of contemporary canons of taste and decorum. The very title page of the anonymous *My Own Song Book* (1840), published in Harrisburg by Hickok's son William Orville Hickok (1815–1891), flouts the tradition of moral edification, promising only "the most popular sentimental, patriotic and humorous songs." Instead of a lengthy preface or apologia, there is only the following:

ADVERTISEMENT
If you want to "drive dull cares away,"—come buy my book.
                                                   COMPILER.[25]

Interspersed among the sentimental ballads in the small forty-eight-page collection are comic songs involving ethnic stereotypes and stage dialect, such as

"I Canna Winna Marry Yet" and "Mine Katy, Vat Lives on de Plain," sung to the Scots air "Jessie the Flower o' Dunblane." Especially prominent here are several popular Negro-dialect songs regarded as predecessors of the blackface minstrel shows of the 1840s. These include "The Battle of Plattsburgh," also known as "Backside Albany" (1815) by Micah Hawkins,[26] "Jim Crow" (1830) "as sung by [blackface entertainer Thomas Dartmouth] Rice," "My Long Tail Blue" (1827), "Sambo's Address to His Bredren" (1833) with its refrain of "Ching-a-ring chaw," "Jim Brown" (1836), and "Jim along Josey" (1838).

While singing schools typically attracted youthful pupils, they did not cultivate a specifically juvenile repertory. Lowell Mason was one of the first to realize the potential of music especially suitable for the interests and aptitudes of children. With the success of his singing schools for children (1830) and his singing classes in Boston public schools (1837), Mason found a use for secular children's songs, which he published in *The Juvenile Lyre* (1831) and *The Juvenile Singing School* (1838).[27] Vocal-music classes gradually became an accepted part of common schools and Sunday schools in wide areas of the United States, including those where shape notation prevailed. A third group of patent-note collections arose to accommodate this need among Pennsylvanians of German culture and descent. The contents of these publications are not strictly secular: they contain hymns, including those suitable for Sunday schools, and songs teaching morality and reform values, such as obedience to parents, avoidance of strong drink, and pity for the poor. They largely avoid expressions of romantic love, as well as racial and ethnic stereotypes.

The undated *Musical Primer and Juvenile Instructor* (ca. 1846), is the work of Henry Smith and Benjamin Shroder Schneck (1806–1874) of Chambersburg, Pennsylvania. Singing master Henry Smith (Heinrich Schmidt) was the author of the popular *Church Harmony* (1831) and co-compiler of the *Vocalist's Pocket Companion* (1839); Schneck was a German Reformed clergyman and editor of the *Chambersburg Weekly Messenger* and the *Reformierte Kirchenzeitung*. According to the compilers, the purpose of this thirty-eight-page pamphlet, published in small, upright format in both patent-note and round-note editions, was "to test the question, whether an attempt to introduce music into the family circle, through the medium of Common and Sabbath-Schools, will meet with encouragement on the part of parents, and those who are intrusted with the education of children."[28] The authors cite with approval the introduction of music into the common schools in "some of the Eastern States" and express the hope that their collection will prepare the way "for promoting this good cause" in the middle and western states.

As its title implies, *The Musical Primer and Juvenile Instructor* attempts to combine the rudiments of reading with those of music. The first twelve pages of the pamphlet are devoted to the letters of the alphabet and their sounds;

the only music is a song introducing the letters. Pages 13–26 constitute the instructional rudiments of music, while pages 27–31, and the inside back cover, comprise "practical lessons"—that is, rounds for two, three, and four voices with solmization syllables printed below the notes. The final section contains eight psalm and hymn tunes and four secular songs.

Another collection mixing secular and sacred content, likewise designed for children, is *The Juvenile Harmony* (1852), compiled and published by Thomas R. Weber (1818–1889) of Hellertown, Pennsylvania. Weber's 118-page collection exhibits a more conventional oblong tunebook format, with a brief rudiments section at the front. Although there are there are no reading exercises, there are two alphabet songs, both entitled "The A, B, C." In one of them, as in a few other songs, the singing syllables are printed below the notes, along with the lyrics. Curiously, although the book is printed in the standard four-shape notation, the syllables printed below the notes are the seven "Italian" syllables "do ra mi fa sol la si [sic]." Also included are several rounds and temperance songs, and a song for teaching the names of the months of the year. Several songs bear attributions, notably to Lowell Mason. There are also several songs adapted from the German.

T. R. Weber continued to supply German-language and bilingual sacred music in patent notes to Eastern Pennsylvania churchgoers until his death in 1889.[29] His *Pennsylvanische Choral Harmonie* appeared in sixteen editions from 1844 to 1891. Weber reissued *The Juvenile Harmony* in 1859 and also published two collections, not seen, whose purpose and contents would seem to be similar. *The Juvenile Singing School* (1855) is a forty-eight-page collection in a small oblong format similar to that of collections designed for Sunday schools. Surprisingly, as late as 1878 Weber issued a large bilingual collection, *Die Sonntags-Schul Harmonie*, whose German subtitle describes the books as "a collection of songs set for three and four voices for Sunday schools, weekday schools and musical societies, and for use in families, with German and English texts." While the exact contents are unknown, they likely contain a variety of sacred, secular, and pedagogical songs.

There is no evidence that any of the volumes described here achieved sales or perennial popularity approaching that of popular patent-note sacred tunebooks such as *Missouri Harmony* or Smith's *Church Harmony*. In Ohio and Pennsylvania, as in other regions where patent notes prevailed, the primary purpose of singing schools remained that of training singers for public worship: the goals of "regulating" secular singing and avoiding profanity during musical instruction did not persuade Americans to abandon their sacred tunebooks. For their convivial singing, on the other hand, singers evidently preferred inexpensive, up-to-date pocket songsters without musical notation: even in those areas where conventional notation prevailed, songsters with notation constitute only a small minority of song collections. The movement to provide educational materials for schoolchildren represented a pervasive and growing trend in the nineteenth century. American teachers who attended normal schools came to rely on standardized materials with wide distribution, such as the Eclectic Readers by William Holmes McGuffey; for musical instruction, they were hardly likely to adopt provincial patent-note collections to provide the materials for cultural improvement. Still, the tunebooks, songsters, and musical primers described here represent a significant and fascinating attempt to provide a diverse repertory of music in those regions where shape notation prevailed and where composers such as Stephen Foster and Dan Emmett had their first musical exposure.[30]

Notes

1. Timothy Olmsted found it necessary to justify his use of conventional notation in his *Musical Olio* (1805), p. [3]: "These characters are not only our old acquaintance, but that of the whole musical world, in which all nations can read and probably never will discard." Hastings derided patent notes as "dunce notes" in his *Musical Magazine* 1 (1835): 87, qtd. in Lowens, *Music and Musicians*, 117–18.

2. Crawford, *America's Musical Life*, 131.

3. Bealle, *Public Worship, Private Faith*, 2.

4. Timothy Flint, *The Columbian Harmonist* (Cincinnati, 1816); Lowell Mason and Timothy B. Mason, *The Sacred Harp: or, Eclectic Harmony* (Cincinnati, 1834).

5. Joseph Anthony Jr., *The Western Minstrel* (Cincinnati, 1831), 3.

6. Jackson, *White Spirituals*; Jackson, *Spiritual Folk-Songs*; and Jackson, *Down East Spirituals*.

7. Wolfe, *Early American Music*, 205–6.

8. Crawford, *America's Musical Life*, 235–7

9. Lowens, *Bibliography of Songsters*, ix–xi.

10. The publisher, Ebenezer Hubbard Flint, was the son of the Rev. Timothy Flint (1780–1840), the Presbyterian missionary who had compiled *The Columbian Harmonist* (Cincinnati, 1816).

11. Anthony, *Western Minstrel*, [iii–iv].

12. Hinshaw and Marshall, *Encyclopedia*, 5:316. Information on the family's migration from Virginia is found in Jacob, *Anthony Roots and Branches*, qtd. by Barbara Ellen Rowe at http://familytreemaker.genealogy.com/users/r/o/w/Barbara-Ellen-Rowe/GENE3-0028.html.

13. William Roscoe and James Currie, "The Negroe's Complaint," published anonymously in 1788. *Federal Gazette and Philadelphia Evening Post*, April 8, 1790. Roscoe, *Poetical Works*, 71–73.

14. *The Port Folio*, August 30, 1806, written for the Fourth of July, 1806, attributed to Mr. [William] Bigelow of Salem, Mass.

15. *Lives of Scottish Poets*, 46–49.

16. A. S. Hayden, *Introduction to Sacred Music* (1835), [iii].

17. Campbell, Scott, Stone, and Johnson, *Psalms, Hymns, and Spiritual Songs*. Hayden would later help to revise this collection as *The Christian Hymn Book: A Compilation of Psalm, Hymns and Spiritual Songs, Original and Selected*, by A. Campbell and others (Bosworth, 1865).

18. Hayden, *Sacred Melodeon*, 4.

19. Henry Smith and Henry Ruby, *The Vocalist's Pocket Companion* (1839), [ii]–iii.

20. Vinton, *Masonick Minstrel*.

21. Mark Clague, personal communication.

22. T. K. Collins Jr., *The Aeolian Glee-Book* (1853), [t.–p.].

23. *The American Minstrel* (1836), [3].

24. J. H. Hickok, *The Social Lyrist* (1840), 4.

25. *My Own Song Book* (1840), [2].

26. Mahar, "Backside Albany."

27. Crawford, *America's Musical Life*, 146–49.

28. H. Smith and B. S. Schneck, *The Musical Primer and Juvenile Instructor*, 1.

29. Grimminger, *Sacred Song*, 150–59.

30. This is not to claim that either Foster or Emmett knew or were influenced by these secular shape-note collections, only that the songs preserved in these books were current in the areas where they grew up.

References

Bealle, John. *Public Worship, Private Faith: Sacred Harp and American Folksong*. Athens: University of Georgia Press, 1997.

Campbell, Alexander, and others. *The Christian Hymn Book: A Compilation of Psalm, Hymns and Spiritual Songs, Original and Selected*. Cincinnati: Bosworth, 1865.

Campbell, Alexander, W. Scott, B. W. Stone, and John T. Johnson, *Psalms, Hymns, and Spiritual Songs, Original and Selected, Adapted to the Christian Religion*. Bethany, W.V.: Campbell, 1834.

Crawford, Richard. *America's Musical Life: A History*. New York: Norton, 2001.

Grigg's Southern and Western Songster. Philadelphia: Grigg and Elliot, 1836.

Grimminger, Daniel Jay. *Sacred Song and the Pennsylvania Dutch*. Rochester, N.Y.: University of Rochester Press, 2012.

Hinshaw, William Wade, and Thomas Worth Marshall, eds. *Encyclopedia of American Quaker Genealogy*. 6 vols. Baltimore, Md.: Genealogical, 1969–1977.

Jackson, George Pullen. *Down East Spirituals and Others*. New York: Augustin, 1939
———. *Spiritual Folk-Songs of Early America*. New York: Augustin, 1937.
———. *White Spirituals in the Southern Uplands*. Chapel Hill: University of North Carolina Press, 1933. Reprint, New York: Dover, 1965.

Jacob, Nancy Vasti Anthony. *Anthony Roots and Branches*. Shreveport, La.: Professional Business Services, 1971.

The Lives of Scottish Poets. London: Boys, 1821.

Lowens, Irving. *A Bibliography of Songsters Printed in America before 1821*. Worcester, Mass.: American Antiquarian Society, 1976.

————. *Music and Musicians in Early America*. New York: Norton, 1964.

Mahar, William J. "'Backside Albany' and Early Blackface Minstrelsy: A Contextual Study of America's First Blackface Song." *American Music* 6 (Spring 1988): 1–17.

[Roscoe, William.] *The Poetical Works of William Roscoe*. London: Ward and Lock, 1857.

Stanislaw, Richard J. *A Checklist of Four-Shape Shape-Note Tunebooks*. ISAM Monographs no. 10. Brooklyn, N.Y.: Institute for Studies in American Music, 1978.

Vinton, David. *The Masonick Minstrel*. Dedham, Mass.: Mann, 1816.

Wolfe, Richard J. *Early American Music Engraving and Printing*. Urbana: University of Illinois Press, 1980.

Bibliography of Shape-Note Publications Containing Largely Secular Songs, 1831–1861

The following is a list of the shape-note publications emphasizing secular content, 1831–1861. Citations are in the following format:

AUTHOR (or TITLE, if no named author)
Short title, edition date
Full title with imprint.
Pagination.
Copyright or other information relevant for dating. Inventory of contents.
Copies in libraries, indicated by MARC codes. Asterisk indicates that I have examined the copy.
Variant issues or later editions.

THE AMERICAN MINSTREL
The American Minstrel, 1836
The American Minstrel: A choice collection of the most popular songs, glees, duets, choruses, &c. many of which are original. With select music. Cincinnati: Stereotyped and published by J. A. James and Co. 1836.
318 pp; frontispiece. Songster with music for a few songs.
Copyright entered 1836, District of Ohio, by J. A. James & Co. Preface signed Cincinnati, June 1836. P. [1], t–p.; p. [2], copyright statement, "Printed by James and Gazlay, Cincinnati"; pp. [3]-4, preface; pp. 5–305, songs; p. [306] blank; pp. 307–18, contents.
*NHi(inc) *MH OC *RPB
[reissue] *The American Minstrel*, 1837.
MH
The American Minstrel, new and revised edition, 1844

The American Minstrel: . . . New and revised edition: Philadelphia: Henry F. Anners, 1844.
318 pp; front.
Copyright entered 1840, District of Ohio, by U. P. James. No preface. P. [1], t–p.; p. [2], copyright statement. pp. [3]–306, songs; pp. 307–18, contents.

*MH
[reissue] *The American Minstrel*, Philadelphia: Henry F. Anners, 1848.
NHi

JOSEPH ANTHONY Jr.
The Western Minstrel, 1831
The Western Minstrel, or *Ohio Melodist*: Containing a choice collection of moral, patriotic and sentimental songs, with the appropriate music for each piece in patent
notes, carefully selected and affixed thereto; together with instructions for learners.
Being well calculated to give a correct knowledge of vocal music: and also designed
to assist learners of the instrumental branch of that science. By Joseph Anthony Jr.
Cincinnati: published by E. H. Flint, . . . printed at the Cincinnati Journal Office.
1831.
159, [1] pp.
Copyright granted December 6, 1830, District of Ohio, to Joseph Anthony Jr. Preface
signed Clinton Co. O February 1, 1831. P. [i], t–p.; p. [ii], copyright notice, "stereotyped at the Cincinnati Type Foundry"; pp. [iii]–iv, preface; pp. [v]–x, instructions
for learners. . . . pp. 12–159, music; p. [160], index.
C 5779 *MWA(inc) *OClWHi
[variant issue] *The Western Minstrel*, or *Ohio Melodist*: . . . By Joseph Anthony Jr.
159, [1] pp.
Same as main entry, only lacks imprint.
*RPB

TILLINGHAST KING COLLINS Jr.
The Aeolian Glee Book [1853]
The Aeolian Glee-Book: Consisting of a choice collection of glees, quartetts, trios,
rounds, and harmonized songs, arranged for soprano, alto, tenor, and base voices.
Designed for singing classes, musical societies, and social singing parties. By T. K.
Collins Jr. Philadelphia: published by T. K. Collins Jr.
63, [1] pp. Aikin characters. 19x25 cm
Copyright granted 1853, Eastern District of Pennsylvania, to T. K. Collins Jr. P. [1],
t–p.; p. [2], preface, copyright notice; "Collins, printer"; "The character notes, as
used in the 'Christian Minstrel,' secured for this work by special contract with the
proprietors"; pp. 3–63, music; p. 64, contents.
ICN
[reissue] *The Aeolian Glee-Book*, 1854.
DLC
[reissue] *The Aeolian Glee-Book*: S. C. Collins, publisher, 1863.
*T

THE EOLIAN SONGSTER
The Eolian Songster, [1832]
The Eolian Songster: A choice collection of the most popular sentimental, patriotic, naval, and comic songs. With music. Cincinnati: published by U. P. James.
252 pp., 12mo; illust. Songster with music for some songs.
Copyright granted June 15, 1832, District of Ohio, to U. P. James as proprietor. P. [i] blank; p. [ii], frontispiece; p. [iii], t–p.; p. [iv] copyright notice, "Stereotyped by J. A. James, Cincinnati"; pp. [v]–vi, preface; pp. vii–ix, contents; p. [x] blank; pp. [11]–252 songs, with music and woodcuts.
*DLC *MWA NN *OC *OHi
[reissue] *The Eolian Songster*. Cincinnati: N. & G. Guilford & Co. 1833.
252 pp. Contents as above.
*ICN MB LNT
[reissue] *The Eolian Songster*; Cincinnati: U. P. James. 1852.
252 pp. Contents as above.
*RPB

The Eolian Songster [abridged version]. [ca. 1847–1853]
The Eolian Songster: A choice collection of the most popular songs, with music. Cincinnati: published by U. P. James, 107 Walnut Street. [cover title]
[11]–42 pp. Songster with music for three voices.
Undated; U. P. James was at this address in the years 1847–1853. Pp.[11]–42, songs with music.
DLC ICN *MWA NN NBUG NJP *OHi *RPB
[variant issue] Cincinnati: published by J. A. and U. P. James.
PU CSmH

AMOS SUTTON HAYDEN
Introduction to Sacred Music, 1835
Introduction to Sacred Music; comprising the necessary rudiments, with a choice collection of tunes, original and selected. By A. S. Hayden. Pittsburgh: published by the Author—printed by Johnston and Stockton—1835.
104 pp.
Copyright entered 1835 by A. S. Hayden, Western District of Pennsylvania. P. [1], t–p.; p. [ii], copyright notice; p. [iii], preface; pp. [iv]–viii, rudiments; pp. 9–103, music; p. 104, index.
*MWA

Introduction to Sacred Music, [2d edition], 1838
Introduction to Sacred Music. Stereotyped edition, enlarged and much improved. Pittsburgh: printed by Johnston and Stockton. 1838.
120 pp.
Copyright granted 1838, Western District of Pennsylvania, to A. S. Hayden. Preface to second edition signed Sept. 1838. P. [1], t–p.; p. [ii], copyright notice, "Stereotyped

by J. A. James, Cincinnati"; p. [iii], preface, preface to 2nd edition; pp. [iv]–x, rudiments; pp. 11–119, music, p. 120, index.
OClWHi *PPiPT *RPB TxFTC

The Sacred Melodeon, 1848–1866

The Sacred Melodeon: Containing a great variety of the most approved church music, selected chiefly from the old standard authors, with many original compositions. On a new system of notation. Designed for the use of churches, singing societies, and academies. By A. S. Hayden. Published by the proprietor. Printed and sold by T. K. & P. G. Collins, Philadelphia. Stereotyped by L. Johnson & Co. 1849.

304 pp. Aiken seven shape notation.

Copyright entered 1848, Eastern Districe of Pennsylvania, by A. S. Hayden. Preface signed Euclid, Ohio, Nov. 1848, A. S. Hayden. P. [1], t–p.; p. [2], copyright notice; pp. 3–4, preface; pp. 5–22, rudiments; pp. 23–301, music; pp. [302]–304, index.
*DLC TKL

reissued as above 1850 (6th ed.), 1851, 1853
*InGo

reissued Cincinnati: Moore Wilstach & Keys [Wm. Overend & Co., printers] 1852
*DLC(inc); 1853 ODW; 1858 CCC inc

Cincinnati: Moore, Anderson & Co. [Wm. Overend & Co., printers] 1855; 1856
*CCC (1855 cover) ICRL *OClWHi (1855 cover) *tem; 1857 *OO (1858 cover); 1858 *CCC(inc?) PPPrHi

Cincinnati: Moore Wilstach & Baldwin 1865
*InGo NcWsM; 1866 NcWsM

Cincinnati: Wilstach, Baldwin & Co.
*InGo

Indianapolis: Bowen, Stewart & Co. 1860.
*OClWHi(inc)

JOHN HOYT HICKOK

The Social Lyrist, 1840–1847

The Social Lyrist: A collection of sentimental, patriotic, and pious songs, set to music, arranged for one, two, and three voices. By J. H. Hickok. Harrisburg, Pa. Published by W. Orville Hickok. Stereotyped by L. Johnson, Philadelphia. 1840.

144 p.

Copyright entered 1840, Eastern District of Pennsylvania, by E. Guyer and W. O. Hickok. Preface dated Harrisburg, 1 Jan. 1840. P. [1], t–p.; p. [2], copyright notice; pp. 3–4, preface; pp. 5–140, songs with music; pp. 141–144; index.
DLC GEU *InGo MH *MWA NjP NN RPB

[reissue] Harrisburg, Pa., Hickok and Cantine 1843.
MH CtY NHi MWA

[reissue] Harrisburg, Ps.: B. Parke, 1847.
LNB

MY OWN SONG BOOK
My Own Song Book, 1840
My Own Song Book: A well selected collection of the most popular sentimental, pa-
    triotic and humorous songs. Each song arranged and set to music. Harrisburg, Pa.
    For sale by W. O. Hickok. 1840.
48 pp. Songster with music.
P. [2], advertisement, "If you want to 'drive dull cares away,'—come buy my song book.
*NHi

THE RURAL SONGSTER
The Rural Songster, 1850
The Rural Songster: A collection of national and sentimental songs, for rural life.
    Dayton, O.: published by B. F. Ells. 1850.
112 pp. Songster with music. Illustrated.
P. [i] blank; p. [ii], frontispiece; p. [iii], t–p.; p. [iv] blank; pp. [v]–viii, index; pp. 9–112,
    songs with music.
NjP *RPB OD TU MWA
[reissue] reissued Dayton, O.: published by B. F. Ells. 1852.
*OClWHi

The Rural Songster, [2d edition], 1853
The Rural Songster. New edition, greatly enlarged and improved. Dayton, O.: published
    by L. F. Claflin. 1853.
160 pp. Songster with music. Illustrated.
Copyright entered 1854, District of Ohio, by B. F. Ells. Pp. 9–160, music.
*MWA
[reissue] Dayton, O.: More, Clarke & Co. 1854. [cover imprint]
*RPB
[reissue] Dayton, O.: Ells, Marquis & Co. 1856
ODM

HENRY SMITH and HENRY RUBY
The Vocalist's Pocket Companion, [1839]
The Vocalist's Pocket Companion: Being a collection of the most popular songs, ar-
    ranged with solos, duetts and trios. By H. Smith & H. Ruby. Chambersburg: Henry
    Ruby, printer.
iv, 108 pp.
Copyright entered 1839, Eastern District of Pennsylvania, by H. Smith & H. Ruby.
    P. [i], t–p.; pp. [ii]–iii, preface, errata; p. iv, contents; pp. 1–108, songs with music.
*DLC *MWA *MiU-C *RPB

HENRY SMITH and BENJAMIN SHRODER SCHNECK
The Musical Primer, and Juvenile Instructor, [ca. 1846]
The Musical Primer, and Juvenile Instructor. By H. Smith & B. S. Schneck. Chambers-

burg: published by the proprietors. Stereotyped by L. Johnson & Co., Philadelphia. Copyright secured, according to law. [cover title]

36 pp. Also published in round notes (inside front cover).

One of recommendations inside front cover dated January 19, 1846. P. 1, preface; pp. 2–5, alphabets, song "A.B.C." with music; pp. 6–12, spelling lessons; pp. 13–26, introduction to music; pp. 27–31, practical lessons; pp. 32–36, songs with music; inside back cover, two rounds with music; outside back cover, index to the juvenile instructor. P. 13, caption title, "Juvenile Instructor."

*CtHT-W *PPL

THOMAS R. WEBER

The Juvenile Harmony, 1852–1859

The Juvenile Harmony: Containing a choice collection of moral and sacred songs, designed for juvenile singing schools, common schools, Sunday schools, family circles and juvenile concerts. By T. R. Weber, author of the "Pennsylvania Choral Harmony," "New Harmony," etc. 1852. [Allentown]

viii, 118 pp.

Copyright entered 1852, Eastern District of Pennsylvania, by T. R. Weber. P. [i], t–p.; p. [ii], copyright notice, index, "J. R. Weber, printer"; iii–viii, rudiments [identical to those in *Die neue Harmonie*; pp. 1–118, music.

*CCC NcU NcWsM

The Juvenile Harmony. Second edition. Printed by the compiler, 1859.

viii, 120 pp.

Copyright entered 1859, Eastern District of Pennsylvania, by T. R. Weber.

*InGo *NcU (inc)

The Juvenile Singing School, 1855

The Juvenile Singing School, Original and Selected, 1855.

48 pp; 12 x 15 cm.

DLC

Die Sonntags-Schul Harmonie, 1878

Die Sonntags-Schul Harmonie: Eine Sammlung drei und vierstimmig ausgesetzte Gesänge für Sonntags-Schulen, Wochen-Schulen, und musikalischen-Geschellschaften [*sic*], und für den Familien Gebrauch: mit Deutschem und Englischem Texte. Hellertown, Pa.: Gedruckt von Thos. R. Weber, 1878.

viii, 270, 24 p.; 17x25 cm.

Caption title following p. 270: Anhang zur Sonntagsschul-Harmonie.

DLC

PART II

Patronage

American culture is unavoidably and often proudly democratic. It is also often singularly entrepreneurial, with many eyes firmly fixed on the commercial potential of any new artistic enterprise. But arguably the fundamental feature of American music, apart from its stylistic hybridity and diverse sources of inspiration, is its need to make its own way in the marketplace. American artists and musicians have never enjoyed conspicuous or even consistent financial support from long-standing organs of high authority, whether sacred or secular, even when sufficient wealth and leisure time emerged to facilitate such a rise.[1]

Patronage of music in particular has been a sometime thing in the United States because it has long been seen as fundamentally divorced from the immediate needs of the social order. John Adams famously declared in a letter to wife Abigail in 1780, "I must study politics and war that my sons may have the liberty to study mathematics and philosophy. My sons ought to study mathematics and philosophy . . . in order to give their children a right to study painting, poetry, music, architecture, statuary, tapestry and porcelain." Putting off the decorative arts—which music surely is, in this context—until the third generation only made practical sense for Adams. His tacitly accepted hierarchical division also helps to explain the impulse to "catch up" with Europe, which begins to appear in the essays of later nineteenth-century cultural writers Ralph Waldo Emerson and Frederick Louis Ritter, an early Beethoven biographer who viewed America as needing finally to declare a national musical identity. But cultural assumptions lie deep, and not all that much has changed in our attitudes toward music as a minor occupation in the twenty-first century.

Because the arts have generally occupied a third (or even lower) tier in American prestige, they have only rarely risen to the point of needing to be taken seriously by the cultural, political, and social powers that be. Music as either a plaything of the wealthy or diversion for the masses just does not figure politically—except in the unique case of military bands, the outlay for which in the US federal budget is nearly three times the entire annual allotment to the National Endowment for the Arts.[2] In any case, the arts are not necessarily deemed worthy of the support of hard-working, middle-class "tax payers," much less patronage from national or state governments.

The popular arts, of course, still function as an integral part of daily life, but there is no consensus that the arts—beyond a handful of painted symbols and national airs—should be singled out for "special" financial benefit. In America, this stance is also never confused with any collective urge to provide government support for musicians. Indeed, by the late twentieth century, financing of musicians, often assumed to be members of a class of feckless intellectuals, was viewed with suspicion at all levels. Composer Virgil Thomson, who earned his daily bread mainly as a writer and music critic, concludes his essay "How Composers Eat, *or* Who Does What to Whom and Who Gets Paid" (1961) with a characteristically wry assessment that implies patronage to be little less than a form of intellectual bribery—at least as far as composers are concerned:

> Between the extremes of being too rich for comfort and being really poor, the amount of money composers have doesn't seem to affect them very much. Photogenic poverty and ostentatious spending are equally repugnant to their habits. The source of their money has, however, a certain effect on their work. We have noted that the composer, being a member of the Professional Classes, enjoys all the rights and is subject to the obligations of what is known as Professional Integrity. This does not mean that he enjoys complete intellectual freedom. He has that only with regard to the formal, or structural, aspects of his art. His musical material and style would seem to be a function, at any given moment, of his chief income source.[3]

Popular music has always existed in some form, generally without official patronage, but flourishing in direct relationship to its audience and serving an essential cultural function. Most music aimed at a mass public forms part of a transient experience in time but is nevertheless heavily freighted. Allied to religious ritual, sung tribal histories, or family genealogies, much meaningful music is shared in public settings. A money economy is not necessarily involved in the process. For music to exist in any given region where music literacy is not widespread—which is to say most of them, even in America up to the twenty-first century—the question of patronage has for the most part been an issue of concern only to fashion-conscious elites.

On the heels of the Enlightenment, however, once music markets were formed to vend musical products—instruments, printed song sheets, broadsides, songsters, or a teachers' services, then the calculus changed. While much of music history is invested in historical biographies of primarily the great performers and composers of music and in larger narratives about its social meaning, the mundane details of the music business deserve another look. (Technical factors—melodic and harmonic structures and formal development—that shape individual musical works define the bailiwick of the music theorist or analyst.) The presence of music within, and the support of music by, larger social institutions is the concern of four chapters in this volume and address larger issues of patronage.

The spread of English musical theater to the American colonies in the middle of the eighteenth century via full companies, such as David Douglass's American Company of Comedians, presented new opportunities for entrepreneurial as well as artistic ideas to take root. In making his case for a growing "cultural maturity" in America during the 1760s, Sterling Murray focuses his discussion in chapter 4 on a single English opera, *Love in a Village* (1762), and its transplantation to the New World only four years after its London premiere. Issues ranging from the lack of copyright controls to the generally free and easy adaptations in actor-centered shows—the norm in European sung theater at the time—make Murray's analysis pertinent today, when ownership and transmission of music are very much in the forefront. Douglass's eighteenth-century American productions are related to his London projects but are also exceptional in that they reflect new American circumstances. The unusually rich orchestral requirements of *Love in a Village* must have made its music, in Murray's words, "strikingly new and different" from the customary stage vehicles of the time. The genre of English comic opera, as opposed to "ballad opera" dating from the 1720s, was itself a novelty on both sides of the Atlantic. The incipient sentimentality and romantic expressions of the late eighteenth century were much at variance with the "more brutal and cynical skepticism that permeates works like *The Beggar's Opera.*" *Love in a Village*, with its added intertextual elements "set American theater music in a new direction." In what ways did Douglass shape his productions and build his business in order to attract the audience support he knew to be essential once it reached the shores of North America?

On the religious side—a most important side of American music history—Esther Crookshank explores in chapter 5 the highly varied treatment of the most familiar texts in English-speaking America outside the Bible during the eighteenth and early nineteenth centuries, the religious poetry of Isaac Watts.[4] Tracing the paths of four especially popular Watts texts is the business of Crookshank's chapter that seeks to address questions of patronage in the broadest sense— the support Watts received from religious leaders in successive revivals and in a manner he never intended. How were Watts's hymn texts interpreted and where were they published such that they could "take root" in settings both educational and religious and in ways that they appealed to both African American and Anglo-American communities? Watts hymns were beloved across generations among both rural and urban audiences and in contrasting, not to say contradictory, theological contexts. In settings where printed hymnals and oral traditions are documented, Crookshank leads us to observe the interactive nature of nineteenth-century hymn performance as a whole. She examines the evidence on all sides and helps us see how specific musical elements render specific texts attractive for a given community setting. In the process, she also fills in the social background of the great revival movements of the period between the colonial era and 1900. Given Watts's strong presence in Protestant church hymnals up to the present day—he wrote the words of the popular Christmas carol "Joy to the World" and the refrain "From All That Dwell Below the Skies," among some 750 other poems—it is fair to claim that Watts continues to be strongly felt by thousands of patrons across the English-speaking world. Ironically, many, if not most, of his devotees, though cherishing his poetry and even committing words and melodies to memory, would be hard pressed to identify his name.

Amy C. Beal, in chapter 6, brings us up to date about "an independent strand of American music production" in the twenty-first century only beginning to be explored in the scholarly literature. Taking into account historical antecedents, in which a musician may need to be not merely composer, conductor, or live performer but also "recording artist, record producer, bandleader, studio builder, software designer and programmer, and publisher," her chapter raises a host of fascinating questions about the patrons and the beneficiaries of patronage when corporate and aesthetic values collide. Where donors more closely resemble commercial machines than individual benefactors and the audience is whomever has access to an electronic playback device, new challenges arise.

The information explosion is a preoccupation of present media-dominated age, and of course the question "Who gets paid?"—for downloads, samples, tweets, parodies, and borrowings of any kind—broadens exponentially the scope of Virgil Thomson's question. Beal's exploration of publisher/composer relations, especially when composers themselves become publishers—their own patrons as it were—or form cooperative organizations to support each other provides a fascinating glimpse into the practical concerns of American modernists during the last four decades of the twentieth century.

Even more relevant to the increasingly common phenomenon of self-marketing by composers is Mark Clague's study in chapter 7.[5] Clague introduces his case study with a lengthy historical discussion of the broader meaning of the word "school" to reveal in depth how the other themes of this book can intertwine with questions of finance and economics. Then, distilling his conversations with Atlanta Symphony conductor Robert Spano, a key mediator on the scene, Clague reports that the Atlanta School members "share a self-proclaimed aesthetic embrace of melody, traditional tonality, and resources drawn from world or popular music." Clague's focus falls on the essential but in some sense extramusical elements that have shaped this "school," however. Spano works to attract donors, to commission works calculated to appeal to local audiences, and to introduce new music widely by creating public events and video presentations in the metropolitan area. Clague provides an insightful context for this contemporary school by contrasting earlier American nationalist rhetorical strategies that deploy the term (as in "the Second New England School," which evokes a linkage, however imaginary, between early Federal period tunesmiths, such as William Billings and Daniel Read, and the German-trained songwriters and symphonists like Edward MacDowell or George Chadwick, who happened to reside in New England around 1900) with the more crafted and subtle marketing tactics of Spano and the Atlanta group.

As John Spitzer reports in 2012, "Nineteenth-century American orchestras supported themselves almost entirely at the box office, selling their performances to the public. This was a marked contrast to many European orchestras of the time, which enjoyed significant state patronage. It is also a contrast to today's American orchestras, most of which derive only about one-third of their income from ticket sales."[6]

Similarly, most opera companies, choral societies, and Broadway theaters subsist on fundraising benefits, recording royalties, private donations, and foundation and government grants. Church musicians, mostly individually salaried within their congregations or denominations, accrue a miniscule fraction of the amount of patronage once doled out by the Renaissance princes of the Roman Catholic Church. The newcomer to the patronage business, but one likely to remain on the scene for the near term, is the American university. Part of a typical music professor's job description, under the rubric of "research" or "creative activity," is to write and publish or perform new music on a regular basis. Merely teaching the next generation of music students is not sufficient to rise in the ranks of elite college and university music departments nowadays. This form of patronage has its merits despite what detractors may say—again, Virgil Thomson's critique comes to mind—but it is likely to remain in place as long as the current structures of higher education draw such a large percentage of young Americans across the social and economic spectrum.

Notes

1. Outside of America things have almost always been different. The Western cultural norm since the Enlightenment has been to view the healthy functioning of communities through their symbols and their artistic life, and so the arts became the responsibility of leaders and cultural creators. It is no surprise, then, that the chief patrons over time have tended to be kings, mayors, bishops, guilds, and, in more bourgeois circumstances, concert companies and singing societies.

2. Based on the most current figures available, in the period between 2010 and 2014 funding for the NEA comes in at roughly $150 million per year, whereas the military budget for its more than 130 bands comprising 6,400 members was $437 million in 2015—nearly three times the outlay (Dave Philipps, "Military Is Asked to March to a Less Expensive Tune," *New York Times*, July 1, 2016).

3. The essay appears in a collection introduced by John Rockwell, *A Virgil Thomson Reader* (New York: Dutton, 1981), 121.

4. Watts (1674–1748), is still included far more frequently in modern Protestant hymnals in the reformed tradition than any other noncontemporary writer except Catherine Winkworth (1827–1878). The only eighteenth-century poet to rival Watts in the number of musical settings is Charles Wesley (1707–1778).

5. Clague's subtitle, "A Point of View and a Case in Point," is a tip of the hat to Richard Crawford's assessment of the place of American musicology in the larger scheme of American cultural studies, a 1975 essay "American Studies and American Musicology: A Point of View and a Case in Point," published by the Institute for Studies in American Music (Brooklyn, New York).

6. *American Orchestras in the Nineteenth Century*, edited by John Spitzer (Chicago: University of Chicago Press, 2012), 219.

4 *Love in a Village* and a New Direction for Musical Theater in Eighteenth-Century America

STERLING E. MURRAY

Nestled among the news reports concerning Charleston in an October 1765 issue of the *South Carolina Gazette* was the following announcement:

> Mr. Douglass, Manager of the American Company of Comedians, is returned, who, we hear, has brought over, at a great expense . . . some very eminent performers from both the theatres in London, particularly in the SINGING-WAY, so that the English COMIC OPERA, a species of entertainment that has never yet appeared properly on this side of the water, is likely to be performed here this winter to great advantage.[1]

With this rather innocuous bit of local news, a new and decisive chapter in the history of American musical theater was first recognized.

David Douglass (ca. 1720–1786) began his career on the American stage as a member of Lewis Hallam's London Company of Comedians.[2] When, in 1756, yellow fever claimed Hallam's life in Jamaica, Douglass married his widow and took over the company, whose name he later changed to "The American Company."[3] Douglass's troupe was one of several active in the colonies before the Revolution. None had a resident home; rather, they traveled from town to town, stopping to perform for a time and then pushing on to the next venue. Like that of Hallam's before him, Douglass's company followed a route that spanned the distance from Charleston to Newport, making stops along the way at Williamsburg, Annapolis, Philadelphia, and New York.

Touring or "strolling" companies were small, requiring each actor to be versatile and capable of fulfilling multiple functions as actor, dancer, and musician. Music occupied an essential place in eighteenth-century theatrical productions, both in London and the colonies. In addition to musical stage pieces, songs and interlude music were interpolated into spoken dramas—sometimes to a surprising degree.[4] An evening at the playhouse typically began with "waiting music" played by the orchestra. The mainpiece that followed was divided into several acts, with additional music placed between them.[5] In addition to the featured work, there was an afterpiece that typically was shorter and lighter in character. In order to keep their audiences entertained and under control during the interval between these two offerings, musicians again were called on to perform. With this amount of music in an evening's entertainment, it was necessary that the payrolls of eighteenth-century theater companies include several actors who could also sing or play an instrument.

Before 1766 the repertory of the American Company included three principal musical pieces: *The Beggar's Opera* (1728), *Flora, or Hob in the Well* (1730), and *The Devil to Pay* (1731).[6] All were ballad operas, in which spoken dialog alternated with songs, or airs, whose tunes were borrowed from preexistent music and supplied with words sculpted to fit their new dramatic settings. The richest source repositories for these tunes were the traditional songs sung in taverns and hawked as broadsides on street corners. The requirements of such short and repetitive songs were so basic that performers did not need to be trained singers. In most instances, if an actor could "carry a tune," this was considered sufficient.

Douglass, who recognized the artistic limitations of such works, had higher aspirations for his company. In the mid 1760s he set out to enrich the musical repertory of the American Company with comic operas that were the newest rage of London's musical theaters.[7] Douglass had good reason to expect that this newer style of theater would be well received. Americans were eager to refurnish their lives in the colonies with the latest fashions of London, and, as asserted in the *South Carolina Gazette*, this "species of entertainment" was completely new to the colonies.[8]

Douglass's scheme was not without its problems. While there were members of his company who possessed sufficient skill to negotiate the limited musical requirements of ballad operas, this newer repertory demanded a higher degree of musical proficiency. Douglass recognized that he would have to make some fundamental adjustments in his company, and in the late spring of 1764 he set sail for London to recruit trained vocalists.[9] Singers who could act rather than actors who could sing were his new priority.

Douglass spent the rest of 1764 and most of the following year in London. Although we have no specific records, he probably invested much of his time talking with fellow actors and theater mangers, attending performances,[10] and frequenting the city's pleasure gardens, seeking out talented young singers who might be convinced to try their fortune in the colonies. Traveling in this circle, Douglass hardly could have avoided contact with Thomas Arne (1710–1778). The fifty-four-year-old Arne was a shining light of fashionable London theater life.[11] By the time of Douglass's visit, Arne had to his credit several successful theater pieces,[12] and his songs were regular fare at the city's pleasure gardens. Arne was in a perfect position to assist Douglass in his search, and, indeed, it seems likely that he did.

When Douglass returned to the colonies that autumn, he brought with him five talented young singers: Sarah Wainwright, Stephen Woolls, Thomas Wall, Henrietta Osborne, and Nancy Hallam.[13] Both Wainwright and Woolls were students of Arne. Miss Wainwright made her stage debut in *Love in a Village*. Woolls was well recognized as a singer, and after coming to the colonies he and Sarah Wainwright frequently performed together in both concert and stage productions.[14] Wall specialized in comic roles.[15] In addition to singing, he played guitar and mandolin and was called upon to accompany singers onstage, between acts, and in the interval separating the mainpiece and afterpiece.[16] Although Mrs. Osborne joined the company in London and traveled with the others, she was not a new discovery. Douglass had worked with her a decade before in Jamaica. Nancy Hallam was one of the most talented of this band of players.[17] As a child she had appeared in the colonies with Lewis Hallam's troupe but was sent back to London for further musical training. After her return with David Douglass, Nancy Hallam quickly emerged as one of the company's stars. Her performances—both dramatic and musical—earned her the respect and admiration of her audiences.[18] Although each of these actor-singers possessed his or her own special talents, all were capable musicians whose accomplishments easily distinguished them among other actors who were appearing onstage in the colonies at the time.

It was late October 1765 when the *Packet Carolina*, under the command of Captain Robson, sailed into Charleston harbor with Douglass and the new members of his company aboard.[19] In addition to the quintet of singers, Douglass also brought back with him sets designed by the Danish artist Nicholas Thomas Dall (d. 1776), principal scene painter at Covent Garden Theatre. Included in Douglass's luggage were new plays for his reconstructed company. Douglass had selected two works in particular, through which he intended to spotlight his singers in the 1765–66 season: *Thomas and Sally* and *Love in a Village*. Both were products of the collaboration of Arne with the young Irish playwright Isaac Bickerstaff (1733–1812).[20] *Love in a Village* was one of Arne's greatest successes. It opened at the Theatre Royal in Covent Garden on December 8, 1762, and caused an immediate sensation, receiving an astounding thirty-seven performances in its first season and was still holding its own when Douglass arrived in London two years later.

Douglass was eager to display the new talent he had recruited from the theaters of London, but upon arriving in Charleston he was confronted with a serious obstacle to his plans. Contrary to his expectation, his company was still in Barbados. It would be six months before they were able to return. His choices were hardly appealing; he could set out for Barbados as soon as passage could be arranged and forgo the season in Charleston,[21] or he could make do with such pieces as the thinness of his reduced company would allow. Pressed on by eager and determined members of Charleston's theater-going public, Douglass opted for the latter and announced in a printed broadside that he would "refit the Theater" with the intention of reopening with a play or farce on November 11.[22] As it turned out, this opening production was delayed, but in the meantime his singers appeared in local concerts, keeping them in the public's eye and building anticipation for their upcoming stage appearance.[23] It was not until February 10 of the following year that Douglass finally was able to mount a production of *Love in a Village* at the theater on Queen Street.[24] Through this performance, audiences in the colonies had their first taste of London's fashionable new theater trend.

By June 1766 the actors in Barbados had returned, and the full company had moved on to Philadelphia, where Douglass was overseeing the construction of a new playhouse. On November 14 the Southwark Theater opened with *Thomas and Sally*,[25] but it was not until early 1767 that *Love in a Village* again was offered. A review appearing in the *Pennsylvania Gazette* on January 22 lauded the American Company's performance as "beyond expectation," claiming that it "must give real delight to every person void of ill-nature."[26] The piece was repeated in March[27] and quickly became a permanent fixture in the company's repertory.

Libretto

Bickerstaff's libretto unfolds a tale of two young people, Rosetta and Thomas, who each separately decide to escape their respective arranged marriages imposed by their aristocratic families by masquerading as servants. Rosetta takes refuge in the home of an old school friend, Lucinda, pretending to be her maid, where she meets Thomas ("Young Meadows"), who recently has been hired as a gardener by Lucinda's father, Justice Woodcock. Rosetta and Thomas fall in love, but unmindful of each other's real identity, they both imagine the other as an impossible social match and try to dissuade their feelings. The unlikely resolution to this dilemma is introduced in the last act, when we learn that the original intention of their parents was to have them betrothed to one another.

The attraction of Rosetta and Thomas is echoed in a second love match between Lucinda and Eustace. Although both are of the same social station, Lucinda is convinced that her father has already selected her future husband, and she keeps the true identity of her intended secret, passing him off instead as her music teacher. Finally, creating a foil to the love affairs of these aristocratic couples is the much less romantic treatment of Lucinda's servant Margery by the rough-hewn Hodge. Although the father of her unborn child, Hodge has discarded Margery in favor of what he hopes will be the affections of the new chambermaid (Rosetta). These developing love interests are played out against a background of secondary figures. Central to these are Lucinda's cantankerous and obstinate father and, as a counterbalance, his neighbor, Squire Hawthorn.

Much of Bickerstaff's play was lifted from another stage piece, *The Village Opera*, by Charles Johnson (1679–1748), which opened February 6, 1729, at the Drury Lane Theater and was one of the many ballad operas that appeared in the wake of the incredible success of *The Beggar's Opera*. Bickerstaff made no apology for his appropriation from Johnson's work. Indeed, in a preface to John Walsh's edition of *Love in a Village*, Bickerstaff wrote, "It may not be improper to observe, that there is an Incident or two in this Opera, which bear some Resemblance to what may be found in a Piece called the Village Opera, written in the Year 1729, by C. Johnson." Bickerstaff is too modest. His libretto is indebted to Johnson's work for much of its plot, characters, and even some dialogue.[28] Bickerstaff pared down the principal roles of Johnson's play but also added the character of Eustace. In Johnson's narrative, Lucinda's love interest is mentioned and alluded to but never actually depicted onstage. The addition of Eustace allows Bickerstaff to establish three couples and explore three quite different expressions of love.[29]

The printed libretto for *Love in a Village* appeared on the shelves of London's bookshops soon after the opera's first performance.[30] The opera enjoyed such immediate success that booksellers quickly sold out of copies. Bickerstaff's text went through multiple editions in England and was sold and republished in both Ireland and Scotland. In 1794 Matthew Carey printed an American edition, which he offered for sale at his shop on Market Street in Philadelphia.[31] New editions were still being published as late as 1829.

Music

Bickerstaff's libretto is clever and witty, but the special appeal of this work rests with its music. Although normally attributed to Arne, *Love in a Village* is actually a pasticcio or pastiche, in which borrowed musical settings are blended with original music.[32] Fewer than half of its songs are actually by Arne. Although pasticcio comic operas share with ballad operas a common element of reusing previously composed music, there are fundamental differences that distinguish the two genres. Unlike comic operas, ballad operas include no original music. Such works were appreciated for their entertainment value, their success being measured less in terms of artistic worth than by a practical yardstick of their marketability. Moreover, while sometimes drawing on the sources common to ballad operas, pasticcio comic operas also included musical material derived from more elevated genres of art music. The very nature of this different type of borrowed material fundamentally altered the character of stage works that employed it.

The score for *Love in a Village* includes an overture commissioned from Carl Friedrich Abel (1723–1787)[33] and forty-two songs, eighteen of which are the work of Arne (see appendix for the airs from *Love in a Village* with musical sources). Arne composed only four songs specifically for this opera. These include one aria each for Rosetta ("The traveller benighted," air 34), Lucinda ("Believe me, dear aunt," air 17), and Meadows ("Still in hopes to get the better," air 7) as well as a trio, "Well, come let us hear" (air 31), in which Arne brings together his principal singing roles (Rosetta, Lucinda, and Hawthorn) in a clever and highly entertaining ensemble finale. Arne drew the other fourteen songs from editions of his Vauxhall songs published in the period between about 1742 and 1758.[34] The remaining twenty-four songs are based on music by various composers, which Arne fitted and adapted to accommodate Bickerstaff's text. While within this miscellany Arne drew on the repertory of traditional tunes regularly harvested for ballad operas, he cast a much wider net, crisscrossing a range of style and taste, both old and new.

In addition to fashionable songs of the pleasure gardens, there are arias from Italian operas, two of Handel's oratorios, and even a movement from a concerto grosso by Geminiani. Next to the music of composers of international stature, such as Baldassare Galuppi, George Frideric Handel, Felice de Giardini, and Francesco Geminiani, one finds works by figures of more regional reputation: William Boyce, Pietro Domenico Paradies, and Arne's violin teacher, Michael Christian Festing, as well as four composers whose music has all but faded completely into oblivion—Giuseppe Agus, Girolamo Abos, Joseph Baildon, and John Weldon.

Although in preparing his opera Arne may have requested permission from individual composers to reuse their music, he was not obliged to do so, as in 1762 there was no legal safeguard to prevent appropriating the work of others in what was otherwise an original composition.[35] In drawing on this repertory, Arne sought pieces that would both accommodate Bickerstaff's words and complement the dramatic needs of the scene, but he also chose items that—although not all recent—might still be familiar to his audience through printed sheet music.[36]

The immense popularity of *Love in a Village* created an immediate demand for access to its songs. John Walsh, an astute businessman, wasted little time in publishing a keyboard-vocal score of the opera, which found its way to the music rooms of many London homes.[37] Walsh's edition consisted of reduced settings of the songs for a treble melody and figured bass, with text underlaid between the staves. Capitalizing on the "star power" of individual singers, Walsh indicated above each song the name of the singer who performed it onstage. Those who had enjoyed seeing a performance of *Love in a Village* could then purchase Walsh's score and take pleasure in playing and singing their favorite selections at home.

Performance scores are less common in this repertory than with Italian opera; thus, the presence of a handwritten full score for *Love in a Village* in the library of London's Royal College of Music comes as a welcome surprise.[38] Although clearly an eighteenth-century source,[39] the original title page that might have provided a precise date is missing. The score encompasses 150 folios of ten-stave oblong paper, copied in the neat and precise handwriting of a professional copyist. One song stands outside this description. Although laid out in the same manner as the rest of the score, Rosetta's "When we see a lover languish" (air 38) is notated in handwriting more concise and fluid than that of the copyist (see fig. 1).

Faint pencil markings added to the manuscript page suggest that this is the hand of the composer.[40] Included among the other holdings of the Royal College of Music library is a volume of various pieces in Arne's handwriting.[41] Comparison of the hand that copied the aria in the score of *Love in a Village* with a sample of Arne's handwriting from this collection discloses that Arne wrote both (see fig. 2).[42] Most probably, the Royal College score was prepared under Arne's supervision and intended for use at Covent Garden.[43]

At some point the score came into the possession of the composer Samuel Arnold (1740–1802), whose signature appears on the first page of the manuscript. Following his name are the initials "Mus: Doc:"—a title accorded Arnold upon earning a doctor of music degree from Oxford University in July 1773 (see fig. 3).

At first glance, this date would seem to offer a terminus post quem for the manuscript. However, upon closer consideration the academic title turns out to be in a lighter ink and a different hand than the signature itself, so it was probably added later. Arnold joined the staff of the Theatre Royal at Covent Garden in 1764, and in this new position he was involved in performances of Arne's comic opera.[44] As composer and keyboardist, Arnold was responsible for rehearsing and directing the orchestra. It would have been in connection with these duties that the manuscript score came into his hands.

One additional anomaly of the manuscript concerns Rosetta's aria, "In love should there meet a fond pair," which occurs near the end of the second act. At the place in the score where this song should appear one finds only eight blank

Figure 1. RCM, MS 342, f.135r, manuscript score for Love in a Village. Reproduced by permission of the Royal College of Music, London.

Figure 2. RCM, MS 2058 f.1r, musical sketchbook. Reproduced by permission of the Royal College of Music, London.

Figure 3. RCM, MS 342, inside cover. Reproduced by permission of the Royal College of Music, London.

pages. It is also absent from the earliest printed librettos but appears in Walsh's vocal score and his 1764 edition of the libretto,[45] where the song is identified as the work of an otherwise unknown "Mr. Barnard."[46] It seems most likely that this piece was added to the score after the first performance.

Love in a Village and the American Company

It is impossible to reconstruct the precise nature of the American performances of *Love in a Village*. No prompter's book, orchestral parts, or other performance materials used for this work by the American Company have survived. Douglass's possible association with Arne's manuscript orchestral score, which could resolve a number of issues concerning the American performance of this work, remains unclear. Although Arnold or even Arne may have told Douglass about the score and perhaps even showed it to him,[47] it is highly unlikely that Douglass could have obtained possession of the manuscript or even a copy of it to bring back to Charleston. Today, handwritten orchestral parts can be pur-

chased or rented from companies that provide this specific service, but there
is no evidence that such a practice was known in eighteenth-century America.
The preparation of orchestral parts seems to have been solely in the hands of
the composer-arranger employed by the theater company. Thus, we are left
with the probability that the American Company's performances of *Love in a
Village* were based on printed editions of the libretto for the dialogue and the
vocal score for the songs.

The libretto calls for ten actors—six men and four women (see table 1). Douglass saw to it that each of the company's new members was featured in a principal musical role. With eleven solo songs and three duets, Rosetta is clearly the
favored singer. Nancy Hallam, who sang the role of Lucinda, is given only five
arias, but these include some of the best music in the score. Her appeal to the god
of love, "Cupid, god of soft persuasion" (air 12), sung to a melody by Giardini,
is one of the high points of the piece. Adam Allyn, who played Lucinda's suitor
Eustace, was a veteran performer who had been with the company since 1759.
Although a competent actor, Allyn was not a singer. This deficiency may have
caused him some problems in this role, as Eustace is involved in two musical
numbers, one of which is a duet with Lucinda based on music from Handel's
Susanna (HWV 66). There is a certain comic irony in the fact that the role of
the music teacher is assigned to one of the weaker singers in the cast. Of the
minor characters, Hodge has the most extensive musical part. He sings three
selections, two of which derive from traditional tunes. Douglass himself played
the curmudgeonly Justice Woodcock. In his single song, "When I followed a lass"
(air 18), Woodcock recalls his youthful days in London. Bickerstaff borrowed
the words from Colley Cibber's *Love in a Riddle* (1729) and, in keeping with
the bawdy nature of the text, Arne chose a country dance tune, "Joan's placket
is torn," for its music.[48]

Several pasticcio arias in *Love in a Village* came from settings that were fully
orchestrated. To do justice to this newer style, Douglass now required a full orchestra where, in the past, a mere skeletal instrumental ensemble of harpsichord
with one or two melody instruments would suffice. The precise instrumentation
of Douglass's ensemble is difficult to establish. Members of the orchestra are
not listed in any of the newspaper notices or playbills. The instrumentation of
Arne's score might serve as a guide. In addition to strings, the score calls for
two flutes or oboes (played by the same musicians), two bassoons, and two
natural horns.[49] Most probably, the orchestra for the American Company's performances of *Love in a Village* matched this instrumentation, albeit with certain
modifications necessitated by local performance conditions.[50] As with touring
companies today, a full orchestra usually did not travel with the company. Instrumentalists could be hired as needed at various performance venues, and, on
occasion, gentlemen of the community might join in for their own amusement.

Table 1. Cast for the American Company's 1766
Production of *Love in a Village*

Rosetta	Sarah Wainwright
Lucinda	Nancy Hallam
Thomas Meadows	Thomas Wall
Sir William Meadows	Owen Morris
Justice Woodcock	David Douglass
Hawthorn	Stephen Woolls
Eustace	Adam Allyn
Margery	Catherine Harman
Hodge	Lewis Hallam
Mrs. Deborah Woodcock	Mrs. Douglass

Local musicians possessed varying playing abilities, which must sometimes have required adjustments to the score. However, attention was focused on the singers, with the possible deficiencies of the orchestra easily overlooked.

Walsh's printed score would have provided little assistance in creating appropriate instrumental accompaniments. Its reduced two-voice texture had to be fleshed out by adding internal voices and orchestral color. Although without orchestral parts it is impossible to replicate precisely what the music of this opera sounded like in its first American performances, Arne's manuscript score provides a few helpful clues.

Presumably, Arne himself composed the orchestral accompaniments that would be needed for those songs based on traditional melodies or borrowed from printed sources preserved only in vocal-keyboard settings. Selections borrowed from large-scale musical compositions—Italian opera, oratorio, or concert music—already possessed full orchestrations in their original settings. The obvious choice would be to reproduce these items in their original instrumental settings. This was, however, not the case in all instances. The two songs appropriated from the music of Handel demonstrate this situation. While Lucinda and Eustace's duet, "Let rakes and libertines resign'd," reproduced almost precisely its setting in *Susanna*, "My dolly was the fairest thing," borrowed from *L'Allegro*, is much less faithful to Handel's original.

Arne draws on his full ensemble in only a half-dozen numbers. For most arias, the orchestra is pared down to strings alone, in some instances reduced even further to violin and basso. The string group also sometimes is expanded by the addition of a pair of wind instruments. Specific instruments are often suggested by the text or its source. As a matter of course, songs whose texts drew upon bucolic or pastoral images include flutes or oboes in their instrumentation. Occasionally, it is a characteristic feature of the music itself that demands the application of a particular instrumental color. Young Meadows's first-act aria,

"Still in hopes to get the better" (air 7), in which he expresses frustration in his failed attempts to ignore Rosetta's maidenly charms, is a case in point. The rollicking 6/8 rhythms and horn-like melodic figures of Arne's music bring to mind the hunt—perhaps intended as a metaphor for Tom's pursuit of Rosetta—and this, in turn, suggests the addition of two horns to the basic string ensemble.

For the audiences of colonial American theaters accustomed to ballad opera's simple tunes in minimal orchestral settings, the music of *Love in a Village* must have been strikingly new and different. In place of short songs sung to familiar tunes, they were treated to full arias laid out in logical musical structures and provided with an orchestral accompaniment. Rosetta's third-act song, "The traveller benighted" (air 34), serves as an excellent example. This is certainly the musical centerpiece of the work. Arne composed this aria specifically for Charlotte Brent (1735–1802), a luminary of London's musical stage and Arne's long-time mistress. In American performances Douglass cast Sarah Wainwright in this role. This was a logical choice, given that Wainwright was a pupil of Arne's and had appeared in the first production of *Love in a Village*, albeit in the secondary role of the pregnant serving girl, Margery.[51] American audiences were delighted with Wainwright's interpretation of Rosetta. In the judgment of one reviewer, her stage presence "exceeds the famous Miss Brent."[52]

The musical demands of "The traveller benighted" confirm Douglass's need to infuse his pre-1765 company with accomplished singers if he wished to explore this new variety of musical theater. The extremes of range and the agility required of the singer to leap from one register to another, as well as the intricate coloratura melismas and embellishments of this aria, would present substantial hazards for an untrained singer (see ex. 1).

Indeed, the great musical distance that separates such a setting from the conventional strophic songs of ballad opera is abundantly clear when Rosetta's aria is placed against a typical air from *Love in a Village*'s most popular predecessor, *The Beggar's Opera* (see ex. 2).

"If the heart of a man" is a testament to feminine charm sung by *The Beggar's Opera*'s highwayman hero, Captain Macheath. Ballads such as this were musically limited and had to be adapted for use on the stage. Most were quite short, normally with only enough music for a single strophe of text. They typically existed as single-line melodies that in their new settings needed to be supplied with a harmonization and rudimentary accompaniment.[53] As in the case of Macheath's air, such additions were basic and contributed little to the overall effect of the music. The balanced phrase structure, repetitive pitch and rhythm patterns, lack of ornamentation, and limited harmonic color of Macheath's song are also features common to most of the ballad repertory.

Although "The traveller benighted" is *Love in a Village*'s most elaborate setting, its musical demands are by no means unique. Early in the first act, Rosetta

Example 1. "The traveler benighted" from *Love in a Village*, reduced score, meas. 1–24.

Example 2. "If the heart of a man" (air 21) from *The Beggar's Opera*.

sings "My heart's my own" (air 3), where she states forcibly and without apology the subversive notion that her love is her own to bestow ("No mortal man shall wed me till first he's made my choice"). In this aria, Arne draws on one of his own pleasure-garden songs, whose gracious elegance seems somewhat at variance with Rosetta's rebellious proclamation, "Let parents rule cry nature's law and children still obey and is there then no saying clause against tyrannic sway" (see ex. 3). Emphasizing her point, Rosetta sings "tyrannic sway" to a five-measure sequential melisma that would be very much at home in an Italian opera (mm. 29–34). In the stormy political climate of the American colonies in 1766, this passage must have rung especially true to many in the audience.

Example 3. "My heart's my own" (air 3) from *Love in a Village*, reduced score, meas. 12–42.

One of the most striking differences between *Love in a Village* and the sort of musical stage presentations Douglass featured with his company before 1765 rests with the manner in which the music is integrated into the drama. In ballad operas, musical numbers generally are introduced in a rather random fashion and often without particular dramatic necessity.[54] Indeed, for the most part the songs were a secondary consideration, designed more as interludes partitioning the narrative into digestible morsels. As the scene depends little on their presence, individual songs could be added, deleted, or changed without serious damage to the plot. This is less true of comic operas. In *Love in a Village* Arne employs music in a structural manner to identify and add emotional depth to his characters. This is evident in his use of borrowed melodies. Whereas Arne associates characters of aristocratic birth with music drawn from the cultivated galant repertory of the theater and pleasure gardens, traditional tunes were considered most appropriate for servants.[55] Indeed, the finale to the first act is given over to a tune medley sung entirely by servants. In this scene a housemaid, footman, cook maid, and carter take turns trying to convince prospective employers to hire them.[56] Each makes his case to a well-known traditional tune. The kitchen maid quite appropriately touts her special skills to the melody of "Roast Beef of Old England,"[57] while the housemaid sings to "Nancy Dawson," a tune named for a dancer who had achieved great popularity in a 1759 revival of *The Beggar's Opera*.

The situation with Justice Woodcock's neighbor, Squire Hawthorn, is a bit less clear. As Hawthorn is a member of the gentry, most of his music is based on the same repertory as the other characters of his social station. But as his first-act entrance Arne has Hawthorn express his carefree lifestyle in "There was a jolly Miller" (air 8), based on a ballad originally known as "The Budgeon." Eighteenth-century theatergoers were sure to recognize this melody from its appearance in *The Devil to Pay*. This simple song, with its odd combination of lilting dotted rhythms and brooding minor mode, became one of the most popular selections with American audiences (see ex. 4).

In addition to helping delineate the social station of his characters, Arne also drew on associations with source melodies to underscore dramatic situations and convey less obvious facets of their personalities. In act 2, when Rosetta is left responding to the unwelcome amorous advances of Justice Woodcock, she does so by means of a melody taken from Galuppi's opera, *Enrico*. This work, having been popular in the 1740s, was as out of date as the attempted lovemaking of her employer. But, when Rosetta muses on Thomas and how impossible it is for her to erase him from her thoughts, it is to the thoroughly up-to-date strains of a pastorella from an opera by the same composer that had opened in London only a year before.[58]

Margery presents another special situation. Although she is of the servant class, both of her songs come from the pleasure-garden repertory and are rich

Example 4. "There was a jolly Miller" (air 8) from *Love in a Village*, reduced score.

in pathos. Her first-act aria "How happy were my days till now" (air 13) is based on a traditional Scottish ballad tune "The Bonny Broom," which Arne has recast in the fashionable galant style. Arne's choice of borrowed melody here provides an interesting viewpoint from which to consider Margery. While her class and station are emblematically projected in this reference to a traditional tune, her unrealistic faithfulness to the unrepentant Hodge—even in the wake of his cruel rejection of her and their unborn child—brings Margery well within the sentimentalized romanticism of her mistress, a fact deftly conveyed through Arne's reconsideration of the Scotch air in the Vauxhall style.

* * *

The 1766 season marked a turning point for the American Company and, indeed, for theater in the colonies. Douglass's decision to add singers to his company and upgrade his repertory resulted in a new kind of musical entertainment whose unconventional approach to both text and music was well received in the colonies of the 1760s, when a sense of political self-identity was slowly taking shape. *Love in a Village* offered a fresh alternative to the tired conventions of ballad opera. Bickerstaff's libretto projects an overtly sentimental portrait of love quite at variance with the more brutal and cynical skepticism that permeates works like *The Beggar's Opera*.[59] In addition, Bickerstaff's depiction of rural life as idyllic resonates with a philosophical ideal of the mid-eighteenth century that found truth and meaning in the simple and unadorned existence of man in harmony with nature. Only after shedding the trappings of social position and authority do Rosetta and Thomas discover their love for one another. This freedom of expression in our young couple's determination to experience love for love's sake harmonizes well with Whiggish political ideals of the day. The music of Arne's score offered something equally novel. By tapping into the comic opera repertory, Douglass was treading challenging musical ground. Still, this was an experiment that paid off. The blending of artistic and popular (high and low) styles with both original and adapted music appealed to the tastes, democratic and artistic alike, of his American audiences.

The years before the Revolution witnessed an increasing awareness of the colonies as a cultural extension of London society, and, with works like *Love in a Village*, musical theater began to emerge from the shabby fringes of entertainment to assume its new role in this budding cultural maturity. The Bickerstaff-Arne collaborations of *Love in a Village* and *Thomas and Sally* opened the door to other similar productions, and in the following decades comic operas assumed an increasingly prominent role in the repertoires of American theater companies. By introducing English comic opera to colonial audiences, Douglass had set American theater music in a new direction, one that would eventually reach its fruition in what today constitutes the American musical stage.

Appendix

The airs from *Love in a Village* with musical sources[60]

Act I

1. "Hope, thou nurse of young desire" (Rosetta and Lucinda). John Weldon (1676–36), "Let Ambition," from *The Judgment of Paris* (1701).
2. "Whence can you inherit" (Rosetta). Girolamo Abos (1716–1760), "Non son le lacrime," from *Tito Manlio* (1751).
3. "My heart's my own" (Rosetta). Thomas A. Arne (1710–1778), "The Female Phaeton," publ. in *A Favourite Collection* I (1757).
4. "When once love's subtle poison gains" (Lucinda). Arne, "The generous distress'd," publ. in *Lyric Harmony* I (1745).
5. "O! had I been by fate decreed" (Meadows). Samuel Howard (1710–1782); source unknown.
6. "Gentle youth, ah, tell me why" (Rosetta). Arne, "The Fond Appeal," publ. in *Lyric Harmony* (ca. 1745).

7. "Still in hopes to get the better" (Meadows). Arne, newly composed.
8. "There was a jolly Miller" (Hawthorn). Traditional English tune: "The Budgeon."
9. "Let gay ones and great" (Hawthorn). Joseph Baildon (ca. 1727–1774), "Hark! Hark the horn calls," publ. in *The Laurel* (ca. 1752).
10. "The honest heart whose thoughts are clear" (Hawthorn). Michael Christian Festing (1705–1752), "The Morning Fresh," publ. in A *Collection of English Cantatas and Songs* (1750).
11. "Well, well, say no more" (Hodge). Traditional Irish tune: "Larry Grogan."
12. "Cupid, God of soft persuasion" (Lucinda). Felice de Giardini (1716–1796), "Voi amante."
13. "How happy were my days till now" (Margery). Arne, "Bonny Broom," publ. in *Vocal Tune* III (ca. 1750); based on traditional Scots tune.
14. "Servants' Medley." Traditional English tunes.
　　Chorus: "My masters and mistresses hither repair."

Act II

15. "We women like weak Indians trade" (Lucinda).[61] Pietro Domenico Paradies (1707–1791), "Quel ruscelletto," from *La Forza d'amore* (1751).
16. "Think, my fairest, how delay" (Eustace). Arne, "Advise to Sylvia," publ. in *Blind Beggar* (1741).
17. "Believe me, dear aunt" (Lucinda). Arne, newly composed.
18. "When I followed a lass" (Woodcock). Traditional English tune: "Joan's placket is torn."
19. "Let rakes and libertines resign'd" (Lucinda and Eustace). George F. Handel (1685–1759), "Ask if yon damask rose be sweet," from *Susanna* (1749).
20. "How bless'd the maid whose bosom" (Rosetta). Baldassare Galuppi (1706–1785), "La Pastorella," from *Il filosofo di campagna* (1761).
21. "In vain I ev'ry art essay" (Meadows). Arne, "The stream that glides," from *Cymon and Iphigenia* (1750).
22. "Begone—I agree" (Meadows and Rosetta). Arne, "A Pastoral," publ. in *The Agreable Musical Choice* VII (1756).
23. "Oh! how shall I in language weak" (Meadows). Henry Carey (1697–1743), "The Power of Beauty."
24. "Young I am, and sore afraid" (Rosetta). Galuppi, "Son troppo vezzose," from *Enrico* (1743).
25. "Oons! neighbour ne'er blush for a trifle" (Hawthorn). Arne, "Ye prigs," publ. in *Vocal Melody* I (1749).
26. "My dolly was the fairest thing" (Hawthorn). Handel, "Let me wander," from *L'Allegro* (1740).
27. "Was ever poor fellow so plagu'd" (Hodge). Giuseppe Agus (ca. 1725–ca. 1800), source unfound.

28. "Cease, gay seducers, pride to take" (Rosetta). Arne, "Jockey and Mary," publ. in *The Agreeable Musical Choice* VIII (ca. 1758).
29. "Since Hodge proves ungrateful" (Margery). Arne, "The Love Rapture," publ. in *A Favourite Collection* (1757–58).
30. "In love should there meet a fond pair" (Rosetta). "Mr. Barnard" = King George III.
31. "Well come, let us hear" (Rosetta, Hawthorn, Lucinda). Arne, newly composed.

Act III

32. "The world is a well furnish'd table" (Hawthorn). Arne, "A Touch on the Times," publ. in *The Agreeable Musical Choice* VIII (1758).
33. "'Tis is not wealth, it is not birth" (Rosetta). Felice de Giardini, "Quanto mai felici," publ. *Sei Arie* (1762).
34. "The traveller benighted" (Rosetta). Arne, newly composed.
35. "If ever a fond inclination" (Lucinda). Francesco Geminiani (1687–1762), Concerto Grosso in C Minor, Op. 2/1, IV: Allegro (1732).
36. "A plague of those wenches" (Hodge). Traditional Irish tune: "St. Patrick's Day."
37. "How much superior beauty" (Meadows). Howard, "I like the Man whose soaring soul."
38. "When we see a lover languish" (Rosetta). Arne, "Lotharia," in *The Universal Magazine* (1749).
39. "All I wish in her obtaining" (Rosetta and Meadows). Arne, "O the raptures of possessing," publ. as a duet in *Agreeable Musical Choice* VIII.
40. "If ever I'm catch'd in those regions" (Hawthorn). William Boyce (1711–1779), "An Answer to Orpheus and Euridice" (1740).
41. "Go, naughty man, I can't abide you" (Rosetta). Arne, newly composed.
42. "Hence with cares, complaints, and frowning" (Hawthorn). Boyce, "Rail no more," publ. in *Lyra Britannica* V (ca. 1751).

Notes

1. *South Carolina Gazette*, October 19–31, 1765. The phrase "both theaters" refers to the playhouses at Drury Lane and Covent Garden. The Licensing Act of 1738 recognized only these two theaters within London's city limits. A similar notice appeared in the *South Carolina and American General Gazette*, October 23–31, 1765: "On Friday last [October 25], Mr. Douglass, director of the Theatre in this town, arriv'd from London with a reinforcement to his company. We hear he has engaged some very capital singers from the theatres of London, with a view of entertaining the town this winter with English operas."

2. Lewis Hallam (1714–1756) was born into a British theatrical family. In 1752, he and his brother William formed the London Company of Comedians, and in June of

that year Lewis, acting as manager, brought the company to the American colonies. They gave their first performance in Williamsburg in the playhouse near the Capitol.

3. The troupe first appeared under their new name in Charleston in November 1763. Rankin, *The Theatre in Colonial America*, 101.

4. One production of Shakespeare's *The Tempest* in 1756 included thirty-six songs and duets. Mates, *America's Musical Stage*, 25. Music designed to accompany activity on the stage is yet another type of music commonly encountered in eighteenth-century productions. See Anne Dhu Shapiro, "Action Music," 49–72.

5. Incidental music seldom received specific mention on playbills or in newspaper advertisements and reviews. One welcome exception is the following summary of between-act music that appeared on June 4, 1767 in the *Pennsylvania Journal*: "End of Act I., God save the King, by Mr. Woolls and Miss Wainwright. End of Act II., 'The Spinning Song,' by Miss Wainwright. End of Act III., a Duet, written on the Marriage of the Princess Augusta and the Prince of Brunswick, composed by Dr. Arne, and sung before their Majesties. End of Act IV., 'Lovely Nancy,' by Miss Wainwright." Sonneck, *Early Opera in America*, 38.

6. These same pieces found a place in the repertories of most colonial theater companies. They were sometimes joined by other ballad farces, such as Henry Fielding's *The Mock Doctor* (1750) and Henry Carey's *Damon and Phillida* (1751).

7. The term "comic opera" is a blanket label embracing a variety of dramatic and musical styles. In its simplest meaning it refers to English-language stage productions in which musical selections are interpolated into a dramatic narrative.

8. *South Carolina Gazette*, October 19–31, 1765.

9. The exact date of Douglass's departure from Charleston is not known. His company played in the new theater on Queen Street through April, but by late June he was in London. On July 5, 1764, *The New York Post-Boy* reprinted an article from an unnamed London source, which described the recent appearance in the city of a gentleman from Carolina seeking "to engage a select company of players of both sexes, for the new theatre open'd last winter in Charles-Town." Although not identified specifically by name, there can be little doubt that this refers to Douglass. See Johnson and Burling, *The Colonial American Stage*, 237.

10. Douglass had ample opportunity to attend performances of *Love in a Village*, which played at Covent Garden at least fifteen times during this period.

11. Throughout his career Arne was associated with London musical theater, a circumstance strengthened by the fact that his sister Susannah (1714–1766) married the actor and playwright Theophilus Cibber, son of Colley Cibber. In 1734 Susannah was hired as a singer at Drury Lane and her brother, Thomas, as composer and arranger. Both later defected to the Theatre Royal at Covent Garden. Arne created numerous masques, pantomimes, and incidental pieces for Drury Lane, but it was for the Theatre Royal that he designed his best-remembered stage works.

12. The early 1760s saw the appearance of three of his most popular compositions: *Thomas and Sally* (1760), *Love in a Village* (1762), and his opera, *Artaxerxes* (1762), based on a libretto by Metastasio.

13. Rankin reports that this group numbered six, including, in addition to the five listed here, William Verling (*The Theater in Colonial America*, 104). Verling was a native Virginian who is not known to have lived in England (personal correspondence from Odai Johnson, December 2012). He joined the American Company in Charleston but left two years later to form his own troupe (The Virginia Company). Neither Verling, who was not a singer, nor Osborne is known to have appeared in the American Company's productions of *Love in a Village*.

14. It was customary for actor-singers to supplement their stage earnings by appearing in concerts. For more information on the contribution made to colonial concert life by members of Douglass's company, see Sonneck, *Early Concert-Life in America*.

15. Each actor had his or her "line" or specialty within the company. For example, an actor's line might be to perform comic roles and portray bad-tempered old men. Their individual contracts specified the lines they would be required to fulfill. The 1798 contract of the actress and singer Georgina Sidus, usually referred to as Mrs. Oldmixion, reads in part "Mrs. Oldmixion engages for the ensuing season at New York: to play the first line of Opera, or such characters as she has given in a list of, the best of the Comedy Old Women, the best of the Chambermaids, or her choice in Comedies." Mates, *America's Musical Stage*, 40.

16. In 1765 the *South Carolina and American General Gazette* ran an advertisement announcing that "Thomas Wall, from the Theatre Royal, Drury-Lane and the Haymarket, London, undertakes to teach Ladies and Gentlemen to play upon the Guitar, etc" (October 23–31, 1765). The London fashion for the English guitar was enthusiastically transplanted to the colonies. It was considered an especially appropriate instrument for young ladies. Wall's wife and daughter, who both sang and played the mandolin, also appeared with the American Company.

17. Colonial newspapers and playbills consistently refer to her as "Miss Hallam." Nancy Hallam often is confused with Sarah Hallam, the wife of Douglass's stepson, Lewis Hallam Jr. Another female member of the Hallam family, Isabella, sang the role of Lucinda in London performances of *Love in a Village*. Isabella Hallam married the actor who played Eustace and is most often referred to as "Mrs. Mattocks." She is not known to have performed under either name on the American stage.

18. Charles Willson Peale (1741–1827) captured her image in a portrait, in which she is depicted in the role of Imogene (disguised as the boy Fidele) in Shakespeare's *Cymbeline*. Today, Peale's portrait is part of the collection of the DeWitt Wallace Museum in Colonial Williamsburg.

19. The *Carolina* reached Charleston on October 25. Kenneth Silverman suggests that the ship carrying Douglass and his fellow actors was also transporting stamped paper and an official to see that it was distributed in the colony (*A Cultural History of the American Revolution*). This could not have been the case, as the ship carrying the stamp official docked on October 18, a week before the *Carolina*. Davidson, *Propaganda and the American Revolution 1763–1783*, 176.

20. Bickerstaff arrived in London in 1755 with aspirations of achieving fame as a playwright. His initial venture into the theatrical world, *Leucothoé*, was fashioned as

a dramatic poem. It failed miserably. But his next attempt, *Thomas and Sally; or, The Sailor's Return*, set to music by Arne, was a resounding success. The following year, the two collaborated again on an oratorio titled *Judith*. *Love in a Village* was their third and last project together. Bickerstaff went on to write other pieces for the English musical stage with other composers, including two of the more successful comic operas of the period, *Maid of the Mill* (1765) with Samuel Arnold and *The Padlock* (1768) with Charles Dibdin.

21. Thanks to regulations of the newly imposed Stamp Act, all ships in Charleston harbor were being detained. This legislation required that printed materials originating in the colonies be on paper manufactured in London and bearing a revenue stamp, which had to be purchased with valid sterling coin rather than colonial paper money. Ship's papers were among the items covered by the Stamp Act.

22. Broadside, November 4, 1765, South Carolina Historical Society, loose papers (Ac 97) as cited in Curtis, "The Early Charleston Stage: 1703–1798," 76–77. This document is reproduced in Crain, "Music in the Colonial Charleston, South Carolina Theater: 1732–81," 243–45.

23. On November 13, less than a month after their arrival in Charleston, Miss Wainwright and Miss Hallam appeared on a benefit concert for Peter Valton, organist at St. Philip's Church. *South Carolina Gazette*, 19–31, October 1765, as cited in Sonneck, *Early Concert Life in America*, 16.

24. Reported in the *South Carolina Gazette*. See Willis, *The Charleston Stage in the XVIII Century*, 51. Theater coverage for the 1766 season was spotty as a result of the imposition of the Stamp Act, but Willis points out that this date is confirmed by an entry in the journal of Mrs. Gabriel Manigault, wife of a prosperous local merchant.

25. *Pennsylvania Journal*, November 13, 1766.

26. *Pennsylvania Gazette*, January 22, 1767, as cited in Sonneck, *Early Opera in America*, 38. A response to this review appeared in the same newspaper a week later (January 29, 1767).

27. The advertisement in the *Pennsylvania Gazette* on March 19, 1767, indicated that this was the play's "Fourth Night" but failed to identify any dates for the three previous performances.

28. A review that appeared in *The Theatrical Review* of a performance of *Love in a Village* at the Drury Lane Theater on October 8, 1771, compared Bickerstaff to "a Taylor, who, though not able to make a complete new Suit of Cloaths himself, has an admirable hand at altering and amending an old one." In the reviewer's opinion, Bickerstaff's play could only be considered "an Alteration" of Johnson's play. He praised some of the libretto's dramatic elements, but found little positive to say about the song texts, which were an original contribution of Bickerstaff's: "Neither the Sentiments, nor Versification of the Songs deserve much commendation." *The Theatrical Review; or, New Companion to the Play-house* (London: Printed for S. Crowder in Pater-noster-Row, 1772), 52–53.

29. For a contemporary comparison of the two plays, see *The Theatrical Review; or, Annals of the Drama* (London, 1763), 22–36. Adas, "Arne's Progress: An English Composer in Eighteenth-Century London," 218–23.

30. LOVE IN A VILLAGE; / A / COMIC OPERA: / As it is Performed at the / THEATRE ROYAL / IN / COVENT-GARDEN / LONDON / Printed by W. GRIFFIN; / For J. NEWBERY, and W. NICOLL, in St. Paul's / Church-Yard; G. KEARSLY, in Ludgate-Street; / T. DAVIES, in Russel-Street, Covent-Garden; and / J. WALTER, at Charing-Cross. / MDCCLXIII.

31. LOVE IN A VILLAGE / A COMIC OPERA / Written by / MR. BICKERSTAFF. / As performed / AT THE NEW THEATRE, / in Philadelphia / From the Press of M. Carey, / March 1, M.DCC.XCIV.

32. In the early 1760s *pasticcio* had thoroughly captured the imagination of London theatergoers. In addition to English comic opera, this technique also found its way into Italian *opera buffa*. According to Fiske, "in the 1761–2 season, six out of the ten Italian operas were pastiches." *English Theatre Music*, 332. *Pasticcio* operas like *Love in a Village* represent a stylistic middle ground between ballad and comic opera.

33. Walsh included Abel's Overture (Knape 45a) in a collection titled *Abel, Arne and Smith's favourite overtures . . . from Love in a Village, Thomas & Sally, Judith, Eliza, Enchanter, Faires* (London: Walsh [n.d.]).

34. At various times in his early career, Arne was associated with three of the London pleasure gardens: Ranelagh, Marylebone, and Vauxhall.

35. The Statute of Anne (1710) established copyright protection for authors of books, but it was not until 1777 that music was included under this legislation. Some composers sought to shield their work from piracy through various other means, such as royal privileges that could be granted for a specific period. In any case, rights of protection were concerned with publication rather than performance. Hunter, "Music Copyright in Britain to 1800," 272.

36. Decidedly out of step with the other sources is the tune used for Rosetta and Lucinda's opening duet, "Hope, thou nurse of young desire." This melody, originally set to the words "Let Ambition Fire the Mind," was composed by John Weldon for William Congreve's *Judgment of Paris* in 1701. Weldon's setting was written as part of a competition, in which his work was selected over those of such better-known composers as Daniel Purcell and John Eccles. Arne's choice of a melody first heard on the London stage more than sixty years before is testament to the appeal of Weldon's song. Thanks to its appearance in *Love in a Village*, this melody gained a new life and was reprinted numerous times in the 1780s. It even appeared as late as 1799 in a memorial tribute to George Washington with the new words "Hush'd be every joyfull sound." See Murray, "A Checklist of Funeral Dirges," 338.

37. LOVE IN A VILLAGE. / A COMIC OPERA / *As it is Perform'd at the* THEATRE ROYAL *in* / COVENT-GARDEN. / The Musick by / Handel Howard Geminiani Paradies / Boyce Baildon Galuppi Agus / Arne Festing Giardini Abos / *For the* HARPSICHORD, VOICE, GERMAN FLUTE, or VIOLIN. / LONDON. *Printed for* I. WALSH *in Catherine Street in the Strand* [n.d.]. Editions of both the libretto and score were available in the colonies.

38. GB Lcm MS 342. The score is in excellent condition and shows little evidence of repeated use. Manuscript markings on the opening pages establish that it was a gift from Stephen Groombridge (perhaps the astronomer) to John Bayler on July 14, 1829,

and that it found its way into the hands of William Barclay Squire, who donated it to the library in July 1897. A bookplate indicates that at one time it was in the possession of Robert Smith, who probably was an antiquarian collector. His bookplate, including name and family moto (*suaviter in modo, fortiter in re*, "gently in manner, firmly in action"), also appears on a copy of *Musica Transalpina* in the Folger Shakespeare Library in Washington, DC (STC 26094). This document came into the collection in 1917.

39. The manuscript is copied on paper that bears the watermark of James Whatman the Younger, who died in 1798. Whatman inherited his business from his father, also named James Whatman (1702–1759). The family paper mills were recognized in particular for the manufacturing of a wove paper (known on the continent as Vélin), distinguished by its smooth surface that resulted from the particular placement of chain lines in the manufacturing process.

40. The unsigned jottings are found on folio 135 v. ("Arne's writing") and folio 136 r. ("This Song is like [?] the hand of T. Arne"). Fiske reports that this song was "thought to be in the composer's autograph," but does not mention these pencil markings. Fiske, *English Theatre Music*, 328–29n1.

41. GB Lcm MS 2058. This is an oblong quarto volume that includes transcriptions of several five-part motets by Palestrina, a series of harmony studies, and the "Battle Scene" from Arne's music for *The Rehearsal* (1741).

42. I am grateful to Dr. Peter Horton, Deputy Librarian (Reference and Research) of the Royal College of Music for responding to my questions concerning this manuscript and for bringing MS 2058 to my attention. Still undetermined, however, is why it was Arne rather than the copyist who notated this particular song in the score. Perhaps a different song was intended for this spot, and Arne substituted this one in its place.

43. The cue lines inserted before each musical selection point to the manuscript being designed as a performance source rather than a presentation volume.

44. All performances of *Love in a Village* took place in the theater at Covent Garden. See *The London Stage 1660–1800*, part 4: 1747–1776, edited by George Winchester Stone Jr. (Carbondale: Southern Illinois University Press), 1962.

45. *Love in a Village* (London: printed for J. Newbery, G. Kearly, W. Griffin and W. Nicol, 1764).

46. According to Fiske, Dr. Thomas Busby claimed that Barnard was a pseudonym for King George III, who was the actual composer of this song. Fiske, *English Theatre Music*, 330–31.

47. Douglass probably met Arnold during his time in London. Arnold's new comic opera, *The Maid of the Mill*, received its first performance at Covent Garden early in 1765, and Douglass would certainly have had an interest in this work. It may, in fact, have been among the new pieces in his luggage when he returned to Charleston. In May 1769 the American Company gave their first performance of *The Maid of the Mill* in New York's John-Street Theater; it thereafter became a regular part of their repertory.

48. This tune appears in at least eight ballad operas and is likely to have been recognized by many in Douglass's audience

49. The *basso* part is not supplied with figures but might still have doubled as a *continuo*.

50. Julian Mates provides a detailed discussion of early American theater orchestras in chapter 3 of his book *The American Musical Stage,* 71–95. Although concerned primarily with the period after the revolution, much of his account is also applicable to the early years of the American Company. See also Hoover, "Music in Eighteenth-Century American Theater," 6–18.

51. Wainwright first appeared in role of Margery at the performance on January 2, 1765. Douglass was in London at this time and may have been in the Covent Garden audience that evening.

52. *Pennsylvania Gazette,* January 22, 1767.

53. In London performances, such modifications generally were left to staff musicians employed by the theaters as composers and arrangers. In provincial and colonial companies this work fell to the keyboardist, who typically fulfilled the role of music director. Our knowledge of these adaptations derives principally from printed editions of the librettos that include music for individual airs.

54. There are, of course, exceptions to this characterization, although in most instances it is the juxtaposition of the original text with its new dramatic setting that engages with the narrative rather than the function of the music within the scene itself. For example, in the tavern scene of *The Beggar's Opera,* the whores and highwaymen sing and dance to a courtly French melody. This particular choice of music furnishes a secondary level of commentary that would not have been lost on an audience of 1728. Such referential meaning often depends on time and place. The satire that arises from the use of this aristocratic French dance melody by tavern revelers of the meanest sort might be less sharply drawn in later productions or those mounted in the colonies.

55. A notable exception is Justice Woodcock's recall of his amorous past in "When I followed a lass." In this instance, Arne has selected a ballad tune with its own ribald past associations in order to emphasize Woodcock's licentious character.

56. Originally, the hiring-fair finale included nine tunes stitched together by orchestral interludes, each sung by a specific type of servant. In addition to those mentioned here, there was also a gardener, huntsman, laundry maid, groom, and dairymaid. The scene is organized in this manner in early editions of the libretto and Arne's score. After the first performance, this grouping was deemed too extensive, and the number of parts was reduced. It is this version that Walsh included in his vocal score.

57. The music is by Richard Leveridge, who may also have penned some of the text. "A Song in Praise of Old English Roast Beef," with words and music attributed to Leveridge, was included in volume 3 of Walsh's *British Musical Miscellany* (1734–1737).

58. This point is also made in Adas, "Arne's Progress," 223.

59. In his history of American music, Richard Crawford points out that the contrived happy ending of Bickerstaff's libretto offers an expression of sentimentality that conforms to "the theatrical conventions that *The Beggar's Opera* had mocked." See *A History of America's Musical Life,* 99.

60. Tune sources are based on Fiske, *English Theatre Music,* 605–6.

61. In the manuscript score this appears as "We women like poor Indians made."

References

Adas, Jane H. "Arne's Progress: An English Composer in Eighteenth-Century London." PhD diss. State University of New Jersey, 1993.

Crain, Timothy M. "Music in the Colonial Charleston, South Carolina Theater: 1732–81." PhD diss. Florida State University, 2002.

Crawford, Richard. *America's Musical Life: A History*. New York: Norton, 2001.

Curtis, Julia. "The Early Charleston Stage: 1703–1798." PhD diss. Indiana University, 1968.

Davidson, Philip. *Propaganda and the American Revolution, 1763–1783*. Chapel Hill: The University of North Carolina Press, 1941.

Fiske, Roger. *English Theatre Music in the Eighteenth Century*. New York: Oxford University Press, 1973.

Hoover, Cynthia Adams. "Music in Eighteenth-Century American Theater." *American Music* 2, no. 4 (Winter, 1984): 6–18.

Hunter, David. "Music Copyright in Britain to 1800." *Music and Letters* 67, no. 3 (July 1986): 269–82.

Johnson, Odai, and William J. Burling. *The Colonial American Stage, 1665–1774: A Documentary Calendar*. Madison, Wis.: Fairleigh Dickinson University Press, 2001.

Mates, Julian. *The American Musical Stage before 1800*. New Brunswick, N.J.: Rutgers University Press, 1962.

———. *America's Musical Stage: Two Hundred Years of Musical Theatre*. New York: Praeger, 1985.

Murray, Sterling E. "A Checklist of Funeral Dirges in Honor of General George Washington." *Notes: Quarterly Journal of the Music Library Association* 36, no. 2 (December 1979): 326–44.

Pennsylvania Journal, 1766–1767.

Pennsylvania Gazette, 1767.

Rankin, Hugh F. *The Theatre in Colonial America*. Chapel Hill: University of North Carolina Press, 1960.

Shapiro, Anne Dhu. "Action Music in American Pantomime and Melodrama, 1730–1913." *American Music* 2, no. 4 (Winter 1984): 49–72.

Silverman, Kenneth. *A Cultural History of the American Revolution*. New York: Columbia University Press, 1987.

Sonneck, Oscar G. *Early Concert-Life in America (1731–1800)*. 1907. New York: Da Capo, 1978.

———. *Early Opera in America*. 1915. New York: Blom, 1963.

South Carolina Gazette, 1765.

South Carolina and American General Gazette, 1765.

The Theatrical Review, or, New Companion to the Play-house. London: Printed for S. Crowder at Pater-noster Row, 1772.

Walsh, J[ohn], collector. *Abel, Arne and Smith's Favourite Overtures . . . from Love in a Village, Thomas & Sally, Judith, Eliza, Enchanter, Fairies*. London: Walsh [1763].

———. *British Musical Miscellany, or, The Delightful Grove*. 6 vols. London: Walsh, [1734–37].

Willis, Eola. *The Charleston Stage in the XVIII Century*. 1933. New York: Blom, 1968.

5 "We're Marching to Zion"

Isaac Watts in America

ESTHER R. CROOKSHANK

Introduction: Watts's Theology and Language of Worship

In 1872 Henry Ward Beecher, this country's most loved preacher at that time, claimed that hymns, particularly those of Isaac Watts, shaped Americans' theology in his day more powerfully than even the Bible did.

> If you analyze your religious emotions I doubt not you would trace them back to the early hymns of childhood more than to the Bible itself. If you consider the source of your thoughts of heaven I think you will land in Dr. Watts rather than in the revelator St. John.

Hymns even apart from music—read aloud, memorized, and contemplated—found a place in the inner lives of nineteenth-century Americans that seems to have been closer to Scripture than to anything else. Beecher here made a powerful assertion about the roots of "religious emotions," particularly those of generations of Americans who had learned hymns from childhood. He also addressed concepts of heaven, naming as the genesis of those images—for the average American—the hymnody of Isaac Watts even before biblical revelation. The greatest American fiction work of the era, *Uncle Tom's Cabin*, by the clergyman's famous sister, Harriet Beecher Stowe, reflects this view when the author has the hero quote a Watts hymn on his deathbed: "Something in the voice penetrated to the ear of the dying. He moved his head gently, smiled, and said, 'Jesus can make a dying-bed / Feel soft as downy pillows are.'"[1]

Exactly how American Protestants of the mid-nineteenth century did "land in Dr. Watts," to quote Beecher's lively phrase, is the subject of this chapter.

This study will trace the path of four of Watts's texts in Protestantism from the colonial period through about 1900: "Alas! And Did My Saviour Bleed," "Am I a Soldier of the Cross," "Come, We That Love the Lord," and "When I Survey the Wondrous Cross." I will address the questions of the nature of Watts's system of public worship; how and why his psalms and hymns took root on American soil; how Watts's theology and language affected American worship and was altered by it; the role of Watts's texts in the two Awakenings and in related musical styles and practices; the place of Watts in school education through the nineteenth century; the centrality of Watts in African American worship and the shape-note singing tradition; and adaptations of Watts in the gospel hymnody of urban revivalism. My conclusions will address the cultural work Watts's writings may be seen to have accomplished in American life and worship through these contexts.

Between 1707 and 1739 in Southampton the young British clergyman and scholar of logic and philology Isaac Watts produced four publications by which he hoped to achieve a systematic reform of congregational song in England's Dissenting church of his day. The four books were: *Hymns and Spiritual Songs: In Three Books* (London, 1707), *Psalms of David: Imitated in the Language of the New Testament* (1719), *Horae Lyricae*, and *Divine and Moral Songs for Children*. Accomplishing far more and reaching beyond what he could have anticipated, his work indelibly stamped Protestant worship on both sides of the Atlantic for nearly two centuries.

In his famous preface to *Psalms of David*, Watts disclosed the essence of his "Grand Design": "to teach my Author to speak like a Christian."[2] His defense was powerfully reasoned and irrefutably scriptural: Watts the logician argued that Old Testament scripture viewed in New Testament light both allowed and obligated him to Christianize the psalms. After systematically "ransacking" existing metrical psalters, church histories, and psalm commentaries, Watts developed a new approach, what he called the psalm imitation, by which to shape the Psalms into Christological declarations and prayers. Watts's preface demonstrates a clear awareness of his plan's radicalness and potentially enormous influence, as well as an unshakeable confidence in the soundness of his underlying "great Principle":

> But still I am bold to maintain the great *Principle* on which my present Work is founded; and that is, That if the brightest Genius on Earth or an Angel from Heaven should translate *David*, and keep close to the Sense and Style of the inspired Author, we should only obtain thereby a bright or heavenly Copy of the *Devotions of the Jewish King*; but it could never make the fittest *Psalm-Book for a Christian People.*[3]

At the end of the same volume he included the groundbreaking article, "A Short Essay toward the Improvement of Psalmody." Although Watts had intended to revise and republish it later, this is the only volume in which it appears. Escott views it as the manifesto of Watts's work. In it Watts argued that while the integrity of Scriptural text must be preserved in public reading, that it was just as important that worship song must be nonliteral—in other words, the congregation's own response: "By Reading we are instructed what have been the Dealings of God with Men in all Ages, . . . but Songs are generally Expressions of our own Experiences, or of his Glories. . . . We breath [*sic*] out our souls towards him."[4]

Armed with the New Testament mandate to "sing with understanding," Watts approved only singing "with due knowledge and Conviction";[5] reason itself, he claimed, demanded that the psalter and all congregational song must make sense to and be true for the congregation singing it. He saw the need in public worship of his day for what Escott calls "something approaching uniformity of interpretation." For Watts, the beauty of scriptural songs was that they met the needs or expressed the feelings of people in a specific situation—they had concreteness, particularity, and were dated, as Escott writes.[6] On that basis, Watts took it upon himself not only to evangelicalize but also to modernize, nationalize, and concretize the psalter for his world of Great Britain and his target audience, the dissenting church. Watts's *Psalms* in a sense provided his generation with a *Living Bible* set to music—neither a literal translation nor a metrical versification (and he made no apologies on either count) but a new model, for which he adopted the word "imitation" from his literary background. As Escott points out, Watts was writing in England's Augustan Age, "when the Imitation was a literary genre popular in intellectual circles. Watts did for the Hebrew Psalmists what Pope had done for Horace, and what Johnson was shortly to do for Juvenal." As Pope applied to the personalities and events of the Georgian era Horace's descriptions, "so Watts set forth the Christian worship and life of his own age in terms descriptive of Hebrew life and . . . worship in the days of David and Hezekiah."[7] Thus in Watts, Psalm 100 became:

> Sing to the Lord with joyful voice,
> Let ev'ry land his name adore;
> The British isles shall send the noise
> Across the ocean to the shore.

Finally, insisting that even the Christianized Psalter could not meet every need of New Testament worship, particularly for Communion, Watts argued that that the gospel by nature called for "hymns of human composure." Did not the epistles proclaim that the church had a higher revelation of God than

David or the prophets had? He clinched his argument for hymns with the line: "Where can you find a Psalm that speaks the Miracles of Wisdom and Power as they are discover'd in a crucify'd Christ?"[8]

The second underlying premise of Watts's "Essay," besides that of comprehensibility and realism in song, was the principle of liberty in Christ developed in Galatians. Watts read this epistle as freeing Christians from bondage to singing New Testament texts just as surely as it broke the Calvinist shackles of metrical psalmody. Liberty in the Spirit rejected neither psalms nor hymns but proclaimed open season on singing either scriptural or non-scriptural texts, and freedom from all "fixed forms of praise."[9] For Watts, as Escott explains, "it is the breath of reality in our praises that matters most of all" to God. . . . before using [the Psalms] we must make them our own." Nothing less could be true new-covenant worship.

Watts's system of congregational song, while influenced by his study of earlier metrical and even medieval models, was most shaped by his exhaustive command of Scripture in the original languages. His system of worship was also shaped by his mastery of and passion for both logic and philology; as the author of a logic textbook used at Oxford for more than a century, he exercised great care in his use of language.

Equally important, however, was his deep concern over the lack of understanding of church song that he observed among lay working-class worshippers in England's nonconformist congregations of his day. As a result, he resolved to adapt his language, when writing poems for congregational use, to the understanding of the common Christian, resulting in what he called "sunk expression." Harry Escott has described Watts's stylistic development as a process of "artistic *kenosis*. Watts had to lay his poetic glories aside and dress the profound message of the gospel in the homespun verse and language of the people."[10] Ronald Tajchman has analyzed Watts's use of Aristotelian rhetorical schemes and devices, and he explains the tension in the poet's hymns: "On the one hand, [Watts] sought to elevate his fellow believers by means of language. On the other hand, he wanted to reach the lowest level of understanding." By yoking his theological and scriptural prowess to his rhetoric skills, Watts could navigate a middle path.[11]

Like earlier psalm versifiers, Watts divided longer psalms into parts, to facilitate congregational use. He divided some psalms still further by inserting the rubric "Pause." Escott notes the astounding metric variety and options in Watts's psalter. While adhering, as he promised, to the best known meters, Watts provided multiple versions in different meters for many psalms for a total of 338 psalm versions, of which 164 are in common meter, 121 in long meter, thirty-four in short meter, and several each in assorted others.[12] Nearly fifty psalms, or one-third of the psalter, are provided with two versions; thirteen psalms are cast in all three favorite meters; many other psalms or sections of psalms appear in four, five, and even six different meters. Although prevented by his theology from using twelve entire psalms and 285 verses of other psalms, which he declared unfit for the New Testament church, Watts was nonetheless remarkably inclusive for the rest of the Psalter. According to Escott's tabulations, of the 2,461 total verses in the book of Psalms, Watts treats fully 2,050.[13]

While poets since the Middle Ages had written devotional and communion hymns and had also made limited efforts to bring Christ into the Psalms, Watts's new system was a quantum leap forward, a step with a revolutionary nature of which he was well aware. Appearing early on were pamphlets from opponents, including: *A Vindication of David's Psalms from Mr. I. Watts's Erroneous Notions* and *Reasons Wherefore Christians Ought to Worship God, not with Dr. Watts's Psalms, but with David's Psalms*. To read and accept Watts's opponents, one would have to believe that David himself had placed his imprimatur on the Psalms of Sternhold and Hopkins, the first completed Psalter in English. Even six years later, when Watts's *Logic* was published, he wrote in its preface:

> It is for the same reason that the bulk of the common people are superstitiously fond of the Psalms translated by Hopkins and Sternhold, and think them sacred and Divine because they have been now for more than a hundred years bound up in the same covers with our Bibles.[14]

Susan Tamke discusses the deep-seated prejudice against hymns among many churchmen in British Puritanism, for whom even owning or using a hymnal in one's private devotions was considered subversive behavior.[15] Foote quotes Rev. William Romaine, rector of St. Anne's in Blackfriars, London, in the "Essay on Psalmody" prefixed to the latter's own *Collection out of the Book of Psalms* in which the rector denounced "Watts's Whims." Romaine expressed great concern that he might see (or perhaps was already seeing) "Christian congregations shut out the divinely inspired psalms, and take in Dr. Watts's flights of fancy. . . . Why should Dr. Watts, or any other hymn-maker, not only take precedence over the Holy Ghost, but also thrust him utterly out of the church?"[16] Whether Romaine was more concerned about the Holy Ghost or market competition is unclear.

Watts in the Regular Singing Controversy, Revisions, and Tunebooks

In nonconformist worship song of seventeenth-century England, a leader read the psalm one line at a time, in alternation with the congregation's singing of each tune phrase. This custom was called lining out or deaconing, after the precentor, clerk, or deacon—often musically unlearned—chosen to line out the tunes. Instituted first as a provisional measure for church singing by the English

Puritans at the Westminster Assembly of 1644 to assist illiterate worshippers,[17] lining out had been brought to the colonies and had become entrenched practice in New England by the 1720s. In the next fifty years, the paradox evolved that psalmsinging declined sharply through the very measure devised to help illiterate singers.

In his preface cited above, Watts held forth little hope that the state of congregational singing could change. In fact, he admitted that he expressly tailored his poetic style to a congregational practice he deplored. His solution was to avoid constructing a poetic thought that extended beyond one line and therefore put an end to the absurd exchange of sentence fragments between leader and congregation that often resulted from lining out of earlier Psalm paraphrases: "I have seldom permitted a Stop in the middle of a Line, and seldom left the end of a Line without one, to comport a little with the unhappy mixture of Reading and Singing, which cannot presently be reformed."[18] The very reason he had restricted himself to the three most usual Metres—long, common, and short—was to ensure rhythmic clarity. He provided metrical alternative versions to give himself some degree of license and still be found responsible to scripture, explaining: "If in one Metre I have given the Loose to a Paraphrase, I have confin'd myself to my Text in the other."[19]

Despite his resignation about the prevailing state of singing, Watts could not resist giving a few parting instructions. The worship he advocated was first and last grounded in clear understanding of the texts. Underscoring the crucial roles of reason and literacy in the worship of God, he wrote: "First, Let as many as can do it bring Psalm-books with them, and look on the Words while they sing . . . to make the Sense compleat. . . . Secondly, Let the Clerk read the whole Psalm over aloud before he begins to parcel out the Lines, that the People may have some notion of what they sing; and not be forced to drag on heavily . . . without any Meaning, till the next Line come to give the Sense of them." Finally, he appealed for a faster tempo, "that we might not dwell so long upon every single Note," and called for "greater Speed of Pronunciation," which he believed "would be more agreeable to [the Psalmody] of the antient Churches, more intelligible to others, and more delightfull to our selves."

The earliest histories of music in the colonies detail the decline of psalmsinging in the Calvinist congregations and the organized effort mounted by leading Congregational ministers to redress the dilemma. Nineteeenth-century music historians George Hood and Nathaniel Gould concur in deploring the near-disappearance of the tune repertory, the wretched intonation, appalling vocal production, distended tempi, rhythmic anarchy, and generally lifeless, irreverent spirit that prevailed in the churches' psalmody by the turn of the eighteenth century. Samuel Sewall, a Massachusetts chief justice, leading figure in Boston's civic and church life in the late seventeenth century, and for twenty-four years precentor of the Old South Church in Boston, described in his diary in 1713 what must have been typical pitfalls for the precentors of the time: "I try'd to set Low-Dutch Tune and fail'd. Try'd again and fell into the tune of 119th Psalm. . . . In the Morning I set York Tune, and in the 2d going over, the Gallery carried it irresistibly to St. David's, which discouraged me very much."

To quote Frederic Louis Ritter, another early historian of American music, this practice gradually attained to "some members of the congregations" such importance "that they looked upon its performance as a religious duty."[20] And when ministers and others sought to do away with the custom after psalm-books became plentiful and most people had learned to read, the effort was at first vehemently opposed. In Louis Benson's words, "Disorder had acquired the force of a tradition."[21] In 1720 the Massachusetts Puritan minister and Harvard graduate Thomas Symmes released into this scenario his treatise *The Reasonableness of Regular Singing*, described by David Music as the "opening salvo" in the ministerial campaign to reform New England's congregational song.

How did Watts's texts reach the colonies? As early as December 1711, the prominent New England divine Cotton Mather recorded in his diary that he had received a copy of the "new Edition" of Watts's *Hymns and Spiritual Songs* (in other words, the second edition of 1709) from the author. Watts's correspondence with Mather and other colonial clergy indicate the poet's interest in spreading his system of worship to the churches in the New World. He even subtitled a few psalms "for New England." According to David Music, British-imprint copies of both Watts's *Hymns and Spiritual Songs* and *Psalms of David* were available for purchase in New England well before 1729.[22] Nine texts by Watts had been published individually in six Boston collections between 1712 and 1714, including "Hark! From the Tombs a Doleful Sound," "Why Do We Mourn Departing Friends," and "When I Survey the Wondrous Cross," apparently the first publication of each of these hymns in America.

Rochelle Stackhouse's recent (1997) thorough study documents the reception, adaptation, and dissemination of Watts's psalms and hymns in the colonies. Despite the support of Mather and other progressive New England Puritan clergy, Watts's texts met with resistance in the colonies, as they had in England. Even the enthusiastic Mather made clear in his diary that he intended to enjoy Watts's texts in his family worship and to share them with his friends for the same purpose.

> Isaac Watts, hath sent me the new Edition of his Hymns; wherein the Interests of Piety are most admirably suited. I receive them as . . . a Supply sent from Heaven for the Devotions of my Family. There will I sing them, and endeavor to bring my Family in Love with them . . . and perswade my well-disposed Neighbours to furnish themselves with them; and in this way promote Piety among them.[23]

For public worship, however, Mather himself undertook the task of scripture versification in his *Psalterium Americanum*, which he hoped would be the church psalter of the new nation. This "sterile product," to use Foote's phrase, was cast in Mather's curious idea of blank verse, and the work never sold.

The most obvious cause of resistance to Watts in New England, however, was what Hugh T. McElrath calls the "stranglehold" on colonial Calvinist worship of the older psalters, notably that of Sternhold and Hopkins. Also popular were its successor of higher poetic quality, the so-called "New Version" of Nahum Tate and Nicholas Brady from England, and the first American-published psalter or book of any kind, the *Bay Psalm Book* of 1640.[24] Later editions of both these books included tune supplements. The people's fervent loyalism to the older psalters was by degrees through two main agencies—the singing school movement and revivalism.

The revisions of Watts's works produced in the colonies in the following decades both reflected and embodied major cultural, religious, and political shifts. Before the Revolution, Watts's *Psalms of David* had become quite widely used in New England churches, replacing almost entirely the *Bay Psalm Book*. Beginning his work during the Revolution, Massachusetts schoolmaster and printer John Mycall issued in 1791 a revised Watts psalter in which he had replaced Watts's references to the British Israel with rousingly patriotic sentiments of the Revolution. By 1784, the General Association of Connecticut Congregationalists had commissioned Joel Barlow, a poet of growing reputation who had hopes of becoming the new nation's poet laureate, to prepare an "official" Watts revision for the use of Connecticut congregations. Barlow not only Americanized the national references to Israel, he also made stylistic and even discrete theological changes in Watts as well. Barlow's subsequent travels in France and flirtation with liberal political philosophies of the French Revolution brought immediate suspicion on the home front as to possible heretical tinges in his work. The association promptly engaged a new person to complete a second official Watts revision.

The association's choice and the epitome of orthodoxy was Timothy Dwight, grandson of Jonathan Edwards. Dwight was a serious, young Congregational pastor and Yale graduate who in 1795 assumed the presidency of that school. He venerated Watts and strove in this project to exceed his model, completing the paraphrases of the twelve psalms Watts had omitted and adding thirty-six new texts of his own. "Dwight's Watts," as it came to be called, enjoyed considerable use after its release in 1801. Stackhouse shows how Dwight's alterations of Watts reflect a viewpoint of reactionism and conservatism during the tremendous social and religious changes of the nation's earliest years. Dwight undid many of Barlow's revisions in what can best be interpreted as an ironic attempt to arrest the social reorganization and ultimate ecclesiastical disestablishment that followed the Revolution. Stackhouse concludes insightfully that Dwight's best-known original hymn from that collection, and his only widely sung hymn now, is "I Love Thy Kingdom, Lord," a celebration of God's kingdom on earth, which Dwight so clearly envisioned as the Congregational church of the colonial period and whose political stability and social power he had striven so diligently to protect from inevitable decline. In the words of John Bealle and Alice C. Crozier, "Music was one element in a crisis of national scope resulting from the 'loss of the old dignity and purpose of the colonial Calvinist society.'"[25]

But Watts was not only the province of the established church, which would have been ironic for that dissenter. Baptists in the colonies, like their Congregational neighbors, had generally used Sternhold and Hopkins; when they finally did relinquish that book, most adopted Tate and Brady. David Music notes that in 1771 the congregation of the First Baptist Church of Boston voted to adopt "Dr. Watts's Psalms together with his Hymns be sung in Public instead of Tate and Brady."[26] Twenty years later, they voted that the "Selection of Hymns by the Revd. Rippon of London, be used at baptisms and communion seasons, as a supplement to Dr. Watts's Hymns." Rippon's, interestingly, was itself an arrangement of Watts's texts in a topical format more easily useable during worship. Although the book had been published abroad only four years before they adopted it, apparently it had an immediate appeal. In 1818 James M. Winchell, the First Baptist Church's pastor, published his own version, *An Arrangement of the Psalms, Hymns, and Spiritual Songs of . . . Watts*, which immediately found wide usefulness among New England Baptists. "Winchell's Watts" contained 687 psalms and hymns by Watts and 327 hymns by other authors. Based on its success, Winchell published a companion tunebook, his *Sacred Harmony*, in 1819.

The rise of choirs was linked closely with the adoption of Watts's books. As Benson put it, "The movement to improve singing was inevitably a movement toward the use of Watts or of other hymns."[27] Writing in the 1840s, George Hood recorded that, despite the reformers' efforts, which were concentrated in cities (particularly Boston), "there were few country churches with a choir before 1765 or '70. They were generally formed as the custom of 'lining out' the psalms was done away. Or perhaps they were the means of removing that barbarous and penurious custom. At any rate, choirs and that custom were ever at a war, in which the former have ever proved victorious."[28] Church minutes of the Congregational South Church in Andover reflect that members voted to add choir seats in the sanctuary in 1779, the same year that they changed books from Tate and Brady to Watts.[29] The First Baptist Church of Boston formed a choir in 1771 when it adopted Watts.[30] Several church records cite the establishment of the choir and the adoption of Watts in a single entry.

By the time the furor of the tract wars and sermonic battles over "Usual Singing" (or the Old Way) versus the new "Regular Singing" had settled, the singing-school movement was launched. The inevitable result of the singing school, targeted as it was at young people, was the establishment of choirs in churches across New England; the precentor surrendered by degrees to the choir. In the course of the conflict, other strongholds fell. The increased circulation of the new sacred music slowly opened the door to Watts in various incarnations. Singing schools had taught young people of both sexes to read by note, paving the way for mixed or "promiscuous singing" in the worship of God. Lastly, in some city churches, a bass viol was admitted into the gallery to support the psalmtune and the more musically complex pieces that the choir introduced.

In one sense, then, the shift to Watts's Christianized psalms and hymns meant a move to notated music and choral polyphony and to a select group that could and sometimes did eventually dominate worship as had the precentor it replaced. On the other hand, the presence of Watts's texts in a church could indicate a congregation's interest in the revival, according to Richard Raichelson.[31] David Music asserts that Watts made no serious inroads into the churches until the triumph of "regular singing" and the beginning of the Great Awakening in the 1740s.

Watts, Theology, and Musical Styles in the Awakenings

Stephen Marini has argued that the Regular Singing controversy was actually "rehearsal for revival" for the first Awakening. "The singing controversy of the 1720's revealed deeper theological, sociological, and cultural tensions in Congregational and Baptist communions that in the revival would become permanent lines of fracture in New England. The Singing Controversy announced the cultural disintegration of Puritanism." In the Awakening, "spiritually heightened singing appeared as a distinguishing mark of regeneration," fostering the development of one important new genre, the camp-meeting hymn or spiritual. Watts's "human composures," writes Marini, kindled a lasting Evangelical tradition of hymns and spiritual songs that at first supplemented and at times overshadowed the Wattsian canon. After 1770, hymn and hymnic psalms of Watts and others acquired an indigenous musical style, to be discussed herewith, appearing in multiple settings by various composers in the wave of tunebook publication accompanying the singing school movement. These musical settings ensured the texts' longevity through the rise of fixed musical forms. The most distinctive form produced by the singing-school movement was the fuguing tune. And on the doctrinal front, "the new hymnody acquired theological interpretations accompanying the new synthesis of music and texts and reflecting the Evangelical and Liberal positions that shaped Protestant thought in the new nation." In short, Marini concludes, the universality and publicity of sacred singing made it, of all religious media, perhaps the most sensitive to the complex changes wrought by the Great Awakening in America.[32]

Watts's texts played important, though different, roles in the revivals of Edwards, Whitefield, and the camp meetings, respectively. Jonathan Edwards recalled in a letter finding his congregation singing the hymns of Watts only, having cast aside the psalms, when he returned from an extended trip. He writes: "When I came home I disliked not their making some use of the Hymns: but did not like their setting aside the Psalms." He resolved the situation to everyone's satisfaction, recalling later:

> It has been our manner in this congregation, for more than two years past, in the summer time, when we sing three times upon the Sabbath, to sing an Hymn, or part of a Hymn of Dr. Watts's, the last time, *viz*: at the conclusion of the afternoon exercise . . . the people . . . seem'd to be greatly pleased with it.[33]

Clearly, modern evangelicals did not invent "blended" worship music. Whitefield was enthusiastic about Watts's texts and ultimately produced a collection in 1753 containing Wesley and Cennick but predominantly Watts. Richard Raichelson has pointed out the paradox that "Whitefield, the great exponent of revivalistic preaching, was more allied with the musical temperament of [tunes set to] Watts than [to] the Wesleys. . . . Ironically, his preaching style was consistent with the Wesleys and contrary to that of Watts." Of the established congregations that had adopted Watts and come increasingly under Watts's influence after the Revolution, he observes, the revivalistic churches moved to other musical styles—those of the Methodist hymns, of their own folk hymns, and then the camp-meeting spiritual.[34]

While the Second Awakening had vast reverberations in reshaping conversion theology, redrawing denominational lines, and fueling reforms such as abolition, that revival's clearest effect in lay worship life may have been its legacy of "social religion." Sandra Sizer has analyzed the complex of practices that came to be called by this name: lay testimony, exhortation, prayer, and singing by both men and women. Stemming from the new evangelical understanding of conversion and the desire to keep revival fires alive in local churches, the "social meeting" was an evening, lay-led gathering in which Puritan distinctions between public and private worship were set aside, as they had been in the revivals.[35]

The limited place of singing in the First Awakening was eclipsed by its central role in the Second Awakening, as documented in dissertations by Paul Hammond, Richard Hulan, Ellen Jane Lorenz Porter, and others.[36] The camp-meeting spiritual that emerged from this movement may be categorized in at least two main types: the improvisatory repetitive, rousing choruses, often added to popular hymn texts of Watts and Wesley, and the freely ornamented, folklike, often modal type. Containing aspects of both is the musically striking setting of "Alas!

And Did My Saviour Bleed," titled "I Yield," from Hillman's famous collection *The Revivalist*. Watts's first stanza is sung intact. The refrain is a simple, moving poetic utterance in which surrender to Christ at the vision of his crucifixion is framed in language of both intimacy and conquest:[37]

> I yield, I yield, I yield,
> I can hold out no more;
> I sing by dying love compell'd,
> And own thee conqueror.

The wide-ranging F-minor melody reaches its dramatic and melodic peak un-expectedly at the beginning of the refrain, on the leading tone and sustained high F, then catapults downward with anguished cries of surrender in three wrenching grace-note figures. The rest of the refrain, far from the trite rhythms in many camp-meeting choruses, represents a gradual release of both melodic and rhythmic tension as the calm opening tune phrase returns and the soul reaches repose. The fermatas in Hillman's transcription recall the rhythmic freedom and emotional power of early camp-meeting singing that was gradu-ally purged from later notated versions in collections in the following decades.

At Home and School with Watts: Hymns for Children and Hymns in Children's Lives

In Boston in 1715 an obscure twenty-four-page booklet of songs for the use of children appeared: *Honey out of the Rock Flowing to Little Children That They May Know to Refuse the Evil and Chuse the Good: Certain Select Hymns for the Use of Such, Taken from Those of the Excellent Mr. Isaac Watts, as More Pecu-liarly Adapted for Their Instruction* (Boston, 1715). The twenty-two hymns in this miniature selection, all taken from his *Hymns and Spiritual Songs*, include no texts still in use. David Music attributes the editorship of this curious col-lection to Mather, based on typography and the nature of the "Body of Divinity Versify'd" at the end.[38] While it must remain only an intriguing footnote to the narrative of Watts in America, *Honey out of the Rock* is the earliest collection of his work published in the colonies.

Like his poems for adults, Watts's hymns for children were intended above all to be ones they could understand and use. He wrote his *Divine and Moral Songs for Children* to be sung in the home or family circle; they were probably not used in worship, according to Escott. The book's profound influence in American life was through its adoption as a primer or chapbook in American schools for generations.[39] Escott points out that in these texts, Watts celebrates the glories of God's creation. He wrote "I Sing the Mighty Power of God," with its colorful detail as well as panoramic view, for children. It first appeared in

Divine and Moral Songs and was not adapted congregationally until later. Escott has traced probable influences on Watts from poet Robert Herrick ("Cloaths for Continuance") and writers of other Puritan children's poems as well as several poems from Bunyan's *Book for Boys and Girls*, but he argues that Watts was the first poet to write from the child's perspective.

Despite what Escott has called "admittedly priggish religious sentiments in some texts," which he blames at least in part on an era "that understood little of child life," he argues that Watts "joyed to stand at the child's level and to look at life and religion from the child's height of mind and soul. It was Isaac Watts who *humanized* children's praises: they were *divine* songs just because, for the first time, they were human and childlike. . . . in 1715[, t]here was nothing even approaching them in content, delightfulness, and versification." Like Watts's adult hymns, his works for children also "followed a system: the chief occasions of a child's worship were taken into account. . . . In theme and execution, the *Divine Songs* run parallel with Watts's work in adult praise."[40] Ironically, John Wesley criticized Watts for this very perspective—or weakness, in his mind—which he set about to reverse in his own texts. The latter, he claimed, when understood by children, would make them "children no longer, only in years and stature."[41]

Childlike as they were, Watts's poems in no way shrank the size of God or of his demands on every person, however small. The hymn that must have lodged a particularly vivid vision of God's omniscience in children's minds was that which begins:

> Almighty God, thy piercing eye
> Shines through the shades of night;
> And our most secret actions lie
> All open to their sight.

Susan Tamke notes that in the British Victorian children's novel *The Fairfield Family*, "when [the character] little Emily steals a plum, she dreams later "that a dreadful Eye was looking upon her from above. Wherever she went, she thought this Eye followed her with angry looks, and she could not hide herself from it." At this point the novel quotes this Watts hymn stanza to drive home the moral. In *Divine and Moral Songs* Watts graphically and terrifyingly describes the punishments of hell. Song 15, "Against Lying," reads:

> The Lord delights in them that speak
> The words of truth; but every liar
> Must have his portion in the lake
> that burns with brimstone and with fire.
>
> Then let me always watch my lips
> Lest I be struck to death and hell,

> Since God a book of reckoning keeps
> For every lie that children tell.[42]

According to writings of the period cited by Tamke, many Victorians, even years later as adults, associated hymns with threatening situations because of hymns they learned in childhood that reinforced a fearful attitude toward God and a vision of God as dispenser of justice.[43] Tamke observes that despite this harsh view of the world, or perhaps because of it, Watts's hymns for children continued to be republished throughout the nineteenth century.[44]

The profound effect of Watts's thirty-eight "divine songs" and eight "moral songs" on generations of Americans can only be guessed at from the staggering publication history of this slim volume. According to Phyllis Bultmann, more than sixty-eight separate editions of this work were published between 1715 and 1880, not counting the great many reprints that appeared.[45]

The prefaces of many American children's hymnals recommended to parents and teachers that to obtain full moralizing influence, children's hymns be memorized. At home and school, children were called on to recite hymns to reinforce a lesson being taught. W. T. Stead notes that one American correspondent sent him a list of twenty-three hymns he had memorized before the age of four in the mid-nineteenth-century, adding, "I really enjoyed learning them, . . . partly because it gave my father so much pleasure to hear me repeat them."[46] Edmund Gosse, another American Victorian, related that "one of the 'games' of a social afternoon among evangelical families was for the children to recite hymns, 'some rather long.'"[47]

Whether children's experiences with hymns were pleasant or troubling, hymn singing and hymn memorization were shared experiences of generations of nineteenth-century children in both England and America. Tamke notes, "The process of memorizing hymns in the family circle and in the schoolrooms created a shared culture among children, at least middle-class children and those children of the lower classes who were educated by middle-class principles." She points out "how widely and deeply embedded this culture was among Victorian adults and children" by recalling Lewis Carroll's two famous parodies of Watts's children's hymns in *Alice in Wonderland*. Carroll satirized "How Doth the Busy Little Bee" in his "How Doth the Little Crocodile," and Watts's " 'Tis the Voice of the Sluggard: I Heard Him Complain" became " 'Twas the Voice of the Lobster." As Tamke observes, the spoof was successful only because Carroll's readers were utterly familiar with the hymns.[48]

Although *Divine and Moral Songs* continued to be published and used in America through much of the nineteenth century, Tamke explains, the "complexion of children's hymns as a whole underwent a change." Later Victorian children's hymns became more positive, largely purged of violent language and imagery, with a didacticism that operated now from guilt rather than fear or threat, in Tamke's analysis; "the newer Victorian hymns for children suppressed the overt motive of fear."[49] Swept by literary Romanticism, many of them celebrated the child as God's good creature in the context of nature imagery. Here also Watts the naturalist provided the foundation for children's hymns that followed his.

"Dr. Watts" Singing in the Black Church

The dissemination of Watts's collections to African slaves in the American colonies has been described in a much-quoted letter by the Rev. John Davies of Virginia to John Wesley of 1750. Davies recounted to Wesley, then an Anglican missionary in Georgia, news on the distribution of hymnals and their enthusiastic reception in the slave community:

> I have supplied them to the utmost of my ability [with books]. They are exceedingly delighted with Watts's songs. And I cannot but observe that the Negroes, above all of the human species I ever knew, have the nicest ear for music. They have a kind of ecstatic delight in Psalmody; nor are there any books they so soon learn, or take so much pleasure in, as in those used in that heavenly part of divine worship.[50]

Most studies on African American worship during slavery focus on the ring shout and pay less attention to the phenomenon that came to be called variously "metered" or "long-meter" singing, "surge singing," lining out, or, most often, "Dr. Watts" singing. While this stemmed from the lining-out practice of the white New England churches, it became so transformed and embedded in black musical practice as to have become the root of much African American musical expression since its inception. The varied use of terminology in sources raises several questions. Was lining the text speaking or singing? Clearly, in its British origins this term meant to read the Psalm line by line, as the Westminster resolution states. We recall Watts's own description of England's "unhappy mixture of reading and singing." In both black and white traditions "lining out" refers to the responsorial reading, chanting, or singing of a psalm or hymn. The related, distinctively black practice of "Dr. Watts" or meter singing describes lining by the leader answered by highly ornamented, melismatic, much slower, congregational renditions of the tune phrases.[51]

One early reference, an article from the [New York] *Nation* of 1867 (quoted in Allen's preface to *Slave Songs of the United States*), describes lining out as part of the official service, "And at regular intervals one hears the elder 'deaconing' a hymn-book hymn, which is sung two lines at a time, and whose wailing cadences, borne on the night air, are indescribably melancholy. But the benches are pushed back to the wall when the formal meeting is over,"[52] the journalist continues, describing the shout ritual that would customarily follow.

By the 1950s folklorist Gertrude P. Kurath had noted the influence on hymn singing of West African chants imported by slaves to southern plantations in the eighteenth century: "They alternated between solo and chorus, sometimes in overlapping polyphony, always with ornaments and glides."[53]

When in 1975 Alfred Pinkston conducted fieldwork in rural churches in the South, he found long-meter singing still widely practiced in the deacon-led "devotional" services held before the regular worship service.[54] Pinkston observed that when a hymn is lined, "the words are given melodically" instead of just being recited. "To be effective in lining the hymn, it is necessary to recite the words in a musical fashion."[55] As an example, he cited that "What a Friend We Have in Jesus" was introduced by one melodic formula for the first two lines, but a different melodic formula for lines three and four, and neither formula bore any relation to the hymn tune. Congregations sang the melody in unison, but also improvised a second part a fourth below, creating strict organum throughout. The slow but weighty tempo resumed with each congregational response, despite the chanted interruptions. Text declamation, due to tempo and ornamentation, was so unclear as to obscure the sense of the words.

The devotional period consisted of one to three lined hymns alternated with as many prayers, setting the tone for the entire worship service. "The deacons feel that this is their main function in the service and to weaken or destroy the devotional period would render them ineffective," Pinkston wrote.[56] He noted that even churches with "college trained ministers" that modernized their services in other respects managed to "[avoid] many conflicts" by retaining this opening devotional period. It was clearly a link to a spiritual and cultural heritage. Even churches that had plenty of hymnals (most of those he visited) did not use the hymnal for meter singing. While lining out, the leader might interpolate testimonies or a story supporting the thought of the hymn stanza. Or prayers by congregation members might erupt, after which congregational singing resumed. After the hymn was sung, it was customary to hum until the pastoral prayer began. (The last stanza of the hymn was usually sung standing; those not able to stand would raise their hands to show support for the call to stand.) Two ministers Pinkston interviewed claimed that "the spiritual rewards from reading and singing the hymn from the hymnal are not as inspiring as having someone line the words."

Horace Clarence Boyer's dissertation, a study of black worship services in Rochester, New York, documented meter singing especially in Baptist and Methodist congregations there. Boyer found that the "humming chorus" after the lined hymn was obligatory and always drew from the last two phrases of the hymn tune.[57] As early as 1961 William Tallmadge analyzed a solo hymn recorded by gospel great Mahalia Jackson and saw it as a direct adaptation of ornamented, congregational Dr. Watts technique to the solo voice. Tallmadge was an early scholar to connect the black tradition to the seventeenth-century Scottish lining-out of Psalms; writing in the early days of rock, he also saw solo gospel artists as transmitting older congregational practices into new secular styles: "I would venture that the very florid and highly ornamented treatment of melodies by some popular . . . 'rock and roll' singers during the past five years may have derived from the old 'lining-out' style by way of such Gospel solos as Mahalia's 'Amazing Grace.'"[58] More recently, William Dargan has transcribed and analyzed a long-meter rendition of Watts's Psalm 116, "I Love the Lord, He Heard My Voice," noting it as still one of the most sung metered hymns in South Carolina as recently as 1995.[59]

A final aspect of African American worship must enter this discussion: What possible connection exists between Watts and the black spiritual? Ritter in 1884 hypothesized, in the characteristically condescending white viewpoint of his day, that some black hymns "began years ago as compositions of more cultivated minds. . . . This theory accounts for the poetry, for often a negro hymn opens with a stanza or two which would not have discredited Watts" after which later stanzas were added and the original ones eventually dropped. While his theory applies to that subtype of camp-meeting song discussed earlier that used Watts texts as the basis on which to add choruses, it is a pattern that survived long afterward in both the African American and white folk spiritual. Ritter's next observation points to another angle of the Watts connection:

> There is, however, still another set of hymns, the words of which the plantation ne-
> gro himself composed entirely at the beginning. They are usually short-metred, [by
> which I assume he meant normal tempo] poetical descriptions of familiar Bible
> incidents, some of them of incredible length, and bristling with anachronisms.
> The blacks call this class of hymns "figurated" from the Bible; and I have heard one
> which was descriptive of the battle of Christian and Apollyon, and consequently
> "figurated" from Bunyan. No word, by the way, is a sweeter morsel on the negro
> tongue than this original verb,—to "figurate." . . . It is used in a dozen senses."[60]

Ritter here attributed a unique ability for biblical paraphrase to African American creativity. It seems it is not a very large step from Watts's Psalm "imitations" to the biblical "figurations" of the black spiritual. After all, Watts had been found guilty of an anachronism or two himself. Perhaps African American worshippers had captured the spirit of Watts, while his more learned revisers such as Barlow and Dwight, in their doctrinally and politically motivated versions, were quibbling over the letter.

The spread of the singing-school movement to the southeast and south after 1800 and the birth of the shape-note singing movement beginning in the 1830s and '40s has been well documented. Richard Crawford, among the first musicologists to bring American psalm tunes to scholarly attention, has introduced a new research methodology and effective tool for the study of singing-school and shape-note tunes in his *Core Repertory* study of the 101 most republished tunes in American imprint tunebooks through 1810.[61] Like Dr. Watts singing, "Sacred Harp singing is a substantial living tradition with unbroken links to the eighteenth century," notes folklorist John Bealle in his recent study that contextualizes the Sacred Harp tradition, its revivals and survival socially, both textual and musically in the changing cultural landscape of its entire history.[62] George Pullen Jackson's historically important but dated studies were pioneer works on tune families and regional tune repertories.[63] Buell Cobb's book *The Sacred Harp* (1978), which chronicles the singing school's migration south, is a thorough if not definitive introduction to Sacred Harp singing.[64]

Of the thirty-eight four-shape books published between 1798 and 1855, according to Charles Ellington, "only *Southern Harmony* and *Sacred Harp* gained sufficient footing to insure their popularity and use well into the second half of the nineteenth century.[65] The 1991 edition of *Sacred Harp* contains eleven settings of the four Watts texts under discussion. *Southern Harmony* contains four; and one text is duplicated between the books, making a total of fourteen tunes.

The 1991 edition of *Sacred Harp*, the edition most used from the late nineteenth-century through today's national shape-note revival, presents the clearest picture of the role of Watts in the ongoing shape-note tradition in this country. In that edition, twenty-one new composers were added, only three of whom had contributed to the previous edition. Their contribution represented sixty new songs, for which twenty-seven are settings of Watts's; 136 of the total 560 texts in the 1991 edition are his. As Bealle explains, "contemporary composers 'breathed new life' into the old [Watts] poetry by choosing the texts for their compositions, reengaging the poetic idiom and providing for renewed personal associations with texts that resonated throughout the singing community."[66]

Revival Again

By 1875 another revival movement was poised to sweep the nation. The young evangelist Dwight L. Moody and his musical associate Ira D. Sankey, both in their thirties, had traveled to England as complete unknowns two years earlier to lead evangelistic meetings; before the end of their trip they had forged an entirely new paradigm for revivalism. Back in the United States, as they held series of fabulously successful revival campaigns in one major city after another, the culture ultimately came under the sway of their new style of religion. A far cry from the histrionic preaching, all-night services, and improvised singing of the camp meetings, Moody's and Sankey's services were orderly, carefully timed, and

Table 1. Watts Settings of Four Texts in *Southern Harmony* and *Sacred Harp*

Title	Book	Tune Title	Composer Attribution
Alas! And Did My Saviour Bleed	SoHarm	REMEMBER ME. CM.	L. J. Jones
	SacHarp	VICTORIA. C.M.	Leonard P. Breedlove
	SacHarp	WEEPING SAVIOR. (2nd.) CM	Arr. Edmund Dumas
	SacHarp	LOVE THE LORD. C.M.	J. P. Reese, 1859
Am I a Soldier of the Cross	SoHarm	ORTONVILLE C.M.	—
	SacHarp	CHRISTIAN SOLDIER. C.M.	F. Price, 1835
	SacHarp	SOLDIER OF THE CROSS. C.M.	G.B. Daniel
	SacHarp	LIVING LAMB. C.M.	Arr. C. Davis, 1850
	SacHarp	JOYFUL. C.M.	Arr. B. F. White, 1844
Come, We That Love the Lord	SoHarm	WEBSTER. S.M.	—
The Hill of Zion Yields	SoHarm	MOUNT ZION. S.M.	[Bartholomew] Brown
	SacHarp	MOUNT ZION. (First). S.M.	Bartholomew Brown
	SacHarp	THE HILL OF ZION. S.M.	B. F. White, 1859
The Men of Grace Have Found	SacHarp	CONCORD. S.M.	Oliver Holden, 1793
When I Survey the Wondrous Cross	SacHarp	WONDROUS CROSS. L.M.D.	Paine Denson, 1932

paced with a businessman's professionalism—and, for the first time in history, supported by millions of dollars donated by America's wealthiest businessmen of the day. Crucial if not central to the whole venture was the musical leader— who served as song leader, soloist, choir director, and often hymn writer—and a new, spit-polished style of hymn, the gospel hymn. With the latter's rampant popularization, the paradigm shift was complete. Ultimately, much evangelical worship became stamped with the pacing, ethos, and musical repertory of the new revivalism, and has never been fully delivered since.

Sankey's fabled success in Britain and back in the United States was due in part to the gospel hymns of Philip P. Bliss, another talented young singer and hymn writer pioneering in the revival music field. Upon Sankey's arrival home, he and Bliss collaborated on the collection *Gospel Hymns and Sacred Songs*, containing songs in the new style by Bliss, Sankey, Hartsough, Perkins, and others. It was followed with five more volumes over the next eighteen years, all of which would be published together in 1894 as the epoch-making *Gospel Hymns Nos. 1 to 6*, still in congregational use today. In his preface to the scholarly reprint edition, musicologist H. Wiley Hitchcock calls this book a "portable revival." Sandra Sizer has explained how this hymnal successfully brought the "social religion" of the post–Second Awakening era into the mass revivals of the progressive 1890s. Through hymn texts of testimony, invitation, and exhortation, addressed to oneself and to other people, and through prayer hymns of conversion and response, the song leader of urban mass revivalism could meld a congregation of thousands into a temporary "emotional community," to use Sizer's phrase. In that community people could share their conversion story in testimony hymns and invite the unconverted to salvation through invitation hymns. Through hymns the unsaved could appropriate salvation for themselves, model their own conversion experiences on those of the believers. Gospel hymns instantly made people feel close without actually having to become so.

But was the gospel hymn so new? It was certainly current, with its popular tune styles—the dotted-rhythm march, the waltz in ⁶⁄₈ or ¾ time, and other rhythmic styles. Even the "devotional" style introduced in Mason's and Hastings hymn reforms was well-represented in the new gospel songs. Perhaps the most "generic" gospel hymn-tune style was that "characterized by a singable, repetitive melody, catchy rhythms and simple harmonic language; a chorus or refrain is typical but not requisite, as is call-and-response writing, or the immediate echo of a few words between upper and lower voices, in the chorus.[67] But the chorus and call-and-response were, after all, familiar to congregations from the camp meetings of their parents' generation and provided a comforting connection to "old-time religion," stability, and values to thousands of newly urbanized Americans nostalgic for their roots.

The four hymns under discussion appear in *Gospel Hymns Nos. 1 to 6* in six tune settings (see table 2). All but the setting of Mason's older tune, "Hamburg," will be discussed here.[68]

Table 2. Settings of Select Watts Texts in *Gospel Hymns Nos. 1–6*

First Line	Traditional Tune	No. in GH	Chorus	Composer or Arr.
Alas! And Did My Saviour Bleed	AVON	79	Help me, dear Saviour, Thee	Asa Hull
Alas! And Did My Saviour Bleed	AVON	305	At the cross, at the cross	Ralph E. Hudson
Am I a Soldier of the Cross	ARLINGTON	494	In the name of Christ the King	Ira D. Sankey
Come, Ye That Love the Lord	ST. THOMAS	567	We're marching to Zion	R. Lowry
When I Survey the Wondrous Cross	HAMBURG	709	none	Lowell Mason, arr.
When I Survey the Wondrous Cross	HAMBURG	491	O wondrous cross where Jesus	Ira D. Sankey

The two most famous gospel hymn settings of Watts's texts are undoubtedly Ralph E. Hudson's "At the Cross," a setting of "Alas! And Did My Saviour Bleed," and Robert Lowry's "We're Marching to Zion." "Alas! And Did My Savior Bleed" appears in Watts's *Hymns and Spiritual Songs*, volume 2 (on "Divine Subjects"), under the topic heading, "Godly Sorrow Arising from the Sufferings of Christ." Watts's original text had six stanzas. The second, which was deleted in most subsequent publications, reads:

> Thy body slain, sweet Jesus, Thine,
> And bathed in its own blood,
> While all exposed to wrath divine
> The Glorious Suff'rer stood?

In all editions after the first Watts had designated this stanza as optional for church use, perhaps due to its graphic imagery.

Hudson's "At the Cross" illustrates perhaps most clearly the links between camp-meeting, shape-note, and gospel hymns, bridging the gap between oral and print traditions over several decades. At least versions of this text with various choruses attached appeared in tunebooks or revival collections by midcentury.

Leonard Breedlove's tune "Victoria" appears in the original *Sacred Harp* with the chorus:

> I have but one more river to cross (*repeat twice*)
> And then I'll be at rest.[69]

Here the stanza's opening line is sung three times, followed by line two, but the rest of the stanza is deleted. Clearly the linear thought and internal coherence of Watt's sermonic hymn is freely sacrificed for the repetition of a signature snippet of text that is presumed to suffice for the spiritual needs of the singers.

J. P. Reese is credited in *Sacred Harp* with writing the tune "Love the Lord" in 1859. Its romping 6/8 tune is undistinctive, supplied with the poetically bumpy but at least doctrinally unabrasive refrain:

> O who is like Jesus? Hallelujah, Praise ye the Lord;
> There's none like Jesus, hallelujah, Love and serve the Lord.

Perhaps the most unusual setting bears the tune name "Weeping Savior" (second tune), attributed in *Sacred Harp* to the arranger Edmund Dumas in 1869 but strongly suggesting an earlier folk origin. After Watts's stanzas, the refrain grips the listener with the plea to "See the Savior on the cross! Oh, sinner, hear Him cry, 'Eloi, Eloi, Lama Sabacthani!'" ending with Christ's cry to His Father on the cross.

"Remember Me" is perhaps the most famous shape-note setting of Watts's text, attributed in *Southern Harmony* to L. J. Jones. The tune, in the tenor voice, bears strong resemblance to "Avon," although in a more restricted compass, and is a jewel of simplicity in its total of seven measures, repeated for the stanza and again for the chorus. The somberness of the purely pentatonic melody is matched by the two-line refrain, a profound theological distillation of and response to Watts's poem: "Remember, Lord, thy dying groans, And then remember me." But the electrifying power of this three-voice tune lies in the striking parallel sonorities in the outer voices. The entire tonal plateau lurches downward on the words "dying *groans, And* then" in haunting parallel fifths.

Ralph Hudson, born in Napoleon, Ohio, in 1843, served in the Civil War and then taught music at Mount Vernon College in Alliance, Ohio, before devoting himself fully to evangelistic singing, songwriting, and music publishing. He was also a licensed Methodist Episcopal preacher. He published his tune to "At the Cross" in 1885 in his *Songs of Peace, Love, and Joy*. The traditional tune to which Watts's text had long been wed till then was the Scottish "Avon," by eighteenth-century music teacher, shoemaker, draftsman, and lay church worker Hugh Wilson (1766–1824), who likely captured in it more than a whiff of a Scottish ballad, according to Donald Brown. "Avon" had already been circulating in American hymnals with this text by Hudson's time, and one may note a distinct melodic similarity between the two tunes. But where Wilson's tune unfolds in an architectural design spanning all phrases, Hudson's hovers around the tonic triad so closely as to become trite. It seems impossible that Hudson would not have known "Avon" and highly likely that his tune was at some level influenced by it.

Hymnologist Donald Brown has found the chorus "At the cross" appended to a Wesley hymn, "O, How Happy Are They," in *Glad Hallelujahs* (edited by John R. Sweney and William J. Kirkpatrick) published in 1887 and to another text by Ralph Kelso Carter in the *Emory Hymnal* in the same year. From these settings Brown argues that the chorus was already known and in circulation when Hudson chose it for Watts's text.[70] But Hudson's combination of this hymn and chorus is his own—a shed or lean-to built of roughly hewn, low-grade timber onto the stately structure of Watts's hymn. The chorus's burst of dotted rhythms is annoyingly incongruous even with Hudson's own preceding tune, a fact Brown cites to support his argument for differing origins. Theologically, the disparity between stanza and chorus is glaring. We have moved ever further from Watt's sermon meditation. There can be no greater chasm that that between Watts's declaration "Thus might I . . . Dissolve my heart in thankfulness and melt my eyes to tears" and Hudson's rollicking "Now I am happy all the day."[71] The most jarring aspect of the Watts-cum-gospel-chorus is the theological whiplash one experiences at every transition from Watts's poetic argument in the stanzas to the musical-textual trampoline of Hudson's chorus. The somberness of Watts's theme, "Godly Sorrow Arising from the Sufferings of Christ," seems lost.

Yet Sankey, in his *Story of the Gospel Hymns* in 1906, refers to "At the Cross" as the "new tune" by Hudson for the old hymn by Watts, implying it was widely known and accepted by then. Sankey noted that the pioneer children's evangelist E. P. Hammond credited Hudson's "At the Cross" with his conversion at age seventeen.[72] This cobbled hymn, then, was to prove durable and even of service.

Decades earlier, in November 1850, Fanny (Frances Jane) Crosby, already a prominent teacher and laywoman in New York City, after weeks of attending revival meetings at the Broadway Tabernacle, and on her third anguished visit to the altar, surrendered to the divine love to the singing of the final lines of this hymn, "Here, Lord, I give myself away, 'Tis all that I can do." She notes in her autobiography, cited by Bernard Ruffin, something of the power of the older tune in her phrase the "grand old consecration hymn," "Alas! And Did My Saviour Bleed," presumably a reference to the tune "Avon." Whether in its old garb or newer, unmatched patchwork dress, this Watts text catalyzed rebirth and transformation for two spiritual leaders of the urban revival movement, one being its leading poet and lay theologian.

Hudson was not the only gospel-hymn composer to revamp this Watts text. Asa Hull's tune with a new chorus by the title "Remember Me" was also successful enough to appear in *Gospel Hymns Nos. 1 to 6*. Like the composers of the shape-note tunes, Hull attempts to frame in his chorus a fitting response to Watt's meditation, possibly based on a folk model. The biblical phrase "Remember Me" recalls Jones's shape-note setting and biblical refrain, but Hull's reference to the prayer of the dying thief is more explicit:

> Help me, dear Saviour, Thee to own,
> And ever faithful be;
> And when Thou sittest on Thy throne,
> O Lord, remember me.

Hull's chorus effectively leads the singer into prayer and conversion by following the biblical model of the penitent criminal's plea. The short, nondistinctive tune is squarely in gospel-hymn tune style, complete with the prolonged subdominant chord in the penultimate phrase so typical of many gospel tunes. One may regret that of the two gospel choruses for this text, the one with greater theological integrity and cohesion has not survived.

Ira D. Sankey, his fantastic success as a hymn writer notwithstanding, was far less illustrious in his remodeling of Watts. His version of "Am I a Soldier of the Cross" apparently enjoyed currency both in the United States and England; it appears in *Sacred Songs and Solos* as well as *Gospel Hymns*. It contained his highly predictable chorus:

> In the name of Christ the King,
> Who hath purchased life for me,

> Thro' grace I'll win the promised crown,
> Whate'er my cross may be.

Sankey's new tune for Watts is a step-wise, run-of-the-mill dotted-rhythm melody that employs call-and-response in the chorus on the words "In the name" and "of Christ the King," resulting in a rousing march that Watts's call-to-arms imagery invites. Sankey's application of the identical techniques and style to a text of completely opposite mood proves disastrous, however. This is Sankey's take on "When I Survey the Wondrous Cross."

Seemingly possessed of a desire to prolong both the middle and end of every line of that poem, Sankey charges into this most exalted of hymn texts with rollicking call-and-response from the first measure of the piece onward and drives every alternating measure in the stanza with the identical jog-trot dotted rhythm. A possible explanation for this piece may be that, for the vernacular musician Sankey and his audiences, this effort represented a jerry-rigged sort of choral complexity, and they even found it exciting. It is unclear whether Sankey, who had his finger on the pulse of revival audiences like no one else of his day, thought this song style to be actually raising the congregation's musical tastes and abilities in the sense of Mason's and Hasting's ideals, or if simply knew that the people would enjoy belting this out. The chorus, highly predictable in lyrics, may also be one of his more homely efforts, in which the opening minor seventh leap (on "O wondrous cross") is actually a prolonged upper neighbor to the sentimental ascending sixth (on "where Jesus died"), a stock-in-trade melodic formula of parlor song of the day. Erik Routley's words come to mind here: "As the Gospel Song developed, the possibilities of chromatic harmony . . . for arousing emotion were not overlooked."[73] If the raucous treatment of the earlier stanzas were not enough, the chopping up of the words "See from His head" in stanza 3 is intolerable. The sharp irony here is that nearly two hundred years earlier Watts had designed his entire worship reform to do away once and for all with precisely such senseless chopping up, mangling, and bowdlerization of sacred thoughts and phrases.

The last revised Watts hymn in *Gospel Hymns Nos. 1 to 6*, even more famous than "At the Cross," became a signature tune of the gospel-hymn era. Watts's hymn "Come, We That Love the Lord" enjoyed success on American soil in many worship traditions. Of all of Watts's texts discussed here, this one was edited most extensively from its original ten stanzas. Watts gave the poem the topical heading, "Heavenly Joy on Earth." The form of his original argument is of particular importance. As the heading indicates, this was not primarily written as a "heaven song"; it was about the foretaste, the pleasures accruing already now to those walking in God's ways. These are the "joys" we wish to "make known" as we "join in a song with sweet accord." The second stanza, although indicated by Watts as optional, seems key to this train of thought:

The sorrows of the mind
Be banish'd from the place;
Religion never was design'd
To make our pleasures less.

From that refreshing vantage point, the admonition in stanza 3 makes even greater sense, in which only those who never knew our God ought refuse to sing. Watt's delightful original here reads: "Favorites of the heav'nly King / May speak their joys abroad," an endearing endorsement of the doctrine of election. After a glorious, sweeping view of this heavenly King and his sovereignty, "who rules upon the stormy sky, And manages the seas," we are reassured that "This awful God is ours, Our Father and Our Love," that he does and will provide for us, and will ultimately bring us into his presence and into sinless joy. "The thoughts of such amazing bliss," then, "should constant joys create"—the fact that "the men of grace have found glory begun below." The imagery of stanza 8 recalls Psalm 85:10–11 as an image of earth and heaven meeting: "Truth shall spring out of the earth, and righteousness shall look down from heaven." Interestingly, although Watts bracketed the latter stanza also, it was a favorite of singing-school composers and compilers. The felicitous language of the last two stanzas, 9 and 10, has been immortalized to congregations for centuries—the "thousand sacred sweets" abound for God's people on the hill of Zion, it should be noted, "before we reach the heav'nly fields or walk the golden streets." Such joys are the reason Watts closes with the admonition that every tear ought to be dry, for we are already "marching thro' Immanuel's ground / to fairer worlds on high."

There is a traditional English tune for this hymn. Now known as "St. Thomas," it was originally part of Aaron Williams's longer tune "Holborn," published in his *Universal Psalmodist* (London, 1763), and quickly became popular in the United States. It had been reprinted in dozens of American tunebooks by 1820.[74] Hymn scholars Theron Brown and Hezekiah Butterworth writing in 1906 noted the use of another tune for this text beside "St. Thomas"—the Italian tune "Ain," by Arcangelo Corelli. They describe the latter as a "fugue piece" that has "more music" than "St. Thomas," "and the joyful traverse of its notes along the staff in four-four time, with the momentum of a good choir, is exhilarating in the extreme."[75] It seems that the "joyful traverse of the notes" was fast becoming a tradition for this text.

No composers of shape-note settings added a chorus or any text to this hymn of Watts's, but they took liberties in selection of stanzas. The oldest tune, Bartholomew Brown's "Mount Zion" (First SM) appears in both *Southern Harmony* and *Sacred Harp*. This rousing, extended four-part setting in C major of the ninth and tenth stanzas no doubt afforded a few joys and sweets to the singers, with its swooping contrary motion triplets rising to high G in the treble through most of the first strain, followed by a modified fuguing section (with three rather than four entrances and with voices singing differing melodic material) culminating in a swirling, eleven-note melisma on the superimposed words "fairer" and "high"—both strong words in the stanza—and coalescing in a dramatic rest and emphatic homophonic march to the finish. It seems that Brown's is the first setting to exploit the polyphonic possibilities of this stanza, and its tune name is the first of several to identify Watt's text by the name Zion. The distribution of stanzas here also foreshadows future settings: stanza 9 is set homophonically in just eight measures, while the "fuge" with homophonic conclusion devotes forty measures to stanza 10 (counting the customary repeat).

A year later, in 1793, Oliver Holden, prominent Baptist layman and composer of the tune "Coronation," set stanzas 8 through 10 of this text to the tune "Concord" SM. A quasi-fuguing tune on a much smaller scale, its opening phrase is four measures long, the repeated second half only seven (or fourteen with repeat). This quasi-"fuge" uses inexact imitation and paired voices (bass-alto and tenor-treble) rather than four staggered entrances. Decades later, in 1859, *Sacred Harp* compiler Benjamin Franklin White tried his hand at this text with the tune "The Hill of Zion" SM, a setting, like Brown's, of only stanzas 9 and 10. Unlike the others, however, this A-major setting is a plain tune in 3/4 of only thirteen measures; while pleasant, it is not exuberant, and certainly not rambunctious in the style of Brown's.

Thus, when in 1867 Baptist minister Robert Lowry, then pastoring the Hanson Place Baptist Church in Brooklyn, composed the tune "We're Marching to Zion," he was building on a growing musical tradition for this text. It is difficult for the listener, having once heard Brown's setting, not to hear the direct lineage of a tune in 6/8 meter with simple polyphonic effects in the refrain, now updated in gospel hymn dress. Despite the family resemblance, however, Lowry's tune is fully a child of its generation, with its martial dotted rhythms in the refrain, and call-and-response technique replacing the now antiquated "fuge." Lowry, after taking up hymn and tune writing seriously during his pastorate in Brooklyn, succeeded gospel hymn pioneer William B. Bradbury as editor of Sunday school song books at Biglow and Main in New York, the nation's leading hymnal publisher to that time. There Lowry composed gospel hymn tunes, edited bestselling collections, and exerted great influence on shaping the gospel-tune style.[76]

He first published this text with his tune in a collection for Sunday school, *Silver Spray* (1868). Brown and Butterworth noted that "for revival meetings the modern tune . . . by Robert Lowry should be mentioned. A shouting chorus is appended to it, but it has melody and plenty of stimulating motion." This glimpse into performance practice indicates that the loud singing still associated with this tune was customary from the beginning; however, these authors credit Lowry's tune with rhythmic vitality, shouting aside. They also praise the melodic shape of Lowry's tune, which is worth noting in a tune style known for repetitive melodies such as Sankey's "The Ninety and Nine" and Carter's "Standing on the Promises."

Not all voices were as supportive of gospel hymnody as Brown's and Butterworth's. Presbyterian scholar David R. Breed, professor at the Western Theological Seminary in Pittsburgh, found much to say on the topic in his hymnology textbook of 1903. Like his contemporaries in academe, Breed was compelled to discuss gospel hymns due to their fantastic popularity. He rejected their texts as true hymns (even those he called beautiful and effective, such as "Almost Persuaded"), discredited their musical quality based on the composers' lack of training, and found the solo-chorus feature objectionable on the same grounds: "It requires much less skill to write a solo with a simple refrain than to write a good hymn-tune." He also objected to the call-and-response feature in the choruses, which he thought of as the "imitation of the fugue-tune" and "little else than simple antiphony." But Breed reserved his harshest words for the most objectionable of all features, "[which] has been," he writes, "the dissociation of old standard hymns from the stately tunes to which congregations have been accustomed to sing them, connecting them with trifling melodies." Breed spoke out not only with the indignation of one who has been robbed of the church's musical birthright; he was livid at the pallid substitutes gospel-hymn composers were handing him: "The tune which has been joined to [the text] is altogether out of keeping with the words. So it has been," he continues,

> with two of Watts' most serious hymns, "Alas, and did my Saviour bleed" and "Come we that love the Lord." In both cases a chorus has been added that we hesitate to characterize. The words of the chorus are a deep and pitiable decline and the music is almost sacrilege. . . . How can any devout worshiper, before the cross of his crucified Saviour, take up such a strain as that which this Gospel chorus furnishes. It is inexplicable. The other chorus is simply tawdry, picnic music—unworthy of pilgrims to the heavenly city.[77]

Conclusion

This chapter has examined four of Watts's hymn texts in the rich counterpoint of American historical, theological, and literary contexts that produced and enveloped them. Stackhouse, Marini, and Music have shown that Watts came to ascendency in US Protestantism on the crest of two concurrent and often conflicting movements: the rise of regular singing and the First Awakening. Watts seemed to thrive as well in a move toward order and regulation as in a movement that rocked American Protestantism violently enough to produce a second, still greater revival. Then, with the onslaught of urban revivalism and mass-produced gospel hymnody, Watts not only survived but came out on the top of the charts, in Hudson's and Lowry's updated versions. Watts's efforts produced reform where he did not at all intend it and in ways he—by his own admission—had not hoped to have effected change—namely, in musical style and practice. He despaired of a tradition of lining out, yet a beautified, cultural transformation of it came to bear his name and ultimately to permeate nearly every form of vernacular black musical expression to this day. Perhaps it could be said that the colonies and new nation were the eager Gentile recipients of Watts's musical gospel, in contrast to the British Israel for whom he had first poured out his efforts.

The questions raised at the outset of this chapter have embraced a swath of American life nearly two hundred years long and as wide as the republic, connecting Congregational churches in the northeastern colonies, schoolrooms for more than a century, developing African American worship traditions in the southeast and south, the presidency of Yale University and American religious intellectualism, and the unfettered euphoria of Kentucky's camp-meeting revivals in the early 1800s.

Watts was adapted in the doctrinal shift from Calvinism to evangelical theology in the Second Awakening, modified by Republican politics and sanitized at the rise of a new educational philosophy in the nineteenth century. His texts were quickly becoming the congregational staple at the time of disestablishment and national independence, when a new language and liturgy were needed. Watts became the liturgist for a new nation. His works fulfilled on this soil a destiny they could never have realized had they remained in Britain, and they did so—owing to his prodigious gift and intentional populist approach—in a way no other British collection could have. As liturgy, his work ensured not only the viability of new hymns in America but also the longevity of at least some Psalms, which his texts carried through the turbulent psalmody controversy to the present day.

Watts became, for the first centuries of America's existence, our national poet. This occurred not only through worship but also through business and education. Watts reached the colonies at the beginning of a burgeoning movement of tunebook publication, with the built-in market of the singing-school movement to promote him. His children's texts use in schools insured their transmission to future generations for more than a century. And Watts was there when a whole African population was learning English and literacy on American soil. The texts of the Bible, Watts, and Wesley were the first poetic models for African American language arts. Watts as national song acquired a distinctive singing-school tune style and then outgrew it, putting on the musical dress of the patchwork gospel hymn. The tunes changed, but Watts's texts were not tune driven; they were rugged enough to survive all the theological and musical tinkering. Their theological power has always resided in their scripturality, their staying power in the accessibility of their language and rhetoric to common people, their pedagogical power in the vivid images—pictures of heaven, pilgrims, the cross—that captured the minds of preachers, children, and older Christians from the nation's early days of literacy.

Among the ironies in this story is that Watts's corpus was written to be populist, yet it became for entire eras in many quarters *auctoritas*. Was it sacralized during the formation of genteel nineteenth-century American culture, as Lawrence Levine has argued happened to Shakespeare?[78] To an extent, yes, but only after having been revised and having had the hellfire and brimstone swept out. Watts was sacralized by Victorians after being reworded—ironic, since he was himself the ultimate reworder. But for worshippers in the colonies and young republic, Watts had become the prayer book long ago. The wordsmiths failed, and Watts remained; all aspirants to the offices of poet laureate and national psalmist lost their crowns to him. And even while being sacralized in some circles, Watts's poetry put out yet deeper roots into American culture through the ongoing shape-note tradition and the oral tradition in black worship that bears his name.

John Bealle has observed, "Indeed, today there is surely no Watts revival at hand among prevailing contemporary evangelical Christian movements. Yet *Sacred Harp* and Watts, largely undiluted, have found a curious, if small, niche in contemporary America."[79] I would differ with Bealle and maintain that Watts has never been revived because evangelical Americans have never lost Watts. They have theologically revised him, politically tweaked his words, and remodeled his tunes, but they have always sung him.

Susan Tamke contends that even Watts's greatest admirers admit that the quality of his work is uneven, that his subjectivity and sentimentality at times are obnoxious, and that his starkly Calvinistic theology is, particularly in children's hymns, foreign to modern ears. The continued used of Watts's hymns, however, speaks for itself: they appealed to his own generation and every one since.[80]

As Bealle has also pointed out, "Watts seems an unlikely poetic voice for the postmodern age." However, Donald Davie, whom Bealle calls "possibly Watts's most articulate and enthusiastic supporter in literary circles," proposes two possible avenues for approaching Watts: from an antiquarian view and from the perspective of the axiom. As for the first, Bealle observes, "there is plenty in Watts to satisfy an antiquarian appetite." He notes Davie's suggestion that "it is all too easy to project Watts's sentiments [and his imagery, I would add, of mortals as worms] into the past and not apply them to one's own experiences"—until, Bealle points out, the singing community experiences a loss of a beloved member, and suddenly the archaic language, "Why should we start and fear to die?" becomes relevant.[81]

Davie explains the second possible approach to Watts, through axiom, as follows:

Religious belief, it has been bluntly said, is irreconcilable with "the modern mind." But even if that were so in some general or abstract sense, it is quite clear that even the most modern mind, if . . . it chooses . . . *can* still enter the imaginative world of Watts, the world of the axiom. One way to make that passage is by relishing the literary (aesthetic) pleasures that only the worlds of the axiom can supply.[82]

Precisely because Watts takes biblical doctrine as unassailable truth, he takes for granted that stones will cry out if mortals do not sing:

> Let mortals ne'er refuse to take
> Th' Hosanna on their tongues;
> Lest rocks and stones should rise, and break
> Their silence into songs.

By the late eighteenth century, in contrast, Augustus Toplady framed the same concept hyperbolically:

> Should we, dear Lord, refuse to take
> The Hosanna on our tongues,
> The rocks and stones would rise and break
> Their silence into songs.

"For Watts," Davie writes, "the stones' supposed behaviour is simply the necessary consequence of the axiom: if God is the Creator, then every one of His creatures—stones as well as men—responds to Him and moves at his command." Davie contends that the serious student of Watts's poetic style will, in fact, "break out of the world of 'the aesthetic' into the regions of human experience more liberating, though also more alarming."[83] Elaborating on this thought, Bealle explains what may be part of Watts's power still today:

> Watts possesses an encoded resistance to modernity. We moderns may erect mediating schemes for engaging Watts, but these schemes only affirm that a more powerful reading lurks beneath them. Sacred Harp singings, which attract so diverse a spectrum of believers, are ritual encounters in which the mediating schemes that might influence reading—"vain discourse," as Watts himself put it—are kept away. Only self-examination stands between singer and text."[84]

By way of epilogue, in 1998 rising hip-hop artist Lauren Hill released her first solo recording, *The Miseducation of Lauren Hill*. The fourth piece on the album is Hill's free meditation, or perhaps "imitation," on Mary's Magnificat from Luke 2, written during Hill's pregnancy with her first child. The song is titled "To Zion." In stanza 1, Hill moves seamlessly from telling Mary's story to telling her own—voicing her emotions of joy, awe, and pain at being misunderstood by friends, in which she identifies with Mary. But she journeys through her struggle, arriving triumphantly on the words, "Now the joy of my world is in Zion." As in other songs, Hill draws openly on her Christian faith. She expresses it here through her Baptist heritage of gospel hymns, as the song ends with polyphonic layering of her theme line and a textual hook from Robert Lowry: "Marching, marching to Zion, Beautiful, beautiful Zion." This version is hardly Watts's original. But it is Watts once removed, Watts through the voice of Robert Lowry as embraced for more than a century in the rich traditions of the African American church that have nurtured Hill and so many others, Watts as known and loved for generations by countless saints across America in their march to Zion. This, too, is Isaac Watts in America.

Notes

A previous version of this chapter appeared as "'We're Marching to Zion': Isaac Watts in Early America" in *Wonderful Words of Life: Hymns in American Portestant History and Theology,* edited by Richard J. Mouw and Mark A. Noll. Grand Rapids, MI, and Cambridge, UK: Eerdmans, 2004, pp. 17–41.

1. Watts, *Hymns and Spiritual Songs, Book II,* "Christ's Presence Makes Death Easy," cited in Bishop, *Isaac Watts,* 190.

2. Watts, preface to *Psalms,* [iii]–xxxii, cited in Music, *Hymnology,* 130.

3. Cited in Music, *Hymnology,* 135.

4. Watts, *Psalms,* 243, cited in Escott, *Isaac Watts,* 122.

5. Watts, *Psalms,* 266, cited in ibid., 127.

6. Escott, *Isaac Watts,* 124.

7. Ibid., 121–31.

8. Watts, *Psalms,* 258, cited in Escott, *Isaac Watts,* 125.

9. Escott, *Isaac Watts,* 126–27.

10. Ibid., 26.

11. Tajchman, "Isaac Watts's Communion Hymns," 22.

12. 6 8's, 6 10's, 6.6.8.6.6.8. and 6.6.6.6.4.4.4.4.

13. Escott, *Isaac Watts,* 148.

14. Wright, *Lives,* 132.

15. In 1799 Thomas Tregenna Biddulph, vicar of St. James Church in Bristol, was virulently attacked in a pamphlet that accused him of being a dissenter in disguise. The reason for this charge? He used hymns in public worship. Tamke, *Make a Joyful Noise,* 22.

16. Foote, *Three Centuries,* 64.

17. "'It is the duty of christians [*sic*] to praise God publicly by singing of psalms all together in the congregation and also privately in the family. In the singing of psalms the voice is to be audibly and gravely ordered; but the chief care must be to sing with understanding and with grace in the heart, making melody unto the Lord. That the whole congregation may join therein, every one that can read is to have a psalm-book and all others not disabled by age or otherwise are to be exhorted to learn to read. But for the present where many in the congregation cannot read, it is convenient that the minister or some fit person appointed by him and the other ruling officers do read the psalm line by line, before singing thereof.'" Cited in Ritter, *Music in England,* 51–52.

18. Cited in Music, *Hymnology,* 118.

19. Cited in ibid., 135.

20. Ritter, *Music in America*, 52.

21. Benson, *English Hymn*, 162.

22. Music, "Isaac Watts in America," 30.

23. Diary of Cotton Mather, Massachusetts Historical Society Collection, 7th Series, VIII, 142, cited in Foote, *Three Centuries*, 65–66.

24. The *Ainsworth Psalter* and *Rous's Version* were also in use to a lesser extent.

25. Crozier, *Novels*, 91, cited in Bealle, *Public Worship*, 78.

26. Music, "First Baptist Church," 36.

27. Benson, *English Hymn*, 192–93.

28. Hood, *History*, 180–81.

29. Stackhouse, *Language of the Psalms*, 102.

30. Choirs were established at First Baptist in Haverhill, Massachusetts, and Providence, Rhode Island, in 1786 and 1791, respectively.

31. Raichelson, "Black Religious Folksong," 206.

32. Marini, "Rehearsal for Revival," 87.

33. Music, *Hymnology*, 184.

34. Raichelson, "Black Religious Folksong," 207.

35. Sizer, *Gospel Hymns*, 14–15, 50–52.

36. Hulan, "Campmeeting Spiritual Folksongs"; Lorenz, *Glory Hallelujah*; Hammond, "Music in Urban Revivalism."

37. Jackson, *Spiritual Folk-Songs*, 240.

38. Music, "Watts in America," 32.

39. Benson, *English Hymn*, 120–21.

40. Escott, *Isaac Watts*, 216.

41. Ibid., 216.

42. Song XV, "Against Lying," stanzas 5 and 6. Isaac Watts, *Divine and Moral Songs*, 55–56.

43. Tamke, *Make a Joyful Noise*, 82–83.

44. Ibid., 77.

45. Bultmann, "Everybody Sing," 145, cited in Tamke, *Make a Joyful Noise*, 80.

46. Tamke, *Make a Joyful Noise*, 80.

47. Gosse, *Father and Son*, 234, cited in Tamke, *Make a Joyful Noise*, 77.

48. Tamke, *Make a Joyful Noise*, 77.

49. Ibid., 83.

50. Wesley, *Works*, 584.

51. It should be noted that this style is distinctly different from the call-and-response technique found in the camp-meeting song and later urban gospel hymn, an immediate echo of a few words between upper and lower voices. Pinkston used the term *lining out* synonymously with "statement and response," but no other source I consulted equates these two terms. Pinkston, "Lined Hymns," 89.

52. *The Nation*, May 30, 1867. Cited in Allen, Ware, and Garrison, *Slave Songs*, xiii.

53. Kurath, "Rhapsodies of Salvation," 178.

54. Pinkston, "Lined Hymns," 92–94.

55. Ibid.

56. Ibid.

57. Boyer, "Analysis.".

58. Tallmadge, "Dr. Watts."

59. Dargan, "Congregational Singing."

60. Ritter, *Music in America*, 393.

61. Crawford, *Core Repertory*.

62. Bealle, *Public Worship*, back cover blurb.

63. Jackson, *Spiritual Folk-Songs*.

64. Cobb, *Sacred Harp*. For comment, see Bealle, *Public Worship*, xii.

65. Ellington, "Sacred Harp Tradition," 18.

66. Bealle, *Public Worship*, 231. Composers of pieces in *Sacred Harp* and other tunebooks did not indicate which editions or revisions of Watts's they set to music.

67. See also Rothenbusch, "Role of Gospel Hymns," 223.

68. Other appearances of unadulterated Watts in GH1–6 are "Salvation! O the Joyful Sound!" (694, text only) and "Not All the Blood of Beasts" (689), set to Mason's short meter tune, BOYLSTON.

69. Jackson cites the tune title as VICTORIA or ONE MORE RIVER TO CROSS, Jackson, *Spiritual Folk-Songs*, 226.

70. D[onald] B[rown], "Alas! And Did My Savior Bleed," *Handbook to the Baptist Hymnal* (Nashville, Tenn.: Convention Press, 1992), 83–84.

71. Hudson managed to capitalize on the chorus's existing popularity by setting it to another Watts text as well, "I'm Not Ashamed to Own My Lord," creating almost as poor a match. This combination was successful enough at least in England that the publishers of *Sacred Songs and Solos*—the British counterpart to *Gospel Hymns Nos. 1 to 6* included it. Sankey, *Sacred Songs*, 883.

72. Sankey, *Sankey's Story*.

73. Routley, *Music of Christian Hymns*, 137.

74. Glover, *Hymnal 1982 Companion*, 3B: 411.

75. Brown and Butterworth, *Story of the Hymns*, 38–39.

76. Reynolds, "Come," 112, 392.

77. Breed, *History*, 335–39.

78. Levine, *Highbrow/Lowbrow*.

79. Bealle, *Public Worship*, 230.

80. Tamke, *Make a Joyful Noise*, 21.

81. Bealle, *Public Worship*, 230–32.

82. Cited in Bealle, *Public Worship*, 233.

83. Ibid.

84. Ibid., 236.

References

Allen, William Francis, Charles Pickard Ware, and Lucy McKim Garrison. *Slave Songs of the United States*. 1867. Reprint, Freeport, N.Y.: Books for Libraries, 1971.

Bealle, John. *Public Worship, Private Faith: Sacred Harp and American Folksong*. Athens: University of Georgia Press, 1997.

Benson, Louis F. *The English Hymn: Its Development and Use in Worship*. 1915. Reprint, Richmond, Va.: Knox, 1962.

Bishop, Selma L. *Isaac Watts: Hymns and Spiritual Songs, 1707–1748*. London: Faith, 1962.

Boyer, Horace Clarence. "An Analysis of Black Church Music with Examples Drawn from Services in Rochester, New York." PhD diss., Eastman School of Music of the University of Rochester, 1973.

Breed, David R. *The History and Use of Hymns and Hymn-Tunes*. Chicago: Revell, 1903.

Bultmann, Phyllis Wetherell. "Everybody Sing: The Social Significance of the Eighteenth-Century Hymn." PhD diss., University of California at Los Angeles, 1950.

Cobb, Buell E., Jr. *The Sacred Harp: A Tradition and Its Music*. Athens: University of Georgia Press, 1978.

Crawford, Richard. *The Core Repertory of Early American Psalmody*. Madison, Wisc.: A-R, 1984.

Crozier, Alice C. *The Novels of Harriet Beecher Stowe* (New York: Oxford University Press, 1969), 91.

Dargan, William T., "Congregational Singing Traditions in South Carolina." *Black Music Research Journal* 15, no. 1 (Spring 1995): 29–73.

Davie, Donald. "The Language of the Eighteenth-Century Hymn." In *Dissentient Voice: The Ward-Phillips Lectures for 1980 with Some Related Pieces*. Notre Dame, Ind.: University of Notre Dame Press, 1982.

Ellington, Charles Linwood. "The Sacred Harp Tradition of the South: Its Origin and Evolution." PhD diss., Florida State University, 1969.

Escott, Harry. *Isaac Watts, Hymnographer: A Study of the Beginnings, Development, and Philosophy of the English Hymn*. London: Independent, 1962.

Foote, Henry Wilder. *Three Centuries of American Hymnody*. Cambridge, Mass.: Harvard University Press, 1940.

Glover, Raymond R., gen. ed. *The Hymnal 1982 Companion*. New York: Church Hymnal, 1994.

Gosse, Edmund. *Father and Son: Biographical Recollections*. New York: Scribner's, 1907.

Hammond, Paul Garnett. "Music in Urban Revivalism in the Northern United States, 1800–1835." DMA diss., Southern Baptist Theological Seminary, 1974.

Handbook to the Baptist Hymnal. Nashville, Tenn.: Convention, 1992.

Hood, George. *A History of Music in New England: With Biographical Sketches of Reformers and Psalmists*. 1846. Reprint ed. by Johannes Riedel, New York: Johnson, 1970.

Hulan, Richard Huffman. "Campmeeting Spiritual Folksongs: Legacy of the 'Great Revival in the West.'" PhD diss., University of Texas at Austin, 1978.

Jackson, George Pullen. *Spiritual Folk-Songs of Early America*. 1937. Reprint, New York: Dover, 1964.

Kurath, Gertrude P. "Rhapsodies of Salvation: Negro Responsory Hymns." *Southern Folklore Quarterly* 20, no. 9 (1956): 178.

Levine, Lawrence W. *Highbrow/Lowbrow: The Emergence of Cultural Hierarchy in America*. Cambridge, Mass.: Harvard University Press, 1988.

Lorenz, Ellen Jane. *Glory Hallelujah: The Story of the Campmeeting Spiritual*. Nashville, Tenn.: Abingdon, 1978.

Marini, Stephen A. "Rehearsal for Revival: Sacred Singing and the Great Awakening in America." In *Sacred Sound: Music in Religious Thought and Practice*, edited by Joyce Irwin, 71–91. Chico, Calif.: Scholars, 1983.

Massachusetts Historical Society Collection, *Diary of Cotton Mather*, 7th Series, VIII.

Music, David W. *Hymnology: A Collection of Source Readings*. Lanham, Md.: Scarecrow, 1996.

———. "Isaac Watts in America Before 1720." *The Hymn* 50, no. 1 (January 1999): 30.

———. "Music in the First Baptist Church of Boston, Massachusetts, 1665–1820." In *Singing Baptists: Studies in Hymnody in America*, edited by Harry Eskew, David W. Music, Paul A. Richardson. Nashville, Tenn.: Church Street, 1994.

Pinkston, Alfred Adolphus. "Lined Hymns, Spirituals, and the Associated Lifestyle of Rural Black People in the United States." PhD diss., University of Miami, 1975.

Raichelson, Richard M. "Black Religious Folksong: A Study in Generic and Social Change." PhD diss., University of Pennsylvania, 1975.

Reynolds, William J. "Come, We That Love the Lord" and "Lowry, Robert." In *Handbook to the Baptist Hymnal*. Nashville, Tenn.: Convention, 1992.

Ritter, Frederic Louis. *Music in England and Music in America*. Vol. 2. London: William Reeves, 1884.

Rothenbusch, Esther Heidi. "The Role of *Gospel Hymns Nos. 1 to 6* (1875–1894) in American Revivalism." PhD diss., University of Michigan, 1991.

Routley, Erik. *The Music of Christian Hymns*. Chicago: GIA, 1981.

Sankey, Ira D, comp. *Sacred Songs and Solos: Twelve Hundred Hymns*. London: Marshall, Morgan, and Scott, 1921.

———. *Sankey's Story of the Gospel Hymns*. Philadelphia: Sunday School Times, 1906.

Sizer, Sandra S. *Gospel Hymns and Social Religion: The Rhetoric of Nineteenth-Century Revivalism*. Philadelphia: Temple University Press, 1978.

Stackhouse, Rochelle A. *The Language of the Psalms in Worship: American Revisions of Watts' Psalter*. Lanham, Md.: Scarecrow, 1997.

Tajchman, Ronald. "Isaac Watts's Communion Hymns: An Application of Classical Rhetoric." *The Hymn* 46, no. 1 (1995): 18–22.

Tallmadge, William H. "Dr. Watts and Mahalia Jackson: The Development, Decline, and Survival of a Folk Style in America." *Ethnomusicology* 5 (1961): 95–99.

Tamke, Susan. *Make a Joyful Noise unto the Lord: Hymns as a Reflection of Victorian Social Attitudes*. Athens: Ohio University Press, 1978.

Watts, Isaac. *Divine and Moral Songs for Children*. 1715. Reprint, Morgan, Penn.: Soli Deo Gloria, 1998.

———. *Hymns and Spiritual Songs, Book II*. [London: 1720]

———. *The Psalms of David Imitated in the Language of the New Testament*. London: Printed for J. Clark, R. Ford, and R. Cruttenden, 1719.

Wesley, John. *Works*. Vol. 3. New York: Carlton and Lanahan, 1856.

Wright, Thomas. *The Lives of the British Hymn-Writers, Vol. III: Isaac Watts and Contemporary Hymn-Writers*. London: Farncombe, 1914.

6 Living in the (Publishing) House of Music

A Short History of Composer-Driven Independent Publishing and Distribution in the United States

AMY C. BEAL

> It takes time to demonstrate that a substantial
> alternative exists.
> —Kenneth Gaburo, founder of Lingua Press

Approximately twenty-five years ago, I began my exploration of "American experimental music": its history, practitioners, compositions, and performance practices. At that time, Richard Crawford's just-published book, *The American Musical Landscape* (1993), taught me to look also at other aspects of American experimental music: its definitions and their sources, historiography, financial situations, institutions, patronage, and other matters of practicality, commerce, and cultural structure. A few years later, my dissertation followed this focus and examined issues of support, dissemination, and reception history. (This focus is what later caused Richard Taruskin to suggest I title my first book *Where the Money Was*, a suggestion I politely declined, though it did make a certain amount of sense.) I quickly came to see that much of what held the "American experimental tradition" together was a shared experience of independent, creative, do-it-yourself culture—sometimes by choice and sometimes by necessity—and that contextual reality frequently carried more salient historical information than the music products themselves.[1] I became interested in real-life issues, deceptively simple questions like: "What, exactly, butters the composer's bread?"

Since that time of my initial excursions into the history of American experimental music, the issue of independent, composer-driven publishing and distribution has remained a common thread running through much of the American experimental tradition's story and has thus remained one of my peripheral interests. I'm grateful to have the opportunity to explore it in greater depth. For independent composers, such publication series and distribution services have proved critical to the dissemination of music that often lives in the uncharted territory beyond institutional walls and, ultimately, beyond the whole idea of imprimatur.[2]

William Billings, Anthony Philip Heinrich, Arthur Farwell, Henry Cowell, Harry Partch, Dick Higgins, Carla Bley, Michael Byron, Peter Garland, Kenneth Gaburo, Larry Polansky, and others have fostered an independent strand of American music production despite the muscular power of commercial music industries in this country since the late eighteenth century. By focusing on composer-driven publications, I am foregrounding "the authority wielded by musical notation."[3] Yet some of the composers I'm interested in have distributed music in other forms—most notably, self-produced recordings, or Gaburo's language-based compositions—and certainly much of the music published by Cowell, Byron, Garland, and Polansky is notated in highly unconventional forms. The categories of "composers' music" and "performers' music" become murky in the study of experimental music of all kinds.[4] The definition of "composers' music" ceases to apply to indeterminate scores written in prose or graphic notation, and the meticulously notated music of composers like Carla Bley, Roscoe Mitchell, Henry Threadgill, Myra Melford, and many others clearly take "jazz" composition out of the realm of "performers' music." Can an independent musician working in today's America get by without forfeiting either "technical control or economic reward?"[5] Between one end of the continuum and the other, experimental and largely independent musical practitioners have adopted many of the agencies necessary for the production of music: composer, performer, teacher, distributor, manufacturer, writer. To this list I would add recording artist, record producer, bandleader, instrument or electronic music studio builder, software designer and programmer, and publisher. Composers stemming from experimental networks have rarely stayed in the European model of "Composer" as an autonomous profession. Instead, they perform their own and each other's music, they copy, print, photocopy, bind, and mail their own scores, they write the computer code they need to compose the work, they put their records into boxes and seal them themselves (as Harry Partch famously did on film in 1958), they organize festivals, create performance spaces and music communities, and they invent means of distribution.

Some of these activities have been well documented. William Billings, acknowledged as the first American to publish a book containing entirely his own compositions (*The New-England Psalm-Singer*, Boston 1770), ambitiously strove to define himself as a composer, and many who followed in his footsteps, including most of the protagonists in the story of independent American music publishing, would agree with his maxim that "nature is the best dictator" when it came to musical composition. In the words of Karl Kroeger:

> Billings, a young, unknown composer, burst upon the Boston musical scene with a publication of major dimensions without, apparently, any previous public exposure of his compositions in print. The history of printing in eighteenth-century America suggests that such a scenario is extremely unlikely, and it may indicate that Billings's reputation as a teacher of psalmody in Boston was firmly established in 1770. He could expect a sufficient number of students and patrons to subscribe to his tunebook to guarantee its publication.[6]

Some hundred years after Billings, Charles Ives self-published the first issues of his *114 Songs* and *Concord Sonata*, and Arthur Farwell's Wa-Wan Press published the works of thirty-seven composers over an eleven-year period.[7] Henry Cowell's New Music series carried on this tradition (in the areas of score publication, recordings, and live performances), as did Larry Austin's *Source: Music of the Avant-Garde* starting in the late 1960s, while Harry Partch founded Gate 5 Records in a warehouse in Sausalito, California, as a home for his idiosyncratic work. Dick Higgins's Something Else Press and LaMonte Young and Jackson MacLow's *An Anthology* made important contributions as well; Sylvia Smith's Smith Publications, established in 1974 for the publication of "serious, progressive American Music," still goes strong today.[8] Max Roach and Charles Mingus established an independent label called Debut Records in 1953. And the list goes on. How is creative independence affected when composers take matters into their own hands? What happens to the connection between musical style and the musical marketplace? Composer Kenneth Gaburo responded to these circumstances with healthy skepticism:

> I certainly acknowledge the need for monetary support, but not as if there's no exit from patronage. I'm not against money. I'm against the price artists generally pay for it. Survival depends on being *needed*, not merely on economics.[9]

Speaking to an international audience in 1974, composer Christian Wolff (b. 1934) commented on the relationship between independent-minded composers and economic support in the United States:

> The avant-garde has until fairly recently existed in a kind of social vacuum—that is to say, it has not been taken up or supported by any of the normal social agencies, be they academic, or be they the concert world. The normal, establishment musical life has until fairly recently, and even now only in very tentative ways, made no effort whatsoever to do anything for this kind of music. So the composers of this kind of music have always felt a kind of indifference to, or [. . .] lack of pressure from certain social demands. They didn't feel that they had to write music that would be pleasing to a particular kind of establishment. This isn't

to say that they didn't feel economic pressures: I mean they weren't free in that sense, but they were artistically or aesthetically free. [. . .] I think if you reflect on that a little bit you can see there are both advantages and disadvantages to that condition, and it's probably time to begin to think about the disadvantages. It's obviously a very good atmosphere in which to grow up, and in which to find what you need to find, and what you can do musically, but on the other hand [. . .] you pay a very great price for this sense of isolation, of being cut off [. . .].[10]

In this context, we can observe that the widely acknowledged leader of mid-twentieth-century American experimentalism, John Cage, made some surprising career decisions with regard to the preservation and dissemination of his own work, thus directly addressing the disadvantages of isolation while maintaining artistic and aesthetic freedom at the same time.

A Contradictory Case: John Cage, Peters Edition, and the Legal Challenge of Indeterminacy

As I have chronicled elsewhere, at the time of John Cage's search for a permanent, internationally distributed publisher after a few of his works had been issued by Henmar Press (a branch of Peters specifically for ASCAP members[11]), he was deeply involved in an ongoing epistolary conversation with John Edmunds and Peter Yates, who were searching for ways to classify different strands of American music, including the unique branch of experimentalism, which particularly interested Yates.[12] Cage had approached Hans W. Heinsheimer at Schirmer but was rejected. His relationship to Walter Hinrichsen at C. F. Peters proved to be more fruitful. Cage was frustrated by the need to search for a publisher at all, feeling the strains on his ability to get his work performed if it were not published and distributed, but he also felt that such circumstances were "part and parcel of the general lack of an intellectual life in the field of American music."[13] In his correspondence with Edmunds, then the director of the Americana Section at the Music Division of the New York Public Library, Cage outlined four possible paths for American music publishing and the role public libraries might play in that endeavor. Cage speculated about the following possibilities:

1. Composers' cooperatives;
2. Publication outside the United States;
3. Publication by an American university [Cage specifically mentioned Wesleyan University, Dartmouth College, or the University of Illinois];
4. "The free publication (or distribution) of music by the Public Libraries of this country."[14]

Cage explicitly wanted to get his own music out of his own hands and also felt that publishing through public libraries was a good option that "should be made known as available to any composer, regardless of his fame or quality (just as the libraries contain all the novels, good, bad, and indifferent)."[15] Soon, however, Cage seems to have abandoned the quest for independent publishing.

When Cage accepted a contract from Peters Edition in 1960, he made a decisive and somewhat anomalous break with the tradition of independent publication and distribution in the experimental circles with which he had been associated. The C. F. Peters Corporation, founded in Leipzig in 1800, had published works by Beethoven, Grieg, Mahler, and Schoenberg. (Following Cage, notable American composers to sign with Peters included Christian Wolff, George Crumb, Morton Feldman, Lou Harrison, Fred Lerdahl, and Roger Reynolds.) With the recognized authority of Peters's imprimatur, Cage's work was poised for international acceptance.[16] (At the same time, the formidable college press at Wesleyan University took on the publication of Cage's collected writings, which resulted in the release of his influential book *Silence* in 1961.) Biographer Kenneth Silverman describes the terms of the Cage-Peters relationship:

> By an agreement signed in June 1960, Cage would receive an advance for each of his compositions the company printed—twenty-five to seventy-five dollars, depending on length—and a 10 percent royalty on sales. The agreement covered future works as well: the company would publish two of his works a year for ten years. They would also sell his tapes, marketing *Fontana Mix*, for instance, as a set of four single-track or two double-track tapes, for sixty dollars a set. Distribution would be wide. There were Peters firms in Frankfurt and Zurich, and one in London, managed by Hinrichsen's brother. The corporation also worked through outlets in Norway, Sweden, Switzerland, Belgium, and Japan. Peters could thus make copies of Cage's scores easily available internationally.[17]

In 1962 Peters published and distributed internationally an eighty-page catalog of Cage's published works with a foreword and annotations on the pieces by Cage himself. This comprehensive catalog was also a powerful research tool at the time, as it included lists of recordings of Cage's work, his writings to date, performances of his music, secondary literature about him, and the transcription of an interview in which he explained his ideas. But the fact that his music was now controlled by a corporate publishing house with legal contracts that determined rules of use also quickly dramatized the discrepancies between a publisher's rights and responsibilities and the by-definition collaborative, open-ended nature of indeterminate music.

In 1967 Peters's lawyers threatened Italy-based American composers Frederic Rzewski and Jon Phetteplace with legal action for making and broadcasting realizations of Cage's indeterminate work on Italian radio, specifically *Imaginary Landscape No. 5* and *Where Are We Going? What Are We Doing?* A lively exchange of letters highlighted the difference in positions between the young composers and the established publisher with regard to the copyright owner-ship of the original tapes for *Where Are We Going?* which was held by Henmar Press and its selling and rental agent C. F. Peters Corporation in New York. A frustrated Phetteplace wrote to Peters's lawyer:

> I no longer make scores for the tape music I write, nor do I hope to publish the old ones, and the problem of collecting fees from performances doesn't exist, since friends who arrange for performances send money if there is some, none if there isn't. *This is symptomatic of how the music publisher no longer figures in the minds of many young composers, for he can offer no solutions.* All the same, a tape center, with many publishers operating it together, would be desirable, and in that case my tapes would have a home other than their present one which is, at the moment, rather chaotic. What I would like to know now is, do you have any other suggestions?[18]

On May 1, 1967, Cage got involved in the dispute and urged his fellow com-posers not to view publishers as obstructionist. He counseled Phetteplace: "Ap-proached as friends, rather than as enemies, of people, of music, publishers generally will go out of their way to facilitate projects. Ignored, they become active legalistically."[19] As Silverman describes it, Cage's relationship with his publisher Hinrichsen was a match made in heaven, and Hinrichsen's devotion to Cage's work may explain his energetic reaction to learning about Phetteplace's unauthorized realizations.

Source: Music of the Avant-Garde was one such initiative by which composers took matters into their own hands if established resources like Peters Edition were not available to them. Published from 1967 until 1971 in Davis, California, *Source* "was a place for communities and individuals, for composers, and per-formers, for practitioners and audiences, to find each other."[20] Furthermore, in the words of Douglas Kahn,

> They had not been served well by then-current publications on new music, which were directed toward an academic readership or limited in the range of music discussed. *Source* was intent on presenting work and the thinking of creators directly, and operated through a sense of inclusion and creative possibility, rather than programmatically.[21]

Source published eleven unique volumes containing articles, scores, record-ings, and interviews by and with composer-performers working largely in non-academic ways. The history, contents, and importance of *Source* have been well documented, and it remains a milestone in the history of independent American music publishing.

Independent Publishing after 1970

As a member of the New York School generation that included Earle Brown, Morton Feldman, and David Tudor, Kenneth Gaburo (1926–1993) has been an important figure in the history of independent American music publishing. His Lingua Press, founded in 1975, supported the work of more than twenty independent American composers and also published many volumes of writing by Gaburo himself. Focusing on both language and music-based work, Lingua produced scores, records, books, audio and video tapes, and film. A conversation between David Dunn and Gaburo printed with the title "Publishing as Ecosystem" is one of the most illuminating documents with regard to the importance of this kind of work. Copyright issues like the ones raised by the Cage-Phetteplace-Peters conflict incited a radical stance in Gaburo:

> Copyright is one official means by which people can claim something as their own. In this sense, one may speak of copyright as legitimized ownership. It amounts to a kind of protection, as long as it is understood that what is primarily protected is the actual material, form, and content of the specific document so copyrighted; but not its *idea*. However careful a publisher may be with maintaining a work's integrity it is not necessarily protected from the possible outrageous consequences of its having been issued. Here I have in mind such matters as opinion, bad-mouthing, hearsay, naivete, censorship, plagiarism. Since I think a work's decay, i.e. its corruption, . . . at least in terms of the idea . . ., begins at the moment it is issued, the protection which copyright affords is not of very much value. [. . .] My sentiment is in direct conflict with the fact that *Lingua* is in the world. The extent to which it is regarded as a business suggests the degree to which it has to be involved in the ownership-copyright issue. Even in this limited view, however, I make a distinction: I will not claim ownership for a work unless it's my own. Authors whose work Lingua publishes hold their own copyrights, and thereby, claim ownership.[22]

Further, Gaburo challenged common assumptions about music's ability to survive on its own terms:

> I challenge that assumption by postulating another one, namely: that an artist, no matter the specific persuasion, can earn an honest wage, as artist, without compromise, pandering, or loss of dignity when a "cultured environment" wants, needs, and highly values what artists do. In the absence of this very powerful assumption, one is left with what is currently assumed: that an artist cannot earn an honest wage as such, and thus must resort to patronage of one kind or another, or simply do something else concurrently. This is also referred to as a "cultured environment." But here an artist's dignity is at the mercy of whim, caprice, and art-as luxury. [. . .] The weight of history supports the assumption of patronage. The assumption I make seems impossible, given current-day evi-

dence, exceptions notwithstanding. And so, one is more or less left with that's how it is. To say "that's not how it should be" begins [. . .] the process of finding ways to turn things around.[23]

Gaburo sometimes published materials he wasn't personally fond of but toward which he felt the need to "put forth alternatives."[24] Just as Cage believed that "the libraries contain all the novels, good, bad, and indifferent," Gaburo did not feel it was his role to act as a controller of quality. Similarly, the independent New Music Distribution Service founded by Carla Bley and Michael Mantler in 1972 refused to categorize its inventory based on stylistic distinctions, and would distribute anything sent to them as long as it could be classified as "independent."[25] These egalitarian repositories of unconventional art and music provided a needed space for creative work that would not survive otherwise in a hierarchically organized and market-driven culture of survival-of-the-fittest economics.

Three composers who all happened to have been students of James Tenney's at some point in their young careers—Peter Garland (b. 1952), Michael Byron (b. 1953), and Larry Polansky (b. 1954)—have made significant contributions to the field of American independent music publishing. Exploring the first item on Cage's list—namely, "composers' cooperatives"—these young experimental composers took matters into their own hands: Byron with a series of anthologies that published otherwise unavailable music by composers like Malcolm Goldstein, Philip Corner, David Mahler, Daniel Goode, and many others during the mid-1970s; Garland with Soundings Press, which published a series of journal-like volumes filled with essays and scores alike (not to mention some of the only available transcriptions of the player-piano studies of Conlon Nancarrow); and Polansky (and co-founder Jody Diamond) with the composers' collective Frog Peak Music, which currently serves as a repository and distributor (and in many cases also as publisher) for some 127 underrepresented individuals, groups, and independent record companies.

Soundings and *Pieces*

Composer Peter Garland enrolled as a student at the California Institute of the Arts in 1970. That fall, he took a course with Dick Higgins, founder of the independent publishing firm Something Else Press (est. 1963). Inspired by Higgins's class on publishing, Garland, initially with fellow CalArts student John Bischoff, embarked on a mission that would occupy him, off and on, for the next two decades, and would have a tremendous impact on the availability of experimental music worldwide. Bischoff recalls:

> Once I started hanging out with Peter, and we were both working with Jim [Tenney], I remember how they both seemed to be in agreement that more

emphasis needed to be put on studying the work of composers in the American tradition (Ives, Ruggles, Cage, etc.) as opposed to a European one (Webern, Boulez, Stockhausen). I was keen about composers in both traditions—I was particularly interested Earle Brown's music at that time—but it was the first time I had heard anyone push the idea that the American tradition was primary. It affected me quite dramatically.[26]

As early as November 1970, Garland and Bischoff had contacted more established (and, in some cases, academically employed) experimentalists like Pauline Oliveros and Robert Ashley, soliciting scores and asking for names of other composers they should include. Dick Higgins himself was a tremendous resource for Garland in terms of the logistics of starting an independent publication series. (Higgins, who had studied composition with Henry Cowell, reissued Cowell's *New Musical Resources* through Something Else Press in 1969 and was thus a direct link to an earlier generation of independent publishing within experimental music.[27]) In 1971 Higgins wrote: "Glad to hear *Soundings* is shaping up. For your mailing, I think the best thing for me to do is lend you my music mailing list. I'm sending it under separate cover."[28] Shortly thereafter, Higgins wrote with further advice: "To promote: swap ads with every music mag in the country (get lists out of Ulrich's, Standard Periodical Directory), especially *Source*. You may wind up with 25 pages of ads, but ultimately that doesn't hurt and you'll see, every library in the country will need *Soundings*."[29] Soon Higgins was mixing praise with further practical advice:

> I find *Soundings* 3/4 marvelous. Really you've got it together. That Byron piano piece [*Song of the Lifting Up of the Head*] is so unpretentious, says so little, means so much. I keep playing it. Re funding: I suggest you (in retrospect) pay yourself $200 for having edited each issue. That's $800. (Be sure it shows on your income tax, and then give it back to *Soundings* as a business expense—that's quite legitimate). Then apply for matching grants to cover production expenses.[30]

Conductor and musicologist Nicolas Slonimsky wrote in response to Garland's requests for help:

> You ask me "where to go for money to finance the project." This is some question. If I had known where to go for money, I would have gone there myself. You are, of course, aware of various foundations and fellowships that do give money to earnest people. Someone defined the Ford Foundation as "a large body of money completely surrounded by people who want some." You can try to get a nibble at that or at Guggenheim.[31]

The first issue of *Soundings* opened with a one-page song by Lou Harrison called "May Rain," which the eighteen-year-old Garland had already acquired by December 1970. Soon, many composers realized how valuable this resource was. Harrison himself wrote: "About *Soundings*—the marvelous new one arrived today [. . .] and it is very grand! Could I interest you in my *Peace Pieces*? Not a publisher in this country will touch them (of course!) but they are among my best pieces."[32] Writing on Merce Cunningham Dance Company letterhead, composer Gordon Mumma was also encouraging: "*Soundings* is a good idea, I like the diversity of materials you indicate for the first two issues. Thusly, enclosed is my check for $7.00, for a subscription for one year."[33] Harry Partch, upon receiving the second issue, wrote: "As before, you have brought out a handsome magazine."[34]

Between 1972 and 1990, Garland's Soundings Press published sixteen issue numbers in thirteen discrete volumes. As early as 1973, *Soundings* volumes were becoming known worldwide. Important first publications, like the songs of Paul Bowles, transcriptions of the piano studies of Conlon Nancarrow, and an important comprehensive study of the early works of James Tenney, came to the attention of older composers and others in the contemporary music community around the globe, including Ursula Block, Earle Brown, Cornelius Cardew, Herbert Henck, Hans Otte, Roger Reynolds, Charles Seeger, Toshi Ichiyanagi, Virgil Thomson, Walter Zimmermann, and dozens of others who corresponded extensively with Garland throughout the lifetime of *Soundings*. Carla Bley and Michael Mantler partnered with Garland for distribution of *Soundings* through their New York–based New Music Distribution Services. Garland's aesthetic alignment was clear from the start and can be summarized by the enthusiasm of fellow composer John Luther Adams: "Long live the gourd-rattling, hubcap-knocking wing of American music! And kudos to you for keeping the pot stirred up and carrying on the cranky-craggy tradition of Varèse, Ruggles, Cowell, Rudhyar, Partch, et al."[35] Composer David Mahler, who had been in school with Garland at CalArts, echoed the sentiment: "I am unable to adequately express my appreciation for *Soundings*: Ives, Ruggles, Varèse. For myself, at least, it arrived at a very timely moment, and has helped send my thoughts off in a straight line again."[36]

Following in the footsteps of forefathers Tenney, Malcolm Goldstein, and Philip Corner, whose Tone Roads concerts during the 1960s had celebrated the work of their forefathers Ives, Ruggles, Cowell, Partch, and others, Garland and his generation continued the work of both documentation and distribution of the American experimental tradition on shoestring budgets and a tremendous amount of self-motivation.

Entrepreneur Betty Freeman became interested in *Soundings* as early as 1971, initially because of Garland's dedication to Harry Partch. Over the years she contributed money toward the publications through the Harry Partch Foundation and the Aesthetic Research Center of Canada. In the late 1980s, the community *Soundings* covered became anxious about Garland's intention to cease publication. In 1988, for instance, Kyle Gann, music writer for the *Village Voice*, wrote to Garland: "I don't know whose attention you were trying to get by announcing *Soundings*' imminent demise, but you sure got mine. That's a tragedy."[37] To be sure, *Soundings* had found success in part due to its defiant stance, and the perpetuation of a narrative of neglect. David Mahler expressed this sentiment shortly before *Soundings* ceased publication:

> Now my mind has been filled with more thoughts about how U.S. composers find themselves in such an untenable quagmire of no performances, no recognition, no commissions, etc. I have been focusing on our lack of a good sense of history of our own heritage (from Ives on, let's say), and how this history has been almost systematically eliminated from schools, the media and the so-called major performing institutions.[38]

Mumma, too, was saddened by the news of *Soundings* coming to an end, and he summarized its enormous historical impact:

> What a shock, *Soundings* is reaching its last issue. All great things come to an end. I think *Soundings* has been a very great achievement in the realm of American music culture, in some respects the most important periodical publication since *Source* and, previously, Henry Cowell's *New Music*.[39]

The final volume of *Soundings*, which was printed in 1988, included music by Charles Amirkhanian, Mary Jane Leach, Gordon Monahan, Gordon Mumma, Lois V. Vierk, and John Zorn (among others), as well as a previously unpublished essay by Peter Yates titled "The American Experimental Tradition."

In the spirit of initiatives like Lingua Press and *Soundings*, composer Michael Byron, too, voluntarily and energetically turned to publishing while living in Toronto in the mid-1970s. A friend and former CalArts classmate of Garland's, Byron had also been a student in Higgins's class on publishing. Byron produced three historically significant volumes that complemented the offerings of *Soundings*: *Pieces: An Anthology* (1975–76); *Pieces: A Second Anthology* (1976); and *Pieces 3* (1977).[40] The first two volumes were supported in part by York University and the Aesthetic Research Centre (ARC) in Vancouver, which was founded by instrument builder, musical sculptor, and ARC chief editor John Grayson. Lou Harrison also supported *Pieces* financially. (In Byron's words: "We had no money, we just had an idea."[41]) Byron also served as editor of the *Journal of Experimental Aesthetics*, a serial publication launched by the ARC in 1974, and in 1975 he edited and published a book (unique to this day) called *From Wheelock Mountain: Music and Writings of Malcolm Goldstein*.

Byron was optimistic about the work he and Garland were doing, and he corresponded frequently with his friend and co-publisher: "I really think it's fantastic that both *Pieces* and *Soundings* are coming out within such a short time span of each other. It's rare that so much work by our friends comes out in such quantity (in fact, it never has before)."[42] But the preface to *Pieces* 3 revealed that the series was in trouble. "I intend to do all that is possible to continue publishing *Pieces* on a more regular basis," Byron wrote. "Much will depend on increased funding and book sales, but if as I very much hope, this materializes, I will attempt to publish at least two issues each year. Efforts are being made to find some channel for the International distribution of *Pieces*. To date these have been unsuccessful; a response from anyone with ideas concerning this would be very welcome." All three *Pieces* volumes emphasized a dedication to living composers (or *friends*, as he put it), to diversity in sound sources, and to a wide variety of experimental and idiosyncratic methods of notation. Byron's respect for and devotion to the music of his peers is evident in the dedications of these volumes: The first, "Dedicated, warmly, to the composers whose music and ideas appear in this volume"; the second, "My personal association with the composers whose work appears here, has been a constant source of inspiration and energy."

By 1979, Byron had collected music for a fourth *Pieces*, which was to be funded in part by Betty Freeman and was to include music by Byron and Garland, as well as Maryanne Amacher, Barbara Benary, John Cage, Rhys Chatham, Philip Corner, Bob Davis, Malcolm Goldstein, Daniel Goode, Lou Harrison, William Hawley, William Hellerman, Dick Higgins, Alison Knowles, Jackson MacLow, David Mahler, Meredith Monk, Conlon Nancarrow, Phill Niblock, Tom Nixon, Pauline Oliveros, David Rosenboom, Carlos Santos, Richard Teitelbaum, and James Tenney.[43] Sadly, due to financial difficulties and the high cost of printing in New York, among other factors, *Pieces 4* was never completed.

Frog Peak Music: A Composers' Collective

Though Frog Peak Music sometimes functions as a publisher, it is different from *Soundings* and *Pieces* in that it is almost unique in its creation of a home for an enormous body of work by a large number of disparate composers. In an interview with the online site New Music Box, run by the American Music Center, composer Larry Polansky, co-founder of Frog Peak, shared some broad thoughts on the philosophies behind the collective, its advocacy for pluralism, and its beginnings in the mid 1980s:

> At that time there was a whole community of people who really had no outlet for their work. And there were a couple of significant theoretical works . . . that I thought should be out in the world, like Jim Tenney's *Meta-Hodos* and John Chalmers's *Divisions of the Tetrachord*. . . . We [Polansky and co-founder Jody Diamond] started with this idea that composers would take control over the distribution of their own work. Not to be so much a publisher, but to be what I

like to call an availability site. That by pooling resources, instead of composers going to a photocopy store and mailing it out when somebody asked you for something, there'd be one place where people could get it. Make it a collective and dedicate ourselves to having no interest in advertising or promotion whatsoever, and also to try to have no interest in the notion of imprimatur. We weren't certifying anything. . . . It was a philosophical, social, artistic experiment in every possible way. . . . It gets a lot of people's work out into the world in an honest, simple, sincere way, with no cosmetic nonsense and no hype. I've been committed to that all through my life—never selling anything, never convincing anybody of anything, of really staying true to the musical idea as much as possible. . . . We decided at the very beginning to never apply for a grant and to never devolve into arts administration. . . . I think with Frog Peak, its main virtue is that we've stayed afloat for a very, very long time. We've kept small. We've kept to our basic principles, as high in integrity as we possibly can. And to our surprise we've gotten noticed. We have a lot of standing library orders. Complete collections are in a number of really good libraries. So now it's a good thing for composers because they get out in the world, to safe, widely available places.[44]

In 1983, around the time Frog Peak was founded in Oakland, California, Polansky gave a ninety-minute lecture-demonstration titled "Dealing with the Avant-Garde: Problems of Librarianship with Contemporary Music Materials—Locating, Storing, and Retrieving New Music" to the Music Library Association Northern California Chapter fall meeting. He wrote of the event to Peter Garland:

Recently did a guest talk for the Cal. State Music Librarians Association (talk about a weird bunch) called "Dealing with the Avant Garde," telling them all about ind[ependent] publishers and recordings and ways to catalog, archive, and make available non-published stuff and the like. It went over well, and they all wrote down *Soundings* after I stated that any library in the country that didn't have a complete set and a standing order was screwing up its job. Hope you get some orders from that. They've asked me to write a long piece for their national journal, as well as compile a resource list of "avant-garde" materials, so I may ask for some names from you when I do that. Such a publication could really help get some things off the ground and so on, so even though it sounds like a royal pain in the ass to do, I think it would be worth it.[45]

Today, Frog Peak lives in Lebanon, New Hampshire, and describes itself in this way:

Frog Peak Music is an artist-run composers' collective dedicated to publishing and producing experimental and unusual works by its member artists, and is committed to the idea of availability over promotion. Frog Peak Music is a not-for-profit organization in which member artists determine the form and content of their own work.[46]

Like Cage and Gaburo before him, Polansky does not feel it is his role to act as a controller of quality. By remaining flexible about its inventory, Frog Peak is able to distribute a wide variety of writings, scores self-published by others (like Lou Harrison's Hermes Beard Press), and odd art objects like (inedible) olive oil made by Anthony Gnazzo, as well as works by long-dead composers considered part of the Frog Peak family—most notably, Ruth Crawford Seeger and Johanna Beyer—and even works by a fictional composer (I won't say which). Frog Peak's publications of Tenney's *Meta+Hodos* and John Chalmers's *Division of the Tetrachord* are unique milestones in the history of American music theory.

Aside from making the work of so many people available to libraries and other institutions since the mid-1980s, Frog Peak has also been responsible almost single-handedly for a revival of extensive interest in the work of German-American composer Johanna Beyer, who disappeared almost completely from the historical record when she died in obscurity in 1944. With her manuscripts readily available in the New York Public Library, and with no heirs from whom to ask permission, the Frog Peak/Johanna Beyer project has, to date, published thirty critical editions of her scores, thus making them available to musicians who have taken up the challenge and have been performing and recording her work with great vigor. The case of Beyer is a good example of what an impact an independent, nonprofit, completely DIY operation can accomplish. In 1990 Frog Peak Music took possession of the entire *Soundings* catalog and continues to distribute its backlog today.[47] As Polansky wrote to Garland, "Frog Peak has been really good so far, and I'm trying to keep it from being a 'business' and use all the money to distribute and publish people's work."[48] Though the directors of Frog Peak maintain artistic and aesthetic control over who is allowed to belong to the collective, those decisions are not made according to any pre-established definitions of genre. In this sense, its musical worldview is not dissimilar to the New Music Distribution Service, whose directors professed in 1986:

> The New Music Distribution Service (NMDS) distributes all independently produced recordings of new music, regardless of commercial potential or personal taste. A wealth of new music is being created in the areas of jazz, classical, and rock, as well as outside of any clearly delineated experimental categories. Because of its generally uncommercial nature, this music has had minimal representation in the music industry. Independent record production and distribution may be the only way for musicians to maintain artistic and economic control of their work. [. . .] We deal with everyone equally, regardless how much or how little the records sell. The music in this catalog is intended to be successful on its own musical merit, rather than on strictly commercial terms.[49]

One major difference between an initiative like NMDS and one like Frog Peak is that Frog Peak accepts *people*, not stand-alone products. And by accepting people into the collective, Frog Peak creates *community*, and not just a warehouse full of supplies. Despite subtle differences in their aesthetic choices, idealists like Polansky, Bley, and Mantler have committed much of their lives (not to mention private storage spaces, garages, attics, and so on) to Gaburo's declaration that "it takes time to demonstrate that a substantial alternative exists."

Conclusion: Continuing the Tradition of Independence

Though this chapter focuses primarily on issues in American music publishing and distribution between approximately 1960 and the end of the twentieth century—and before file sharing, internet publishing, and online communities became an enormous part of musicians' means of distribution and community building—many younger-generation groups of composers and performers continue to collaborate and support one another in ways typical of the American experimentalist past. I'll close with an example of just one such community and a mention of one of its central figures. Composer Mike Winter (b. 1980), who has worked closely with James Tenney, Larry Polansky, Michael Byron, and others central to this story, is the founder of an independent performance space in downtown Los Angeles called "the wulf." The wulf has created a music community much like the many cheap, small, no-frills and out-of-the-way, DIY loft-like venues scattered in cities and small towns across the United States. Managed and populated largely by a number of recent graduates from Garland's and Byron's alma mater, California Institute of the Arts (CalArts), these young musicians and composers (including the promising Laura Steenberge and Catherine [Cat] Lamb, among others) are dedicated to independent, open-ended, and cooperative performance situations. Several people involved in this community recently founded *The Experimental Music Yearbook*, a composer-curated online journal dedicated to this next generation of American experimentalists.

I'm frequently asked if I think that the "American experimental tradition" still exists. Though people (mostly composers!) argue today about the validity of the designation "American experimental," I believe it *is* indeed a tradition, and I believe it does still carry on its work with integrity. The aforementioned young musicians in Los Angeles are doing just that: creating a physical space for new work to be heard; building a community beyond official institutions; developing a network in support of their music; and cultivating a climate of care about each other's work. In other words, living in the house of music, one they built for themselves in the image of independent and collective efforts of the past.

Notes

1. In the words of Kenneth Gaburo, "An experimental work, de facto, is in apposition to some aspect of history which preceded its existence; it pushed existent boundaries. It is precisely this feature which distinguishes an experimental work from, say, an imitative or anecdotal one." Dunn and Gaburo, *Collaboration Two*, 15.

2. "Beyond Imprimatur" is an idea I am borrowing from Larry Polansky's views on the aim of independent music publishing and his own philosophies driving Frog Peak Music (a composers' collective). See http://eamusic.dartmouth.edu/~larry/misc_writings/talks/music.talks.html.

3. Crawford, *America's Musical Life*, x.

4. See Crawford, "American Music."

5. Crawford, *American Musical Landscape*, 65.

6. Kroeger, "Introduction," xxix.

7. Apparently, Ives paid Schirmer's engravers to create the scores of these pieces, but Schirmer did not wish to have its name on the publishing page. Thanks to Gayle Sherwood Magee for this information.

8. See http://www.smith-publications.com.

9. Dunn and Gaburo, *Collaboration Two*, 11.

10. Christian Wolff, speaking at the Internationale Ferienkurse für Neue Musik, Darmstadt, July 28, 1972. Transcribed by the author from tape held at the Internationale Musikinstitut Darmstadt.

11. Thanks to Sabine Feisst and Don Gillespie for clarifying the relationship between Henmar Press and C. F. Peters Edition.

12. See Beal, "Experimentalists."

13. Letter from Cage to Yates, December 28, 1959, box 3, folder 1, Peter Yates Papers.

14. Letter from Cage to Edmunds, December 31, 1959, file C-6, John Cage Correspondence.

15. Ibid.

16. Today, the online Peters catalog carries 440 individual Cage products for sale or rent, including T-shirts sporting the tacet symbols for *4'33"* and graphic notation taken from *Aria*.

17. Silverman, *Begin Again*, 173.

18. Jon Phetteplace to H. Swarsenski (Edition Peters, London), April 24, 1967. Jon Phetteplace Papers. Emphasis added.

19. Cage to Phetteplace, May 1, 1967. Jon Phetteplace Papers.

20. Kahn, "Preface," ix.

21. Ibid.

22. Dunn and Gaburo, *Collaboration Two*, 4–5.

23. Ibid.

24. Ibid., 20.

25. See Beal, "Copyright Royalties: New Music Distribution Service," chap. 6 in Beal, *Carla Bley*, 51–56.

26. John Bischoff, written communication with the author, February 14, 2013.

27. Something Else Press published fifty books during the 1960s and 1970s, including John Cage and Alison Knowles's monumental *Notations*, also published in 1969.

28. Letter from Dick Higgins to Peter Garland, December 3, 1971, Peter Garland Papers. Stanley Lunetta of *Source* was not as helpful, writing: "Our mailing list would be a list of subscribers, and a lot of work to type out. Probably too much for our already overworked secretary to do. We are all trying to recover from Brain Rot obtained from gluing Fur into #9." Letter from Stanley Lunetta to Peter Garland, December 21, 1971, Peter Garland Papers.

29. Letter from Dick Higgins to Peter Garland, July 26, 1972, Peter Garland Papers.

30. Letter from Dick Higgins to Peter Garland, December 17, 1972, Peter Garland Papers.

31. Letter from Nicolas Slonimsky to Peter Garland, May 21, 1972, Peter Garland Papers.

32. Letter from Lou Harrison to Peter Garland, [no date], Peter Garland Papers.

33. Letter from Gordon Mumma to Peter Garland, December 20, 1971, Peter Garland Papers.

34. Letter from Harry Partch to Peter Garland, May 16, 1972, Peter Garland Papers.

35. Letter from John Luther Adams to Peter Garland, March 18, 1983, Peter Garland Papers.

36. Letter from David Mahler to Peter Garland, August 20, 1974, Peter Garland Papers.

37. Letter from Kyle Gann to Peter Garland, June 24, 1988, Peter Garland Papers.

38. Letter from David Mahler to Peter Garland, December 11, 1988, Peter Garland Papers.

39. Letter from Gordon Mumma to Peter Garland, February 2, 1988, Peter Garland Papers.

40. For further information on the content of Byron's *Pieces*, see Beal, "Dreaming of Virtuosity."

41. Michael Byron, interview with Rebecca Stuhlbarg, on Santa Cruz (Calif.) public radio KUSP, April 23, 2006.

42. Letter from Michael Byron to Peter Garland, August 20, 1976, Peter Garland Papers.

43. Letter from Michael Byron to Peter Garland, postmarked April 30, 1979, Peter Garland Papers.

44. Oteri, "Frogspeak."

45. Letter from Larry Polansky to Peter Garland, November 8, 1983, Peter Garland Papers.

46. See http://www.frogpeak.org.

47. "Peter—Got the boxes, and your invoice. Haven't opened yet, but boxes look fine. Are you sure 50-50? We want to help *Soundings* as much as you want to help FP!!" Postcard from Larry Polansky to Peter Garland, January 1990, Peter Garland Papers.

48. Letter from Larry Polansky to Peter Garland, December 9, 1989, Peter Garland Papers.

49. "Introduction to the New Music Distribution Service," *New Music Distribution Service 1980 Catalog* (New York: Jazz Composer's Orchestra Association, 1986), unpaginated.

References

PRIMARY SOURCES

Frog Peak Music Papers, Lebanon, New Hampshire.
Internationales Musikinstitut Darmstadt, recording archive, Darmstadt.
John Cage Correspondence, Northwestern University Music Library.
Jon Phetteplace Papers, Geisel Library Special Collections, University of California, San Diego.
Peter Garland Papers and *Soundings* Records, Manuscript Collection, Harry Ransom Humanities Research Center, University of Texas, Austin.
Peter Yates Papers, Geisel Library Special Collections, University of California, San Diego.

SECONDARY SOURCES

Austin, Larry, and Douglas Kahn, eds. *Source: Music of the Avant-Garde, 1966–1973.* Berkeley: University of California Press, 2011.
Beal, Amy C. *Carla Bley*. Urbana: University of Illinois Press, 2011.
———. "Dreaming of Virtuosity." CD Liner Notes for *Michael Byron, Dreamers of Pearl* (Joseph Kubera, piano), New World Records 80679-2 (2008), 2–18.
———. "Experimentalists and Independents Are Favored—Mapping Americana: John Edmunds in Conversation with Peter Yates and John Cage, 1959–61." *Notes: Quarterly Journal of the Music Library Association* 64, no. 4 (June 2008): 659–87.
Crawford, Richard. *The American Musical Landscape*. Updated edition. Berkeley: University of California Press, 2000.
———. "American Music and Its Two Written Traditions." *Fontes Artis Musicae* 31 (1984): 79–84.
———. *America's Musical Life: A History*. New York: Norton, 2001.
Diamond, Jody, and Larry Polansky. "If We Can Make It We Can Print It, and If We Can Print It We Can Give It Away: Experimental Independent Music Publishing in the United States; or, Beyond Imprimatur." Invited talk given at the Music Library Association Meeting, New York City, March 10, 1992. Unpublished; available at http://eamusic.dartmouth.edu/~larry/misc_writings/talks/If_We_Can_Make_it _we_Can_print_it.MLA.NYC.Talks.pdf.
Dunn, David, and Kenneth Gaburo. *Collaboration Two: Publishing as Ecosystem*. Pamphlet. Ramona, Calif.: Lingua, 1983.
Ginsburg, Maya Lisa. "Documenting the American Experimental Tradition: A Historical Examination of SOURCE and *Soundings*." MA thesis, San Diego State University, 2011.
Kahn, Douglas. "Preface: *Source* in the Cause of New Music." In Source: *Music of the Avant-Garde, 1966–1973*, ix. Berkeley: University of California Press, 2011.

Kroeger, Karl. "Introduction." *The Complete Works of William Billings*. Boston: American Musicological Society and Colonial Society of Massachusetts, 1981.

Oteri, Frank. "Frogspeak: Larry Polansky on Frog Peak Music (a composers' collective)." Interview. New Music Box, January 2010, American Music Center, available at http://newmusicbox.org/article.nmbx?id=6226.

Silverman, Kenneth. *Begin Again: A Biography of John Cage*. New York: Knopf, 2010.

7 American Music Goes to School

A Point of View and a Case in Point

MARK CLAGUE

The term "school"—in reference to a group of classical music composers—carries the weight of historical privilege. Never just descriptive, the usage affirms both the coherence and the influence of the assemblage, arguing for its prestige through collective action. The term was already firmly established in the vocabulary of music history by 1789, when Charles Burney completed his four-volume *A General History of Music*. In an attempt at stylistic analysis of primarily medieval chant and Renaissance polyphony, Burney refers to the "Roman school," the "Flemish school," the "Neapolitan school," and the "French school" specifically.[1] His usage grows out of extensive discussions of both training academies and influential teachers and their followers, especially in ancient Greece and throughout medieval Europe—for example, the "school of Chiron," the "school of Linus," or the "Pythagorean and Platonic schools."[2] Writing of his own time and evoking a burgeoning European nationalism, the Englishman Burney laments that

> as for Music, we [the English] have little that we can call our own; and though more money is expended upon this favourite art in England, than in any other kingdom upon the globe; yet, having no school either for the cultivation of Counterpoint or Singing, we acquire by those arts neither honour from our neighbours, nor profit to our natives. Both take wing together! And without a scarcity of genius for contributing to the pleasures of the ear, we purchase them with as little necessity as we should corn at a dear and foreign market, while our own lands lay fallow.[3]

Thus Burney interweaves the practice of music training and its aesthetic lineages with interpretive accounts of style and influence, resulting in an argument, both implicit and explicit, about artistic excellence and national identity.

The ideological stakes of the notion of a compositional "school" were raised again in 1834 when Austrian musicologist Raphael Georg Kiesewetter first grouped Haydn and Mozart under the rubric the "Viennese school,"[4] not simply interpreting stylistic affinity but arguing for the hegemony of (Austro-)German culture in Western music. He writes:

> By Haydn and Mozart the art of sound was raised in all departments to the highest perfection; their style was the exclusive model for all the composers of Germany and France; and whatever has been produced in later times, deserving of being called grand and beautiful, owes its origin to this epoch. We must, therefore, characterize these two eminent composers as the founders of a new school, which may be called that of Germany, or more properly the Viennese school.[5]

That whatever is "grand and beautiful" "in later times" "owes its origins" to the "highest perfection" of Haydn and Mozart, who are characterized in terms of place, reveals stylistic interpretation as a nationalist construct.

This use of the word "school" as a concept to reinforce German nationalism was renewed in 1859 by the composer Franz Brendel during his address at the inaugural Musicians Congress (Tonkünstler-Versammlung) in Leipzig when he proposed the moniker "the New German school" (die neudeutsche Schule) to affirm his preferred group of progressive composers after Beethoven. According to Brendel, it was common to call German baroque composers from the period of J. S. Bach and Händel the "Old German school" [die alt deutsche Schule], while, following a period of Italian influence (upon Mozart, for example), Beethoven had restored the aesthetic of the German north, inspiring the work of such composers as Wagner and Liszt while forging a New German school.[6] Thus, Brendel interrupts Kiesewetter's narrative to purge German culture of foreign influence and place himself and his idols at the core of national identity. Of course, German composers outside of Liszt's circle were excluded, prompting critics to expose Brendel's construction as self-promotional and to identify it by the more precise and confined phrase as the "Weimarian school."[7] Serving as editor of the *Neue Zeitschrift für Musik*, however, Brendel controlled the vehicle for amplifying his interpretive terminology and the self-aggrandizing aesthetic argument it encapsulated.[8] As a result, his notion has persisted.

The term "school" is most commonly used in twenty-first-century music texts today in reference to the "Second Viennese school," a use introduced by Arnold Schoenberg's composition pupil and biographer Egon Wellesz, who as far back as 1912 signaled the collective efforts of Schoenberg and his students, Alban Berg and Anton Webern, in the phrase the "Young Viennese school" [la jeune ecole viennoise].[9] Wellesz evocation of a new, "young" Viennese school signaled a desire to recapture the glory of Beethoven's era and carried further ideological and aesthetic implications. As adopted to English-language publications, the term "Second Viennese school"[10] came to distinguish the efforts of Schoenberg and his followers from Mozart, Haydn, and additionally Beethoven to the now "First Viennese school." Yet the notion of Schoenberg's school as the "second" also intertwined the two eras in the attempt to shape the reception of modern music by reinforcing Schoenberg's claims that atonality was merely an extension of an inherited tradition of Austro-German music, reaching back through Beethoven, Mozart, and Haydn.

Wellesz's construction of Schoenberg, Webern, and Berg as a compositional school is arguably the most convincing use of the concept to date in music historiography. This triumvirate explored atonality and twelve-tone composition led by Arnold Schoenberg as instructor—a construction accurate both literally and philosophically. These three composers shared close, if sometimes strained, personal relationships, executed joint projects—notably the Society for Private Musical Performance (Verein für Musikalische Privataufführungen), and were received by critics and audiences alike as exhibiting a mutual aesthetic. That serial composition dominated the American academy after World War II could only have strengthened the position of Schoenberg's "school," as well as the ideological legacy of the concept.

From such origins, the notion of a "school" of composers has itself become a deeply embedded tradition central to the writing, teaching, and learning of music history (certainly in the English-speaking world). Uses include the fifteenth- and sixteenth-century Burgundian school, the Darmstadt school (Boulez, Maderna, Nono, and Stockhausen), the English Madrigal school, I Giovane scuola (late nineteenth-century opera composers), the Manchester school (Birtwistle, Goehr, and Maxwell Davies), the Mannheim school, the Neapolitan school, the New York school (Cage, Feldman, Brown, Wolff, and Tudor), the Roman school, the Venetian school, and by implication such groups as the Mighty Five and Les Six. The term is more than description; it is aesthetic, promotional, evaluative, and ideological.

The notion of school implies coherence; it identifies an ensemble of artists, signaling creative unity in concord with music history's focus on the singular compositional genius that breaks with tradition to advance art. A school has students and thus perpetuates its teachings, influencing others and thus achieving significance and even dominance. A school also furthers its own identity, serving to crystallize an interpretation (when advanced by a historian) or to advance an aesthetic (when proposed by the composers themselves) or even to promote the careers of its members.

The term "school" has particular resonance in American music historiography as an analytical concept and vehicle for narrative, but also for aesthetic affirmation and ideological position. The use seems to have been introduced by Frederic Louis Ritter in 1883 in his history *Music in America*—the first book-length attempt to tell the story of music in the United States. Defending the efforts of the "native psalm-tune composer," Ritter invokes the notion of the "Billings School" against conservative critiques of the composer William Billings and his contemporaries.[11] Ritter fails to articulate any shared characteristics of this group, except the shared antipathy that rose against them. Such objections centered on the fuguing tune, accused of having "little meaning" and a tendency "rather to provoke levity rather than to enkindle devotion." The critics of the Billings School saw this music as "ignorant," a "perversion," "evil," and burdened by an interest in "novelty" that discounted the models of European masters. Ritter, in contrast, found the dismissal of the Billings School to have done lasting damage to the American composer, who was now limited to "short, sacred glees," "harmonized in the most simple manner." As a result, Ritter argues that "the American church-composer's . . . imagination did not gain in breadth. . . . There are no battles with contrapuntal intricacies."[12] Exacerbated by a religious aversion to instrumental music, Ritter argues that the American composer's growth was stunted.

Later commentators saw an American school as either impossible or a barrier itself. Writing in 1904, Louis C. Elson lamented the poor prospects for a "distinctively American school" of musical composition, dismissing the possibility that one had existed to date.[13] In 1955 Gilbert Chase, writing in his textbook *America's Music: From the Pilgrim's to the Present*, characterizes the work of America's late-nineteenth-century classical composers as a "school." Chase writes,

> We must attempt to define the prevailing New England attitude toward musical art, that is to say, the attitude that dominated the musical thinking of those New England composers who, in the final decades of the nineteenth century and the first of the twentieth, succeeded in forming a rather impressive school variously known as the "Boston Classicists" or the "New England Academicians." It might be denied that formed a "school" in the strict sense of the term, but, like all New England cultural manifestations, this musical movement that centered in Boston and that flourished from about 1880 to World War I assumed rather definite characteristics, and I think it can be shown that it stemmed from a fairly homogeneous cultural and aesthetic background.[14]

Chase proceeds to discuss a constellation of New England–based composers who received training in the Austro-Germanic tradition, typically in Europe. He identifies John Knowles Paine as the "ancestor" of these "Boston academicians," most directly as the teacher of Arthur W. Foote and Daniel Gregory Mason. Chase names some half dozen members of this school, including George Chadwick, Amy Marcy Cheney (Beach), and Horatio Parker. He also describes a shared and coherent aesthetic among them but ultimately dismisses their creative path as "imitative provincialism."[15] Chase celebrated originality and independence rooted in folk traditions and thus membership in a school was itself a creative indictment. Chase's use of the term, however, would be superseded, and Ritter's defense remounted.

Musicologist H. Wiley Hitchcock rehabilitates the term *school* as one of affirmation in his 1969 textbook, *Music in the United States: A Historical Introduction*. As with Burney, Hitchcock's use of the term seems to grow organically out of the historical description of musical practice, specifically of the singing-school movement led by such ministers as the Rev. Thomas Symmes, who in 1721 gave a sermon on "The Reasonableness of Regular Singing," and Rev. John Tufts, who the following year published the instruction book *An Introduction to the Singing of Psalm-Tunes*. As Hitchcock writes, "Like clergymen before and after them, the Puritan ministers of New England set out to reform music in their churches. In so doing, they created the first music instruction books in America, established a unique kind of musical education, and paved the way for our first school of composers."[16] Hitchcock refers to this "school of composers" variously as "the first group of American composers," the "Yankee Tunesmiths," and—almost obliquely in only a section heading—as "the First New England School."[17] It is this later phrase that would prove the most influential. Hitchcock does not list the members of the First New England school precisely, but here he discusses the music of William Billings extensively, as well as that of Timothy Swan and Daniel Read, while concluding that "Americans were consistent in their taste, and their music is perfectly homogeneous stylistically; in its own terms, it is as 'stylish' as the more complex and sophisticated European music of its time."[18] Thus the notion of a "school" of composition is launched among this initial fluorescence of American composers as part of an aesthetic argument immediately attached to the question of value—that American music achieves a comparable quality and coherence to its European root.

Hitchcock deepens his aesthetic claim and echoes music history's construct of the Viennese schools again in his identification of a "Second New England School." He writes:

> If [John Sullivan] Dwight and contributors to his journal . . . were the literary voices of the art-music of the age, a group of New England composers was the musical voice. I shall call them the Second New England School, grouping them together by virtue of their common inheritance, attitudes, and general style much as I grouped the late eighteenth-century composers of the First New England School.[19]

Based on detailed stylistic analysis, Hitchcock goes on to identify the members of this second school as John Knowles Paine and younger composers Arthur Foote, George Chadwick, Arthur Whiting, Horatio Parker, Mrs. H. H. A. Beach, and Daniel Gregory Mason. Note that in contrast with those who later echoed

Hitchcock's notion (maybe too casually), originally Edward MacDowell is explicitly excluded from the group as aesthetically distinct and independent, that is, MacDowell's music is more akin to Wagner and Liszt's New German school—as a "tone poet" rather than a devotee of "traditional" if still "Romantic" forms connected with earlier German composers such as Mendelssohn.[20] Music historians had earlier identified this American grouping of late-nineteenth-century composers under such rubrics as "the Academics" (Rupert Hughes, 1900), the "Boston classicists" (Benjamin Lombard 1915, echoed by Gilbert Chase in 1966), and the "Boston Group" (John Tasker Howard, 1946).[21] Yet using stylistic analysis, Hitchcock contends the school was neither academic nor classicist, and his argument becomes all the more convincing by leveraging the historiographical weight of the term "school," by this time so firmly established in musicological discourse by Burney, Kiesewetter, Brendel, and Wellesz.

As with the New German and Second Viennese uses, Hitchcock's rendering of the term "school" argues for value by adopting a term already steeped in the Austro-German tradition to suggest that music in America merited attention not only in comparison to that of European masters but also because of its comparison to the European masters themselves. Writing first for a textbook, rather than a scholarly article, Hitchcock appears to be inspired by pedagogical exigency—to create a rubric to enable his student readers to understand, remember, and also appreciate the flowerings of music composition in the United States. The aesthetic hegemony of the term strengthened the effectiveness of Hitchcock's terminological adaptations as teaching tools,[22] implicitly arguing for the value of American classical music and its inclusion in the academy and by extension classical music's canon. That the student audience in his Hunter College classroom and beyond would have already been deeply indoctrinated into these canonical traditions of artistic excellence and influence in European compositional schools by music history survey courses and their texts made Hitchcock's proposition of the First and Second New England schools all the more convincing and powerful.

One example of such a popular music textbook conceivably in use by Hitchcock's students in their other courses was Donald Jay Grout's *A History of Western Music* (1960/1964). Like Burney, Grout identifies educational academies with the term "school"[23] but uses the term primarily to identify significant groups of composers and stylistic lineages. Discussing the early polyphony of Leonin and Perotin and their associated "system" of rhythmic modes, for example, Grout writes: "The system and its notation were developed gradually during the twelfth and thirteenth centuries to fill the needs of a school of polyphonic composers whose activities were centered at Paris. Two composers in this school . . . were Leonin . . . and Perotin. . . . Their compositions, together with those of their anonymous French contemporaries, are known collectively as the music of the

Notre Dame school."[24] Grout goes on to address the Burgundian school (a "name
. . . given to both the style of music and the school of composers") and links
the notion to "the rise of national styles" with the Venetian, Roman, Viennese,
English, and French schools.[25] Exploring "Schoenberg's Influence," Grout asserts
that "the Schoenberg followers must be regarded . . . as a school existing side by
side with others which still maintain an allegiance to Classical tonal principles."[26]

Although Grout addresses music in the United States in both the nineteenth
and twentieth centuries, mentioning composers such as Stephen Foster, Arthur
Farwell, Horatio Parker, Edward MacDowell, George Gershwin, Roy Harris,
Virgil Thomson, Walter Piston, Roger Sessions, and Howard Hanson, with
more extended treatment of the music of Charles Ives and Aaron Copland, he
does not use the term "school" to describe their efforts. Grout emphasizes the
diverse resources and individual voices of these composers but considers overt
nationalism in the United States as "only a subsidiary part."[27] While respecting
the distinctive artistry of its composers, Grout's discussion also suggests that
American music as a whole is fragmented and often derivative of European
forms, lacking coherence and incapable of perpetuating its aesthetics or asserting influence beyond its individual personalities.[28]

Hitchcock's reifications of the First and Second New England schools have
been echoed by his students, including Richard Crawford in the first edition
of *America's Musical Life: A History*,[29] and finds further resonance in similar
phrases used in many textbooks. In his *Oxford History of Western Music*, Richard
Taruskin refers to "'The Boston School'—sometimes called the 'Second Yankee
School' to distinguish it from the New England hymn writers of the colonial
period."[30] Michael Broyles refers to both schools in his chapter for *The Cambridge
History of American Music*.[31] Joseph Horowitz invokes both the "First . . ." and
"Second New England School" in his *Classical Music in America*,[32] yet many
scholars also resist the terminology, at least to some extent. Crawford avoids the
phrase "First New England School" and places the "Second New England School"
among several such labels. Crawford's 2013 textbook, *An Introduction to America's
Music* (co-authored with Larry Hamberlin), groups Paine, Parker, Chadwick,
Beach, and Foote (excluding MacDowell), arguing, "In a nod to their psalmodist
forebears, these composers have come to be called the 'Second New England
School.'"[33] Peter Burkholder, in his revision to Grout's *A History of Western Music*, similarly recognizes American hymnody's "distinctive New England idiom"
but avoids the word "school" and likewise discusses Paine, Chadwick, Parker,
MacDowell and Beach as simply "Boston composers" without institutionalizing
them as an ensemble.[34] Each of these authors takes care to contextualize the term
"school," often crediting the phrase to earlier and unnamed "historians."

Care in using the term "school" is certainly warranted, as the notion also
essentializes and distorts. A "school" obscures the individuality of its members

and excludes less favored contemporaries who might well deserve attention. The construct exaggerates difference and denies commonalities. Similarly, the dominance of the term "Second New England School" emphasizes academic composers to the exclusion of composers arguably heard more often during their day, such as the church organist and sacred composer Dudley Buck, who was born in New England but worked more often in the Midwest. Further, Hitchcock's telling distinction between early Romantic and Wagnerian influence among American composers is lost more often than not when MacDowell is lumped among the Second New England school. A focus on schools of composers diminishes the contributions of other musical figures. Such schools admit few conductors, performers, or writers; influential figures who were not composers, such as the conductor Theodore Thomas and critic John Sullivan Dwight, are marginalized. While textbooks perpetuate the notion in service of pedagogical exigency, the term "school" seems on the decline as used in research publications, such as journal articles and monographs. Many of today's scholars seem weary of the term and favor more nuanced notions of genealogy influenced by Foucault or simply avoid such layers of generalization.

Yet the notion of "school" retains significant and powerful ideological weight accrued over more than two centuries of use in teaching and writing about music, especially as used in grand narratives of the Western European classical tradition. These narratives continue to serve, subtly and not, the rhetorics of aesthetic debate in the absorption of new musics into the living practice of classical music. This construction effort is clear in the phrase and idea of "the Atlanta School of Composers," a term coined by conductor Robert Spano to encapsulate an aspect of his commissioning activities as music director of the Atlanta Symphony Orchestra (ASO). By leveraging the tradition and aesthetic gravitas of the notion of a compositional school in Western European music history, Spano and his collaborators—including the composers, the institution, musicians, their donors, and the city of Atlanta—have successfully commissioned, premiered, recorded, and launched a cohesive body of new orchestral works. That the creation of the "Atlanta school" has occurred during an era of shrinking budgets, the "death" of the classical recording industry, and conservative retrenchment in programming makes this accomplishment and by extension the power of the concept of school of composers all the more remarkable.

The Atlanta School

Robert Spano first imagined the notion of a new American school of composers in 2005 while walking from his apartment to the Atlanta Symphony Orchestra's home—the Woodruff Art Center—for a speech he was about to give to a scheduled retreat of the symphony's board of directors. As music director of the ASO, Spano had invested regularly in contemporary composers—commissioning works, making world-premiere recordings, and developing relationships between these composers and the Atlanta audience. As he recalled:

> I started recognizing that this [The Atlanta School] is not just a collection of composers in whom we had taken an interest; it is actually an aesthetic phenomenon that is observable in American music of my generation. . . . It became a kind of revelation . . . it's observable in the same way that we have talked about such things in the history of music, *Empfindsamkeit* or *Sturm und Drang* or The Big Five or The Six . . ., but it struck me that this was true. And I tried to figure out why . . . because they [the composers of The Atlanta School] don't sound like each other, they sound like themselves. . . . So what was it that was making me see them as some kind of shift? And it occurred to me that it was tonality, tunes, and an interest in world music, popular culture, or both—that influenced their music. . . . I got very excited by this. This is a new American School, school in the sense of aesthetic identity. . . . In our later planning meetings, we decided to have a little more hubris about it. . . . Why not call them "The Atlanta School of Composers"?—which was really a more convenient handle for us to talk about it in our own world, to promote them, to raise money for them, to nurture the whole project. . . . The Atlanta School is not well defined . . . it is not a specific group of people. . . . It's meant to be a loose definition, by definition.[35]

Spano's remembrances were made as part of a panel discussion on Friday, June 18, 2010, at the Sixty-Fifth National Conference of the League of American Orchestras—the national professional organization of symphonic ensembles in the United States. Hosted in their city by the Atlanta Symphony and validating the ensemble's own position as a leader within the field, the conference as a whole marked a symbolic coming of age for what has been billed as "The Atlanta School" of composers, especially after the ASO performed a concert featuring their work for industry delegates later that evening. Under the banner title "Atlanta School of Composers Concert," Robert Spano led performances of three movements from Michael Gandolfi's *The Garden of Cosmic Speculation* (2007), Osvaldo Golijov's *Three Songs for Soprano and Orchestra* (2001–02), Jennifer Higdon's recently premiered *On a Wire* (2010), featuring the six members of the chamber ensemble Eighth Blackbird as soloists, and Christopher Theofanidis's *Rainbow Body* (2000), which is arguably the founding composition of the school.

Robert Spano took the helm of the Atlanta Symphony Orchestra in September 2001 with a mandate to bring the innovative ideas he had explored with the Brooklyn Philharmonic in New York City to invigorate the more conservative tradition in Atlanta; doing so would help raise the stature of both his new city and its orchestra. Even before his first concert, Spano made plans to shake up the orchestra's repertoire, to commission new works, and to engage video artists and lighting designers to provide visual analogs to select live performances. The first appearance of a composer who would be included in The Atlanta School took place that first season in one of the orchestra's subscription concerts—and in only his second concert series as music director—in a program that Spano opened with Theofanidis's *Rainbow Body*. This thirteen-minute kaleidoscopic poem is rooted in the idea of natural perfection (Dzogchen) from Tibetan Buddhism and quotes a chant fragment by the medieval mystic Hildegard of Bingen.[36] Spano had premiered the work with the Houston Symphony just the year before, and the piece would go on to win London's 2003 Masterprize for Composition en route to becoming one of the most frequently performed twenty-first-century classical compositions.[37]

Theofanidis's use of common-practice harmony and his shimmering reiterations of the Hildegard chant melody from "Ave Maria, O auctrix vite" (Hail Mary, source of life) intersect the qualities of tonality and tune that Spano observed in the school. Popular and world music influences find voice in the casting of chant as the exotic, while the work's mixture of popular and classical influences are exhibited in Theofanidis's use of orchestral colors to evoke the classical realm of klangfarben melody as well as his "wet acoustic" echo effects that imitate a cathedral acoustic but were inspired by patches on the composer's synthesizer, specifically a composite of the "echo" and "slap back" effects.[38] As evidenced by the audience voting for the 2003 Masterprize, Theofanidis's colorful use of the orchestral palette and the dramatic musical gestures between more restful interludes featuring increasingly enriched renditions of the Hildegard melody succeed in engaging a concert audience upon first hearing.

Spano, himself a composer, is driven in part by the goal of sharing contemporary music that speaks to him with his audience. To accomplish this, he humanizes the experience of Atlanta School compositions by fostering a direct, personalized relationship between the creators of these works and his audience. The Atlanta premiere of *Rainbow Body*, for example, was introduced during the concert by a short video shown on screens hanging right and left above the Woodruff Center stage. Recorded and edited in advance, the clip features Spano speaking informally in a relaxed setting with the composer and discussing the work to be performed. Rather than a formal and potentially stiff introduction done live at the concert or the traditional composer bow following the performance, the preview video introduces the composer to advantage and allows the concert producers to excerpt only the most effective comments to showcase the composer in the best possible light. Ironically, the video projector failed at the initial concert from the opening run of *Rainbow Body*, forcing composer and conductor to complete the introduction live; at subsequent concerts the video was used in full, and indeed such introductory films have become an essential tactic of Spano and The Atlanta School.

For Spano's second season as music director (2002–03), he announced what was then called "the Living Composers Initiative" and commissioned one-time

Atlanta resident and his former student Jennifer Higdon to create a three-part work about the city of Atlanta. As a result, in his first commision and the orchestra's first since 1996, Spano first tied his new music project to local pride and civic identity. Atlanta's audience had, in fact, already met Higdon musically, as her eulogistic tone poem *blue cathedral* had been performed the year before on Spano's inaugural season.[39] The new commission specified a twenty-four- to thirty-minute work in multiple movements, but also that one of the movements function also as a stand-alone overture and that another would have an alternate version for chamber orchestra that could be performed by a reduced ensemble for the ASO's children's concerts. In response, Higdon delivered what she called a "musical portrait of Atlanta" titled *City Scape*. The premiere performances took place November 14, 15, and 16, 2002, and its three movements were titled "SkyLine," "River Sings a Song to Trees," and "Peachtree Street." In keeping with Spano's strategy of connecting composer to audience, Higdon was interviewed by local music critic Pierre Ruhe for the *Atlanta Journal-Constitution*, and an introductory video was made for the work's premiere. That the music depicted the urban landscape of their hometown could only have made the piece more attractive to Atlanta's concertgoers and further deepen the sense of personal connection between composer and listener.

The opening movement, "SkyLine," performed the duty of the requested overture and was subsequently performed six times by the orchestra on tour, while "Peachtree Street," which depicts Atlanta's main downtown traffic artery and, in fact, the street on which the Atlanta Symphony's own concert hall is situated, was performed in a reduced orchestration at twenty-one children's concerts conducted by ASO assistant conductor Laura Jackson. Subsequently, the longer middle movement has been performed on its own as part of the ASO's subscription series. This repetition of its commissions has become a vital component of The Atlanta School's approach. Rather than a single, one-time-only gala premiere, Spano and Atlanta's orchestra have performed their successful new commissions repeatedly, both at home and on tour. A second vital step in the project also developed at this time: recording. Excitement for Higdon's work had been heightened by the successful premiere of her *Concerto for Orchestra* by the Philadelphia Orchestra the previous June. Spano capitalized on the success of both new works, by contracting with Telarc to record the pair and subsequently programming the works for the same concert in September of his third season. In this way, two additional aspects of what would become "The Atlanta School" approach—repetition and recording—were instituted.

Another tributary that helped feed Spano's Atlanta commissions was his work at the Tanglewood Music Center. In 1998 Spano was appointed head of the summer festival's conductor-training program, but while there he also came into contact with many up-and-coming composers. One of the most promising of these talents was Argentine American composer Osvaldo Golijov, and in the summer of 2002 Spano conducted the composer's *La Pasión según San Marcos*, a hugely popular work with audiences that had been commissioned for the 250th anniversary (in 2000) of Johann Sebastian Bach's birth. Spano's energetic conducting and Golijov's ecstatic music made for a productive partnership. In 2003 and 2004 Spano served as head of Tanglewood's Contemporary Music Festival, thereby being introduced to a range of international compositional talents. It was at Tanglewood that Spano conducted the premiere of composer Michael Gandolfi's *Garden of Cosmic Speculation*, which was subsequently expanded and recorded as an ASO Atlanta School Composition.

At the time of the League of American Orchestras conference feature in June 2010, The Atlanta School comprised five composers: the original quartet of Gandolfi, Golijov, Higdon, and Theofanidis, with the recent addition of the then-twenty-nine-year-old Adam Schoenberg, who, despite his surname, has no familial nor aesthetic connection to the Austrian inventor of twelve-tone serialism. Spano is also a key member of the school as facilitator, manager, and interpreter.[40] While the defining activities of the Atlanta School are fluid, arising out of Spano's musical interests, its membership is clearly and consistently bounded at any given time, as affirmed by ASO publicity. As the orchestra's artistic director Evans Mirageas describes it, "The Atlanta School is ad hoc, guided by what Robert [Spano] feels at the moment; it's more like a school of fish than an institute."[41] The full phrase in all its hubris arose out of a planning meeting between Mirageas, Spano, and ASO president at the time (December 2007), Allison Vulgamore, in which she asked her artistic team to encapsulate their commissioning activities to better market, raise money, and advocate for the projects.[42] Such meetings are characteristic of the ASO's institutional culture, particularly its "war room" meetings in which the music director, artistic director, executive director, and the heads of marketing and development brainstorm ideas for upcoming events, building commitment from the institution's constituent parts while shaping projects to the needs of each department. Spano himself coined the phrase "The Atlanta School," soon phoning each of its four original composer members to ask permission to include them in the rubric.[43]

The Atlanta School of Composers is defined by two components: a shared aesthetic spirit and a set of institutional presentation strategies that serve to connect audiences to contemporary music with an immediacy more common to the traditional canon of familiar European masterworks. While insisting that any definition be flexible and open rather than too narrow, Spano himself has described the common aesthetic of The Atlanta School as sharing three tendencies:[44]

- Tonality—that, although not necessarily following the rules of common practice harmony, these composers do not eschew recognizable chords and harmonies and, in fact, traditional harmony is a driving force in their music;

- Tunes—that there is a primacy—or at least use—of melody in this music; and
- Popular and world music resources—that these composers routinely blur distinctions between popular and classical musics and frequently draw ideas, materials, and inspirations from across the globe.

Spano, whose own taste in music also includes Pierre Boulez, Elliott Carter, Arnold Schoenberg, Iannis Xenakis, and many other twentieth-century composers who fall well outside of The Atlanta School orbit, recognized the school as part a larger generational shift among his American contemporaries.[45] For Spano, this shift represents a turning away from the theoretical procedures typical in the United States following World War II among composers such as Milton Babbitt, Tania Leon, Roger Sessions, Ralph Shapey, Hale Smith, Charles Wuorinen, and others, toward a more intuitive approach reflecting the intent of composers to write music for their own personal pleasure rather than for the approval of academic or insider colleagues.

Spano thus sees The Atlanta School as a kind of musical family inspired by parental figures such as John Adams, John Corigliano, and David Del Tredici, while being distinct from the minimalist aesthetics of Philip Glass, Steve Reich, Terry Riley, and early Adams. For Spano, Adams's *Harmonielehre* offers an example of the aesthetic shift that inspired The Atlanta School in its re-embrace of major and minor triads. In terms of melody, The Atlanta School is prefigured by other non-academic American composers such as Samuel Barber, Leonard Bernstein, Aaron Copland, and George Gershwin, while being distinct from experimentalists such as Charles Ives, Henry Cowell, Lou Harrison, or John Cage. Not coincidentally, Spano has conducted works by all of the school's ancestral forefathers on concerts with the Atlanta Symphony and recorded all of them (with the single exception of Gershwin) for compact discs featuring composers promoted through The Atlanta School rubric.

While Spano did not create the aesthetic turn in which his school is rooted, the conductor has exerted a strong pull on its music, especially in terms of scope and expression. Driven by his own personal excitement and aesthetic connection to the music of these composers, Spano has placed his nearly boundless personal enthusiasm, time, attention, institutional authority, career prospects, and even personal savings in service of his composers. The school is thus less a calculated move than an outgrowth of the conductor's own passions and interests. Spano himself has claimed not to have any influence on the music's sound or aesthetics of The Atlanta School's composers, yet by means of the initial selection and subsequently his own enthusiasms, Spano seems to have had a defining influence that suggests at least two additional tendencies be added to the list of Atlanta School characteristics:

- an intellectual inspiration, which may provide musical material for the composition, but most importantly provides listeners with a conceptual entry point to the work, and
- an unabashed, intuitive emotional passion in the grand romantic tradition that first invites Spano to connect with each work and then to feel confident that his Atlanta audiences will love the work as well.

Critically here, the intellectual content and emotional expression of Atlanta School compositions must balance, such that listeners attuned to each parameter find reason to engage more deeply. The relationship of concept and expression must be symbiotic such that the ideas in the work propel its emotional reception. Of The Atlanta School's compositions, Spano speaks of a similarly satisfying "emotional ride" that "much older music and certainly [The Atlanta School] composers take one [the listener] on, so that heart engagement leads to a different level of experience and enjoyment."[46]

The second critical component of The Atlanta School's success is a set of presentation and marketing tactics that have made the orchestra's performances of these works more rewarding. These tactics include:

- introducing the composer to Atlanta's audience in advance of a premiere by performing an existing, successful, and known work;
- creating brief introductory videos for each composition featuring the composer with the music director in a relaxed environment, to be shown at the concert just prior to a performance or premiere;
- commissioning a mid-length orchestral work, followed by a longer choral-orchestral piece, often followed by a solo concerto;
- previewing works in progress to improve the quality of the resulting composition (this can be done in several ways, either by the review of the music director, at a festival workshop, or in a preliminary rehearsal);
- a flexibility and willingness to work with composers on last-minute additions and changes to a score in order to fulfill the composer's artistic inspiration;
- collaborative problem solving during the rehearsal process to address potential areas of weakness in a score as conceived and notated;
- advertising each premiere in the community and as part of The Atlanta School brand;
- recording each commission for CD and digital distribution, typically as part of its premiere subscription presentation;
- scheduling repeat performances of The Atlanta School compositions in the orchestra's future subscription concerts, tours, and educational programs over the course of several years in order to create an ongoing relationship between composer and audience;
- continuing to support the careers and works of these composers in an ongoing artistic partnership; and

- an institutional commitment by both orchestra and community to raise money to support the project.

Although "The Atlanta School" approach has developed into a comprehensive plan, these lists of characteristics and strategies misrepresent somewhat their organic development over what was more than a full decade of activity. What is now known as The Atlanta School began as "The Living Composers Initiative" and for a time was known internally as "The Spano School of Composers" before being combined with an external relations and fundraising efforts that linked music to city. Spano and the Atlanta Symphony gradually cultivated a devoted coterie of donors, at one time known collectively as The Academy, as well as an engaged audience in the Atlanta community, such that the orchestra's ticket sales receive a 5 percent uptick whenever a work by an Atlanta School composer is to be performed.[47] This synergy of art, institution, and community represents the combined aesthetic vision of Spano and the composers he has chosen, along with an institution and community aspiring to grow and achieve greater national import and reputation.

In 2012 and again in 2014, Atlanta Symphony musicians were locked out as part of ongoing labor disputes with the board of the Woodruff Art Center, the umbrella organization that oversees the Atlanta Symphony Orchestra. The crisis silenced the orchestra and effectively put Spano's commissioning initiatives and The Atlanta School of Composers on ice. Although lengthy discussion of the challenges posed by these ruptures would take us far beyond the focus of this chapter, brief mention should be made of the activities of Atlanta composers at the time because they provide an encouraging and relevant postscript.

The need to repair relationships in the Atlanta arts community under painful circumstances led to the addition of two Atlanta-based composers to the orchestra's school. A member of ASO's bass section since 1994, Michael Kurth (b. 1971) wrote a string quartet titled *Easy Listening* (2009) for the Riverside Chamber Players, run by ASO cellist Joel Dallow. Kurth shared a recording with Spano, who offered to commission a piece for the orchestra. "I thought he was kidding," remembered Kurth, "and it took several reassurances from him to convince me. I had never written for large orchestra before."[48] Spano programmed Kurth's subsequent compositions for performances in 2011, 2013, and 2015. The composer's aesthetic was already compatible with the Atlanta School approach. "My style fits in with almost everything Robert says he like about the 'Atlanta School' of composers," Kurth reported.[49]

Composer and conductor Richard Prior's role in the school was also assisted, if indirectly, by the crisis. In 2009 Spano was appointed a Presidential Distinguished Professor at Atlanta's Emory University, where Prior serves as director of orchestra studies and where many of the orchestra's musicians teach part time.

Prior played a recording of his *Stabat Mater* for Spano, who instantly suggested a future collaboration, which came to pass when the ASO commissioned Prior's *. . . of Shadow and Light . . .* and when Prior, during the strike, conducted three benefit performances of his own Symphony no. 3 with members of the orchestra. Prior was also signatory on a letter from fourteen composers, including the original members of The Atlanta School, in support of the embattled musicians.[50]

The hegemonic power of the word "school" in reference to a group of composers has played an essential role in the ability of Robert Spano and the Atlanta Symphony Orchestra to market, sell, support, and perform commissions by the composers of The Atlanta School. Although impossible to quantify, the notion of school galvanized these commissioning activities and provided a coherent and unified identity. The project has been critiqued as a return to lighter classical fare (a complaint that Spano vehemently denies), while the notion similarly obscures a range of other commissions, premieres, and even performances of more academic music that audiences find more challenging. To some extent The Atlanta School project has opened space in the orchestra's programs for these more challenging works by putting a positive spin on the notion of new music. It is a compelling example of the power of story to shape the reception of art.

Furthermore, The Atlanta School of Composers articulates the complex interaction of individuals and institutions in American music history, in which art, money, and community are synchronized. Such interaction characterizes the concept of the Institutional Muse, in which an organizational collective not only inspires but shapes artistic practice. Copyright law gives full ownership of The Atlanta School compositions to their individual composers, and similarly music history grants full creative credit to the composer as well. Yet the history of The Atlanta School demonstrates that the orchestra, its musicians, and its community participated in the creativity and construction of both the school and its compositions. The compositions of The Atlanta School would be different if not for the creativity of Spano and his institutional collaborators. Rather than diminishing the power of the composer or the composition, the Institutional Muse amplifies art. The Atlanta School thus offers a model for two constituencies: first, for arts organizations as a means of bringing new works to a broad audience, and second, to music historians who, in attempting to understand art in context, must consider the possibility that context itself is creative.

Appendix: Atlanta School Compositions, 2000–2016

Composer	Title	ASO: Chorus	Comm	Perform	Repeat (*tour*)	Recorded
Higdon	*blue cathedral*			May 2002	Apr 2011	©2003 Telarc 80596 ©2004 Telarc ASO-60
Higdon	City Scape 1. SkyLine 2. River Sings a Song to Trees 3. Peachtree Street		✔	**Nov 2002**	*Sep 2003*, Nov 2007	©2004 Telarc 80620
Higdon	City Scape 1. Skyline		✔	**Nov 2002**	*Mar/Apr 2003*, May 2003, Jun 2004	©2004 Telarc 80620
Higdon	City Scape 3. Peachtree Street		✔	**Nov 2002**	*Nov 2005, Jan 2008,* Fall 2008 YPC, *Dec 2008, Jul 2010*	©2004 Telarc 80620
Higdon	Concerto for Orchestra			Sep 2003		©2004 Telarc 80620
Higdon	Dooryard Bloom			*Jan 2006*	Sep 2006	©2009 Telarc 80673
Higdon	The Singing Rooms	✔	✔	**Mar 2009***		©2010 Telarc 32630
Higdon	On a Wire		✔	**Jun 2010**	Jun 2010	©2011 ASO Media 1001
Higdon	TenFold**		✔	**Jun 2011**		
Gandolfi	Impressions from The Garden of Cosmic Speculation*** (2004–07)		✔	Apr 2006	*Apr 2006*	
Gandolfi	The Garden of Cosmic Speculation (2004–07)		✔+	**May 2007**	Jun 2010#, Jul 2010#	©2008 Telarc 80696
Gandolfi	QED: Engaging Richard Feynman (2010)	✔	✔	**Jun 2010**		©2011 ASO Media 1001

Composer	Title	ASO: Chorus	Comm	Perform	Repeat (*tour*)	Recorded
Gandolfi	Pageant**		✔	**Jan 2011**		
Gandolfi	The Nature of Light (2012)(Clarinet and Strings)		✔	**Jan 2013**		
Gandolfi	Oratorio (expansion of Q.E.D.)	✔	✔	**Feb 2014**		
Gandolfi	Imaginary Numbers			**May 2015**		
Golijov	Last Round (1996)			Sep 2002	*Sep 2002*, Nov 2004, *Jul 2010*, Feb 2011	Recorded
Golijov	Ainadamar	✔		Feb 2004#, Nov 2005	*Jun 2006*, Mar 2011#	©2006 DGG 6429-02
Golijov	Three Songs for Soprano and Orchestra (2001–02)			Feb 2004	Jun 2010	© 2007 DGG 289 477 6426
Golijov	Oceana (1996)	✔		Nov 2004	*Jun 2006*	© 2007 DG 289 477 6426
Golijov	"Water and Horse Prelude" from Ainadamar, arr. Spano**			Nov 2005	??? 2010	
Golijov	Pasión según San Marcos	✔*		*Feb 2006*	*Feb 2006*	****
Golijov	Dreams and Prayers of Isaac the Blind			Jun 2008, premiere		
Golijov	Azul			May 2009		
Golijov	Lua Descolorida (no orch.)			Jun 2009		
Golijov	Mariel			May 2009	Jul 2010	
Golijov	Youth without Youth: Concert Suite			Jan 2010 (US premiere)		
Golijov	She Was Here			Mar 2011	*Mar 2011*	
Golijov	Sidereus			**SepOct 2011**		

Composer	Title	ASO: Chorus	Comm	Perform	Repeat (*tour*)	Recorded
Kurth	Everything Lasts Forever		✔	**Apr 2013**		2018
Kurth	A Thousand Words		✔	**Feb 2016**		2018
Kurth	May Cause Dizziness			**Mar 2011**		2018
Kurth	Prometheus Unhinged		✔	**Oct 2015** Feb 2016		2018
Kurth	Choral Work (2018)		✔			2018
Prior	…of Shadow and Light… (incantations for orchestra)		✔	**Oct 2013**		
Prior	Symphony no. 3			Nov 2014		
Prior	fanfare and intermedio		✔	**Jun 2013**		
Prior	Symphony no. 4		✔	**2017-18**		
Schoenberg	Finding Rothko (2006)			Oct 2009		
Schoenberg	Up!** (2010)		✔	**Sep/Oct 2010**		
Schoenberg	La Luna Azul (2012)		✔+	***Mar 2012***		
Schoenberg	An American Symphony (2011)			Oct 2013		
Theofanidis	Rainbow Body (2000)			Sep 2001*	*Apr 2002, Jan 2004,* Feb 2007, *Feb/Mar 2007,* Jun 2007, *Jul 2008,* Jun 2010, *Jul 2010,* Aug 2012, Apr 2013, *Apr 2013*	©2003 Telarc 80596
Theofanidis	The Here and Now[1] (2005)	✔	✔+	**May 2005**	Mar 2008, *Apr 2008*	©2005 Telarc 80638
Theofanidis	Symphony No. 1 (2009)		✔	**Apr 2009**	*Apr 2009*	©2011 ASO Media 1002

Composer	Title	ASO: Chorus	Comm	Perform	Repeat (*tour*)	Recorded
Theofanidis	Une Certaine Joie de vivre** (2010)		✔	**Sep 2010**		
Theofanidis	Creation/Creator			**Apr 2015**		©2015 ASO Media 1006

Boldface = ASO first performance was also the world premiere

1. The title used for the ASO premiere performance was *The Music of Our Final Meeting*

* Rainbow Body was premiered by Robert Spano with the Houston Symphony in Houston, Texas on April 8, 2000.

** ASO commission for the tenth-anniversary celebration of Robert Spano and Donald Runnicles's tenure at the ASO

*** 4 movements of Gandolfi's Garden of Cosmic Speculation were commissioned and premiered at the Tanglewood Music Center, conducted by Robert Spano in the summer of 2004; Robert Spano commissioned Gandolfi's additional segments of what is now an eleven-movement work.

**** Video of Spano conducting *Pasion* is included with DGG release

\+ Robert Spano personal commission

\# excerpt of the longer work performed

Notes

1. Burney, *General History*, 671, 735, 759, 765. Burney also refers to institutions of musical learning by the term "school," and while there is some blurring of the distinction, his usage is not limited to educational institutions but explicitly signals groups of composers and stylistic coherence as well.

2. Ibid., 258, 280, 355.

3. Ibid., 375.

4. Heartz and Brown, "Classical"; see R. G. Kiesewetter, *Geschichte der europäisch-abendländischen oder unsrer heutigen Musik* (Leipzig, 1834, rev. 1846; Eng. trans., 1848).

5. Kiesewetter, *History*, 243.

6. Brendel, "Zur Anbahnung einer Verständigung," 265+. The proposal led to the founding of the General German Music Association (Allgemeiner Deutscher Musikverein) at the second Musicians' Congress held in Weimar in 1861. See Lucke-Kaminiarz, "Der Allgemeine Deutsche Musikverein," 221+.

7. *Grenzboten*, June 10, 1859, translated from German, after Rainer Kleinertz, "Zum Begriff 'Neudeutsche Schule,'" in Altenburg, *Liszt und die Neudeutsche Schule*, 23–31.

8. The "New German School" appears to be one of the more robust and enduring constructions of the use common to twentieth- and twenty-first-century music-history textbooks.

9. Wellesz, "Schönberg"; for a fuller discussion see Auner, "Second Viennese School."

10. Usage of the "Second Viennese School" can also include Schoenberg's other pre–World War II students such as Wellesz, Jalowetz, Karl Horwitz, and Erwin Stein.

11. Ritter, *Music in America*, 93–111.

12. Ibid., 97–100.

13. Elson, *History of American Music*, 348.

14. Chase, *America's Music*, 366.

15. Ibid., 367.

16. Hitchcock, *Music in the United States*, 7.

17. Ibid., 9.

18. Ibid., 14.

19. Ibid., 130

20. Ibid., 131, 138

21. Hughes, *Contemporary American Composers*; Chase, *America's Music*; Howard, *Our American Music*, 306–23.

22. Neuroscientist James E. Zull argues that the resonance of concepts between well-established and new learnings is pedagogically effective because of its biological basis in neural network; see Zull, *Art*, especially chap. 6, "What We Already Know," p. 91+.

23. See reference to "St. Thomas's school" in Leipzig: Grout, *History of Western Music*, 269.

24. Ibid., 42.

25. Ibid., 121, 164, 175, 177, 216, 289, 290.

26. Ibid., 454. See also the "Schoenberg-Webern school," 437.

27. Ibid., 404–5, 427–29.

28. The exception that proves the rule in Grout's discussion is that Grout praises Copland because "his work and counsel have influenced many younger American composers" (428).

29. See p. 352; Crawford includes MacDowell in the group and makes no distinction among them in terms of classicist, academic, or romantic aesthetic stances.

30. Taruskin, *Music in the Nineteenth Century*, 769.

31. Broyles, "Art Music," 236. Nicholls uses the term in his introduction as well, 41–42. Note that while the phrase "First New England School" appears in the index, Nym Cooke avoids it in his chapter "Sacred Music to 1800," 78–102.

32. Horowitz, *Classical Music in America*, 98.

33. Crawford and Hamberlin, *Introduction to America's Music*, 185.

34. Burkholder, *History of Western Music*, 504, 748–49.

35. Spano, presentation.

36. The remainder of Spano's program that night included Olivier Messiaen's *Oiseaux exotiques* leavened with the Fourth Symphony of Johannes Brahms.

37. Hewett, "As Hopeless as the Others."

38. Christopher Theofanidis, "Rainbow Body," composer's note included in CD booklet *Rainbow Body* Telarc CD-80596 ©2003, 3–4. Synthesizer details from a June 25, 2003, interview with the composer posted to http://behindthebeat.com/2003/06/jennifer-higdon-and-chris-theofanidis-rainbow-body.

39. *blue cathedral* was performed May 9–11, 2002.

40. Spano is also a composer but does not function as a contributor to the school.

41. Evans Mirageas, Skype interview with the author, on August 14, 2012.

42. Ibid.

43. Panel discussion following Spano presentation at the Sixty-Fifth National Conference of the League of American Orchestras, Atlanta, June 18, 2010.

44. These are spelled out in various publications of the ASO and were articulated again in the LAO panel on June 18, 2010.

45. Each of the school's initial members was born in the eleven-year period from 1956 through 1967—Gandolfi (b. 1956), Golijov (b. 1960), Spano (b. 1961), Higdon (b. 1962), and Theofanidis (b. 1967).

46. Panel discussion, LAO conference, June 18, 2010.

47. Interview with Charlie Wade, director of marketing, Atlanta Symphony Orchestra.

48. Kurth e-mail, December 11, 2016.

49. Ruhe, "ASO This Week."

50. Pousner, "Conductor Richard Prior Fears Lockout."

References

Altenburg, Detlef, ed. *Liszt und die Neudeutsche Schule*. Weimarer Liszt-Studien. Vol. 3. Laaber: Laaber-Verlag, 2006.

Auner, Joseph. "The Second Viennese School as Historical Concept." In *Schoenberg, Berg, and Webern: A Companion to the Second Viennese School*, edited by Bryan R. Simms, 1–36. Westport, Conn.: Greenwood, 1999.

Brendel, Franz. "Zur Anbahnung einer Verständigung." *Neue Zeitschrift für Musik* 50 [1859].

Broyles, Michael. "Art Music from 1860 to 1920." In *The Cambridge History of American Music*, edited by David Nicholls, 214–54. Cambridge: Cambridge University Press, 1998.

Burkholder, J. Peter. *A History of Western Music*. 7th ed. New York: Norton, 2006.

Burney, Charles. *A General History of Music from the Earliest Ages to the Present Period*. [1789]

Chase, Gilbert. *America's Music from the Pilgrims to the Present*. 2nd rev. ed. New York: McGraw Hill, 1966.

Cooke, Nym. "Sacred Music to 1800." In *The Cambridge History of American Music*, edited by David Nicholls. Cambridge: Cambridge University Press, 1998.

Crawford, Richard, and Larry Hamberlin. *An Introduction to America's Music*. New York: Norton, 2013.

Elson, Louis C. *The History of American Music*. New York: Macmillan, 1904.

Grout, Donald J. *A History of Western Music*. Shorter ed. New York: Norton, 1964.

Heartz, Daniel, and Bruce Alan Brown. S.v. "Classical." In *New Grove Dictionary of Music and Musicians*, edited by Stanley Sadie. New York: Oxford University Press, 2001.

Hewett, Ivan. "As Hopeless as the Others: Ivan Hewett Reviews Masterprize at the Barbican Hall." November 3, 2003. Posted to *The Daily Telegraph*, http://www.telegraph.co.uk.

Hitchcock, H. Wiley. *Music in the United States of American: A Historical Introduction*. Englewood Cliffs, N.J.: Prentice Hall, 1969.

Horowitz, Joseph. *Classical Music in America: A History of Its Rise and Fall.* New York: Norton, 2005.

Howard, John Tasker. *Our America Music: A Comprehensive History from 1620 to the Present.* 3rd ed. New York: Crowell, 1946.

Hughes, Rupert. *Contemporary American Composers.* Boston: Page, 1900.

Kiesewetter, Raphael G. *History of the Modern Music of Western Europe.* Trans. Robert Müller. London: Newby, 1848. Reprint, New York: Da Capo, 1973.

Kurth, Michael. Personal communication, December 11, 2016.

Lucke-Kaminiarz, Irina. "Der Allgemeine Deutsche Musikverein und seine Tonkünstlerfeste 1859–1886." In *Liszt und die Neudeutsche Schule,* edited by Detlef Altenburg. Laaber: Laaber-Verlag, 2006.

Mirageas, Evans. Personal communication, August 14, 2012.

Pousner, Howard. "Conductor Richard Prior Fears Lockout Will Cause ASO Talent to Scatter." ArtsCulture Blog, Atlanta Journal-Constitution, October 14, 2014. http://artsculture.blog.ajc.com/2014/10/13/conductor-richard-prior-fears-lockout-will-cause-aso-talent-to-scatter.

Ritter, Frederic Louis. *Music in America.* New York: Charles Scribner's Sons, 1883.

Ruhe, Pierre. "ASO This Week: Double Bassist Michael Kurth Composes a New Fanfare," ArtsATL.com, March 28, 2011. http://www.artsatl.com/aso-this-week-serkins-bartok-abbados-brahms-and-a-double-bassists-world-premiere.

Spano, Robert. Presentation at the Sixty-Fifth Meeting of the League of American Orchestras. June 18, 2010. http://www.youtube.com/watch?v=aWtZIuxILSc.

Taruskin, Richard. *Music in the Nineteenth Century.* Vol. 3 of *The Oxford History of Western Music.* New York: Oxford University Press, 2010.

Theofanidis, Christopher. Liner notes, *Rainbow Body.* Telarc CD-80596. 2003.

Wade, Charlie. Personal communication. N.d.

Wellesz, Egon. "Schönberg et la jeune école viennoise." *Societé international de musique* 8, no. 3 (1912–13).

Zull, James E. *The Art of Changing the Brain: Enriching the Practice of Teaching by Exploring the Biology of Learning.* Sterling, Va.: Stylus, 2002.

PART III

Identity

Tribe, family, mother tongue, race, class, gender, and age are among the most common markers of identity. These categories and many others tell us about human self-conception, means of affiliation, forms of expression, and outward signs of personality. Identities are often proudly claimed and boldly represented. Natal identities are just as frequently denied, obscured, and transformed, and in myriad ways. Identities are regularly constructed to expose or mask political and social objectives. It is easy to see why the term "identity" itself has at least the appearance of neutrality, since it demands to be filled with specific details in order to make an impression. Secret or unclear identities invite comment and concern, since both legal and literary minds thrive on the challenges posed by subterfuge. Achieving intimacy, the stuff of everyone's emotional life, is about unmasking feelings. Because music manifests itself in a generally positive, communal context for most cultural groups, understanding the musical identity of a person, place, or thing offers the opportunity to explore those complex objects, perhaps even to go far beneath the surface to discover essential things.

One can talk about American musical identity from a variety of perspectives. Indeed, many of us cannot keep from talking about it; accounting for personal tastes shaped by invisible forces such as music is an endlessly fascinating exercise. Perhaps surprisingly though, given the widespread human fixation with identity in general, determining how American music should be identified unfailingly as *American* is a frustratingly illusive task. The chapters in this section come at this challenge from many angles.

As we observed in the general introduction to this volume, Charles Hiroshi Garrett's book *Struggling to Define a Nation* poses critical questions about Americanness and proposes that deeper meanings are to be found in sites of contestation around the details of a given composition, performance, or creative figure. This is so because music frequently seems to possess an ineluctably magnetic quality. We are drawn, most of us, to some (or many) forms of music rather quickly after first exposure. Musical audiences and practitioners—from the least schooled to the highest professional ranks—invoke powerfully loaded language to convey the intensity of music's effects in words that often sound like the description of a first love. Clearly, identity is important when it comes to musical matters, and American musical identity matters to those who care about America.

Of course, just as we can fall in love with things other than individual persons, so nonhuman objects can have identities. Musical compositions, places associated with musical performance, even institutions or abstract categories, such as "Tin Pan Alley," "Carnegie Hall," "vaudeville," and "jazz" are words richly associated with musical experiences, sounds, memories, and fantasies that vary widely—to say the least.

Guthrie Ramsey's "Songs of Magic/Bodies of Music" (chapter 8) stimulates our thinking by placing gender identity at the center of an interdisciplinary discussion of culture making in the African diaspora in the face of the subtly defamatory but unavoidable practice of "racecraft" (analogous to "witchcraft," from the book *Racecraft: The Soul of Inequality in American Life*, by Karen E. Fields and Barbara J. Fields) and calling attention to the particular neglect of female actors. Guthrie asks, "Could women [whose images we can find but whose names we do not know] have been central to [Negro music's] emergence before American music became a viable commercial product?" Drawing also on the work of visual artists and literary scholars who can provide a richer context for music making in a "safe," often hidden place (called "Elsewhere" by Kevin Young), Ramsey challenges us to think of music as fundamental—functioning to define racial and gender identities under the old slavery system and the structures of American society that came from it. He suggests, "We have much to learn . . . from the division of labor in the musical communities of slavery."

One of the most singular observations of Thomas Riis's study (chapter 9) on the late nineteenth-century work of African American entertainers is the fact that these men and women of the theater generally took the words "minstrel" and "minstrel show" for granted. It was eminently clear to them, who were neither shocked nor offended by the institution per se, that despite the stereotypical equation of the color and word "black" with ridiculously comic behavior, the larger theater world in which minstrelsy functioned provided points of entry into a remunerative profession. Furthermore, it gave them opportunities to develop innumerable talents despite their skin color. A scenario that may appear as ineluctably racist to twenty-first-century observers did not so seem to its nineteenth-century practitioners. Modern sensitivity about the pervasive genre of blackface entertainment (where even players with naturally dark skin tones were required to blacken their faces with burnt cork) should not be conflated with actual violence and discrimination against African American citizens offstage.

Todd Decker examines in chapter 10 how racial identity was negotiated amid a dynamic intellectual coterie in 1920s New York. The urban milieu, postwar euphoria, economic prosperity in the North, and a new freedom of movement egged on by ever more available automobiles creates for Decker a laboratory in which to examine musical, political, and social developments.

Aaron Copland's Piano Quartet (1950) is the subject of Jennifer DeLapp-Birkett's analysis in chapter 11. The "identities and dichotomies" that concern her are embodied in a single piece of music but also have to do with Aaron Copland's position in the long-running contest between the styles of modern music and their cultural associations and practitioners. At an especially fraught moment in American political history, the onset of anticommunist hysteria, many American composers including Copland, previously wedded to neo-tonal, folkloristic style, turned to serialism. Formerly linked with Arnold Schoenberg, who lived in the United States from 1933 until his death in 1951, the serial idiom had been automatically viewed as the polar opposite to Copland's only two decades earlier. DeLapp-Birkett examines identity from stylistic, political, and personal, including gender, perspectives.

8 Bodies of Music / Songs of Magic

GUTHRIE P. RAMSEY JR.

Freedom, like fiction and all art, is a process in
which the dream of freedom is only the first part.
—Kevin Young

Something was terribly wrong among the black Methodists in the early nineteenth century. John F. Watson, a disapproving minister, published a diatribe in 1819 discouraging congregants from musical practices that they obviously enjoyed. His words, obviously meant to emphasize what he found abhorrent, provide modern-day readers with a sonic outline of how the music sounded, its communal nature, and its in-real-time compositional techniques, among other priorities. In short, we are able to "hear"—as best we can this many years removed—what kinds of music making were valuable to Africana people in North America at that time. Watson wrote with striking clarity about what he heard and saw. And unbeknownst to him, these qualities would constitute foundational principles for future music making in black communities. In his disgust, Reverend Watson wrote this now-familiar passage:

> In the *blacks'* quarter, the coloured people get together, and sing for hours together, short scraps of disjointed affirmations, pledges, or prayers, lengthened out with long repetition *choruses*. These are all sung in the merry chorus-manner of the southern harvest field, or husking-frolic method, of the slave blacks. . . . With every word so sung, they have a sinking of one or [the] other leg of the body alternately; producing an audible sound of the feet at every step, and as manifest as the steps of actual Negro dancing in Virginia. . . . If some, in the meantime, sit, they strike the sounds alternately on each thigh. What in the name of religion, can countenance or tolerate such gross perversions of true religion! . . . I have known in some camps meetings, from 50 to 60 people crowd into one tent, after the public devotions had closed, and there continue the whole night, singing tune after tune. . . . Some of these . . . are actually composed as sung, and are indeed almost endless.[1]

He was not wrong about them being "endless." Variants of principles governing these practices still exist today, undoubtedly because of the social power and cultural relevance they symbolize. Musical culture emerged from the context of the Atlantic slave trade.

In the nineteenth-century popular imagination, Negro music comprised both the music of the enslaved as well as that which circulated in the public sphere under the commercial rubric "minstrelsy." Slave music, as it was commonly called in the nineteenth century, received systematic and regular treatment in literature, although contemporaneous periodicals regularly featured articles that marveled at and disparaged the music heard among the country's black population. It is fascinating to compare Reverend Watson's sentiments about religious music to those in this editorial about the other Negro music:

> We cannot but regard the singular fondness of our people for this kind of en-
> tertainment, as one of the most serious hindrances to the proper reception of a
> correct musical knowledge and the spread of sound musical education; for so
> general and popular have these entertainments become, that there is scarcely a
> city of any size in the northern section of the Union which has *not*, or has not
> had, its band of negro minstrels liberally patronized and supported, for the
> laudable purpose of corrupting and vitiating this public taste, by absurdly bur-
> lesquing and exhibiting the barbarous and apish peculiarities of a much despised
> and inferior race, to excite the public ridicule and laughter—and in our larger
> cities, even at this season of the year, when the theatres and concert rooms are
> generally closed, and a high order of dramatic or musical performance would
> hardly prove sufficiently tempting to draw together even small audiences, the
> exercises of a "Brudder Bones," and the vulgar antics of his associates, are wit-
> nessed nightly by hundreds of intelligent persons, who would doubtless conceive
> it to be an impertinence, and feel highly resentful toward any one who ventured
> to hint that their attendance on such exhibitions was a mark of coarseness and
> vulgarity, or that they were not possessed of a correct musical taste, or power of
> discriminating between good and bad music.[2]

The writer apparently feared that America's musical profile and pedigree was heading in the wrong direction—a categorically "Negroid" one.

As I begin to set my sights on writing a history of the phenomenon formerly known as "Negro Music" in America (from the age of slavery to the present), there is no small degree of pressure to find new ways to talk about it. In this chapter I briefly suggest some preliminary routes of inquiry. They attempt to bring fresh eyes, perspectives, and questions to some familiar topics in black music history. New critical views about aesthetics, religion, structural inequality, diaspora, identity, cultural memory, and visual arts allow black music studies to build on the work of earlier scholarship, expanding what we think about his-torical actors long gone. As a cultural tradition, a scholarly topic and academic discipline, and as a contested conceptual idea, this music-making sphere—the individuals, institutions, practices, and the global influences that compose it—have been a remarkable force to contend with. Far from being thoroughly worked over and understood, these topics require that we consider new concerns that may both question and clarify our previous presumptions. To put forth but one example here, the musical practices of slave-era populations can still be excavated for knowledge about the past's historical actors and the social structures in which they interacted. All of this is far from being a done deal.

To begin, let us think about the language that the writers used to describe the formal properties of the sounds and sights they encountered. These snapshots of people attempting to discipline music bring forward some well-known frictions of the nineteenth-century culture wars. In the first passage, Reverend Watson shows concern for the eternal souls of the Negroes and their boisterous, improvised religious practices rather than the harshness endured by the enslaved black body. For him, "true religion" should be a quieter, less corporal affair. The writer of the second example hopes to steer the "coarse," "vulgar," and "apish" musicking away from the broader white public that, despite all such efforts, was uncontrollably attracted to these expressions, what with their audacious affronts to middle-brow sensibilities and aspirations. America's taste for the "Negro sound and dance," even among "the intelligent," has continued unabated to this day—this, despite the discourses of "madness" and sociocultural "infection" characterizing those early warnings. Musical praxis and social orders were considered close allies. The well-being of the state could be determined, in part, by "tasteful" bodies of music.

These early discourses of madness and containment that found their way into some of the documentation about slave-era music did not, of course, prevent African American music (its current rubric) from "spreading." One challenge encountered when writing a new history of this music is to settle on ways to break out of nineteenth-century patterns of thought framed by ideologies of race that were organized around crude notions of biological essentialism. When writing the "African American Music" entry in the most recent edition of the *New Grove Dictionary of American Music*, I emphasized in my opening descriptive paragraph the porous, flexible, and participatory qualities of these cultural practices rather than some of the exclusionary ethics of black cultural nationalism. African American music is:

> A term applied to distinct configurations of sound organization linked historically and socially to people of African descent living within the United States. While scholarship has identified a shared body of conceptual approaches to sound among the numerous idioms of African American music, musicians have employed them across various functional divides in American culture such as

written and oral, sacred and secular, art and popular. Although African American people have been the primary innovators among these idioms, due to mass mediation, the contiguous nature of culture sharing among American ethnic groups, an ever developing and sophisticated global market system, technological advances, and music's ability to absorb the different meanings ascribed to it, people of all backgrounds have shaped, contributed to, and excelled in this fluid yet distinct body of music making.[3]

Of course, throughout history, "participating" was ruled by structural inequalities that prevented black musicians from fully enjoying the same commercial benefits that others did in the culture industry. Yet moving away from biological determinism and its traps does not prevent us from rethinking how black people themselves participated self-consciously in their own sense of "black exceptionalism" within the harsh racialist systems that defined America's slave era.

In my view, future histories of African American music need to come to terms with the idea of blackness and what and how it means as a *social practice* in this story and not an "essential" (or biologically determined) identity. Although there are many great historical studies that unknowingly reduce these social processes to a state of biological ontology, I find the contemporary artistic imagination a wonderful means to destabilize this tendency. Indeed, musicians, poets, and visual artists have used the freedom that is the artistic impulse to balance the historical and contemporary, the material and ineffable, the personal and political responses to blackness.

In this excerpt from her poem "Today's News," Elizabeth Alexander concedes consensus and embraces a vibrant sense of infinity:

> I didn't want to write a poem that said "blackness
> is," because we know better than anyone
> that we are not one or ten or ten thousand things
> Not one poem   We could count ourselves forever
> and never agree on the number.[4]

Alexander relieves her art of the burden of defining what blackness is, even as she is clear about what blackness is not: one thing. Nevertheless, the historical record teaches us that blackness was derived from the fateful and globe-altering encounter among the colonial exploitation by European nation-states, the instituting of "nonhuman" status on the occupants of a perceived "Dark Continent," and the abundant natural resources of the New World. It was within this triangulation that something called *blackness* was calcified as a living concept. Furthermore, the ever-evolving, complex ecology of business practices, religious beliefs, cultural and social patterns, and migrations policed and attempted to stabilize this new idea.

The idea of black exceptionalism, I believe, was a necessary route to social equality if not psychological relief; religious practices became a communal space to perform this necessary act of freedom seeking. In her book about black spiritual empowerment and traditions, *Black Magic: Religion and the African American Conjuring Tradition*, Yvonne Chireau argues that the distinction between African American "religion" and something called "magic" was not always mutually exclusive: "These are complementary categories, and they have historically exhibited complementary forms in African American culture." Chireau's notion of religion is broad—it constitutes not only "the formal creeds, doctrines, and theologies of a church-based faith tradition but includes beliefs that are embedded in the ordinary experiences and the deeply held attitudes, values, and activities of members of a group or community." For Chireau, the actions that can result from these values fall under the category of magic, a particular way in which people could interact with the unseen and powerful spirit world.[5]

Why was there a need for this kind of magic in a predominantly Christian and scientific nation and context? As we know, the idea of a "race-based" economic system of enslavement and labor exploitation depended on establishing nonporous race identity as logical beyond its use for commerce. Once racial identity (buttressed by the related idea of racial "purity") was a given, it could more easily absorb the notion of scientifically supported racial inferiority, an idea that gained its height of authority in the nineteenth century. In their book *Racecraft: The Soul of Inequality in American Life*, Karen E. Fields and Barbara J. Fields have provocatively called this racial belief system "racecraft," which they define as follows: "Distinct from *race* and *racism*, *racecraft* does not refer to groups or to ideas about groups' traits, however odd both may appear in close-up. It refers instead to mental terrain and to pervasive belief. Like physical terrain, racecraft exists objectively; it has topological features that Americans regularly navigate, and we cannot readily stop traversing it. Unlike physical terrain, racecraft originates not in nature but in human action and imagination; it can exist in no other way."[6]

Fields and Fields argue that racecraft has attracted a body of believers who attest to its truth. It has permeated American culture since the first black people landed on these shores and continues today through the ideologies that reproduce structures of inequality in society. Through the actions and imagining of racecraft, individuals and collectivities reaffirm the historical traces of this system in everyday actions. Yet Fields and Fields insist that *racecraft* is not *racism*: "It is a kind of fingerprint evidence that *racism* has been on the scene."[7]

What were the enslaved to do—yield to the power of racecraft, the idea that they had subhuman status? Were they to dutifully build an industrial revolution and America with their backs, hands, and ingenuity without a trace of resistance? If racecraft—like witchcraft—is "imagined, acted upon, and re-imagined, the action and imagining inextricably intertwined,"[8] then how did the enslaved react with action beyond their obvious attempted revolts in the physical world?

The performance world of music, I argue, evolved as a practice that provided New World black people the magic, the power, and the gifts to create alternate cultural and social realties to combat what racecraft had perpetuated so cruelly. Making music with their bodies became an important way for the enslaved to affirm the value of their bodies beyond that of being human tools and targets for brutality. Their humanity was at stake. Far from being blank slates without history, as racecraft would claim, Africans brought with them, transformed, and developed a large number of cultural practices and sensibilities that differed from and synthesized with those of Euro-American origin in the New World.

Poet Kevin Young writes that "rather than stay in their place, the slaves imagined a new one. Remapping was for the slave a necessary form of survival—reconfiguring the American landscape as Egypt or Canaan in order to shore up (and keep secret) their search for freedom. At times allegorical, always coded, such remappings—a kind of storying—provided a set of radical metaphors for the slave's exile."[9] Young characterizes the magical elements of these survival techniques as a "hiding tradition," from slave culture to more modern iterations of poetry, song, storytelling. Although it is too rich a theory to detail here, Young's reading of the slave practices and their legacies in sound, word, and idea provides a template to understand their pathways to the allegorical space he refers to as "Elsewhere": "Elsewhere," he writes, "is central to the African American tradition. Conjured again and again in the spirituals, simultaneously ethereal and earthbound, Canaan and Canada, heaven and Harriet Tubman heading north, Elsewhere is the goal of going—framed in the remapping of what's here. A cosmology that is simultaneously exterior and internal, and what's more, eternally hopeful, however hidden."[10]. Indeed, the conjuring magic of music making allowed the participants to "steal away" and find an alternate reality that they could sustain, nurture, and pass on. As the following excerpt from George W. Crawford's "Jazzin' God" (1929) illustrates, Elsewhere was a hard concept to die:

> It is night. My errand brings me through a busy street of the Negro section in a city having a colored population of seven thousand. Suddenly I am arrested by bedlam which proceeds from the open transom of a store front whose show windows are smeared to intransparency. What issues forth is conglomeration itself—a syncopated rhythmic mess of tune accompanied by strumming guitars and jingling tambourines and frequently punctuated by wild shrieks and stamping feet. Above the din occasionally emerge such words as "Jesus," "God," "Hallelujah," "Glory," and then I realize that this frenzy is being perpetrated in the name of religion. A young man of my own race who has stopped in amazement turns to me half-quizzically and says, "What do you know about that? Jazzin' God."[11]

The uninitiated listener from 1929 offers an accurate description of the sonic event, but the goal of the storefront church service was to bring the power of God down—to fill the storefront and to fill the participants with His presence. And the manner in which the black church sought to coax God into their material worlds sounded much like the congregation Reverend Watson had observed a century earlier. And these sonic and spiritual approaches, many believe, have larger implications beyond the local worship. These implications are historical, global, and secular.

Writing in 1994, Joseph Murphy argued that these cultural ways form a bond with other global black cultures. Murphy and many others have argued that various cultures created by the dispersion of Africans throughout the black Atlantic world share "a distinctive spirituality" that has its roots in Africa and was developed in the slave and emancipated societies of the Western hemisphere. "It flourishes today," Murphy writes, "wherever people of African descent have worked to pass it on to a new generation."[12] Its most profound expression is found in the various religions practiced by these peoples throughout the diaspora. Although these religions obviously have pronounced differences, remarkable similarities abound among them. Perhaps the most prominent of these similarities is how each "works the spirit."

Working the spirit involves organized actions within a ceremony or service wherein the reciprocal relationship between the community and "the spirit" is affirmed. The work is physical and found in the combination of word, music, and movement that is used to circulate energy between a community and the spirit world. The spirit in Murphy's usage has multiple definitions. It "can, at once, refer to God in the person of invisible power, to one power among other powers that emanate from God, and to the spirit of a diasporan people, the *geist* that characterizes and inspires them."[13] The actions involved in working the spirit have empowered the African diaspora throughout its liberation struggles: "Within the ceremonial 'work' lies the diaspora's resources for developing relationships of wisdom, power, and freedom."[14] Murphy believes that anyone who has experienced contemporary forms of black vernacular secular music are definitely familiar with this diasporan spirituality. "It has crossed over," Murphy believes, in "blues, gospel, rhumba, samba, and even rock and roll music."[15] The sonic, kinetic, and philosophic conventions of antebellum religious ceremonies in the United States formed the basis of a new musical tradition. Despite innumerable attempts to appropriate or abstract the spirit of that tradition, it has resurfaced time and time again with renewed rigor and meaning. Other scholars concur.

Robin Sylvan's work in *Traces of the Spirit: The Religious Dimensions of Popular Music* can be read as a primer on how the magic of early black religious practices form an important element in later popular music. He writes that although it remains hidden, the spirituality, the religious aspects—indeed, the magic—form and bind listening communities devoted to popular musics such as rock and rhythm and blues, styles derived from cultural sensibilities based in the African diaspora:

> Thus the musical subculture provides almost everything for its adherents that a traditional religion would. In the heat of the music, it provides a powerful religious experience which is both the foundation and the goal of the whole enterprise, an encounter with the numinous that is at the core of all religions. It provides a form of ritual activity and communal ceremony that regularly and reliably produces such experiences through concrete practices, something that all religions do. It provides a philosophy and worldview that makes sense of these experiences and translates them into a code for living one's day-to-day life, something that all religions do. Finally, it provides a cultural identity, a social structure, and a sense of belonging to a community, something that all religions do.[16]

One of the standard critiques of this kind of thinking is that it seems to endow black people with innate spirituality passed down from slavery. Another explanation, however, shows how these identifications are self-consciously made through intelligent design. It is useful to consider some lessons from visual culture as an example of this culture making. I turn to the work of art historian Cheryl Finley, whose research explores how the symbols and themes from chattel slavery inform contemporary visual artists. She writes: "Without doubt the slave ship stands as the most prominent visual metaphor for historical memory of the Middle Passage. The memory of slavery has been used by artists as a strategy to reclaim the past, to resist cultural hegemony, and to forge personal and group identity in their works."[17] Finley emphasizes that this kind of historical memory work is a self-conscious act, that does important cultural work. However, she is clear that this is an elective, non-essentialized process through which artists may participate in a creative act and not a biologically determined one passing itself off as "nature." These artists deploy cultural memory to imagine their link to others who share the common memory.

One such artist to work within the paradigm of historical memory Finley outlines is the visual artist and writer Hank Willis Thomas. His work engages ideas about identity by critiquing both commodity culture and violence in African American communities. In a series of works that draw on visual symbols from slavery, Thomas forwards a provocative critique through powerful visuals that "draw on the archives of slavery itself, which he then links to contemporary representations of black men."[18] Some of Thomas's pieces draw on the visual and language of commercial advertising that he brilliantly inscribes with political meaning by combining it with iconic images from slavery.

In the work *Absolut Power* (2003), for example, Thomas collapses two images: the famous Brookes slave-ship icon—with slaves packed as tightly as sardines

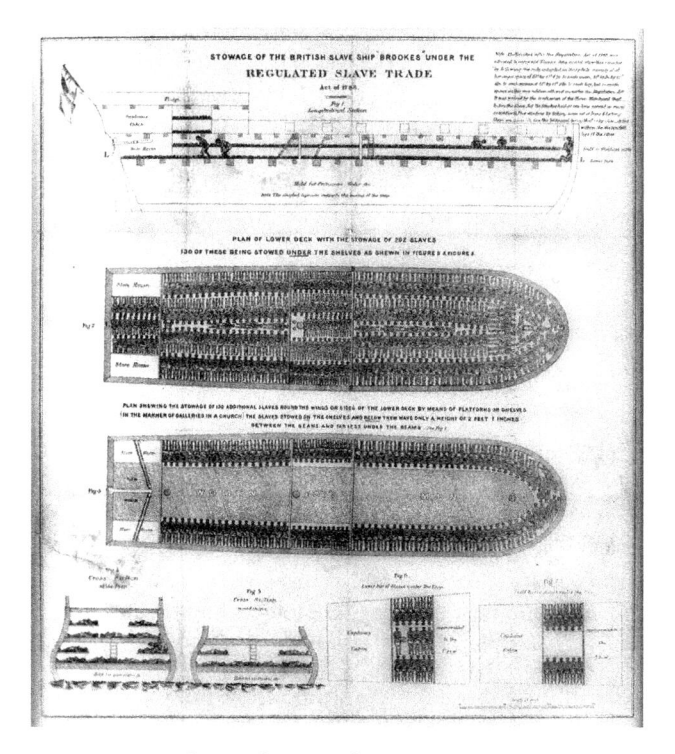

Figure 1. One of several pages of cross-sectional stowage documents of the British slave ship *Brookes*, published in 1788 and frequently thereafter.

in the official stowage documents—published by Quaker abolitionist James Phillips in 1788, and a bottle of Absolut vodka, rotating the ship image (figure 1) counterclockwise by ninety degrees and adding the neck of the bottle to the curved end. In the pieces *Branded Head* (2003) and *Scarred Chest* (2004), the artist takes the ubiquitous Nike Swoosh logo and comments on the way late capitalism has been complicit in the branding of young black men into a naturalized, stereotypical, and overly determined relationship with athletic prowess, particularly inner-city basketball. Considered together, Thomas's works here use iconic images from slavery as design elements in contemporaneous settings of stunning aesthetic power and a cutting critical vision. But what are the lessons here for music? Does Finley's claim help us better hear historical memory in contemporary gospel music, for example?

These kinds of connections have been critiqued and interpreted as well-rehearsed ideas about "African retentions" that were advanced some three generations ago by the anthropologist Melville Herskovits and others. What are we to make of them today? As an example, the following passages drawn from the fields of art history, religion, and literature may be reframed, I argue, in other ways and usefully applied to contemporary thinking about music of the past.

> *Flash of the Spirit* is about *visual* and *philosophic* streams of creativity and imagination, running parallel to the massive musical and choreographic modalities that connect black persons of the western hemisphere, as well as the millions of European and Asian people attracted to and performing their styles, to Mother Africa. . . . The rise, development, and achievement of Yoruba, Kongo, Fon, Mande, and Ejagham art and philosophy fused with new elements overseas, shaping and defining the black Atlantic visual tradition.[19]

> In the New World slave control was based on the eradication of all forms of African culture because of their power to unify the slaves and thus enable them to resist or rebel. Nevertheless, African beliefs and customs persisted and were transmitted by slaves to their descendants. Shaped and modified by a new environment, elements of African folklore, music, language, and religion were transplanted in the New World.[20]

> Anyone who analyzes black literature must do so as a comparativist, by definition, because our canonical texts have complex double formal antecedents, the Western and the black.[21]

A standard reading of these sources would show how scholars of black culture have argued for the artistic, philosophic, and stylistic continuities of an African diaspora. Yet when these writings are historicized "as practice" from the vantage point of the present moment, they become emblematic of a historical arc that encompasses the Black Consciousness movement of the late 1960s to the Age of Multiculturalism in the 1990s. The latter describes a point at which African American artists had "escaped from the aesthetic ghetto to which they were once confined, where the patronizing assumption was that they would find inspiration only in their milieu. As they move from the periphery to the mainstream, they are free as last to follow their various muses."[22] Although the writer of these words was describing artists, poets, and writers, I would say that it captures the sentiment of scholarship and the theoretical paradigms that emerged from "Consciousness" to multiculturalism as well. From the protests of the 1960s that spawned the establishment of the study of black culture in universities to the 1990s' voracious appetite for difference and multiculturalism, the historical writing often took slave-era cultures as a point of departure. Art historian Huey Copeland says it well in his study *Bound to Appear: Art, Slavery, and the Site of Blackness in Multicultural America* as he describes novelist Toni Morrison's *Beloved*, a book of this same moment. For Copeland, it possessed "inimitable conjunctions—of collective memory and historical fact, modernist lyricism and subjective fragmentation, gothic horror and cool structural analysis."[23] The same could be said about other books, from Amiri Baraka's *Blues People* (1963) to Samuel A. Floyd Jr.'s *The Power of Black Music* (1995).

Considering historiographical analysis, collective memory, and the explorations of the relationships among all the arts seem, to this writer, key to unlocking some of the mysteries of music cultures long gone. In fact, the musical past may be crucial to understanding unlettered lives and societal structures that restricted them. As Copeland notes: "The sonic has long served as a viable if not unproblematic medium for black folks to refute the falsifications of the visual, to make claims on the human, and to give voice to dreams, desires, and aspects of the self that would otherwise go unheard even if they remain unintelligible."[24]

In a provocative essay titled "When Malindy Sings," Farah Jasmine Griffin discusses the ubiquitous, symbolic, iconic, and literal power of black women's singing voices in the national consciousness. She writes that "the recognizably black woman—singing rather than speaking—is a familiar sight for American audiences."[25] From Marian Anderson to Whitney Houston and Aretha Franklin to "the anonymous black woman singing 'Amazing Grace' immediately following the Littleton, Colorado shootings or the Texas church shootings,"[26] the image and sound of black women marking time, framing ceremony, symbolizing patriotism and black rage and frustration is inescapable. Quoting Lindon Barrett and Eileen Southern, Griffin highlights the disrupting evocative presence that was the Negro voice in the era of slavery. "In New World slave societies affront to Western aesthetic sensibilities one often finds a further corollary in fears concerning the potential threat posed by the singing voice in Western society or polity. . . . The singing voice proves a disturbing announcement of the vacuity of African and African diasporic cultures, but nevertheless, also an announcement of a threat to Western societies and psyches."[27] Southern specifically points out the "spell" of black women's voices being deployed effectively as a trope in American literature, an evocative phrasing related to the ideals of magic discussed herewith. Griffin's essay is a call to arms for future work on black women's singing as "the originary, founding sound of the New World Black Nation."[28]

Again, literary and visual interventions might lead the way. Huey Copeland has asked: "How did visual practitioners reckon with the slave's position as a form of sexed and gendered property located at the nexus of Western civilization's material, aesthetic, and phantasmatic economies? Was art about slavery meant to point up or offer an escape from the continuing effects of white supremacy for black subjects on the ground, in representation, and within aesthetic discourse?"[29]

Can music be said to function in the same way? And what of literature? Literary scholar Salamishah Tillet's work on slavery, particularly her analysis of the contemporaneous coverage of and literature inspired by Sally Hemings, the slave lover of President Thomas Jefferson, may provide a suitable framing. Tillet

Figure 2. *The Old Plantation*, attributed to John Rose, Beaufort County, South Carolina, ca. 1790. Photo courtesy of The Colonial Williamsburg Foundation. Gift of Abby Aldrich Rockefeller.

argues that Heming "symbolized the potential integration of African Americans into the national identity—a nation over which she suddenly loomed as a sort of founding mother."[30] Can the music of enslaved black women be heard as foundational as well? We have much to learn, for example, about the division of labor in the musical communities in slavery. Were women primarily relegated to singing and dancing while men served as instrumentalists? Can well-known paintings like the one in figure 2 provide cues?

Clearly, we can benefit from revisiting evidence that many believe to be exhausted. We should explore two broad and interrelated paths of inquiry or, as musicologist Gary Tomlinson has characterized it in his work on music and Renaissance magic, "two distinguishable levels of historical interpretation . . . the archaeological and the hermeneutic."[31] For Tomlinson, hermeneutic "signal[s] . . . the conventional activities of cultural history and the history of ideas." Such activities include "the interpretation of texts so as to form hypotheses of their authors' conscious or unconscious meanings and the making of hypotheses about relationships among (and hence traditions of) texts." On the other hand, "[a]rchaeological history . . . takes us beneath questions of authorial intent" and considers the structures of meaning that make such a discourse understood and meaningful to an audience, be it a musical or scholarly one.[32]

Fortunately, the black masses did not forsake what Reverend Watson called "exceptional errors" in their musical preferences. The black populace continually toyed with Eurological songs such as hymns and popular forms to create something of their own making governed by sonic principles they found beautiful and life affirming. From field hollers, children's games, spirituals, and early blues, a robust and influential body of musical grammars emerged that has undergone infinite developments, attracted myriad practitioners from all walks of life around the globe, and inspired multiple and conflicting explanations of its powers. What we need to do in order to move forward, however, is to come to terms with the ineffable, magical—even maddening—forces that were as involved in that power as its formal conventions. We also have to better understand the gender dimensions of early Negro music: Could women have been central to its emergence years before African American music became a viable commercial product? Can creative and self-conscious uses of cultural memory in scholarship and art practice provide a glimpse of that power? Finally, an integrative approach involving new looks at well-known evidence and scholarship from previous generations, together with careful considerations of the lessons from visual-art practice—old and contemporary—might just bring into high relief Kevin Young's "Elsewhere," the place the slaves hid their most profound thoughts about freedom, life, and beauty. Imagine that.

Notes

1. Quoted in Southern, *Music of Black Americans*, 85. Watson, *Methodist Error*, 63–64.

2. "Cheap Music," 574–75. I thank Mary Wallace Davidson for generously sharing her research on nineteenth-century black music with me.

3. Guthrie P. Ramsey Jr., "African American Music," Grove Music Online, https://doi.org/10.1093/gmo/9781561592630.article.A2226838.

4. Alexander, "Today's News," 1.

5. Chireau, *Black Magic*, 7, 4.

6. Fields and Fields, *Racecraft*, 18.

7. Ibid., 19.

8. Ibid.

9. Young, *Grey Album*, 21.

10. Ibid., 53.

11. Crawford, "Jazzin' God," 45.

12. Murphy, *Working the Spirit*, 1.

13. Ibid., 8.

14. Ibid., 9.

15. Ibid., xi.

16. Sylvan, *Traces of the Spirit*, 4.

17. Finley, "Committed to Memory," 3.

18. Kelley, "Burning Symbols," 102.

19. Thompson, *Flash of the Spirit*, xiii–xiv.

20. Raboteau, *Slave Religion*, 4.

21. Gates, *Signifying Monkey*, xxiv.

22. Qtd. in Copeland, *Bound to Appear*, 2.

23. Ibid., 3.

24. Ibid., 15.

25. Griffin, *Uptown Conversation*, 103.

26. Ibid., 102.

27. Ibid., Barrett quoted at 107.

28. Ibid., 111.

29. Copeland, *Bound to Appear*, 4.

30. Tillet, *Sites of Slavery*, 26.

31. Tomlinson, *Music in Renaissance Magic*, ix.

32. Tomlinson, *Renaissance Magic*, ix–x. These two avenues of historical investigation, Tomlinson argues, "are not mutually destructive. Instead they are separate strategies that, joined together, can yield a rich, multitiered, and above all dialogical conception of past discourses."

References

Alexander, Elizabeth. "Today's News." In *The Oxford Anthology of African-American Poetry*, edited by Arnold Rampersad and Hilary Herbold, p.1. New York: Oxford University Press, 2006.

Barrett, Lindon. *Blackness and Value: Seeing Double*. Cambridge: Cambridge University Press.

"Cheap Music," *Saroni's Musical Times* (New York) 1, no. 49 (August 31, 1850): 574–75.

Chireau, Yvonne P. *Black Magic: Religion and the African American Conjuring Tradition*. Berkeley: University of California Press, 2003.

Copeland, Huey. *Bound to Appear: Art, Slavery, and the Site of Blackness in Multicultural America*. Chicago: University of Chicago Press, 2013.

Crawford, George W. "Jazzin' God." *The Crisis* 3 (February 1929).

Fields, Karen E., and Barbara J. Fields, *Racecraft: The Soul of Inequality in American Life*. London: Verso, 2014.

Finley, Cheryl. "Committed to Memory: The Slave-Ship Icon in the Black-Atlantic Imagination." *Chicago Art Journal* 9 (1999): 2–21.

Gates, Henry Louis, Jr. *The Signifying Monkey: A Theory of African-American Literary Criticism*. New York: Oxford University Press, 1988.

Griffin, Farah Jasmine. "When Malindy Sings: A Meditation of Black Women's Vocality." In *Uptown Conversation*, edited by Robert G. O'Meally. New York: Columbia University Press, 2004.

Kelley, Robin D. G. "Burning Symbols: The Work of Art in the Age of Tyrannical (Re)production." In *Pitch Blackness*, edited by Hank Willis Thomas, 102–9. New York: Aperture, 2007.

Murphy, Joseph M. *Working the Spirit: Ceremonies of the African Diaspora*. Boston: Beacon, 1994.

Raboteau, Albert J. *Slave Religion: The "Invisible Institution" in the Antebellum South*. New York: Oxford University Press, 1978.

Ramsey, Jr., Guthrie, unpublished manuscript.

Southern, Eileen. *The Music of Black Americans: A History*. 3rd edition. New York: Norton, 1997.

Sylvan, Robin. *Traces of the Spirit: The Religious Dimensions of Popular Music*. New York: New York University Press, 2002.

Thompson, Robert Farris. *Flash of the Spirit: African and Afro-American Art and Philosophy*. New York: Vintage, 1983.

Tillet, Salamishah. *Sites of Slavery: Citizenship and Racial Democracy in the Post–Civil Rights Imagination*. Durham, N.C.: Duke University Press, 2012.

Tomlinson, Gary. *Music in Renaissance Magic: Toward a Historiography of Others*. University of Chicago Press, 1993.

Watson, John. *Methodist Error; or, Friendly Christian Advice to Those Methodists Who Indulge in Extravagant Religious Emotions and Bodily Exercises*. Trenton, N.J.: Fenton, 1819.

Young, Kevin. *The Grey Album: On the Blackness of Blackness*. Minneapolis: Graywolf, 2012.

9 Defying Boundaries and Escaping Stereotypes

African American Entertainers in the Late Nineteenth Century

THOMAS L. RIIS

The shocked reaction of typical twenty-first-century Americans to the grotesque images of blackface minstrelsy—originally developed in the early nineteenth century—have led race-conscious modern viewers to avoid contact with the phenomenon and often to suppress its existence altogether. As a consequence, even the tip of the proverbial iceberg of bona fide African American entertainment has been deeply submerged in all but the most complete historical accounts. In turn, this omission has resulted in a pervasive aura of suspicion and discomfort associated with black acting, black masking, and the relationship between the two. Complicating the picture of suppressed evidence, and unseen but deeply felt reactions to it, are the well-intentioned but often misunderstood attempts to rationalize and make sense of such a long-lived phenomenon, Spike Lee's 2000 film *Bamboozled* being only the most prominent and commercially viable manifestation at the beginning of the twenty-first century.

The complex social gyrations that have worked to bring about this state of affairs are accounted for, to some extent, in John Strausbaugh's analysis *Black Like You: Blackface, Whiteface, Insult and Imitation in American Popular Culture* (2006). But Strausbaugh's lucid and frank retelling of our "mongrel" American culture, a past and present filled with verbal and visual jousting, needs to be supplemented by a fuller airing of the issues on all sides of racial and gender divides. Moreover, historians must come to grips with how fully engaged and developed was genuine African American popular culture at a time when whites were not much paying attention, during the last third of the nineteenth century. What Albert Murray once called the "incontestably mulatto" character of American culture[1] has simply not been addressed comprehensively in the forty odd years since he introduced this idea despite some provocative salvos fired from time to time by big literary guns, Ralph Ellison and Stanley Crouch, among others.[2]

Let's proceed then with a singular fact about postbellum African American entertainment forms, that the near total interweaving of black musical styles—among all economic classes and across all racial groups—was fully accomplished by the end of the nineteenth century. The documentary tours de force of Lynn Abbott and Doug Seroff, published by the University of Mississippi, *Out of Sight* (2002) and *Ragged but Right* (2007), "establish the essential connection among all categories of African American music of the period under study: folk and school-trained, sacred and secular, recreational and professional."[3] For anyone accustomed to thinking of "mainstream" traditions around 1900 as grounded primarily in urban Euro-American immigrant communities along the Atlantic Seaboard, the origin and spread of dominant images elsewhere in America comes as something of a surprise. By the 1890s, the general populace had certainly begun to appreciate and indeed assimilate African American music that had arisen first in the Midwest and South. White Kansans had ample opportunity to see and imitate rags performed by black piano players years before Ben Harney put ragtime piano on the map in New York City in 1896.

The seven-year period before the infamous *Plessy v. Ferguson* Supreme Court ruling of May 1896 is especially interesting for what it represents. Moreover, the era from 1889 to 1895 saw a culmination of developments from the immediate post-Emancipation period. *Plessy-Ferguson* did not end all black political advancement, although it may have seemed so at the time. But the onset of de jure segregation was one significant factor in keeping certain developments and crossovers in entertainment spaces safely "out of sight."

Such blendings, interweavings, and other "essential connections" have even earlier roots, however, and our historical memory is brief. Just one example from Laurence Hutton's fascinating book *Curiosities of the American Stage* (1891) suggests possible lines of inquiry. He cites, for example, the ballad opera character, Mungo, a black comic servant redolent of commedia dell'arte in Isaac Bickerstaff[e] and Charles Dibdin's very popular eighteenth-century London theater piece, *The Padlock* (premiered 1768). The role was written for one John Moody, a former resident of Barbados and student of its local black patois, but it was eventually played by Dibdin himself in London, later by Lewis Hallam in New York, and eventually by America's first great black tragedian, Ira Aldridge, hailed in the 1820s and '30s for his portrayals of Shakespeare's Othello opposite Edmund Kean's Iago.

Aldridge made a specialty of crossing liminal zones and blazing new trails. A world traveler, celebrated wherever legitimate drama was acted, he was much more successful abroad than at home during slavery days in America. But what is perhaps more intriguing about the role of Mungo is the extended text he sings in the second act of the play, which suggests more connections yet to be fully explored:

> Dear heart, what a terrible life I am led!
> A dog has a better that's sheltered and fed.
>> Night and day 'tis the same;
>> My pain is deir game;
> Me wish to de Lord me was dead!
>> Whate'er's to be done
>> Poor black must run.
>> Mungo here, Mungo dere,
>> Mungo everywhere;
>> Above and below,
>> Sirrah, come; sirrah, go;
>> Do so, and do so.
>> Oh! oh!
> Me wish to de Lord me was dead![4]

If these lines sound familiar to opera lovers, it may be because they point to similar sentiments, bequeathed almost verbatim, to the singing mouth of Mozart and Da Ponte's abused servant character Leporello in the first scene of their opera *Don Giovanni* [*Don Juan*] (1791), "Notte, giorno, faticar," and again in the even more ubiquitous "Largo al factotum," patter aria ("Figaro, Figaro, Figaro . . .") in Rossini's *Il barbiere di Siviglia* [*The Barber of Seville*] (1816), in which the barber Figaro's complaint strongly resembles Leporello's and Mungo's. Both *Don Giovanni* and *The Barber of Seville* were among the first European operas played in the eastern United States early in the nineteenth century, and they are regularly performed in opera houses around the world. *The Padlock* also remained on the boards in America during the same period.

Indeed, Dibdin, Bickerstaff[e], and the actors who played Mungo may well have intended this piece as a spoof on Italian opera, a popular target for satirical treatment from that day to this. At any rate, the span of years between the creation of Mungo and the death of Ira Aldridge in 1867 is only one year shy of a century, and the legacy lingers on. (Eighty-two years later, in 1949, through the magic of animated film, Bugs Bunny performed the Rossini aria in the *Long-Haired Hare*.[5]) The abused comic servant, now become a full-fledged trickster sans blackface, having changed the joke of course, is with us still.

Black and white comic faces, real and painted, are intertwined and complexly related over time.[6] The process of using, and especially exaggerating, another's visage, speech, or attitude in conversations with, against, or about them—whether that process is called insult, imitation, parody, borrowing, mockery, or theft—has deep and universal roots. But returning to the middle of the nineteenth century and the activities of African American actors, those who successfully "changed the joke and slipped the yoke" are plentiful.[7] Ira Aldridge, again, was a pioneer in this effort. Dubbed by the British press as the "African Roscius" (in mocking reference to a famous Roman actor and slave who served as tutor to Cicero)[8] for his portrayal of an Angolan prince on stage (in the then-famous play *Oroonoko*), Aldridge smiled and promptly adopted the sobriquet in all his future publicity.[9]

Closer to home, the most readily available avenue for an African American man to enter show business after the American Civil War was the minstrel show, a protean rebarbative genre developed in the 1820s and standardized by the 1840s by white American males, urban Northerners using burnt cork makeup, ragged costumes, African musical instruments, and eccentric body movements. Some original minstrels claimed to have actual knowledge of slave life and entertainments—but, as Lhamon and others reveal, this is a contested and confusing claim.[10] Whatever the source of their material, the men of minstrelsy's first generation certainly recognized an effective vehicle when they found it. The formalized three-part minstrel show (an introductory, gag-filled, topical dialogue and dance followed by a variety show and a concluding playlet) dominated the American comic stage for fifty years at least, until the 1890s. It has never faded completely from the scene despite high levels of opprobrium aimed at it from all direction since the 1940s.

The central minstrel show images form a set of hyperstereotypes by today's lights, but the full story of the rise and fall of blackface minstrelsy is convoluted indeed. Actors in black makeup go back to Shakespeare's time at least. Wildly dressed and noise-making street performers descended from ancient rituals are seen today in Mardi Gras and similar Carnival celebrations around the world. For generations tatterdemalion circus clowns have painted their faces with red, white, and black disguises.

Strausbaugh is right to observe the international and crossed-class roots of blackface acting, and adds, "But none of this—blackface in theaters, blackface on the streets, blackface clowning—would have come together as minstrelsy without the crucial elements of music and dance."[11] The combination of striking image, raucous sound, and peculiar gesture (the flailing, pointing, and twisting body of the original Jim Crow character, most famously developed by T. D. Rice) was a formula of overwhelming impact. Despite its association with grotesque mockery at home, its long life within other American stage genres, and its transfer to early cinema, the blackface minstrel man and associated characters flourished outside of the United States in radically different, and often less racist, contexts, and indeed continue to do so.[12]

The strongest counterweight to minstrelsy in the post–Civil War period among aspiring African American performers was found in the rise of commercial singing groups imitating the highly successful student vocalists called the Fisk Jubilee Singers. The original ensemble comprised some dozen neatly dressed and vocally skilled university students whose white choral director conceived the idea of a fundraising concert tour to aid their financially pressed school in 1871.[13]

As Eileen Southern explains, their choice to seek support on the road "was not a decision lightly made. The students were not minstrel singers; their program included no jokes, no dances, no catchy tunes. The American public had not yet heard the religious music of the slaves and had given no indication that it was ready to hear it."[14] Indeed, the core of their original touring repertory consisted of more formal concert selections. But the Fisk singers were a phenomenon that caught on like wildfire. Brooklyn preacher Henry Ward Beecher hailed the group, and Boston conductor and entrepreneur Patrick S. Gilmore brought the Jubilees east to participate in his concert extravaganza, the World Peace Jubilee in 1872. Despite the vastness of Gilmore's effort and its mixed success, the Jubilee Singers acquitted themselves admirably and achieved resounding popular and critical acclaim. Within a year of the debut, their fame had spread across the country to audiences of every rank and type. Before the decade was out, they had raised more than $150,000 for Fisk's building campaign, sung dozens of concerts at home and abroad, entertained European royalty as well as common folk in England and Germany, and carried a large repertory of "plantation songs" around the world. Other black colleges were quick to follow Fisk's lead, and "student" choirs of all ages and stripes flooded the market.

According to Abbott and Seroff, "during 1889 and 1890 heroic jubilee troupes [now professional, nonstudent ensembles] headed by Fred Loudin, Orpheus McAdoo, and Sissieretta Jones carried the slave spiritual choruses to the public stages of every inhabited continent. But during the course of the 1890s, [an odd sort of blending began to take place.] Jubilee singing faded into the background, while the popularity of 'authentic' minstrelsy soared."[15] So-called "authentic" minstrelsy—minstrel troupes composed of African Americans—was a revitalized vaudevillian product, but one that had already been established in the 1850s. Companies after the war were sometimes managed by black entrepreneurs and used many vernacular elements that had been spread widely and played to black audiences in black-run and black-owned theaters. Both black and white troupes included spirituals or pseudo-spirituals among their offerings. Women, as never before, were welcomed as singers, dancers, actors, and comedians on vaudeville, burlesque, and minstrel show stages.

Even when retaining the lampblack or burnt-cork facial makeup and exaggerated physical antics, "authentic" minstrelsy of this period was concerned with other theatrical goals besides racial parody, including drag acts and other gender-bending characterizations, sexual innuendo, physical (so-called "knockabout") humor, political jokes, and spoofs of operatic conventions. The real challenge for the African American entertainer on the make was to start at a place that the audience would recognize and then give the public, often their own black public, what it wanted to see, while still remaining alert to racist constructions that could be subverted in the right circumstances—like everything else in the topsy-turvy theatrical world of masked entertainment.

We know something of black entertainment in its amazing variety from the more than 150 actively publishing newspapers aimed at African American readers during the 1890s.[16] These papers were mainly weeklies, and the one most attentive to music and entertainment came out of the Midwest, a crossroads for all regions, the *Indianapolis Freeman*. "From its inception," the *Freeman* was intended to be "a National Illustrated Colored Newspaper," offering a "complete review of the doings of the colored people everywhere."[17] To fulfill this ambitious goal, the paper's editors deputized a vast array of correspondents, solicited subscriptions far and wide, and distributed their editions in "safe zones"—barbershops, pool halls, and other black business establishments—in cities large and small, north and south, sometimes at great personal risk to the individuals in more isolated and racist enclaves.

One multitalented player at the turn of the century, Tom Fletcher, has left us one of the longest and most complete autobiographies of a black actor/musician. We can derive from his account a sharp sense of what boundaries could be crossed and where the challenges for performers lay, much of which can be independently confirmed in the black trade papers.

Fletcher was born in 1873 and died in 1954 at age eighty-two, having completed his book, *The Tom Fletcher Story: 100 Years of the Negro in Show Business*, close to the time of his death.[18] Fortunately for our purposes, Fletcher lived during some of the most transformative years of American political, social, and entertainment history; he was well positioned to observe developments as they occurred. He also enjoyed a long, healthy period of retirement and took the opportunity to recollect his experiences, refer to his scrapbooks and souvenirs, reminisce with his friends, and put his thoughts down on paper. His is not a suave literary history but rather a lively and concrete story told by a proud and pragmatic optimist. Near the top of his account, he writes, "I shall tell what went on before I entered the show business and what went on after. I came along early enough to be called one of the pioneers, and I stuck with the theater or one of its branches all of my life from then until now. In order to give the facts I cannot afford to pull punches so I will have call a spade a spade. I am sure no one will be angry about the truth." As he warms to the autobiographical tale, Fletcher declares,

> All of us who were recruited to enter show business went into it with our eyes wide open. The objectives were, first, to help educate our younger ones, and second, to try to break down the ill feeling that existed toward the colored people. The Fisk Jubilee Singers were the first to carry the spiritual songs which were created from our very souls. The greatest trouble was in finding places to stay while in different cities where they appeared. They did most of their concerts in schools and churches. . . . With the Charles Hicks Georgia Minstrel Company, one of the earliest known all-colored companies, things were a little different. Hicks' outfit was a commercial proposition, and started out soon after the Civil War when bad feeling still ran high. The town halls and theaters were owned and operated by white people, many of whom had formerly owned slaves, so Hicks, who had a very good show, had very few places to play.[19]

Fletcher's narrative draws a familiar arc. He begins in the same place as Du Bois does in *The Souls of Black Folk*—with the Fisk Jubilee Singers—and, likewise, he identifies the Fisk students as seminal figures and role models. He presents the economic improvement and social uplift motives as primary, rather than basing his argument on aesthetic or expressive principles.

Furthermore, he includes the pithy and not insignificant observation that once postbellum commercial theatricals were open to black folks, performers discovered that "the town halls and theaters were owned and operated by white people, *many of whom had formerly owned slaves*" (emphasis added). That human beings and buildings are bracketed together as economic possessions, whether literally true in this instance or not, reveals a depth of understanding about how things worked in the real world, not to mention an entirely justifiable suspicion about the motives of owners in general.

Also notable in Fletcher's account, the meaning of the words *minstrel* and *minstrel company* are taken for granted and left undefined. The actual content of Fletcher's act or those of his predecessors is not his focus here, nor is it very much the center of attention or concern throughout the book. Everybody knew what minstrel shows were—or thought they did. While dismissing certain gestures and expressions within the form, Fletcher stoutly defends the minstrel show, blackface and all, as having opened important and lucrative opportunities. He most certainly does not see himself as an apologist for racism but rather appears to be taken up with what Lhamon calls the "lore cycle" of his art, in which a variety of representative images, gestures, poses, and sounds are "bandied about."[20] As Lhamon explains further, "Lore does in culture what stereotypes do in discourse. Both lore and stereotypes hold current beliefs together in a highly charged shorthand. Lore expresses a group's beliefs compactly such that the group does not need to weigh and consider all its ramifications at any given moment."[21] This is similar to Strausbaugh's point cited above. It also helps to displace the idea that all blackface imitation is defamatory.

At least as striking as Fletcher's affirmation of the minstrel form itself is the multitude of doors that he unhesitatingly walked through in the course of his career. Tom Fletcher left home at age fourteen in 1887 to become a traveling performer, touring in Ohio, Virginia, West Virginia, and Kentucky. He possessed a large, resonant voice that led him to professional jubilee singing groups. He teamed up with Al Bailey, also a singer who "doubled in brass," to form a tuxedo-clad vaudeville duo. Fletcher also proudly joined the cast of larger shows when the opportunities to play even small dramatic parts arose.

"Minstrelsy," as he understood it, implied a lengthy list of possible activities. He tells us in short order about his skills gained and demonstrated as: distributor of handbills, boy soprano, brightly costumed leader of the band, sound-recording artist, bass drummer, actor on stage and in early movies and television, eccentric dancer, and stand-up comedian (sans blackface). He was most definitely acquainted with dozens of fellow show people, women and men, who practiced every imaginable activity onstage: bicycling, snake handling, body contortion, hoop rolling, fire eating, trapeze acrobatics, and slack-wire walking. He knows and names friends and colleagues who were opera singers, dramatic readers, serious actors, and composers.

Fletcher was born in Portsmouth, Ohio, a town about fifty miles downriver from Huntington, West Virginia, on the way to the Mississippi and the American Midwest. The Ohio-Mississippi-Missouri basin and cities that grew and flourished on the river banks therefore form his domain. From Topeka and Kansas City in the west to St. Louis, Louisville, Evansville, and Cincinnati in the east, and down to Memphis, we might imagine an inverted triangle of land occupied by people consumed with change and movement. The cities and towns of this region were the cradles of black popular entertainment from the 1870s to the 1890s. In the early nineteenth century these outposts served as way stations for legendary frontiersmen and denizens of the river, the locale where in the 1840s were found the intrepid longshoremen and keelboat workers told of in Dan Emmett's "Boatman Dance":

> High row, the boatman row.
> Rolling down the river, on the *Ohio* [emphasis added][22]

During Reconstruction, former slaves and independent free black men and women wanting a better life left Mississippi and Tennessee and fanned out in all directions—to Kansas and beyond in the west, to cities of Ohio, Indiana, and Illinois, and sometimes but not always south to the Gulf of Mexico. The most convenient means of relatively rapid transportation was, of course, the river system itself. The waterways thus present us with a geographical locus with which to better visualize important intra-American migrations of individuals and groups, beginning in 1865. Not as dramatic in appearance as the heavily mythologized westward migrations before and after the Civil War, nor yet as thoroughly documented as the evacuation of Southern blacks to northern cities in the first decades of the twentieth century, this more modest shift of place bears close scrutiny. It appears to have been an attempt by moderately ambitious and pragmatic people to move themselves into freer but still relatively proximate neighborhoods with more entrepreneurial and political elbow room and wider scope for creative action in general.

When a self-identified group treks en masse across a country or beyond national and prominent natural borders, its people are apt to preserve and carry with them the essentials of the culture developed in their native habitat. Retention of a valued past becomes a high priority for "strangers in a strange land." So much is an anthropological commonplace. But when a migration of individual persons is more limited either by distance or by number of people—say, one family moving from a small town to a nearby city or from one port city to another—the disruption is less acute, possibly lost to our view. In this instance, migrants may experience less keenly a sense of dislocation from an earlier life. Indeed, individual itinerants may well have a far more positive and unstrained agenda for pulling up stakes than an embattled religious or ethnic group driven from home by tumultuous national upheavals.

The ordinary desire in a young adult male, for example, to move up in the world and seek his fortune in a faraway city does not call attention to itself in the same way that refugees escaping the ravages of war might. Perhaps it was these mini-migrations through crossroads villages and riverside towns in the American Midwest and mid-South that nurtured the likes of Tom Fletcher and dozens of other unknown black actors and entertainers in the Reconstruction era. The very unremarkable quality of its development in areas less densely populated and less celebrated than, say, New Orleans or New York may account for why historians have neglected this marginalized group.

Ike Simond, who describes himself as a "banjo [player] comique," is another case in point. His story provides a small but important window into the work of the post–Civil War generation of black entertainers. A precursor of Tom Fletcher as both musician and chronicler, Simond took the stage name "Old Slack" and wrote a rare and valuable "reminiscence and pocket history of the colored profession," published in pamphlet form in 1891. In it he recounts activities that took place a generation before those in Fletcher's book. Although it is principally a book of lists, full of names whose existence is mostly undocumented elsewhere,

Simond's booklet cites just these urban locations described above as being most receptive and nurturing for his fellow entertainers. He also pinpoints the late 1860s and 1870s as an especially high time for the profession and claims to have "watched its movements from 1865 to 1891."[23]

Besides blackface companies, other forms of traveling shows were also active in these decades. Touring companies giving a mixture of public lectures, recitations, and concerts associated with the so-called lyceum circuits often crisscrossed America in the 1870s. "The first [African American] concert company I ever remember seeing," says Simond, a native of Indiana, "was in Cincinnati in 1864." He thus locates a type of non-blackface entertainment among Negroes that is usually assumed to have developed later on and in another region.

Simond also notes that African American minstrel organizer C. B. (Barney) Hicks first assembled a troupe in Indianapolis in 1865 and subsequently concentrated his tours in the country's central states—Indiana, Illinois, and Ohio—as well as Pennsylvania and New York.[24] Simond is not the only witness to Hicks's leadership in the black minstrel tradition, and so his precise observations lend credibility to other uncorroborated statements.[25] A full generation before any ragtime songs were known or published, Hicks had become the most prominent black minstrel manager in the nation, leading his company on a three-year tour of Australia. He took his performers to Germany in 1870, at least two years before the famed Jubilee Singers. In 1902 he died on the island of Java while leading yet another pioneering black minstrel troupe through its paces. And Hicks was not alone. Simond notes five major black minstrel troupes on tour during 1886. When Barney Hicks's white successor, J. H. Haverly, returned with his all-black company from England in 1882, Simond joined the crowds waiting to greet them at the dock in New York. This vivid reunion of friends testifies to the tenacity with which African American entertainers had established themselves in the field by the 1880s. "Authentic" minstrelsy was the point of departure from which other boundary crossing could take place.[26]

Apparently, Fletcher and Simond were unacquainted with each other; Fletcher neither mentions Simond nor cites his book. Much more data exists about the leading lights Fletcher celebrated, although there are precious few up-to-date accounts of even the most illustrious, such as James Bland, Sam Lucas, Abbie Mitchell, Anita Bush, Ernest Hogan, Charles Gilpin, and Bill "Bojangles" Robinson. Fletcher names a few hundred individual show people, Simond well over a *thousand*. There is clearly more to be learned about this cohort, but the aggregation of names alone establishes the fundamental idea that a developed African American entertainment presence was making itself felt in large and middle-sized communities promptly after Emancipation.

In 1895, after Simond's account concludes, but before the advent of all-black cast musical comedies, an outdoor extravaganza called "Black America" was staged in Ambrose Park, South Brooklyn, and later in other northeastern cities, which claimed to simulate real-life conditions for African Americans in the South "before the War."[27] This kind of gargantuan affair characterized the 1890s, and "Black America" attracted enthusiastic press coverage in New York and Boston. That such crowds could be brought together at all tallies with both Fletcher's and Simond's accounts of substantial talent pools from which a producer might draw. Teams and shows came and went, but there always seemed to be a swirl of activity.

The federal census conducted soon after Fletcher began his career in the late 1880s reports a total of 1,490 Negro "actors and showmen" in the United States. By 1910, in the wake of the phenomenally successful musical comedies headed by Bert Williams and George Walker, Ernest Hogan, and Cole and Johnson, that number of full-time professional show people was counted at 3,088.[28] Most of these had their start in local theatricals, concert companies, small-time vaudeville, minstrel acts, and medicine shows. It was within this rich setting, before the musical comedy as a genre had even achieved a distinctly American profile, that all this talent mixing and boundary crossing was both possible and necessary.

Retired showmen frequently wax nostalgic about their time in traveling troupes, and so one might suppose that the record of "authentic" black minstrelsy is easy to uncover. But fewer than a half-dozen African American names are to be found in Edward LeRoy Rice's extensive biography, *Monarchs of Minstrelsy*, published in 1911 (six names versus the enumeration of 3,088 "actors and showmen" in the 1910 census!).[29] In this instance the failure to cross the color line in simple data collection can only be laid at the feet of white chroniclers whose inability to credit African American initiative fostered neglect. Looking at the careers of Fletcher, Simond and others described in their accounts helps us to infer how diverse the opportunities were for African Americans despite the all-too-familiar social barriers.

The two most important phenomena for black urban musicians between 1895 and 1915 were the advent of ragtime—including songs and piano pieces, sometimes lumped together with so-called "coon" songs—and blues songs, whose African American origins are not in dispute. These two defined types of music were permanently merged into the collective culture with the rise of institutions and industries to disseminate them. The striking rhythms of ragtime and the gritty, pathetic mood of the blues traveled around the world—as completely as the spirituals and jubilees of the earlier period had done—but the process was hastened by a network of passenger railroads, steamship lines, and the development of radio.

Within the contiguous territory of the United States—in 1912 New Mexico and Arizona joined the Union as the forty-seventh and forty-eighth states—

trains could transport whole casts of musical comedy or vaudeville companies across hundreds of miles in a matter of hours. If one built a theater in Omaha, San Francisco, Minneapolis, or Macon, the crowds and the shows arrived in short order. African American theater owners and managers were among those actively catering to their home audiences, especially in midwestern and southern cities. Business had grown sufficiently by 1925 such that a substantial reference book could be published—*Colored Actors' Union Theatrical Guide*.[30]

As well, transoceanic travel occurred more frequently than is usually imagined nowadays. American entertainers obtained a wealth of experience on international stages and by hobnobbing with the natives at foreign ports even before they arrived at the local theaters.[31] San Francisco was a bustling port city filled with music after the Civil War. Minstrel troupes paid visits to the Hawaiian Islands in the 1860s. Orpheus McAdoo's jubilee singers had become a minstrel/vaudeville troupe by the time of their appearance in South Africa in 1899, and other groups set out for tours of Australia, New Zealand, and even China. Dozens of players, singers, and actors regularly made the Atlantic crossing from the 1880s until the outbreak of World War I. The full story of African American musicians in Europe has only begun to be told. But there is no mystery as to how they arrived there.[32]

While proximity could be attained by rapid travel to distance climes, sound recording could preserve a more permanent history of contact with foreigners. In 1878, just five years after Tom Fletcher's birth, Thomas Edison was conducting his experiments in this realm (although his preferred method of using foil and later wax cylinders was fairly quickly displaced by more durable flat vinyl discs). The new techniques of analog recording offered a relatively simple and powerful new way to communicate with sound. Aided by the propulsive power of radio, which made its commercial appearance in 1920, a much vaster audience, uncontrollable by any small elite (whether publishers, theater managers, promoters, or tour impresarios), would soon be exposed to music and the spoken words of famous orators on an order of magnitude inconceivable a few decades before.

The development of cheap recording playback machines and radio also made a fundamental impact on listeners' perception, because technology moved attention away from the *face*—and onto the *sound* of the recorded singer or speaker. The dissociation of minstrel sound from minstrel image would eventually open the door to another kind of boundary crossing—the widespread acceptance of black singing style as normative for all popular music by the last third of the twentieth century. Once producer, product, and consumer were separated, all sorts of imagistic transmutations could also take place. The previously unified statement of image, sound, and gesture that had been developed by minstrel men since the 1820s could now be broken apart. Each radio or record listener in whatever space he or she occupied was free to substitute pictures from his or her own imagination to accompany the sounds he or she heard. For this reason alone, the new media were revolutionary within the American entertainment industry as a whole, despite onerous racial barriers imposed on black entertainers in particular places where their recordings were being made.[33]

To bring the story of intermixture and boundary crossing full circle, we should recognize that the audiences created for and by sound recordings were participants in new virtual communities of listeners whose imaginations were unconstrained by geographical limits. This radical reshaping of the audience via recordings and radio took place within a relatively brief period, and it was aided by the arrival of American troupes, especially black military bands, in France in 1917.

Two overlooked categories of infrequently recorded domestic entertainment, documented in Abbott and Seroff's second book, *Ragged but Right*, need to be mentioned here in order to round out the picture of African American musical activity as it moved into the twentieth century but outside of the realm of indoor theatricals.[34] These types are, first, the circus band and, second, the tent variety show, also known as "tented minstrelsy," or what Paul Oliver simply calls "road shows," which grew most rapidly in the two decades after *Plessy v. Ferguson*.[35]

These two entertainment genres, while not employing African Americans exclusively in all regions, were dominated by them in the mid-South and southeast. Circus bands, tented road companies, full-fledged musical comedies, vaudeville, and movies constitute the five principal genres open to black musical talent in the period up to the Great Depression. The latter three types appeared in permanent theaters, opera houses, and civic halls. They are fairly well documented in the newspapers and have been traced directly to the present day in theater history books. But the first two have been overlooked because they seem to be unrelated to the larger picture. But this *seeming* disjunction is illusory. The traveling circus bands and tented shows often functioned as laboratories or workshops, where skills could be developed and apprenticeships served by ambitious newcomers and thus were just as important as minstrel shows and jubilee choirs had been for the first post–Civil War generation.

Some circus bands gave small, separate side shows, but often activities were more mixed in nature. A report in the *Indianapolis Freeman*, May 14, 1910, explains how a typical band functioned and how thoroughly interwoven were the elements of minstrel shows.

> Prof. Pope and his band, gaily uniformed [working with the Ringling Brothers show], held a conspicuous place in the parade and rendered music that brought applause from admirers all along the line. The organization furnishes the greater part of the entertainment in the Annex. The fifteen men, with pretty dark blue,

well-fitting uniforms, are correctly arranged on a raised platform, seated on red-covered chairs, with the director at the center. Selections are given at the introduction of each wonder and accompanying each feat and at intervals. The minstrel part is exceptionally good. The jokes are all new and clean. The middle part is taken care of in a faultless manner by Mr. William Walker, while the comedy is splendidly given by Messrs. James Jackson, Walter Hinson and Whitney Viney. The singing is very good, showing to an advantage the well-controlled voices of the different men. The orchestra, led by Mr. W. E. Barbour, violinist, is particularly pleasing.[36]

Many circus band musicians traveled with coherent playing units over many years, even as the shows they appeared in formed and reformed around them: P. G. Lowery's Band and Minstrels appeared with the Hagenbeck and Wallace Circus and later with the Ringling Brothers. James Wolfscale's Concert Band was associated with Barnum and Bailey. J. S. Riggers Annex Band was affiliated with the early Three-Ring Circus of Coop and Lentz in 1916. L. K. Baker's Band and Minstrels played with the Jess Willard–Buffalo Bill Wild West Show in 1917.[37]

The range and longevity of all-black-cast tent companies is even more impressive. Pat Chappelle's *A Rabbit's Foot Company*, out of Jacksonville, Florida, lasted from 1903 to 1920. The Florida Blossoms Company, originating in Tampa, Florida, and headed by R. S. Donaldson, lived from 1907 to 1928. The most spectacular of all the tent minstrel shows was the brainchild of musical comedy veteran Eph Williams and his "troubadours, the original, famous, happy purveyors of mirth, music and song."[38] In 1911 Eph Williams and the Troubadours presented the show *Silas Green from New Orleans*. The framework—seldom have detailed plots or scripts survived—for *Silas Green* was probably similar to other less celebrated shows. A handful of central characters, including a scurrilous husband and his dutiful wife and friends, are repeatedly presented in a string of comic situations embedded among a plethora of variety acts and novel specialties. Retaining the title but changing the contents, much like successful television series do nowadays, the *Silas Green* company rarely missed a seasonal tour, with new acts added in each year, from 1911 until 1940. By the late 1930s Silas Green was described in one black press account as "an institution throughout the Southland."[39]

One of the strongest arguments in favor of digging more deeply into the history of these neglected forms of entertainments is to restore them to our understanding of reception. Tent shows and traveling bands performed for large audiences of black and white viewers alike outside of urban centers in a time when the majority of the nation's population resided in rural areas. The evidence is clear that the Southern shows were dominated by black entertainers and that the audiences were biracial, albeit segregated, almost everywhere. Aspiring white performers had many opportunities to observe what black show people were all about (and vice versa to some extent) if they lived in or near these inconspicuous settings. One cannot hope to write an accurate history of the whole culture without taking into account such large swaths of activity that never crossed the threshold of a big-city theater or auditorium and so failed to make it into published reports.[40]

Turning once more to African American entertainers who traveled outside the United States will clarify the scope of their impact. The rapid spread of jazz to Europe soon after its appearance in America has often been remarked, and the observation has an important place in music literature and reception history.[41] But it is less well known that European listeners were prepared *in advance* to enjoy the latest trends in black music because they were familiar with precursor styles. The rapid dissemination of banjo tunes, ragtime, and black popular dance well before jazz had been birthed around the turn of the century was accomplished, or at least assisted, by other living African Americans "on the ground" in Europe, some of whom had been there for as long as a decade before that.

Rainer Lotz has assembled a substantial amount of tour data about these pre-jazz performers in his volume *Black People: Entertainers of African Descent in Europe and Germany*. The copious tour lists, reviews, and vital statistics about sixteen prominent individuals or acts employed in Europe for long periods between 1890 and 1940 should stimulate further research. His set of capsule biographies is supported by extensive primary sources and includes lists of dozens of sound recordings made in Europe. Since Tim Brooks's *Lost Sounds* discusses only US records, his and Lotz's books supplement each other, thus raising further questions about activities on both sides of the ocean and providing even greater inducement to fill in the remaining gaps. British recording authority Howard Rye, in his introduction to Lotz's history, observes that a "very high proportion of records made by African-American artists in the last decade of the nineteenth and the first decade of the twentieth century were made in Europe."[42] How this assertion relates to Tim Brooks's estimated total of eight hundred commercial recordings made by African Americans prior to 1920 is unclear. Nor is the importance of Brooks's side comment that one hundred similar items had been released in Europe.[43]

While listenable recordings are hard to come by, their previous existence in large numbers is implied, and that is the crucial point.[44] *Of course* black performers were making records in Europe, because they were already traveling in Europe—as separate acts or as part of larger companies. To complicate the story of reception even further, it is likely that their audiences in Europe comprised at least partially of *indigenous* black populations who lived in most major European cities and port towns but who did not necessarily have any previous connection to the United States. Afro-European communities have figured little in previous American histories. But the links between Africa and Europe are ancient, and the legacy of nineteenth-century colonialism drew many Africans to Europe, where they became permanent residents. Here is yet another line of inquiry begging for further attention.[45]

Before bringing this survey to a close, I will linger a moment with a single performer, whose remarkable career serves to indicate just how much more there is to learn. A New Orleans native named Belle Davis was one of the leading pop singers, operatic mezzo-sopranos, musical comedy actors, and cakewalk dancers in turn-of-the-century African American theatricals and films. She was a nearly exact contemporary of Tom Fletcher. Besides her stateside career, she frequently toured and recorded in Europe between 1899 and 1929. She remained in England during World War I, came back to the United States in 1919, and then returned to France, where she died, having spent her last four years (1925–29) as the staff choreographer for a prestigious nightclub, the Casino de Paris. From coon shouter to operatic diva to recording artist to fashionable dancer—her resume impresses by its breadth. There were many others like her. Lotz tells us, "*Der Artist*, a German weekly trade paper for traveling artists, has references to more than one hundred black performers [mostly Americans] in Germany in 1896 alone."[46] Such active individuals as Arabella Fields, Seth Weeks, and Will Garland, toured as far to the east as Budapest, Belgrade, Moscow, and St. Petersburg before 1915. Yet these names are seldom seen today and were rarely mentioned in American trade papers a century ago.

It is not clear that the African Americans entertaining European audiences were always playing in what we have come to think of as the "hottest" styles of the day back in America, but that is really not the point. They were understood to represent part of a broad spectrum of popular entertainment perceived as "American," somehow inspired by the lives of African American people.

Musical style is brought to life by dynamic personalities attempting to please and delight audiences wherever they congregate. Performers use the most effective means at hand. There is no reason to believe that these international touring artists would have behaved differently than any others. Yet each developed a special type of exotic character, and all understood that this gave them a unique attractiveness. The music that was used to accompany their acts was just as varied as the acts themselves, as diverse as the personalities and the inner lives of the individual performers.

All performers, whether masked or costumed or caked in makeup, intend to attract attention. That is why they do what they do. They compel us to observe them and delight in their performance, and that is why they succeed. But perhaps the most compelling side of blackface minstrelsy, whether played by "authentic" African Americans or anyone aided by burnt cork, rolling eyes, clown white lips, spastic gyrations, or throbbing music, lies in its ability to both attract and repulse viewers at the same time. It seems that almost everyone intuitively grasps this, yet few can bear to hold onto the full reality of our multiple perception. Apropos of this challenge, poet Kathleen Norris recognizes a certain double consciousness as an unavoidable component of *any* sensitive or artistic personality. She reports,

> William James, in *The Varieties of Religious Experience*, quotes novelist Alphonse Daudet on the death of his brother: "My father cried out so dramatically: 'He is dead, he is dead!' While my first self wept, my second self thought, 'How truly given was that cry, how fine it would be at the theatre.' I was then fourteen years old . . . Oh, this terrible second me . . . how it sees into things, and how it mocks."[47]

The sheer volume of black entertainment material and the amount of exchange taking place among groups and individuals regardless of race—especially in locales outside of major cities in America and abroad in the late nineteenth century—cannot even begin to be calculated because we have yet to do all of our homework. The crossing of boundaries by people of double-minded vision—whether we invoke DuBois's "double consciousness" or Daudet's two selves—was a daily experience for a Tom Fletcher or a Belle Davis. Although we all have avoided, suppressed, and ignored the confusing tentacles of blackface minstrelsy and its cultural residue, the time has come to recognize how deeply embedded it is in the American psyche. Minstrelsy's effects as well as the related creations of musicians who never consciously used burnt cork or dialect or coon songs or any sort of racial parody cannot be understood until they are confronted head on and called by their right name—which is legion.

Notes

1. Murray, *Omni-Americans*, 22.

2. Ellison, *Going to the Territory*; Crouch, *Reconsidering*.

3. Abbott and Seroff, *Out of Sight*, xv.

4. Hutton, *Curiosities of the American Stage*, 93; Southern, *Music of Black Americans*, 120.

5. Daniel Goldmark, *Tunes for 'Toons*, 114–15.

6. W. T. Lhamon's brilliant interpretive analysis (see *Raising Cain*) of the work of T. D. Rice, transatlantic star of the plebeian stage, with the signature song "Jump Jim Crow," demonstrates just how complex the story remains.

7. I take the phrase from Ralph Ellison, *Shadow and Act*. His article originally using the title "Change the Joke and Slip the Yoke" appeared in *Partisan Review* 25, no. 2 (Summer 1958).

8. *The Times* [of London], October 11, 1825. References to Roscius as a synecdoche for a highly talented tragedian first began to circulate with the rise of David Garrick, who was characterized as the "English Roscius" during the eighteenth century. Thomas Southerne based his play's script on the 1688 novel of Aphra Behn, *Oroonoko; or, The Royal Slave, a True History*.

9. Lindfors, "No End to Dramatic Novelty."

10. Lhamon, *Raising Cain.*

11. Strausbaugh, *Black Like You*, 69.

12. Martin, *Coon Carnival.*

13. Southern, *Music of Black Americans*, 227.

14. Ibid., 227–28.

15. Abbott and Seroff, *Out of Sight*, xi.

16. Ibid., xii.

17. Ibid.

18. Fletcher's choice of the term "Negro" in his title confirms his sense of racial pride and accomplishment. Lloyd L. Brown, Paul Robeson's friend and biographer, recollects that Robeson (1898–1976) also preferred the word "Negro" to "black" or "colored," tartly adding that many young militants of the 1960s seemed to be unaware that the "word 'black' is more Aryan than its Latinate synonym, 'Negro.'" Brown, *Young Paul Robeson*, 4.

19. Fletcher, *Tom Fletcher Story*, xviii.

20. Lhamon, *Raising Cain*, 69.

21. Ibid., 70.

22. Constance Rourke in her seminal work *American Humor: A Study of the National Character* (1931) paints the "character" of America as a composite of Yankee, frontiersman, Indian, and Negro, the varied recombinations of which can be seen in our entertainment from the earliest days of the republic.

23. Simond, *Old Slack's Reminiscence*, 1.

24. Ibid.

25. Toll, *Blacking Up.*

26. Other midwestern cities prominent in Simond's account include Chicago, St. Louis, and Des Moines. (He also praises Memphis and New Orleans as being rich in employment opportunities.) He links nearly every location to a specific minstrel manager's activities along with at least a dozen troupe members, who are otherwise unidentified.

27. The players were housed in log cabins built for the occasion and supplied with poultry, livestock, and imitation cotton plants so as to demonstrate the manner of cotton picking in slavery days. The audiences were encouraged to meander through this ersatz pastoral midway before viewing one of the two daily shows. A cast, estimated at five hundred, was assembled by black entrepreneur Billy McClain (another midwesterner, a native of Indianapolis) for producer Nate Salisbury. The talent played band concerts, staged dance contests, performed "superstitious rites and incantations of the Voodoos," executed military drills, acrobatic stunts, and boxing exhibitions, and featured dozens of choruses and vocal quartets, all purporting to illustrate black talent and prowess to the curious Northerners. Riis, *Just Before Jazz*, 23–24.

28. Ibid.

29. Rice, *Monarchs of Minstrelsy*; Simond, *Old Slack's Reminiscence*, x.

30. Sampson, *Blacks in Blackface*, 10, 14, 44–48, 457–68.

31. No less a figure than Will Marion Cook, composer of the internationally cel-

ebrated musical comedy *In Dahomey* (London, 1903), explained in 1898—looking
backward to the 1880s—what he believed to be the true origins of "the rag accompaniment" for dancing. Karl Gert zur Heide quotes Cook in *Doctor Jazz Magazine* in
2005 ("Chicago, 1893, Part 2," 188:7–8): "This kind of movement . . . grew out of the
visits of Negro sailors to Asiatic ports, and particularly those of Turkey, when the
odd rhythms of the *danse du ventre* [belly dance] soon forced itself upon them; and
in trying to reproduce this they have worked out the 'rag.'" (Both belly dancing and
ragtime piano playing are famously associated with the World's Columbian Exposition
of 1896 and must have taken place in close proximity to each other.) Such a genesis
as Cook suggests is not necessarily far-fetched; it is supported by the close linguistic
similarity between the etymologically obscure word "rag" and *the* generic Arabic word
for "dance, dancing," which is "raqs," in common use across the Levant. Confirmation
that early American "rags" were fundamentally understood as *dance events*—and wild
ones at that—(rather than a fixed set of steps, pieces, or rhythms) is cited in Abbott
and Seroff, *Out of Sight*, 443–44. One such raucous affair is reported to have taken
place in Evansville, Indiana, as early as August 1891.

    32. See Wynn, *Cross the Water Blues*.

    33. Yet another emblematic pioneer in this realm was George W. Johnson. Neglected
even up to the present moment, his story is finally beginning to be told. See Tim
Brooks, *Lost Sounds: Blacks and the Birth of the Recording Industry, 1890–1919* (Urbana:
University of Illinois Press, 2004). Born in 1846, a slave in northern Virginia, Johnson
as an adult made his way to New York and lived as a street singer blessed with an
especially powerful *whistle*. Acquaintance with some early recording enthusiasts and
entrepreneurs brought him opportunities to present his specialty to a wider audience.
Two of the most successful and repeatedly imitated hits of the late 1890s were "The
Whistling Coon" and "The Laughing Song," both written and performed by Johnson.
His songs were sold as sheet music, on cylinder, and in vinyl versions in the tens of
thousands, translated into German, French, and Swedish. They launched the careers
of recording companies and other individual performers more conveniently placed
to profit from his ideas than he was. Sadly, Johnson's career declined as rapidly as it
had arisen. A star performer in 1899, by 1910 he had sunk deeply into debt, drink, and
obscurity, surviving only on the charity of friends. In 1913 a final insult that marked
his erasure from history during his lifetime is the artist credit line on a recording of
his "Laughing Song," which identified it simply as "an old standard" with no named
creator. He died in 1914 at age sixty-seven and was buried with twenty others in a
pauper's grave.

    34. Abbott and Seroff, *Ragged but Right*.

    35. Oliver, *Songsters and Saints*, 78+.

    36. Quoted in Abbott and Seroff, *Ragged but Right*, 162.

    37. Abbott and Seroff, *Ragged but Right*, 369.

    38. Ibid., 313.

    39. Peterson, *Century of Musicals*, 316.

    40. Abbott and Seroff, *Ragged but Right*, 335.

41. For a thorough account of World War I black military bands, see Badger, *Life in Ragtime*.

42. Lotz, Black People, xiii.

43. Brooks, 10.

44. Lotz, *Black People*, xiii.

45. Research along these lines is actively pursued, however, by members of the Collegium for African American Research, a transatlantic scholarly organization formed in 1992 to encourage the study of African Americans in Europe.

46. Lotz, Black People, 21.

47. Norris, *Cloister Walk*, 39.

References

Abbott, Lynn, and Doug Seroff. *Out of Sight: The Rise of African American Popular Music, 1889–1895*. Jackson: University Press of Mississippi, 2002.

Abbott, Lynn, and Doug Seroff. *Ragged but Right: Black Traveling Shows, "Coon Songs," and the Dark Pathway to Blues and Jazz*. Jackson: University of Mississippi Press, 2007.

Badger, Reid. *A Life in Ragtime: A Biography of James Reese Europe*. New York: Oxford University Press, 1995.

Brown, Lloyd L. *The Young Paul Robeson*. Boulder, Colo.: Westview, 1997.

Crouch, Stanley. *Reconsidering the Souls of Black Folk*. Philadelphia: Running, 2002.

Ellison, Ralph. *Going to the Territory*. New York: Random House, 1986.

———. *Shadow and Act*. New York: Random House, 1964.

Fletcher, Tom. *The Tom Fletcher Story: 100 Years of the Negro in Show Business!* New York: Burdge, 1954. Reprint, New York: Da Capo, 1984.

Goldmark, Daniel. *Tunes for 'Toons: Music and the Hollywood Cartoon*. Berkeley: University of California Press, 2005.

Hutton, Laurence. *Curiosities of the American Stage*. New York: Harper and Brothers, 1891.

Lhamon, W. T. *Raising Cain: Blackface Performance from Jim Crow to Hip Hop*. Cambridge, Mass.: Harvard University Press, 1998.

Lindfors, Bernth. "'No End to Dramatic Novelty': Ira Aldridge at the Royal Coburg Theatre." *Nineteenth Century Theatre and Film* 34, no. 1 (Summer, 2007): 22–25.

Lotz, Rainer. *Black People: Entertainers of African Descent in Europe and Germany*. Bonn: Birgit Lotz, 1997.

Martin, Denis-Constant. *Coon Carnival: New Year in Cape Town, Past and Present*. Cape Town: David Philip, 1999.

Murray, Albert. *The Omni-Americans*. New York: Outerbridge and Dienstfrey, 1970.

Norris, Kathleen. *The Cloister Walk*. New York: Riverhead, 1996.

Oliver, Paul. *Songsters and Saints: Vocal Traditions on Race Records*. Cambridge: Cambridge University Press, 1984.

Peterson, Bernard L., Jr. *A Century of Musicals in Black and White*. Westport, Conn.: Greenwood, 1993.

Rice, Edward LeRoy. *Monarchs of Minstrelsy from Daddy Rice to Date.* New York: Kenny, 1911

Riis, Thomas L. *Just before Jazz: Black Music Theater in New York, 1890–1915.* Washington, DC: Smithsonian Institution Press, 1989.

———. *More Than Just Minstrel Show: The Rise of Black Musical Theatre at the Turn of the Century.* Brooklyn, N.Y.: Institute for Studies in American Music, 1992.

Rourke, Constance. *American Humor: A Study of the National Character.* New York: Harcourt, Brace, 1931. Reprint, Tallahassee: Florida State University Press, 1986.

Sampson, Henry T. *Blacks in Blackface: A Source Book on Early Black Musical Shows.* Metuchen, N.J.: Scarecrow, 1980.

Simond, Ike [Banjo Comique]. *Old Slack's Reminiscence and Pocket History of the Colored Profession from 1865 to 1891.* Chicago: n.p., 1891. Reprint, Bowling Green, Ohio: Bowling Green University Popular Press, 1974.

Southern, Eileen. *The Music of Black Americans.* 2nd ed. New York: Norton, 1983.

Strausbaugh, John. *Black Like You: Blackface, Whiteface, Insult, and Imitation in American Popular Culture.* New York: Penguin, 2006.

Toll, Robert C. *Blacking Up: The Minstrel Show in Nineteenth-Century America.* New York: Oxford University Press, 1974.

Wynn, Neil, ed. *Cross the Water Blues: African American Music in Europe.* Jackson: University Press of Mississippi, 2007.

zur Heide, Karl Gert. "Chicago, 1893, Part 2," *Doctor Jazz Magazine* 188 (2005): 7–8.

10 The "Most Distinctive and Biggest Benefit that Broadway Has Ever Known"

Producing, Performing, and Applauding across the Color Line in the Twilight of the Jazz Age

TODD DECKER

Walter White and Carl Van Vechten often held interracial parties in their respective Harlem and midtown homes during the 1920s in Manhattan. Walter White—a blonde-haired, blue-eyed, African American man—worked in the headquarters of the National Association for the Advancement of Colored People (NAACP). In October 1929 he was named acting secretary and assumed permanent leadership of the organization shortly thereafter. White would lead the NAACP, the nation's most important civil rights advocacy group, until his death in 1955. Carl Van Vechten—a white man—was a famous novelist, magazine writer, and popular culture maven, a tastemaker who spent much of the 1920s pointing his white readership toward black culture. White, also a novelist, and Van Vechten were close friends.

White's and Van Vechten's respective interracial parties often included music. In 1928 Bessie Smith famously sang for a Van Vechten party, then knocked Van Vechten's wife, actress Fania Marinoff, to the floor for trying to embrace her.[1] White family lore holds that George Gershwin played portions of *Rhapsody in Blue* (1924) in public for the first time on the family piano.[2] Public barriers to racial mixing—a fact of life in theaters and restaurants throughout most of Manhattan—were lowered in the private sphere in both men's homes, often without warning to Van Vechten's guests. George S. Schuyler, black novelist and editor of *The Messenger*, argued for the fundamental importance of these gatherings in a 1950 appreciation of what he called the "Van Vechten Revolution": "Those who came [to Van Vechten's interracial parties] as mere faddists left as fellow travelers of interracialism."[3] NAACP founder Mary Ovington described White's interracial parties in a 1927 profile that emphasized his many friendships with whites who felt completely comfortable in his presence. His Harlem apartment had become, she wrote, "a meeting place for distinguished men and women who love their glimpse into a new social world."[4] White once remarked that for a time Van Vechten's apartment on West Fifty-Fifth Street was "the mid-town office of the NAACP."[5] The NAACP was founded in 1909 by concerned black and white activists on a basis of interracial cooperation. White's and Van Vechten's interracial parties were a sociable, lived expression of the philosophical roots of this historically crucial civil rights organization.[6]

In the first weeks of his quarter century leading the NAACP, Walter White conceived an extraordinary interracial benefit concert to raise funds for the always cash-strapped organization. The successful event sheds light on the role of popular culture in the multifaceted social-political transformation that can be broadly understood, to use an umbrella term, as part of the civil rights revolution. White and Van Vechten valued interracial contacts mediated by the literary and performing arts as important adjuncts to formal efforts to seek legal remedies for racial injustice in the courts and the Congress. White's primary focus in the 1920s and 1930s was confronting the scourge of lynching by lobbying for federal anti-lynching legislation. His narrower goal—for two months at the end of the Jazz Age—was getting blacks and whites to share music and laughter in a Broadway theater.

The making of the benefit is preserved in a 450-page file of letters, telegrams, memos, press releases, and contracts in the voluminous *Papers of the NAACP*, an archival collection housed in the Library of Congress and widely available on microfilm.[7] Formal planning for the benefit began on October 3, 1929; the event took place on December 8. The stock market crashed about halfway between these dates.

Work on the benefit was quick, intense, and singularly intent on subverting the rules of New York entertainment. The first memo in the file lists "Possible Theaters."[8] Eight major Broadway houses are named, along with their seating capacities, among them the Majestic (1,800; at present home to *The Phantom of the Opera*), Jolson's at 59th Street (1,775; since demolished), and the brand-new Ziegfeld (1,622; also razed). White was aiming high, imagining he could fill the largest houses in the theater district. When he thought Paul Robeson might agree to sing, White wrote Van Vechten, "I'm beginning to feel that we may need Metropolitan Opera House after all!"[9] A second memo, dated October 5 and titled "Artists to be Asked to Appear on NAACP BENEFIT," contains an alphabetical list of eighteen individuals and groups, an interracial roll call of popular entertainers from the Broadway and nightclub scene circa late 1929.[10] Duke Ellington is listed just above George Gershwin. The Marx Brothers, a white act, are followed by Miller and Lyles, a black act. Both teams moved from vaudeville to Broadway in the 1920s. Bill "Bojangles" Robinson and Will Rogers, solo acts (and friends) who made the same move from the two-a-day to the Great White Way, are listed in succession. In all, the list includes seven white acts and eleven black acts. It would be difficult, if not impossible, to imagine finding such a list in the files of any commercial producer of the day, be it Florenz Ziegfeld, the bookers of the Keith-Orpheum vaudeville circuit, or the managers of the Cotton Club. Standard procedure on Broadway, vaudeville, and Harlem stages strictly segregated black and white performers, with a few notable exceptions—usually blacks who gained fame appearing before white audiences—never the other way around. Whites did not perform for majority-black audiences. An event with equal participation by black and white artists was almost entirely unknown, although the recent success of the interracial musical *Show Boat*, which had closed in May 1929, suggested breaching the Broadway color line was possible and profitable.[11] In a letter to Van Vechten addressed "Dear Carlo," White referred to these initial lists as "our combined suggestions."[12] The evening's entertainment imagined by these two friends can be considered shocking—even revolutionary—and they knew it. Here was the chance to really mix things up—interracially speaking—and not in the confines of their living rooms but in a Broadway theater.

The event White and Van Vechten managed to create looked a lot like their original two lists. They did engage a Broadway house: the Forrest Theatre, a relatively new Broadway venue, owned by the Shubert brothers, on Forty-Ninth Street with a seating capacity of twelve hundred. It was renamed the Eugene O'Neill in 1959. Twenty-six individuals or groups agreed to appear at the benefit. Their names are listed in the benefit's elaborate program: twelve are black, fourteen are white. Table One lists these performers in program order. A near-capacity crowd was in attendance. The entire affair, onstage and in the house, was racially integrated. If one could travel back in time for only one evening to see and hear the full range of Jazz Age New York entertainment, the NAACP benefit would be the ideal ticket. If one wished to observe blacks and whites interacting in public on equal ground in the age of segregation, the NAACP benefit would provide a fascinating and rare opportunity to do so.

White and Van Vechten wanted their benefit to be the "most distinctive and biggest benefit that Broadway has ever known."[13] White's reference to Broadway says much about the audience he wanted to attract. The benefit was targeted at white audiences for big-time Broadway shows, such as George White's *Scandals*,

Kern and Hammerstein's *Sweet Adeline*, the Gershwins' *Show Girl,* and Cole Porter's *Fifty Million Frenchmen*—all hits of the current season; all represented by stars and featured performers on the benefit roster. Almost all the Broadway performers who appeared at the benefit were pictured in the 1929 issues of *Theatre Magazine*, the fashionable monthly of choice for this crowd and surely one measure of White's success in creating a benefit that might attract the Broadway audience.

Many white theatergoers in the audience had probably seen *Connie's Hot Chocolates* at the Hudson Theatre. Like most revues, this Harlem-nightclub-floorshow-turned-Broadway-revue changed over its run, at one point featuring Thomas "Fats" Waller and Louis Armstrong in the pit and onstage in the number "Ain't Misbehavin." The white members of Van Vechten's social set probably knew the entertainment at Connie's Inn first hand and likely also frequented the Cotton Club and Small's Paradise—this last the only Harlem nightclub that permitted racial mixing in the audience.

George Gershwin was among the first artists White asked to perform and the first to say yes. He was slated to play his *Rhapsody in Blue* on a specially rented Steinway piano: White negotiated a "charity rate" for the rental.[14] Gershwin would attract other midtown audiences: lovers of jazz-inflected serious music and gawkers at musical celebrities.

Another group the NAACP thought might patronize the benefit was New York publishing houses with books by black authors on their lists. White reached out personally to Albert and Charles Boni, Harper and Brothers, Alfred A. Knopf, and Viking Press, suggesting they "take space in [the] program, advertising books by and about Negroes which would be of particular interest."[15] In the end, none advertised—although Knopf bought two tickets.[16] White and Van Vechten were both Knopf authors.

Patrons of New York's Palace Theatre, the pinnacle of the national network of vaudeville theaters, might also have been attracted to the Forrest Theatre lineup. The benefit could not help but be a vaudeville show of sorts: a series of individual acts taking the stage for some ten minutes apiece—one artist was asked to sing three songs—and offering their signature material.[17] Vaudeville's close interplay between audience and performer would have been central to the benefit, and the gilded, intimate Forrest Theatre would welcome such interaction. Perhaps some performers took requests or expressed their personal sentiments regarding the occasion. The white dramatic actress Jane Cowl—Broadway's mistress of the grand manner—was unable to appear but wanted to express her feelings about the NAACP nevertheless. Cowl's friend Ruth Hale read a letter from Cowl at the benefit that aptly summarizes the role NAACP activists believed culture could play in the struggle against racial segregation. Cowl wrote, "With the colored people working so concertedly under their own intelligent leadership, seeking advancement not solely in the commercial world but contributing, as they have, so much to music, literature, painting, and the higher arts, and in their schools, teaching not only the trades but endeavoring deliberately to foster an understanding of beauty, I am convinced that the day is not far off when opportunity—the only thing for which they ask—shall no longer need to be asked for, but will be theirs by right of accomplishment."[18] This kind of public endorsement of the NAACP's goals—by a well-known white Broadway star—was exactly what White was after. Indeed, Cowl's letter may have been the only explicit description of the NAACP's larger mission spoken aloud at the benefit itself. A third memo from early October lists prospective "Patrons," mostly white luminaries from the arts and politics who were asked to allow their names to be listed in the program, publicly linking themselves with the civil-rights organization.[19] This effort proved less successful: the wish list of famous names overlaps almost not at all with the eighty-eight "Patrons" listed in the program, a roll call of individuals who had bought at least ten dollars' worth of tickets.

As this was an NAACP event, White could expect supporters of the interracial organization, both black and white, to attend in large numbers. This would be their night to integrate a Broadway theater by default. This group was quite diverse: the W. E. B. DuBois set, readers of the monthly NAACP magazine *The Crisis*, who would want to see the most respectable representations of African Americans; the "Strivers," black professionals living on Edgecombe Avenue or Sugar Hill in Harlem, such as the beauty-products businesswoman A'lelia Walker (who attended and hosted an after party at her Harlem salon, The Dark Tower); the light-skinned elites White had written about in his 1926 novel *Flight*, who formed Blue Vein Societies and didn't like to mix socially with darker-skinned African Americans; and, of course, white philanthropists and progressives, such as Joel Spingarn and Ovington, who in large measure still defined the NAACP's governance in the 1920s. NAACP stalwarts were called upon to publicly support the December benefit by purchasing boxes in the Forrest Theatre. For a black theater party to enter through the lobby and stake a claim to these spaces would have been noteworthy. Most of the tickets were sold privately by the Committee of One Hundred, Women's Auxiliary of the NAACP—a group of black women, to judge by their home addresses above 130th Street. They accomplished their task so effectively that expensive advertising was unnecessary.

It also contributed to Gershwin being a no-show. In a telegram to White, sent early on the morning after the event, Gershwin reported having forgotten where the benefit was being held, then riding around in a taxi for "THE BETTER PART OF ONE HOUR" in search of the right theater, unable to find any clues in the day's newspapers.[20] Presumably, Gershwin meant the city's white dailies: black newspapers—all weeklies—covered the benefit but not on the day.[21] A single advertisement for the benefit appeared in the *New York Amsterdam News* (see figure 1). NAACP press officer Arthur Seligmann tried without success to get white newspapers to cover the event. The file is filled with press releases and notes to media luminaries: two examples suggest a campaign of subtle string pulling. Seligmann sent a note to playwright George S. Kaufman in his capacity as the dramatic editor of the *New York Times*, pleading, "Anything that you can do with the accompanying matter will accrue to the benefit of human society."[22] Just days before the benefit, Seligmann wrote famed *New York World* columnist F. P. A., asking him to "PLEASE ANSWER IN A LOUD, CLEAR VOICE" that he was coming to the benefit.[23] It was to no avail. Even master of ceremonies Heywood Broun, a syndicated columnist, neglected to mention the benefit in his column. After the benefit, the Associated Press distributed a short description of the event as part of the "society news of New York," one indication a fashionable white audience was in attendance. Seligmann re-released the AP text, together with a list of white dailies that ran the item.[24]

White and Van Vechten's benefit argued that black and white performers should share the same status on the national stage, that black and white patrons should enjoy these performers side by side, and that racial integration, beginning in the sphere of the arts, was a powerful historical force that would, in the words of the well-known spiritual that Van Vechten invoked in his note in the benefit program, "Keep A-Inchin' Along." White and Van Vechten envisioned the benefit as a place where personal and social transformation might occur within the hearts and minds of the interracial audience they sought—and did—attract. Both men had included scenes in their novels where the racial attitudes of individual characters were fundamentally changed by the experience of a public musical performance.[25] They believed in the power of performance and, of course, they hoped to raise money for and heighten the visibility of the NAACP. The event netted just shy of two thousand dollars.[26]

White and Van Vechten's benefit rewards close examination. The archival evidence is unusually rich in detail, opening a window on the show-making process and capturing the private voices of public figures. The roster of performers is richly varied and historically significant, with individuals both famous still and long forgotten. Musical worlds and personalities typically separated by scholars rubbed shoulders at the benefit before a highly unusual interracial audience. The time and place are dramatic, too—a Broadway theater, five weeks after the economic collapse that ended the Jazz Age. And the goal was socially important: to integrate American entertainment, stage and house, backstage and lobby, for one night only, decades before the better-known challenges to racial segregation that arose with the advent of rock-and-roll.

How might the benefit contribute to the study of America's musical life? One approach would mine the archive for anecdotes to insert into established

Table 1. Performers at the December 8, 1929, NAACP Benefit

Credits in quotes are taken from the benefit program.
Performers listed in square brackets did not appear based on evidence in the benefit file.
Asterisks mark performers not mentioned in the post-benefit press release (f773).

As listed in program:

*Eubie Blake (piano) and Broadway Jones (singer) / vaudeville musical team ["Moiret and Fredi" / Al Moore and Fredi Washington, ballroom dance team]

Clifton Webb / Broadway song and dance man, currently in *The Little Show*

Taylor Gordon (singer) and J. Rosamond Johnson (piano) / concertized together in U.S. and Europe, Johnson published the two-volume *Book of American Negro Spirituals*

*Jack Engliss / Broadway leading man, currently in *Good News*

Alberta Hunter / "London *Showboat*"

Margaret Wycherly / "One of the greatest actresses on the English speaking stage"

Duke Ellington and his Cotton Club Orchestra, with the Cotton Club floorshow

Clara Smith / blues singer on stage and record

Albert Carroll / female impersonator in recurring revue *Grand Street Follies*

E. J. McNamara / comedian, star of *Strictly Dishonorable*, hit play of the season [Gershwin, George / "*Rhapsody in Blue* and Composer for Broadway"]

Libby Holman, accompanied by Ralph Rainger / appearing in *The Little Show*

Baby Cox, Edith Wilson, *"Jazzlips" Richardson, *Hot Chocolates Girls / stars of the Broadway show *Connie's Hot Chocolates* (which closed a week after the benefit)[+]

Helen Morgan / "*Showboat, Sweet Adeline*, film *Applause*"

*Richard Hale / "Orpheus"

*Frances Williams / Broadway musical star, appearing in *George White's Scandals*.

Charles Butterworth / Broadway leading man, appearing in *Sweet Adeline*

*Evelyn Hoey / Broadway featured performer, appearing in *Fifty Million Frenchmen*,

Jimmy Durante, with Clayton and Jackson / vaudeville trio, appearing in *Show Girl*

Daniel L. Haynes / singer and actor, recently seen in *Hallelujah*, the first all-black cast film

*Betty Compton / Broadway leading lady, appearing in *Fifty Million Frenchmen*

Utica Jubilee Singers / male quintet from a Southern technical college, heard on NBC radio

Not listed in program but included in post-benefit press release:

Bobbe Arnst (singer), accompanied by Johnny Green

The Dixie Singers

[+] Press release lists Florence Parham among performers from *Connie's Hot Chocolates*.

narratives already central to American musical history. Gershwin's tour around Broadway in a taxi has been noted. The benefit file also tells a slightly scary tale of a dispute over money between White's office and the mobsters who ran the Cotton Club, who had bused Ellington and the club's floor show to and from the event and expected reimbursement from the NAACP. Short version: White paid up on the spot and appealed to Ellington for help.[27] But such tidbits—tantalizing as they are—fail to take in the benefit as an event, an experience, as a night to remember when the sum was greater than its parts. The remainder of this chapter describes and analyzes the benefit as a whole in an effort to highlight the ways White and Van Vechten—two inveterate mixers—challenged their interracial audience to listen across the color line. The challenge of such a survey is to communicate the benefit's diversity—the surprising parade of stars and near-stars—while also lingering over individual moments in the evening's entertainment that bring the much-studied Jazz Age into fresh and surprising focus.[28] Accounting for the full benefit roster forces the historian to deal with the complete spectrum of popular performance, challenging the persistent segregation of black and white that has characterized scholarship on Broadway and popular culture. And the audience, in all its diversity, plays a role as well in this tale of a unique night in a Broadway theater.

Masters of Ceremonies

White fervently hoped that Bill Robinson would be the benefit's master of ceremonies, introducing each successive act and tying the whole together. Robinson was the first black man to succeed as a "single" performing before white audiences without blacking up.[29] Robinson's precursor, the comedian Bert Williams, headlined with the *Ziegfeld Follies* from 1910 to 1919 and spent his entire career in blackface, albeit in a restrained, unique persona that gave the lie to minstrelsy. By the end of the 1920s, Robinson had redefined the black male single, building a career that centered on his skill as a tap dancer and a set of Jazz Age idioms rooted in black rhythm. These same idioms were taken up by white entertainers and songwriters, such as Gershwin, in the 1920s. Indeed, Robinson's signature tune—"Doin' the New Low Down" from the black-cast Broadway revue *Blackbirds of 1928* (closed June 1929)—could easily have been performed by a white singer. The song's lyric, by Dorothy Fields, hit all the touchstones of 1920s "jazz" lingo—"pep," "hot," "crazy," "swing"—without tagging the singer as black or white. These were words of the moment, and Robinson was the most gracious of black models, addressing his audience with the spoken invitation "Listen, good folks" at the start of his 1928 recording of the tune. This tone of gracious, up-to-date welcome—hitting a note of deference that tapped into the entertainer's desire to please rather than the history of racial humiliation of black

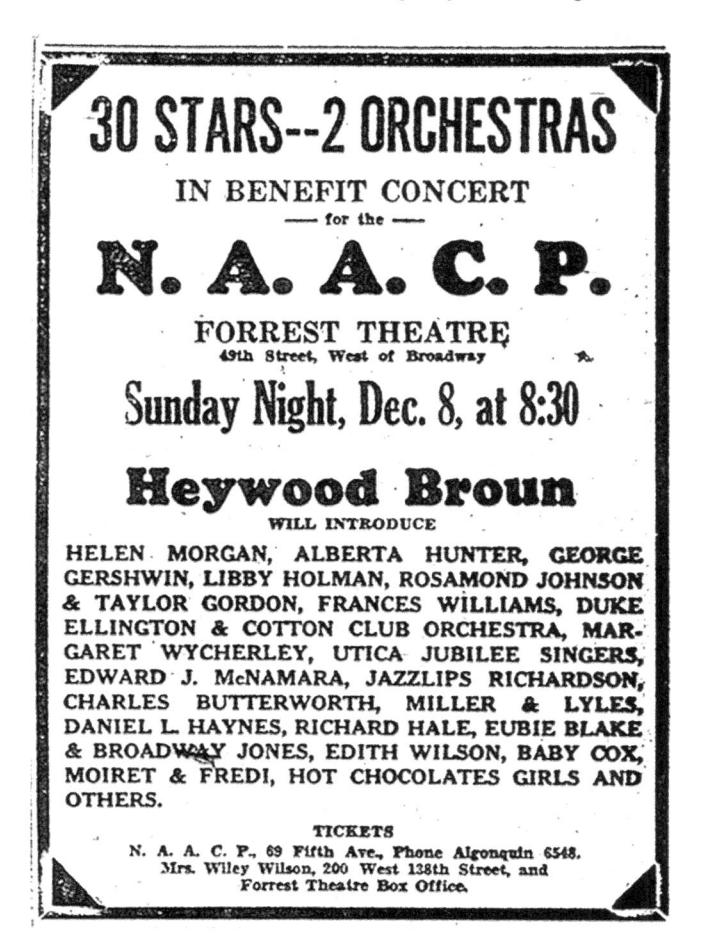

Figure 1. *New York Amsterdam News*, December 4, 1929

men before whites—was exactly what White wanted for the benefit. Robinson had to decline the invitation. He was on the road playing big-time vaudeville and couldn't make it to New York for the night. White held out hopes for Robinson's participation until December 2, the printing deadline for the program.[30]

Had Robinson been the master of ceremonies, the entire benefit would have taken on a different aspect. Robinson would have been responsible for leading the audience and his fellow performers through the evening, introducing black and white, male and female performers, relating to everyone from his virtually unique position as a black musical star embodying the cultural moment and equally beloved by blacks and whites. Here, on an integrated musical stage, Robinson might have engaged in easy banter with a white woman—such as

Helen Morgan—in ways interracial book shows like *Show Boat* wouldn't permit. Perhaps only Robinson had the stature to do this at the time, and only in the italicized realm of the popular musical stage. But even there, such a public leadership role for a black man would have been provocative.

In the end, Heywood Broun served as master of ceremonies. A nationally syndicated, white, liberal columnist, Broun pioneered the "free thought column that may disagree with the newspaper in which it is published."[31] He ran unsuccessfully for Congress in 1930 with NAACP support. A post-benefit NAACP press release praised Broun's "wit and tact"—suggesting Broun successfully negotiated delicate matters of etiquette—and his occasional assistance to stagehands moving the piano onstage, "much to the amusement of the audience." He was credited with keeping the benefit moving "without a single delay or hitch of any kind."[32] Like Van Vechten, Broun was a well-known party host. In his memoir *Born to Be*, the African American singer Taylor Gordon—who sang at the benefit—described a party *chez* Broun honoring "some Big English Lord and Lady." When the great ones arrived, all present began "bowing and scraping" in semi-silent awe. The host, by contrast, greeted his visitors from his prior prone position lying on the floor, as if he were "the only emancipated American."[33] Broun's easy rapport with an interracial cast and audience can be imagined along these lines.

Opening Acts

"So much, as you of course know, depends upon a program of this sort starting off on time and its going with a bang. This first number is so important that, frankly, I am a bit apprehensive about entrusting it to anyone except yourself."[34] White wrote these words to Eubie Blake, and Blake and his partner at the time, Broadway Jones, are the first performers listed in the benefit program. Their musical act, "the marriage of voice and piano," was familiar to black and white audiences alike. Honed to a science after long years with singer Noble Sissle, Blake's approach was similar to Robinson's: setting blackface aside and donning evening clothes, Blake offered casual yet urbane music and patter that worked against minstrel stereotypes. Blake also brought his prodigious piano skills to the stage, demonstrating a mastery of the instrument that spoke for his genuine musical talent. He was, in the words of one black newspaper, "a versatile musician"—a serious player to be enjoyed by discriminating listeners.[35] Blake worked in tandem with a vocalist—originally Sissle, now Jones—who stood in the crook of or next to the piano, easily shifting focus from the audience to Blake, an arrangement that fostered an intimacy that was a hallmark of the act.[36] In 1929 Blake and Jones were touring as the only black act in an otherwise white-cast revue. "Ol' Man River" from *Show Boat* was among the songs they were offering.[37]

Blake, like Robinson, was completely at home on the big-time variety stage; his relaxed manner put white audiences at ease, no doubt one reason White wanted Blake to start off the benefit. But the attraction of Blake for black audiences was important as well. Top-tier black performers working the big time often had few chances to perform for black audiences in black venues. A few weeks after the benefit, Blake and Jones headlined a revue titled *The Birth of Syncopation* at Harlem's Lafayette Theater, assembled by black producer Laurence Deas. Advance coverage of the revue highlighted Blake and Jones's busy schedule working for the white "Keith and Shubert organizations" and the performers' "months of effort . . . to get a 'leave of absence' to gratify their anxiety to appear [in Harlem] before the audiences they love best."[38] This shift between white and black audiences was rendered moot at the benefit, where a mixed audience could enjoy the same act in the symbolically resonant space of a midtown theater. The significance of the interracial NAACP producing the event would not have been lost on those in the audience who were committed to civil-rights activism.

The second act in the program didn't show up. The African American ballroom-dance team of Moiret and Fredi sent a telegram to the Forrest Theatre less than two hours before curtain time: "SORRY CANNOT BE WITH YOU TONIGHT FREDI ILL HOPE AFFAIR IS TREMENDOUS SUCCESS."[39] Moiret and Fredi would have brought Continental cachet to the benefit. The pair had danced across Europe—from London to Berlin and Hamburg to Cannes—in nightclub venues where racial segregation did not limit black performers and patrons as it did in the United States. White had seen the duo in Monte Carlo. Moiret and Fredi would have been somewhat familiar with dancing before interracial audiences.

In the absence of Moiret and Fredi, the show went on with the first white performer on the bill: Clifton Webb, a vaudeville and Broadway veteran who was finally hitting it big in *The Little Show*, where he was singing tunes like "I Guess I'll Have to Change My Plan" and doing sketch comedy (some of the sketches authored by George S. Kaufman, a signature comic voice of the decade). Here, early in the benefit, white Broadway's ironic, brittle, modern comic style took its first turn.

Blake and Jones, followed by Webb, initiated a programming strategy of alternating black and white performers. The first six acts—three white, three black—mapped out the interracial terrain of popular culture the NAACP had assembled for the evening. Webb's Broadway songs were followed by concert spirituals from the African American duo of singer Taylor Gordon with J. Rosamond Johnson at the piano, after which the benefit turned toward Tin Pan Alley with Jack Engliss, a white radio performer and star of the college musical *Good News*. (Engliss participated on the condition he would go on between nine and nine-fifteen, evidence the list of performers in the program reflects their planned order of appearance.[40]) Black followed white when Alberta Hunter took the stage, accompanied by Mrs. Pearl Wright at the piano. (Black singers had black accompanists; white singers had white accompanists.) Hunter began the decade as a blues queen in Chicago and New York but had remade herself into a cabaret singer during a recent stint in Europe, where she appeared in Paris and on the London stage opposite Paul Robeson in *Show Boat* in 1928. White followed black when Margaret Wycherly, billed in the program as "one of the greatest actresses on the English-speaking stage," offered a short, one-woman play, *A Lady Waits*, written expressly for the benefit. No script survives.

These first six acts sum up the musical and dramatic culture of 1929 New York, an indisputably interracial sphere: representatives of both races from Broadway musicals, a bit of the legitimate theater, Negro spirituals sung as concert fare, vaudeville favorites, and perhaps a French cabaret tune and some blues from Hunter. All these voices were included in the first hour of White and Van Vechten's NAACP "Follies." Florenz Ziegfeld introduced the word "follies" to the American theater in his 1907 revue, referencing either the continental style of the Parisian *Folies Bergères* or a newspaper column titled "Follies of the Day," written by Ziegfeld librettist Harry B. Smith.[41] I evoke the term here to underline how White and Van Vechten's event was completely "of the moment" but also "foolish" in the sense of reaching beyond normal practice, pushing the limits of common sense about how race operated in American entertainment. Dwelling for a moment on these limits, consider the contrasts and continuities across these first six acts.

All the performers, except for Wycherly, worked with popular music. The differences between Blake and Jones, Webb, and Engliss were probably slight. All worked the vein of catchy popular songs with lightly syncopated tunes and clever lyrics. Their vocal techniques, physical demeanor, and evening dress probably ran along similar lines as well. Gordon and Johnson offered a contrast that aligned the Negro spiritual with classical music: also in the pair's repertory was the sacred favorite, "If with All Your Heart" from Mendelssohn's *Elijah*, sure to please lovers of high culture. But even Gordon and Johnson had made their careers on vaudeville. As the only female singer in this first group, Alberta Hunter had a perhaps greater personal range than any of the men preceding her. Hunter surely didn't sing the kind of raunchy blues numbers she recorded for the race record market early in the decade. She had self-promoted her recent stint in Europe in black newspapers in the United States, so for her appearance at the benefit Hunter probably sang repertoire drawn from her Paris performances and tunes from *Show Boat*, like "Can't Help Lovin' Dat Man." (She didn't sing much of this popular hit in the London production, but almost no one in New York would have known.[42]) The opening acts seem calculated to moderate any felt differences between the races, with performers known for their graciousness or wry wit getting things going. The next section of the benefit took more chances.

Penetrating Closed Ears

After Wycherly's dramatic playlet—which probably quieted the room—the benefit broke open with the arrival onstage of Duke Ellington and his Orchestra and a crowd of surprise guests: the entire Cotton Club floorshow. White had penciled the Club's female chorus line into his first list of possible performers. While many whites in the audience had probably seen the Cotton Club show, blacks in attendance had not. The NAACP effectively broke the ban against blacks in the audience at Harlem's most famous nightclub, albeit by bringing the Cotton Club to a black audience who were themselves occupying seats in the Forrest Theatre they would not have had easy access to during a regular performance. Before Ellington's band departed, the black blues singer Clara Smith took the stage and sang W. C. Handy's "St. Louis Blues." Smith's inclusion was the single most daring programming choice White and Van Vechten made, and their reasons for putting Smith on the bill are as varied as the makeup of their anticipated audience.

Clara Smith was a prolific 1920s recording artist billed as "the world's greatest moaner." Blues queens historian Daphne Duvall Harrison rated Smith as the "most underrated of all the artists classified as 'classic' blues singers."[43] Born in South Carolina around 1894, Smith began performing as early as 1910, appearing before black audiences on both the Theatre Owners Booking Association (TOBA) circuit and with Al Well's *Smart Set* tent show throughout the South.[44] She hit New York in 1923 and was promptly signed by Columbia Records, a connection that lasted until 1932 and produced more than one hundred sides, including a few duets with Bessie Smith. Harlem audiences were familiar with Clara Smith onstage. In the months before the benefit, she led the cast of a revue titled *Dream Girls* at the Alhambra Theater. The *New York Age* enthused about her in the first paragraph of their review: "The overflowing audiences simply would not let [Smith] go and she sang many encores."[45]

Smith's 1929 discography shows the range of musical forms and textual content embraced by blues queens. Only one of her nine recordings is a twelve-bar blues. The others are about evenly divided between sixteen-bar refrains and Tin Pan Alley AABA chorus with verse forms. All speak directly to the experience of the black, working-class audience. None conforms to the conventional narrative of white, middle-class popular song; none seeks that "jazzy" middle ground occupied by black artists like Robinson and Blake. Many use language and concepts unlikely to be familiar to those outside the black community. In her compelling version of "You Can't Stay Here No More," Smith dismisses her man in no uncertain terms. He has been demanding money, and she resolutely refuses to "sell something I ain't never sold" to get it. Like all the blues queens, Smith struck poses that placed her firmly in control and avoided appearing as a helpless victim. Smith's utter self-possession would set her performance of black womanhood in contrast to two white female singers to follow her at the benefit: Libby Holman, famous for singing a blues number in brownface makeup, and Helen Morgan, famous for playing the mulatto character of Julie in *Show Boat*. For the benefit audience, Smith's blues singing set a benchmark against which later singers could be heard.

For respectable churchgoing African Americans who might be members of the NAACP Women's Auxiliary, blues queens like Smith were beyond the pale. Langston Hughes's 1930 novel *Not without Laughter* offers insight into the possible tensions between the blues and respectable NAACP members. The novel concerns three sisters whose divergent paths exemplify the choices before African American women in the early decades of the twentieth century. Annjee, tied to her love for a blues-singing man who comes and goes at will, works menial jobs and stays caught in the cycle of poverty. Harriet runs away with a carnival minstrel act, works as a prostitute, and ends up a black vaudeville star, billed as the "Princess of the Blues." She aspires to the white Orpheum circuit, confident the "Jews [who] control the theaters" will give her "hot numbers" a chance.[46] Tempy, the oldest, is the soul of respectability, a property owner and upstanding Episcopalian. She strives in every way to be like the liberal white woman she spends years working for as a secretary. Hughes characterizes Tempy in part through her magazine reading: she read *Harper's*, "got her recipes from the *Ladies Home Journal*—and she never bought a watermelon. . . . And in her sewing-room closet there was also a pile of *The Crisis*, the thin Negro monthly that she had been taking from the beginning of its publication."[47] Hughes identifies the respectable strata of black society with NAACP members like Tempy, who doesn't even want "Swing Low, Sweet Chariot" hummed around her house. Did African American women like Tempy in the audience at the Forrest Theater, "high-toned" people who collected Caruso rather than Bessie Smith records, want to hear Clara Smith sing the "St. Louis Blues"?

Even if they didn't, White and Van Vechten contrived a way to make them do so. Langston Hughes would have sympathized with this project. In his essay "The Negro Artist and the Racial Mountain," published in *The Nation* in June 1926, Hughes describes the habits of respectable black music lovers: "A prominent Negro clubwoman in Philadelphia paid eleven dollars to hear Raquel Meller sing Andalusian popular songs. But she told me a few weeks before she would not think of going to hear 'that woman,' Clara Smith, a great black artist, sing Negro folksongs."[48] Against this attitude Hughes exhorted black artists to "let the blare of Negro jazz bands and the bellowing of Bessie Smith singing Blues penetrate the closed ears of the colored near-intellectuals until they listen and perhaps understand."[49] Hughes might as well have been describing the benefit.

How did white audience members respond to a TOBA blues queen? The benefit file suggests White and Van Vechten thought the time was right for Smith—who made her career performing for black, working-class audiences—to break into white vaudeville. A few days after the benefit, White wrote two letters on Smith's behalf. The first, to Van Vechten, outlined White's plan to help Smith get a booking on the white RKO circuit by using his new relationship with George Oberland, an RKO manager who had served as stage manager at the benefit. White asked Van Vechten to "write me a letter saying what you think of [Clara] as a singer and how she would go with white audiences, or, better, white and colored audiences?"[50] White planned to use this letter in a pitch to Oberland on Smith's behalf. Van Vechten could be counted on to help; he had concluded a 1926 *Vanity Fair* piece on the blues queens by praising Smith specifically.[51] Van Vechten responded the very next day with an evangelistic letter: "I heartily concur with you that Clara Smith would make an outstanding success in the 'white' music halls. Of all the Blues singers she is the one most fitted, I believe, to carry this gospel into the alien world. She represents something that is fast going: the primitive old Southern Negro. . . . But she is expert in her delineation of comedy songs too. Personally, as you know, I consider her an important artist."[52] Smith's range—from blues to comedy songs—was in her favor in seeking a white audience. Perhaps Van Vechten was recalling Smith's performance at the benefit just five days before he wrote these lines.

White came up with an excuse to write Oberland on December 12 in what amounts to a thank-you note for Oberland's thank-you note about the benefit. White's postscript tells the real story: "P.S. What did you think of Clara Smith? Wouldn't she go great over the R.K.O. circuit? W.W."[53] This small act on behalf of a blues singer is typical of White's day-in, day-out work at the NAACP. He combined legal and public-policy activism for African Americans as a group with small gestures to improve the lives of individuals he knew. From White's perspective, the benefit presented a chance to put major black performers on a stage where white producers might see them and hire them. Apparently, nothing came of White's effort to get Clara Smith onto the RKO circuit. She continued playing the black variety stage until her death in 1935. Perhaps the benefit was the only time she appeared live before a sizeable white audience. Who knows how many white listeners enjoyed her race records at home?

Two Rooms in Harlem

Smith and the Ellington band were followed by a string of white stars: female impersonator Albert Carroll, comedian E. J. McNamara, and singer Libby Holman. Carroll, a seven-season veteran of the Broadway spoof revue *Grand Street*

Follies, offered his typical inside jokes for the Broadway crowd and impersonated Beatrice Lillie (the English comedienne), John Barrymore (the American dramatic actor), and New York Mayor Jimmie Walker (a great lover of Broadway). These choices would appeal to white Broadway theatergoers who knew the personalities being imitated first hand. E. J. McNamara delivered his famous speech from the season's comedy hit *Strictly Dishonorable*. Again, the appeal was to the midtown crowd. In Gershwin's absence—the disappointment of the audience and the consternation backstage can be imagined—Libby Holman went on next. Holman was accompanied by songwriter Ralph Rainger but may have intended to sing several songs accompanied by Gershwin. It was Gershwin's idea to share the stage with Holman at the benefit: White communicated this to her in a telegram that suggests Gershwin spent some time brainstorming about the event.[54]

When White invited Holman to appear, he asked her to sing a specific song: "It is our desire to make this one of the most distinctive affairs of its kind ever given, limiting the program as we are to only singers and stars of magnitude. . . . We would be most grateful if you would consent to appear. We would want by all means to have you sing 'Moanin' Low.'"[55] "Moanin' Low" was the penultimate number in *The Little Show*, a revue running at the intimate Music Box Theatre at the time. The number—for which Holman donned brownface makeup and impersonated a "high yellow" Harlem prostitute—was a Broadway sensation in late 1929. At the benefit, this musical representation of black life by white performers could be heard in relation to the African American female singers Hunter and Smith, who sang before Holman, and Edith Wilson, who appeared after her. Holman surely didn't don costume and makeup for "Moanin' Low" at the benefit, but for many in the audience, knowledge of the song's presentation in *The Little Show* was surely part of the performance.

In *The Little Show*, Holman and co-star Clifton Webb performed "Moanin' Low" in front of a simple backdrop (designed by Jo Mielziner early in his long career) picturing a somewhat expressionist rendering of a cramped room in a Harlem tenement, complete with an empty gin bottle on the floor beneath an iron bed. Jazz historian Marshall Stearns described the scene in detail, beginning with Webb onstage at lights up. "Libby Holman enters, and as Webb ignores her, conceals a few bills in her stocking. She hands the rest of her earnings to Webb. Momentarily interested, Webb rises languidly and starts to dance with her. As he dances he makes love until he comes upon the hidden money. He tears away the money with a curse, throws Holman violently to the floor, and saunters to stage front and center. This is the cue for the song—and the dance that caused such consternation."[56] At this point Webb performed an imitation of Earl "Snake-Hips" Tucker's erotic loose-limbed dance, which had caused a sensation in *Blackbirds of 1928*, still running when *The Little Show* opened in April 1929.

Stearns claimed "Moanin' Low" ended with Webb "slither[ing] out, slamming the door as Holman [threw] herself against it." Holman's biographer described the simulated lovemaking as Webb "practically raping" Holman. Webb's "terror-stricken" exit reflected fear that he had killed Holman. But she rose from the floor for one last chorus—"Libby recovers, crawls to the door, beating futilely against it, while singing a throaty obbligato, a scatting improvised growl, that no white woman had ever attempted on Broadway before."[57] Revue historian Robert Baral described Holman ending the scene "with a lower-pitched aria of the chorus which got thunderous applause."[58] "The dark purple menace of Libby Holman in the blues" proved the heart of "Moanin' Low."[59] The *New York Telegram* described the audience response as "assailed by panic."[60]

"Moanin' Low" was not a travesty or spoof but rather a serious attempt by white Broadway artists to embody the contemporaneous mythic drama of black New Yorkers in the crowded—and (to whites) mysterious—black metropolis uptown. Van Vechten helped define this world in his controversial novel *Nigger Heaven* (1926); the play *Harlem* (1926), starring Lenore Ulric in brownface, put it onstage in lavish form. Some of the power of "Moanin' Low" was likely due to the reliance on physical gesture, dance, and song to tell the story. For coaching on the movement, Webb went to Billy Pierce, described in *Theatre Magazine* as "the greatest dancer on Broadway . . . who has never hoofed it on any stage."[61] Pierce owned a dance studio catering to white theatrical dancers who wanted to learn black steps. According to the program, benefit performers Evelyn Hoey, Betty Compton, Frances Williams, and Webb had all studied at Pierce's studio. Pierce helped White make contact with some of these performers and assisted in practical matters, such as rental and hanging of the backdrop for the event. The Pierce studio was located in a Forty-Sixth Street building where Pierce had been an elevator attendant. In fact, Pierce's name was a front for black dancer Buddy Bradley, who created solo dances for professionals at a time when featured performers typically provided their own routines. Bradley later claimed to have choreographed "Moanin' Low."[62]

How did "Moanin' Low" go over at the benefit? White audiences would have been thrilled to see and hear Holman—and maybe Webb stuck around to join her onstage. Perhaps they even did a bit of their famous dance, moving in a "black" manner while dressed in "white" clothes and makeup. Black audiences, depending on their personal reactions to the blues, were in a position to judge Holman's attempt to sound black. Holman singing "black" without the dramatic context of the show's set and costuming would have highlighted the element of performance—that "blues" singing was a matter of specific techniques of performance, separable, for "white" performers like Holman, from actual or perceived racial identity. Holman's singing also gave evidence for how black musical style and topics were influencing Broadway singing more generally.

Excerpts from *Connie's Hot Chocolates* followed Holman. This Broadway version of the floorshow at the Harlem nightclub Connie's Inn closed its successful run of 219 performances a week after the benefit. Cast members in the benefit program included Baby Cox and the "high yaller" Hot Chocolates Drops (potentially the second female chorus line at the benefit), Jazzlips "his feet are as gifted as his lips" Richardson, and singer Edith Wilson.

Wilson definitely appeared and may have offered her ballad from *Hot Chocolates*: Thomas "Fats" Waller and Andy Razaf's "(What Did I Do to Be So) Black and Blue," an appropriate counterweight to "Moanin' Low" and entirely apropos for an NAACP event. "Black and Blue" in its original context was also set in a theatrical representation of a room in Harlem. Razaf biographer Barry Singer described the number based on interviews with the lyricist's last wife: "[A] stage awash in white—white walls, draperies, and carpet, and, at stage center, an enormous bed made up in white satin. Swathed in a white negligee, swaddled deep in white bedclothes, the jet-black Edith Wilson nestled on the bed and began to sing."[63] Photos of Wilson contradict this characterization of her skin color. Blues scholar Harrison points out that blues record producer Perry Bradford was attracted to Wilson in part because she was "physically attractive, light complexioned, and charming."[64] The question is a significant one for the reception of "Black and Blue" in 1929. The song was added between *Hot Chocolates'* Brooklyn tryout and Broadway opening in response to a request from gangster Dutch Schultz, who bankrolled the production. In Singer's words, Schultz wanted "a funny number . . . something with a little 'colored girl' singing how tough it is being 'colored.'"[65]

Skin-shade discrimination within the black community was a topic with undeniable resonance at the benefit. The benefit program included a celebratory poem titled "Moving Mosaic or N.A.A.C.P. Dance, 1929" by Nella Larsen Imes that begins, "There was sooty black, shiny black, taupe, mahogany, bronze, copper, gold, orange, yellow, peach, ivory, white."[66] Larsen's novel *Passing*, also 1929, took up the issue in a narrative of escape from and return to the Harlem community. The verse for "Black and Blue" laments: "Browns and yallers, all have fellas. / Gentlemen prefer them light"—framing skin-shade discrimination in narrowly romantic terms. But the chorus opens up the burden of racial prejudice to embrace anyone discriminated against for not being white. The singer is reviled, she sings, "'Cause I can't hide, / What is on my face." Surely these lyrics, if they were sung at the benefit, cut many different ways among the great diversity of people in the Forrest Theatre. One group among the crowd may have been light-skinned African Americans who passed as white to avoid the burdens and indignities of segregation. Mimi, the heroine of White's novel *Flight*, was one among many such "passing" characters in 1920s fiction. White imagined Mimi choosing to stop passing as white and return to the black community as a result of hearing a black spiritual singer in a midtown concert hall. How many individuals like Mimi were at the benefit?

Louis Armstrong, part of the cast of *Hot Chocolates* for a time, recorded an impassioned "Black and Blue" sans verse in 1929. Decades later the song still resonated for Armstrong, who brought it back into his repertoire during his State Department tours of Africa and on the 1955 LP *Satch Plays Fats*. The black-cast musical *Ain't Misbehavin'*, winner of the Tony Award for Best Musical in 1978, also used "Black and Blue" to acknowledge the soul-tearing effects of racial discrimination on black Americans between the World Wars. Razaf's chorus lyric—a product of the late 1920s and likely sung at the benefit—echoed across the twentieth century.

"Black and Blue" rises to an existential climax with the lyric, "I'm so forlorn / Life's just a thorn / My heart is torn. / Why was I born?" The singer who came onto the benefit stage after the cast of *Hot Chocolates* might very well have sung a song titled "Why Was I Born?" Helen Morgan was the star of *Sweet Adeline*, a show written for her by Jerome Kern and Oscar Hammerstein II. Hammerstein wrote the lyric for "Why Was I Born?" after *Hot Chocolates* had opened; perhaps Razaf's "Black and Blue" was the source for the title phrase.

Morgan had been the standout star in the crowded cast of Kern and Hammerstein's *Show Boat* and she was indisputably the biggest name on the benefit bill. Almost all the NAACP press releases trumpet her name in their titles. White made initial contact with Morgan through the black singer Jules Bledsoe, who had played Joe in *Show Boat* and thus knew Morgan. Bledsoe was willing to wire Morgan on White's behalf but warned the NAACP leader, "I DON'T KNOW HOW HER SYMPATHIES LIE."[67] Morgan proved very willing to participate. The file includes a beautiful handwritten note from Morgan to White—her stationery featured a silhouette of her profile—inviting him to call at his convenience and including her telephone number.[68] In typical fashion, White used the benefit to make a new famous friend—also, hopefully, a friend for the NAACP. Later, White requested a photo from Morgan that had never been previously printed, hoping such an image would get the benefit into the white papers.[69]

As I describe at length in my book on *Show Boat*, Morgan was more than a musical star: she was a living icon of Prohibition-refusing New York City, singing her way through arrests and trials connected to nightclubs bearing her name that were raided by federal agents under the Volstead Act.[70] Sidewalk onlookers witnessing such raids were known to heckle the agents as they went about enforcing the law. One song Morgan surely sang at the benefit—simply because she *always* sang it—was her signature tune from *Show Boat*, the torch song "Bill." This weepy ballad aptly captured the essential traits of the white torch singer: a quiet, intimate, confessional vocal style; relentlessly self-centered lyrics about a man the singer loves she knows not why; and a tear in the eye and catch in the throat at the close that betrays the singer's performance as expressive of "real" emotion being poured out for the listener. Morgan's torch-singer persona was diametrically opposed to that of a self-reliant blues queen like Clara Smith, and Morgan's narrowly romantic problems come off as self-indulgent white privilege when heard beside Wilson, and even Holman's, versions of black women's experiences up in Harlem.

The possible juxtaposition on the benefit stage of Helen Morgan's "Bill," Edith Wilson's "Black and Blue," Libby Holman's "Moanin' Low," and Clara Smith's "St. Louis Blues" would have allowed benefit audiences to compare and contrast a tremendously varied range of performed stereotypes of black and white femininity. Like musical examples for a women's studies seminar on intersectionality or a cultural studies seminar on popular culture stereotypes, these four songs and four women occupy various positions along several axes of Jazz Age identity. White and Van Vechten put Morgan, Wilson, Holman, and Smith in the same room, raising questions of the performance and reception of race and gender both for the interracial audience at the benefit and for historians attempting to understand the event and its Jazz Age resonance. These questions don't demand definitive answering so much as persistent asking.

Closing Acts

A string of white performers followed Morgan: Richard Hale, dramatic actor; Frances Williams, headliner at the *George White Scandals* known for doing jazzy, "hot" numbers; Charles Butterworth, Broadway comedian; Evelyn Hoey, a new talent featured in *Fifty Million Frenchmen*, and Jimmy Durante, who played the benefit with his vaudeville partners, Clayton and Jackson, and their own orchestra. This section of the evening offered a strong dose of late 1920s white Broadway—*Show Boat* icon Morgan; Hoey, the latest pretty young thing; the revue-based talents of Williams and Butterworth; the mayhem of Durante.

The final three acts reprised styles already heard. Daniel L. Haynes, an African American singer and actor known for his "muscular physique and powerful voice," probably sang some spirituals.[71] In the summer of 1929 Haynes had starred in *Hallelujah*, the first full-length talkie with an all-black cast. When the film opened to wide critical acclaim in midtown New York theaters, African Americans were refused admission, even for the balcony.[72] At the benefit, Haynes sang live for blacks sitting in the choicest midtown seats. Betty Compton followed Haynes and probably sang "You've Got That Thing" or "Why Shouldn't I Have You?," suggestive songs by Cole Porter she was offering nightly in *Fifty Million Frenchmen*. Compton had had small parts in a string of mid-1920s musicals, including two Gershwin shows. She was a typical Jazz Age flapper-type musical comedy lead—a liberated white girl out for fun, not afraid to shimmy and shake to jazzy rhythms. But Compton's real claim to fame was being the girl that broke up Mayor Jimmy Walker's marriage. Their liaison was one of the most celebrated Broadway affairs of the decade, but it never made print because of the discretion of the New York papers, who loved "Hizzoner." Walker was invited but probably not in attendance at the benefit: NAACP press releases would have certainly emphasized such a high-profile audience member. After the mayor's lover took her applause and exited the stage, five African American men from the Deep South entered and sang religious novelty songs. The Utica Institute Jubilee Singers, hailing from a technical college in southern Mississippi, were heard regularly on NBC radio for three years—an unusual, high-profile spot for young black performers—and would leave for an extended European tour a few days after the benefit. They sang tunes like "Peter on the Sea" and "Somebody's Knocking at Your Door," their repertoire and performance style located at the halfway point between spirituals and pop. Black male vocal-harmony pop groups like the quintet from Utica would find a secure place before white audiences in the decades to come, among the most famous being the Mills Brothers. Gershwin suggested White include the Utica Jubilee Singers on the benefit bill.[73]

Into the Night . . .

The clock necessarily set a limit on the benefit, which ran past 11:30 P.M. An inexperienced producer, White had to pay overtime to union stagehands, cutting into the final profit to the tune of $16.25.[74]

What happened when the show benefit ended? The audience exited through the Forrest Theatre lobby onto Forty-Ninth Street. Most probably turned right: Broadway beckoned one-half block away. A second right at Broadway led straight into the carnival of Times Square, with its neon signs, crush of humanity, and late-night clubs and restaurants. White audience members had their pick: this was their part of town. Some might have furtively entered one of the unmarked speakeasies in the neighborhood. Black benefit patrons knew where to go if they didn't want trouble or a public scene: a bus stop or subway station. Heading uptown to Harlem was the only reliable option for a guaranteed good time. As White wrote about exiting from a performance of *The Emperor Jones* (starring Paul Robeson) in his essay for the 1925 anthology *The New Negro*, "The Civil Rights Act of New York would have protected us [had we decided to go to a midtown restaurant]—but we were too much under the spell of the theatre we had just quitted to want to insist on the rights the law gave us. So we mounted a bus and rode seven miles or more to colored Harlem where we could be served with food without fear of insult or contumely."[75] Assuming black audience members took the subway, which station did they walk to? Did they take a left at Broadway, turning their backs on the lights of Times Square, catching the "A" train at the Fiftieth Street station? Or did they extend the benefit glow by strolling through the heart of the city to catch the subway at Forty-Second Street, noting along the way the theaters where shows they had seen stars from were playing, glancing up Forty-Fourth Street toward the Hudson Theatre's marquee, which advertised *Connie's Hot Chocolates*, the lone black-cast show running in midtown.

Did the interracial audience from the NAACP benefit—strolling in Times Square around midnight—cross paths with audience members from the other benefit that night exiting the Forty-Fourth Street Theatre? George M. Cohan and boxer Jack Dempsey shared the job of master of ceremonies for the all-star— all-white—benefit for the New York American Christmas Fund. Six Broadway shows were represented on the bill—none historically memorable. The big draws at the Christmas Fund were Beatrice Lillie and Ruth Etting; the band was Abe Lyman and his Orchestra—a far cry from Helen Morgan and Duke Ellington alternating at the Forrest.[76] Jimmy Durante managed to play both benefits. The contrast between White and Van Vechten's benefit and the Christmas Fund event could hardly be greater. At the latter, there were no blues queens, no singers of spirituals, no public statements of sympathy with civil rights—and likely no persons of color in the audience (except for those passing as white). The NAACP benefit embraced all of New York City—not just the whites of midtown—and posed challenges to producers, performers, and audience members then, as well as scholars of American music and popular culture today.

The NAACP benefit made manifest for one night only the possibilities for interracial contact latent in the racially segregated musical and theatrical world of Jazz Age Manhattan. White and Van Vechten's program posited several bold points: first, black and white artists can together entertain an audience composed of blacks and whites, satisfying and challenging the tastes of all in the process; second, the black musical and dramatic sources of many white performers' styles are clear to see and hear; third, the sources and styles of black music are varied in origin and tone, from spirituals to blues to Broadway; and fourth, no single musical expression of blackness is definitive. The benefit celebrated performers' talent meeting audiences' desire for entertainment in a commercial public space where racial segregation was not permitted to sort or limit either. No "passing" was necessary at the Forrest Theatre that night.

Several items in the benefit file suggest that some in the audience understood these larger meanings. The NAACP board of directors passed a resolution the week after the event, reading in part, "Besides materially aiding the National Office financially, the event was one of value in interracial understanding, from the bi-racial character both of the performers and of the audience."[77] Forrest Bailey of the American Civil Liberties Union wrote to White on November 30, telling White he had already purchased tickets, and closing, "This promises to be a grand party which nobody who really knows about THINGS can afford to miss."[78] After the benefit, White received a handwritten thank you from Corinne Wright, a member of the Women's Auxiliary, who said of the event, "I have heard nothing but favorable comments about the benefit, both from people who 'know what it's all about' and 'others'!"[79] The benefit as an event designed to challenge the racial segregation of the Jazz Age continues to challenge scholars to be among those who "know what it's all about."

Notes

1. Albertson, *Bessie*, 138–43.

2. Janken, *White*, 68.

3. Schuyler, " Van Vechten Revolution."

4. Ovington, *Portraits in Color*, 116.

5. Kellner, *Carl Van Vechten*, 162.

6. Recent narrative histories of the NAACP include Jonas, *Freedom's Sword*, and Sullivan, *Lift Every Voice*.

7. The complete file can be accessed in the microfilm collection *Papers of the NAACP*, part 11, series A, reel 8, frames 435–864 (Frederick, Md.: University Publications of America, 1986). Hereafter, note references to items in the file will be given as *NAACP* with the date when available (all dates are 1929 unless otherwise noted) and frame number.

8. *NAACP*, October 3, f435.

9. *NAACP*, November 7, f454

10. *NAACP*, October 5, f436.

11. Decker, *Show Boat*.

12. *NAACP*, October 7, f439.

13. *NAACP*, October 7, f438.

14. December 3, f663.

15. *NAACP*, f539–542.

16. *NAACP*, f618.

17. *NAACP*, f496.

18. *NAACP*, f773; *NAACP*, November 22, f536.

19. *NAACP*, October 7, f437.

20. *NAACP*, December 9, f739.

21. All the major black newspapers published articles on the benefit, most simply reprinting NAACP press releases, none offering new information about what happened at the event.

22. *NAACP*, November 25, f556.

23. *NAACP*, December 3, f659.

24. *NAACP*, f802.

25. White, *Flight*, and Van Vechten, *Nigger Heaven*, both published by Knopf in 1926.

26. *NAACP*, f804.

27. *NAACP*, f757.

28. My survey of the event follows the benefit program (*NAACP*, f809–f813), which captures the event as White and Van Vechten hoped it would come off. In two cases, evidence in the file confirms performers listed in the program who did not appear. A post-benefit press release dated December 13 (*NAACP*, f773) does not mention several performers named in the program: table 1 marks these names with an asterisk.

29. See Haskins and Mitgang, *Mr. Bojangles*, 95–97, on Robinson as a single in white vaudeville. Rose, *Eubie Blake*, 62–68, considers black performers who played white vaudeville and gives Blake's perspective on not blacking up.

30. *NAACP*, f642.

31. Harrison, *Twentieth-Century Journalists*, 139.

32. *NAACP*, f773.

33. Gordon, *Born to Be*, 189.

34. WW to Eubie Blake, *NAACP*, November 3, f664.

35. "Blake and Jones Are Hit at Fox Theater," *Chicago Defender*, August 24, 1929.

36. Sissle and Blake were captured on one of the earliest musical shorts, available on *The Scar of Shame: With the Early Sound Short Sissle and Blake*, African American Cinema, vol. 5 (Washington, DC: Library of Congress, 1993).

37. "Eubie Blake Teams with Broadway Jones" *Chicago Defender*, November 9, 1929.

38. "Eubie Blake and Broadway Jones Here Next Week," *New York Amsterdam News*, January 1, 1930.

39. Al Moore to WW, *NAACP*, December 8, f736.

40. *NAACP*, December 4, f699.

41. Bordman, *American Musical Theatre*, 269.

42. On Hunter and *Show Boat*, see Decker, *Show Boat*, 125, 129.

43. Harrison, *Black Pearls*, 239; Harris, *Blues Who's Who*, 467.

44. Harris, *Blues Who's Who*, 466.

45. Ibid., 467; *New York Age*, September 7, 1929.

46. Hughes, *Not Without Laughter*, 296.

47. Ibid., 238, 242.

48. Hughes, "Negro Artist," 33.

49. Ibid., 36.

50. *NAACP*, December 12, f759.

51. Van Vechten, "Negro 'Blues' Singers."

52. CVV to WW, December 13, 1929, in Kellner, *Letters of Carl Van Vechten*, 109.

53. *NAACP*, December 12, f760.

54. *NAACP*, November 22, f545.

55. *NAACP*, November 8, f459.

56. Stearns and Stearns, *Jazz Dance*, 160.

57. Bradshaw, *Dreams*, 71.

58. Baral, *Revue*, 187.

59. *New York Times*, May 4, 1929.

60. Stearns and Stearns, *Jazz Dance*, 160.

61. *Theatre Magazine*, September 1929.

62. On Bradley, see Stearns and Stearns, *Jazz Dance*, chap. 21.

63. Singer, *Black and Blue*, 217.

64. Harrison, *Black Pearls*, 166.

65. Singer, *Black and Blue*, 216.

66. *NAACP*, f816.

67. *NAACP*, October 24, f448.

68. *NAACP*, November 12, f508.

69. *NAACP*, November 18, f507.

70. Decker, *Show Boat*, chap. 3.

71. Peterson, *Profiles*, 297.

72. Kellner, *Harlem Renaissance*, 150.

73. *NAACP*, November 8, 457. The Utica Jubilee Singers' complete recorded works are available on Document Records DOCD-5603.

74. *NAACP*, f769–f772.

75. White, "Paradox of Color," 361.

76. *New York Times*, December 8, 1929

77. *NAACP*, December 12, f758.

78. *NAACP*, November 30, f658.

79. *NAACP*, December 10, f753.

References

Albertson, Chris. *Bessie*. New York: Stein and Day, 1972.

Baral, Robert. *Revue: A Nostalgic Reprise of the Great Broadway Period*. New York: Fleet, 1962.

Bordman, Gerald. *American Musical Theatre: A Chronicle*. New York: Oxford University Press, 2001.

Bradshaw, Jon. *Dreams that Money Can Buy: The Tragic Life of Libby Holman*. New York: Morrow, 1985.

Decker, Todd. *Show Boat: Performing Race in an American Musical*. New York: Oxford University Press, 2013.

Gordon, Taylor. *Born to Be*. New York: Covici-Friede, 1929.

Harris, Sheldon. *Blues Who's Who: a Biographical Dictionary of Blues Singers*. New Rochelle, N.Y.: Arlington House, 1979.

Harrison, Daphne Duvall. *Black Pearls: Blues Queens of the 1920s*. New Brunswick, N.J.: Rutgers University Press, 1988.

Harrison, S. L. *Twentieth-Century Journalists: America's Opinionmakers*. Lanham, Md.: University Press of America, 2002.

Haskins, James, and N. R. Mitgang. *Mr. Bojangles: the Biography of Bill Robinson*. New York: Morrow, 1988.

Hughes, Langston. *Not Without Laughter*. New York: Knopf, 1930.

———. "The Negro Artist and the Racial Mountain (1926)." In *Essays on Art, Race, Politics, and World Affairs*. Columbia: University of Missouri Press, 2002.

Janken, Kenneth R. *White: The Biography of Walter White, Mr. NAACP.* New York: New Press, 2003.

Jonas, Gilbert. *Freedom's Sword: the NAACP and the Struggle Against Racism in America, 1909–1969.* New York: Routledge, 2005.

Kellner, Bruce. *Carl Van Vechten and the Irreverent Decades.* Norman: University of Oklahoma Press, 1968.

———. *The Harlem Renaissance: a Historical Dictionary for the Era.* Westport, Conn.: Greenwood, 1984.

———, ed. *Letters of Carl Van Vechten.* New Haven, Conn.: Yale University Press, 1987.

Ovington, Mary. *Portraits in Color.* 1927. Freeport, N.Y.: Books for Libraries, 1971.

Papers of the NAACP, part 11, series A, reel 8, frames 435–864. Frederick, Md.: University Publications of America, 1986.

Peterson, Bernard L. *Profiles of African American Stage Performers and Theatre People, 1816–1960.* Westport, Conn.: Greenwood, 2001.

Rose, Al. *Eubie Blake.* New York: Schirmer, 1979.

The Scar of Shame: with the Early Sound Short Sissle and Blake. Vol. 5, African American Cinema. Washington, DC: Library of Congress, 1993.

Schuyler, George S. "The Van Vechten Revolution," *Phylon* 11, no. 4 (1950): 362–68.

Singer, Barry. *Black and Blue: The Life and Lyrics of Andy Razaf.* New York: Schirmer, 1992.

Stearns, Marshall, and Jean Stearns. *Jazz Dance: The Story of American Vernacular Dance.* New York: Macmillan, 1968.

Sullivan, Patricia. *Lift Every Voice: The NAACP and the Making of the Civil Rights Movement.* New York: New Press, 2009.

Van Vechten, Carl. "Negro 'Blues' Singers: An Appreciation of Three Coloured Artists Who Excel in an Unusual and Native Medium." *Vanity Fair*, March 1926.

———. *Nigger Heaven.* New York: Knopf, 1926.

White, Walter. *Flight.* New York: Knopf, 1926.

———. "The Paradox of Color." In *The New Negro: An Interpretation*, edited by Alain Locke. New York: Boni, 1925.

11 Dialogue without Words

Identities and Dichotomies in Copland's Piano Quartet

JENNIFER DELAPP-BIRKETT

> We are being taught to think in neat little categories—in terms of blacks and whites, East and West, Communism and the Profit System. In historical perspective, one can find plenty of precedent for that kind of schematized thinking, wrong as it may be. During the religious wars of the 16th century it certainly must have seemed inconceivable that Catholicism and Protestantism could ever peacefully co-exist in the same world. Later the libertarian ideas of the French Revolution and English traditionalism seemed hopelessly incompatible. In the field of music there was a time when you were supposed to make up your mind as between Richard Wagner and Johannes Brahms. To find some virtues in both was considered impossible. Nowadays a similar cleavage is supposed to exist between the mass-appeal music of Shostakovitch and the musical radicalism of Schoenberg.
>
> —Aaron Copland (1949)

American composer Aaron Copland believed dichotomies were dangerous. Copland delivered these words at a controversial gathering: the 1949 Cultural and Scientific Conference for World Peace at the Waldorf-Astoria in New York City.[1] The event's announced purpose was to foster communication across the Iron Curtain, but most historians agree that it was a Soviet-engineered effort to demonstrate Western artists' support for worldwide Communism.[2] The New York meetings were widely publicized and brought considerable media attention to the supposed threat of "Communism in our midst."[3] As his speech continued, Copland proposed an antidote to the dichotomy problem. "All the dichotomies of the past were in some measure resolved, just as we shall have, in some way, to resolve our own," he said. He referred primarily to the international political tensions of the Cold War, and more specifically to Soviet restrictions on the importation of "Western" music.[4]

Such a public stance in a political arena would soon have an unexpectedly detrimental effect on Copland's music career. In the months following the Peace Conference, anticommunist campaigns increased to the point that many causes to which Copland was or had been sympathetic fell under suspicion. Copland's populist, accessible works of the 1930s and 1940s were tied to the community of liberal choreographers and musicians that had since fallen out of favor among increasingly powerful Cold War crusaders. Copland began to realize that given his liberal political past, anticommunists in the current political climate could too easily twist implied Soviet approval of Copland, or his accessible music, into evidence of subversion. Four years later, Copland would describe the Peace Conference as the point at which he ceased "political affiliations of any kind":

> All extra-musical sponsorships, endorsements and participations ended, as far as I was concerned, in March 1949, after I had taken part in the so-called Peace Conference at the Waldorf-Astoria in New York. . . . I had gone hoping to demonstrate that it was possible, at least in the cultural field, for an American composer and a composer from a communist country to sit down and find some basis for agreement. My experience there convinced me that the Conference was a manoeuvre of those in control to advance communist doctrine, and I determined not to do anything in the future that could possibly be interpreted as aiding their cause.[5]

Overlaying the dichotomies Copland named in 1949 was a host of other ideological binarisms, many of which operated as identity markers. These included individualism vs. collectivism, freedom vs. totalitarianism, bourgeois vs. proletarian, intellectuals vs. workers, left vs. right, progressive vs. conservative, high vs. low, science vs. art, and so on. Nadine Hubbs was the first to make a strong case that widely circulating homosexual/heterosexual and queer/straight dichotomies shaped Copland and his compositional choices at midcentury.[6] Indeed, one particularly insidious strain of the postwar climate was the tendency to scapegoat people who fell outside a rigid definition of "normal American," particularly where race, religion or sexuality were concerned. Copland's position as a Jewish, gay man put him in triple jeopardy as the polarizing rhetoric of anticommunism turned membership in both of these communities into political and professional liabilities.[7]

Dichotomies Reinforced

Political and ideological subtexts to the populism/serialism dichotomy were specific and increasingly widespread, particularly among classical composers in East Coast cities in the years 1949–1950. In the months before he began composing the Piano Quartet, the relationship between Cold War politics and composers' musical style rose into sharp relief for Copland.

In the fall of 1949, Virgil Thomson printed some disparaging comments by Arnold Schoenberg in his weekly *New York Herald Tribune* column. Schoenberg was the main proponent of twelve-tone techniques before World War II. Schoenberg accused American cultural leaders of neglecting his music. His concluding remark in Thomson's column: "You cannot change the natural evolution of the arts by a command; . . . you cannot force real artists to descend to the lowest possible standards to give up morals, character and sincerity, to avoid presentation of new ideas. Even Stalin cannot succeed and Aaron Copland even less." Two weeks later Thomson printed Copland's response: "Unlike Stalin I have no desire to suppress [Schoenberg's] music!" Copland wrote, "True, I can't be listed as an apostle and propagandizer for the twelve-tone system; but since when is that a crime?" Then, lest any doubt remain, Copland "dissociated himself absolutely" from the Soviet condemnation of Schoenberg's music that had been voiced by Dmitri Shostakovich at the 1949 Peace Conference. Within a few months, Copland and Schoenberg reconciled via private correspondence, and Copland began sketching the twelve-tone Piano Quartet.[8]

Additional incidents demonstrated Copland's vulnerability to political slander by the time he began work on the piece "in earnest" at the MacDowell Colony the next summer. In mid-March 1950, the editor of the *American Legion Magazine* sent a hostile letter to Paramount Pictures executives accusing Copland of plagiarism in his score to the award-winning film *The Heiress* (1949). The complaint demonstrated to Copland that a powerful private-sector anticommunist network with widespread influence was monitoring him. (It seems more than a coincidence that Copland never wrote for Hollywood again.[9]) The same month, the *New York Times* ran front-page articles on the Senate's efforts to purge homosexuals from the government, specifically from the State Department, which had funded Copland's recent trip to Latin America.[10] In June 1950 the widely disseminated blacklist *Red Channels* appeared, and Copland's entry was one of the longest.[11] Also in June, the FBI opened a file on Copland.[12] He completed the Piano Quartet that October.

In short, the Piano Quartet was written amid Copland's growing awareness of his precarious political standing in the changing postwar climate. The work itself may convincingly be read as Copland's response to the new, politicized, Schoenberg/Shostakovich, serial/tonal dichotomy, which, he had stated at the Peace Conference, was unnecessarily exaggerated by Cold War rhetoric.[13] Such events indicate that many of these dichotomies were fresh in Copland's mind from the day he prepared his Peace Conference speech until his Piano Quartet was premiered.

As he rushed to complete the Piano Quartet in time for its October premiere,[14] Copland had seen clearly that he could not advocate cultural or political reconciliation between the United States and the Soviet Union without endangering his career. But in the wordless, plotless realm of chamber music, he could deconstruct at least one of the dichotomies he listed in his Peace Conference speech and, by extension, register his objection to the others. The way Copland's resistance of categories operates in the Piano Quartet is the subject of this chapter.

Copland on the "Atonal System"

To understand how "serialism" and "tonality" interact in the Piano Quartet, we must first look more closely at the history of Copland's criticisms of serial techniques.[15] Some of the negative attitudes he expressed before 1950 indicate a long-standing (though by no means rigid) prejudice against what he called a "Germanic" aesthetic. Others stemmed from his commitment to a broad audience and his corollary belief that composers who used twelve-tone techniques (or "the atonal system," in popular parlance of the day) separated themselves from the vast majority of potential American listeners.

Copland's affinity for a Franco-Russian sensibility has been well established, as has the existence of a perceived dichotomy among twentieth-century American symphonic composers between French-influenced musical values and styles and those of the dominant but arguably exhausted Austro-German tradition of Haydn, Mozart, Beethoven, Brahms, and Wagner. In 1941, despite some admiration for atonal works by Schoenberg's pupil Alban Berg, Copland concluded that their Germanic aesthetic ultimately doomed them to obscurity.

> *Wozzeck* and *Lulu*, his *Violin Concerto*, and the *Lyric Suite* for string quartet are among the finest creations in the modern repertoire. This does not change the essential truth that Berg's music belongs to the German past. It is that fact that makes it less exciting than it would otherwise be. For it is music that, despite the modern means employed, sends us back to an emotional experience the essence of which we have thoroughly lived through.[16]

It is true, as Copland claimed, that by 1950 he had been exposed to music of Boulez, Dallapiccola, and other non-Germanic composers who had begun using serial techniques outside a Schoenbergian context, leading him to reconsider his bleak predictions.[17]

It is also true, as Copland later asserted, that even at the height of his success writing movie scores and populist ballets, he continued to write works for a smaller, more specialized audience. Indeed, if one searches, one can find kernels of serial procedures in the 1930 Piano Variations and additional evidence from the 1920s that Copland had more than a passing respect for Schoenberg and his school. But as Richard Taruskin has noted, these assertions, though not spurious, were part of a determined campaign of self-reinvention Copland mounted in the early years of the Cold War to keep his music and indeed his career from becoming a casualty of the domestic anticommunist witch hunts. From 1950 through the end of his life, Copland continued to downplay both the idea that music could bear political meaning and the political-ideological influences that had contributed to his own decision to address a broad public during the Great Depression.[18]

This passage from *Our New Music*, published in 1941 and quoted incessantly by subsequent writers over the next twenty years, remains the clearest statement of Copland's own dichotomous views about serialism and tonality [emphases added]:

> Atonal music resembles itself too much. It creates a certain *monotony* of effect that *severely limits its variety of expression*. It has been said that the atonal system *cannot produce folk songs or lullabies*. But more serious is the fact that, being the expression of a highly refined and subtle musical culture, it has very little for a naïve but expanding musical culture such as is characteristic today of the United States (or the Soviet Union). This is not to deny its historical significance or its importance as *an advanced outpost in the technological field of musical experiment*. But for a long time to come it is likely to be of interest principally to *specialists and connoisseurs rather than to the generality of music lovers*.[19]

The second, revised edition of 1962 would be considerably more circumspect. But well into 1949 he continued to express his distance from "the atonal method" using dichotomies of his own that opposed general listeners with connoisseurs, expressivity with monotony, lullabies and folk music with technical experimentation.

The Reconciliatory Potential of Copland's Tone Row

For the Piano Quartet, Copland created a row that allowed him to treat the ideological issues serialism held for him. It enabled him to explore a reconciliation of serialism and tonality—and by extension all the attendant dichotomies—on his own terms.[20]

Copland's row, shown in example 1 below, contains many tonal implications.[21] Triads and segments with common-practice harmonic potential appear within the row, and Copland takes advantage of them at certain key points in the Piano Quartet. For instance, the presence of fourths and fifths in the row's second hexachord allows Copland to retain sounds characteristic of his populist works. The three pitches marked under the staff in example 1 may be heard as scale degrees 4, 1, and 5, with C as a temporary tonal center.

Example 1. Basic tone row of Piano Quartet

In measures 49–50 of movement 3, for example, the piano left hand plays the segment to establish a cadence on F, which proves to be the leading tone of G flat, the following section's tonal center.

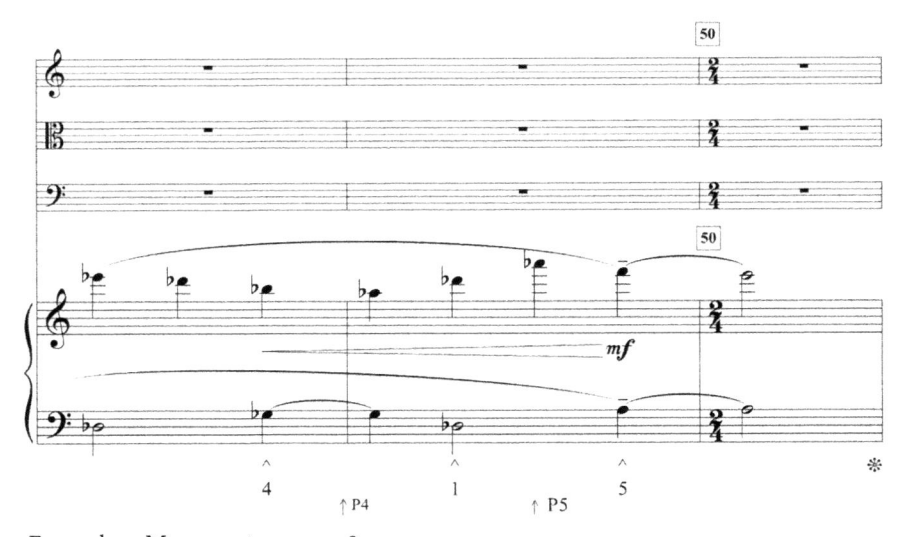

Example 2. Movement 3, mm. 48–50

Major and minor triads and major ninth chords are implied within the row. One of these is marked above the staff in example 1: James McGowan has pointed out that changes in the row's direction cause the pitches D, F (spelled E-sharp), C and B-flat to stand out to the listener, outlining a B-flat major triad with an added ninth.

In earlier movements, the triad plays a structural role: the strings' fugal entrances in movement one outline a minor triad, and at the third entrance the vertical sonority is a minor triad (measure 9). The strings' exposition ends on a C major triad (measure 17). A major chord with an added chromatic pitch is imbedded in the row at the beginning and end of each of the row's two extended whole-tone segments. This sonority is reserved for the last chord of the entire work.

Copland's row is saturated with whole tones. Seven out of the row's eleven consecutive intervals are major seconds; a three-note whole-tone segment appears five times within the row. It occurs most prominently at the beginning of the row. In the third movement, it becomes an incipit for the row itself.

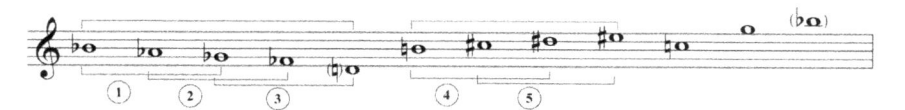

Example 3. Whole-tone segments within the basic row

This versatile three-note segment may also be vertically arranged to suggest a major ninth chord. That usage appears in the opening measures of movement 3, where D-flat major ninth chords begin and end the first two phrases—spelled with F, E-flat, and D-flat, a three-note descending whole-tone segment.

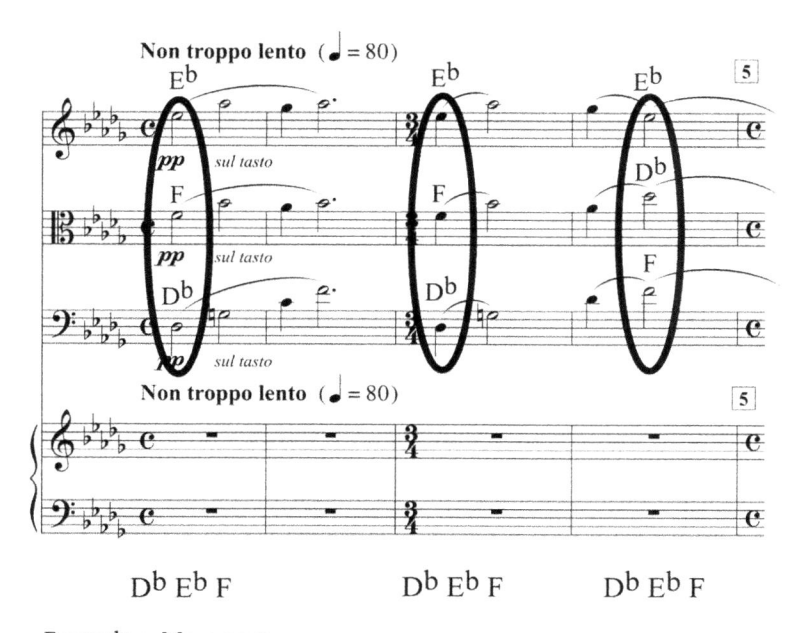

Example 4. Movement 3, mm. 1–4

The pervasiveness of the whole-tone motive facilitates double meanings, which can serve as a catalyst for reconciliation. The pitches B-flat, A-flat, and G-flat can be heard as scale degrees 3-2-1 in the key of G-flat, or as the beginning of a serial tone row. But once the whole-tone pattern is extended beyond three notes, the sense of key becomes obscured. Thus, Copland has built into his row an initial segment so tonal that it can evoke the nursery song "Three Blind Mice," yet in a slightly different context sound unmoored from any pitch center at all.

Example 5. "Three Blind Mice"

In the Quartet's first two movements, in moods ranging from meditative to playful, Copland blends dodecaphony with diatonicism smoothly.[22] The first movement, marked *Adagio serio* (quarter note = 60) is, on the whole, an unhurried exploration of the row's thematic potential. Its first half presents the initial referential contour or theme, together with other closely related melodic material, in smooth lines that layer and thicken gradually. The second half explores the same thematic material but introduces new musical resources: in some sections, increased surface rhythmic activity animates the still unhurried pace; in others, chords add force and textural variety. While the first half is gentle, the second half begins *marcato* and builds to a full, *fortissississimo* climax near the end. A brief denouement, also featuring the theme, ends the movement.

The second movement, a scherzo, is roughly in ternary form: A B A'. The first section (mm. 1–97) opens with, and features, a scurrying theme—rhythmically irregular and disjunct—alternating with contrasting material based on regular, repeated eighth notes. The section culminates in a climactic, homophonic passage, which leads into the developmental B section. The scurrying theme appears nowhere in this section; instead, Copland extensively develops the regular eighth-note material from the first section, deriving numerous new motives in the process. The opening motive's return marks the A' section (mm.

195–266). To the same succession of thematic entrances heard in the A section, Copland adds development of the scurrying theme and weaves in motives first heard in the B section. The A' section culminates in a climactic gesture similar to that of the A section, then closes with a hushed recollection of chords from movement 1.

But in the third movement, the techniques are juxtaposed abruptly. Particularly in the Piano Quartet's third movement, Copland seems to create two distinct characters in order to oppose them. "Tonality" is portrayed as nuanced, expressive, accessible, and diatonic. "Atonality" (also called "serialism" in this essay) is portrayed as monotonous, inexpressive, and alienating. After two movements that integrate dodecaphonic techniques with tonal harmony without using a key signature, why does the third movement begin with one? And why does the movement so prominently feature a strident, three-note, descending whole-tone motive?

Copland used the series of musical events that occur in the third movement of the Piano Quartet to address the ideological connotations and personal identity issues bound up in the serial-tonal dichotomy. Neither wins in the end, but they do reach a sort of musical detente, a peaceful coexistence. The process of dialogue does reveal some common ground, ending with hope for a future resolution.

Movement Three: A Dichotomy Constructed and Explored

The D-flat key signature that begins the movement is the first to appear in the work.[23] Passages in earlier movements established temporary tonal centers, without benefit of a key signature. Movement 1 began with an implication of E-flat minor, using (many) accidentals in lieu of a key signature. But here, Copland unambiguously signals a home key before a single note is heard.

Did the key of D-flat have special significance for Copland? A brief survey reveals that keys with five-flat signatures are fairly frequent in Copland's works, and they often carry connotations of poignancy and richness. Although in earlier works, five-flat key signatures are associated with force and excitement, as in the 1941 Piano Sonata sections featuring *pesante* and *marcato* articulation markings, or sections of the 1936 opera *The Second Hurricane*,[24] by the 1950s, Copland used five flats to convey a gentler ethos. Earlier in 1950, Copland had used five flats for "Sleep Is Supposed to Be," the seventh of the *Twelve Poems of Emily Dickinson*. Its location is central—six songs precede it; five follow—and it has been called "the finest" of the twelve songs.[25] In *The Tender Land* (1952–54) Copland would use five flats for the brief love affair between Laurie, the main

III

Example 6. Movement 3, mm. 1–23

character, and Martin, the drifter, while at the opera's end, D-flat is the key in which Laurie explains her decision to leave home, even though Martin has already left without her. Copland had introduced another doomed love affair in D-flat in his original overture to the film *The Heiress* (1949). Thus, Copland's oeuvre around 1950 associates poignancy, richness, and the exploration of problematic human relationships with the key of D-flat. Perhaps the passages in the Piano Quartet resonate with complex relationships, leave-taking, or a difficult, poignant situation.

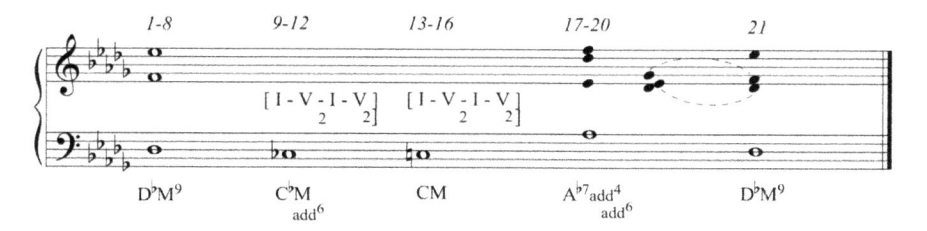

Example 7. Graph of principal tonal areas of movement 3, mm. 1–21

Although this opening passage remains connected to the original row,[26] common practice harmony provides the governing directional element. A reduction of measures 1–22 reveals a D-flat major ninth harmony extended from measures 1 through 8, a C-flat major harmony (or flat-VII in the key of D-flat) from measures 9 through 12, which reappears as a sequence on C major (mm. 13–16) leading to four measures of A-flat dominant harmony resolving over a descending fifth bass to form an authentic cadence in D-flat.

Within this harmonic scaffolding, the passage consists of balanced, periodic phrases, a homophonic texture, smooth voice leading, and a concluding authentic cadence. Its dynamic level is *pianissimo*, increasing only as far as *mezzo piano*. The texture is rich and warm, containing subtle timbral nuances created in part by register shifts and voice exchange. The passage's overall mood, as commentators have noted, is gentle and "hymnlike."[27]

Following this serene, tonal passage full of subtlety and nuance, the descending whole-tone motive arrives abruptly. The "atonal" character is announced by a jarring chord: E-flat–E–C-sharp, which breaks suddenly from the key of D-flat. Its articulation and metric placement accentuate the disjuncture: it enters with accents and a *sforzando* on a weak beat. The chord's interval content is more dissonant than the sonorities that preceded it, and its spelling, with an E-flat and an E-natural appearing in the same chord, visually emphasizes the departure from diatonic tradition. To visually underscore the conceptual leap,

Copland cancels out the key signature while the chord is still sounding. A new, slower tempo, *Molto meno mosso*, marks the beginning of a new section.

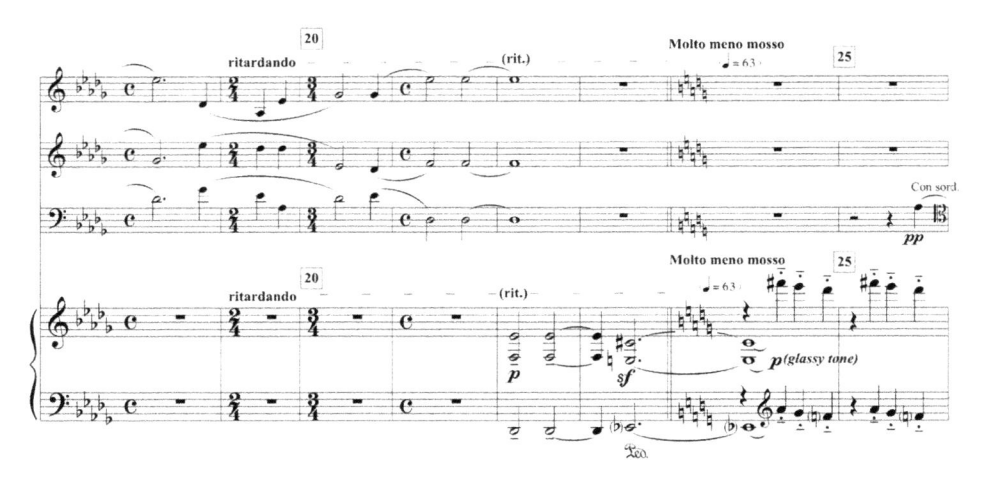

Example 8. Movement 3, mm. 18–25

With this abrupt introduction, the new whole-tone motive enters: the incipit of Copland's row. Admittedly, this representation of twelve-tone atonality is not completely disconnected from diatonicism. The movement's opening chords in the key of D-flat were built from the same row segment. And taken as a melodic entity, the motive can be heard as a three-note descent to tonic in a major key. Despite such possible double meanings, however, here the motive stands in dramatic relief to the tonal passage preceding it, because of its harmonization, transpositions, and articulation.

Copland harmonizes the motive in a way that negates any sense of tonal direction. As example 9 shows, the motive first appears in measure 24 presented in parallel major sixths. The D in the piano right hand is supported by an F-natural, which is not in the key of D major, and whose presence obscures any sense of D major that the right hand's melodic descent from F-sharp might otherwise have created. After repeating this motive, on the same pitches, the piano immediately presents it on B-flat, harmonized again in major sixths. The intervals that result, not present in either the key of D major or D minor, negate any sense of a D tonal center that may have lingered after the motive's first statements. Presentations of the motive then occur on C, A-flat, F-sharp, and D, all members of the same whole-tone scale as the preceding F-sharp and B-flat entrances, and all harmonized with parallel major sixths—members of the opposite whole-tone scale. By using the row's first three pitches at two different pitch levels simultaneously, Copland has presented two complementary

Example 9. Movement 3, mm. 22–33

whole-tone scales and, in the process, introduced all twelve chromatic pitches while avoiding implication of any tonic.[28]

Copland's articulation and expression markings also separate the atonal passage from the tonal one. The expression marking is "*(glassy tone)*," with a detached marcato articulation.[29] The dynamic begins *piano*, then fades to *pianissimo*. The motive here is more tentative and detached than strident, but the contrast with the "tonal" character is effectively the same.

Commentators have criticized this three-note motive over the years. In 1953 Arthur Berger wrote, "The first part of the theme is . . . a bit too elementary in rhythm and too evocative of the whole-tone scale to lend itself happily to quite so much prominence as Copland gives it in the course of the first and last movements ... it fails to bring in its wake either the most novel or the most inspired ideas of the work."[30] In 1982 David Conte wrote of the last movement, "What this movement lacks in motivic ingenuity and thematic development is compensated for by textural variety."[31] Other comments make other excuses: that Copland's lack of experience at using dodecaphony hindered his ability to choose a row that would adequately serve his purposes; that the pressure of a deadline prevented him from arriving at a more elegant compositional solution. The work was indeed written in a hurry: Copland completed it just nine days before its premiere.[32] It may be possible, as Richard Taruskin suggests, that had circumstances been different, Copland would have taken more time to treat dodecaphony more elegantly.[33] Such comments imply that Copland's theme was a lapse from his usual high standard of invention. Yet one cannot discount the possibility that the awkwardness was intentional.

After demonstrating a fairly smooth textural and timbral integration of serial and tonal techniques in the first two movements, why does the work's final movement separate the two? It is as if Copland portrays tonality and serialism as separate characters, pitted against each other in a struggle. These two characters are painted in bold, contrasting strokes at the beginning of the movement: a dichotomy is constructed, and a process aimed at reconciling the differences between serialism and tonality unfolds as the movement progresses.

And what of the "serial" character? The three-note descending whole-tone motive, as the initial row's first three notes, can be taken to represent the row as a whole. In 1941, as noted before, Copland had located three "inherent weaknesses" in serialism. First, he wrote, serialism is monotonous and resembles itself too much. Second, its expressive variety is limited. Third, "the atonal system cannot produce folk songs or lullabies."[34]

In this third movement, Copland's music seems to address all three of his earlier criticisms, whether to confirm or deny them. First, the atonal motive as Copland presents it *is* repetitive and monotonous. Second, whenever it appears in this movement, its articulation markings indicate that it be played with little expression. Thus, on these two points, Copland's characterization of atonality coincides with his earlier view. But on the third point, Copland seems to modify his earlier opinion, for the atonal motive does approximate a folk tune—more precisely, the beginning of one; however, it never blossoms into the balanced, periodic phrases of a fully stated folk song or lullaby. When it appears as a distinct character in this movement (namely, mm. 23–33 and 98–117), atonality is presented as a short, choppy motive, fragmented, without expressive nuance, and with detached articulation. Furthermore, it is not grounded in any larger-scale scheme comparable to the balanced periodic phrases or harmonic directional-ity of the preceding D-flat section. In contrast, diatonic tonality, presented in measures 1–22 and 79–97, *is* grounded in such a character: *legato*, nuanced, longer and broader, and full of subtlety and expression. Since the same pitch material—the eleven-note row—generates both kinds of music, texture and articulation become key factors that distinguish "serialism" from "diatonicism."

Dialogue and Detente

After the diatonic and serial characters are presented, the developmental middle section (mm. 34–79) comments more subtly on their relationship. The first sub-section (mm. 34–40) recalls "tonality" in that the movement's opening tempo returns, and the articulation softens to *delicato*, but the thematic material quickly takes on traits of "atonality," becoming otherworldly, raspy, less warm and less nuanced (*poco sul ponticello*). In the next group of phrases (mm. 40–50) the strings bring back the "tonal" theme, treated canonically, in a warmer *natural* tone, and at the initial, slower tempo.

The third part of the movement's middle section (mm. 51–60) makes an energetic entrance, recalling Copland's Americanist compositions of the 1930s and 1940s. In a clear reference to diatonicism, a key signature appears (this time, G-flat major, a close relative to D-flat in the tonal tradition). Characteristic of Copland's "accessible" or populist style, bold, rhythmically regular, and accented melodic lines are punctuated by syncopated accompaniment. A stately melody containing wide leaps occurs above a bass pedal. Harmony, timbre, and texture also reference the tonal tradition: the texture is made up of independent melodic lines that are rhythmically and harmonically aligned, string mutes are removed, and a tonic-subtonic harmonic progression supports this passage.

The Americana character then fades, the key signature is canceled, and in the next passage (mm. 61–69) increased syncopation and chromaticism culminate in an accented, *fortississimo* seventh chord (modified B-flat half-diminished seventh). These phrases nod toward the jazziness evident in certain Copland works that preceded his populist-Americanist period, like *Music for the Theatre* or the Piano Concerto.

The movement's middle section closes with gentle, *pianissimo* chords that recall the movement's opening. In one sense, the entire section seems to function as a flashback. Starting at measure 40, it fades back in time to an episodic remembrance of Copland's earlier diatonic styles, before fading back into the present just in time for the recapitulation section that closes the movement, which starts in measure 79.

Was this middle section an homage to a disappearing past? Closer examination reveals a surprise: "atonality" provides the structural underpinning. The references to Copland's earlier, "tonal" and jazzy styles occur above a bass line

Example 10. Movement 3, mm. 51–60

taken from the row. Beginning in measure 51, the bass outlines a whole-tone descent from G-flat through F-flat, D, C, and B-flat. This entire section of nostalgic references to "tonality" is given direction by a literal transposition of the first five pitches of Copland's tone row.

The struggle between "serialism" and "tonality" begins anew in measure 79, marking the arrival of what corresponds to the recapitulation in classic sonata

Example 11. Movement 3, mm. 61–69

form. Visually demarcated by a D-flat key signature, the "tonal" character re-appears as shown in example 12, nearly identical in pitch and rhythm to its first occurrence in measures 1–22, but presented by the piano. Once again, the "atonal" character interrupts, in measures 99 through 105, but significant changes indicate the struggle has intensified, and the two characters grapple more closely.

Example 12. Movement 3, mm. 79–91

First of all, the recapitulatory statement of the "tonal" character is less pure. What was first presented as measures 15 and 16 are omitted. Harmonically, this means that the C major harmony of measure 14 is not prolonged when it reappears as measure 92. But it has another result that highlights a more "serial" trait imbedded in this "tonal" passage. The omission allows an uninterrupted, five-note whole-tone descent—the opening of the row—to emerge in the piano's upper voice. And the upper voice contour of measures 91–92 is simplified, in comparison to measures 13 and 14, to reinforce the whole-tone descent.

As an added presence of "serialism" in this diatonic passage, the strings present references to the row in measures 80–86 above the piano's D-flat material,

Example 13. Movement 3, mm. 85–97

though those references are modified to fit within the key. However, in the second half of the tonal passage (mm. 87–91) the whole-tone descent in the high register first violin indicates a renewed attempt to break free from the key of D-flat. But as the string lines continue, they are gradually subsumed into the D-flat tonality by the time the passage approaches the anticipated cadence that closed the movement's first D-flat passage.

The expected cadence does not arrive. Just before the final D-flat major ninth arrives, the passage breaks off, and the harmony left hanging is an A-flat dominant seventh (with an added 4). The atonal voice asserts itself more forcefully than before, interrupting the cadence before the dominant chord's resolution to tonic.

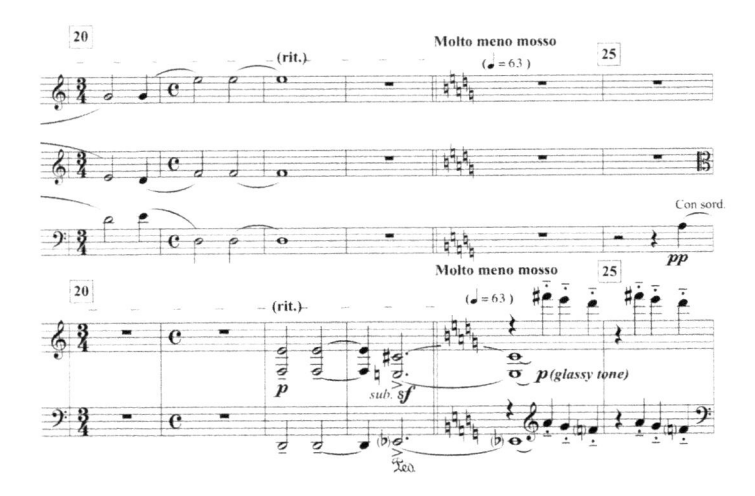

Example 14a. Movement 3, mm. 20–25

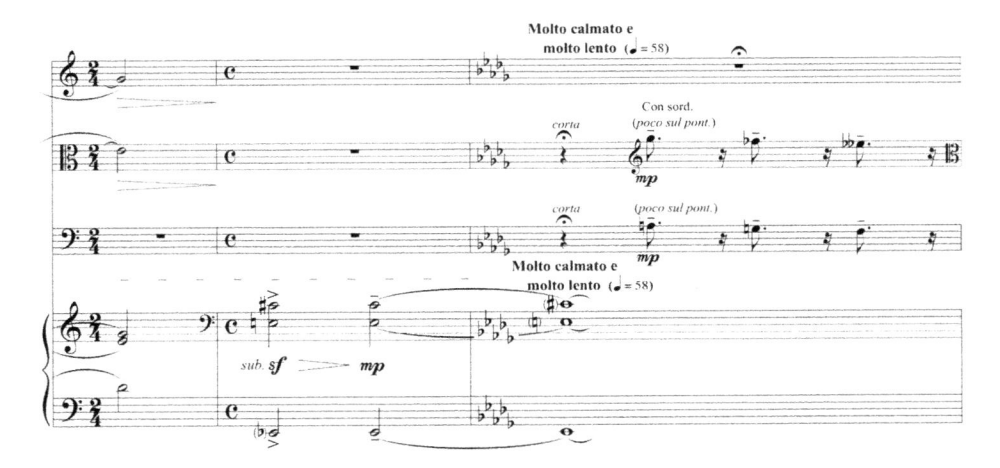

Example 14b. Movement 3, mm. 97–99

As before, the expressive markings indicate that the texture of this recapitulated atonal section should stand out in contrast to the legato, hymn-like quality of the preceding tonal section. The strings are muted and play *poco sul ponticello*. Further accentuating the difference in texture, each pitch of the three-note atonal motive is separated by a sixteenth rest, and is stressed, indicating a string articulation equivalent to the piano's earlier detached marcato.

By interrupting the D-flat passage's closing cadence, atonality prevents tonality from achieving resolution on its own terms. Tonality, if it is to resolve, must now account for serialism. Atonality's voice is stronger now: the three-note motive is presented eleven times, compared with eight in the corresponding earlier passage. While the strings present the atonal motive, the piano right hand quietly offers whole-tone scale fragments (mm. 102–106) in octaves in a high, exposed register—further obscuring any sense of diatonicism.

Example 15. Movement 3, mm. 99–112

Despite the renewed presence of the atonal voice, the diatonic character remains strong and independent as the first violin counters the flat, detached timbre of the viola and cello's atonal motive with a soaring, legato, *dolce et espressivo* line. Harmonically, a dominant triad in the key of D-flat is strongly implied by the piano left hand, which presents the pitches A-flat and E-flat repeatedly in different registers. By the end of the phrase (mm. 109–110), only the first violin holds a pitch not diatonic to D-flat. The strings pause, then reenter with a gentle, open fifth on A-flat, further reinforcing the dominant chord. Once again, a dominant-tonic cadence in D-flat major seems to be approaching.

Before the anticipated tonic chord arrives, the piano breaks in abruptly with the most forceful statement yet of the three-note atonal motive: *forte*, *pesante*, *marcato*, in a high register, and reinforced with octave doubling. As before, its harmonization in major sixths with the left hand obscures any sense of diatonicism. Furthermore, the succeeding statement of the motive is extended into a full presentation of the row's first hexachord, ending with the pitch class A—a significant pitch, as it turns out.

In these final measures, Copland draws from his repertoire of serial techniques to make his ending complete, and the pitch A is a needed resource. Copland had ended the first movement with a statement of his tone row, and for the first time added the missing twelfth chromatic pitch, what Boulanger had called the "note caché." But that earlier "completed" statement had been a transposition. Here, Copland for the first time offers a statement of the row that begins on E-flat. The first presentation of the row, at the beginning of the first movement, was on B-flat. The pitch class missing from that row statement had been A. Here in the third movement, the work's final chord prominently features an A, which appears in the high register of the piano and is reinforced with octave doubling. Serialism appears to have seized the upper hand.

But tonality's presence cannot be obscured. The initially forceful piano line diminuendos to *piano* by the end of its statement of the hexachord. While it holds the sixth pitch—A-natural—the strings, which had been silent for the previous five beats, reiterate a perfect fifth—A-flat and E-flat—joined this time by a C to form a complete dominant triad in the key of D-flat. This forces the piano's A to be aurally reinterpreted within the key of D-flat, as a chromatic neighbor tone to the dominant triad. Tonality was not overcome by the forceful reentry of the atonal motive. Looking at the score, one notes that, indeed, Copland never canceled out the D-flat key signature at the end of the most recent hymn-like section.

The dichotomy is not resolved: neither serialism nor tonality eclipses the other for long. The music never cadences on D-flat; in fact, unresolved neighbor tones are left hanging about the *dominant* chord of D-flat, creating a diatonic yet unresolved effect. And serialism's presence is stronger than ever: the atonal

Example 16. Movement 3, mm. 110–117

motive's dynamic level in the penultimate tonal passage is louder than anywhere else in the movement, and it has grown from the three-note incipit of the row into a six-note hexachord. Yet the second hexachord of the row does not appear. The D-flat key center, like the key signature, lingers to the end. Tonality in one sense subsumes serialism, because the last "serial" pitch—A—is heard as a neighbor tone to a diatonic dominant triad; yet that same A serves to complete the incomplete eleven-note row stated at the outset of the work.

Conclusion: Dialogue vs. Dichotomies

Copland participated in very specific contemporaneous cultural understandings of both serial and tonal music. The extramusical layers to the serial/tonal musical dichotomy arose gradually and shifted continually, taking different shapes in different times and locales. These "definitional axes," to use Hubbs's

term, were culturally constructed meanings that entered Copland's life one experience at a time, nudging his views one way or another.[35] His aesthetic views,
like his identity, were never static. The medium of music allowed for a sense
of unfolding and exploration that to some extent paralleled Copland's shifting
understanding of the mutable dichotomies surrounding him. Just as the Piano
Quartet's third movement enacts a dialogue between opposites fraught with
cultural significance, so Copland's identity, in a sense, was a dialogue between
his own self-identification and the categories that were culturally available to
him in his particular time and place. Musical, political, and sexual dichotomies
were entwined in twentieth-century modern music circles, informing the ne-
gotiation of individual and collective identities, especially at midcentury, and
especially for Copland.[36]

   If extramusical factors encouraged Copland's use of serialism in 1950, they
did not force him into Schoenberg's camp. Copland's use of serialism contradicts many of the stereotypes he had expressed in 1941: lullabies, folksong, and
tonality are potential in his tone row; expressive diationicism and mechanical
monotony spring from the same three-note root. Furthermore, while Schoenberg saw atonality as a necessary advancement that supplanted tonality, in the
Piano Quartet Copland reveals his own belief that the two could coexist, finding
commonalities without losing their distinctiveness.

   Charles Gamble has suggested that Copland's Piano Variations (1930) are not
tonal but "about" tonality. He turns to biography to explain the work's construction, concluding that it takes an "ironic and critical stance toward C# minor." In
the same way, Copland's Piano Quartet seems very much to be "about" a tone
row, "about" the key of D-flat, and about the ideological conflict between the
worlds they represented to Copland at midcentury. In the Variations, Gamble
discerns a "determination to go forward despite the loss of the resources of
tonality." The losses in the Quartet are different but just as real: the loss of populism and community, and the apparent necessity of pursuing an individualistic,
serial-influenced aesthetic.[37]

   The oppositional thinking encouraged by the Cold War climate stifled artists,
Copland protested, because it discouraged dialogue. By 1950, Copland knew he
could attempt neither cultural exchange nor political reconciliation between the
United States and the Soviet Union without endangering his career. But in the
Piano Quartet, he faced and explored one of the false dichotomies he listed in
his Peace Conference speech—a dichotomy reinforced through Stalin's prohibi-
tions and Schoenberg's implied accusations. On many of the definitional axes
operating in the decade after World War II, his identity was suspect. When he
used words to protest the very idea of dichotomies at the Peace Conference, he
found himself categorized at the "wrong" end of multiple axes. But on a musical plane, the Piano Quartet was a forum within which Copland could safely

explore common ground between apparent ideological opposites—tonality and serialism—with fruitful, if sometimes uneasy, artistic results.

Notes

Quartet for Piano and Strings by Aaron Copland ©1951, 1952 The Aaron Copland Fund for Music, Inc. Copyright renewed. Boosey & Hawkes, Inc., sole licensee. Reprinted with permission.

1. Copland, "Speech." (Text of this press release is identical to the script for Copland's Peace Conference Speech found in the Aaron Copland Collection, Music Division, Library of Congress.) I found this undated document in a "Speeches, misc" file in the Aaron Copland Collection at the Library of Congress (hereafter identified as ACCLC) and identified it as Copland's Peace Conference speech in May 1995. A modified version appeared in *Speaking of Peace*, 90–91. The text is now available in Kostelanetz, *Aaron Copland*, 128–31.

2. See Wellens, *Music on the Frontline*, 8–10, and US Congress, House, "Report on the Communist 'Peace' Offensive, a Campaign to Disarm and Defeat the US," April 1, 1951.

3. Jumonville, *Critical Crossings*, 1–48; Saunders, *Cultural Cold War*, 45–56.

4. In a 1996 paper delivered at the Annual Meeting of the American Musicological Society in Baltimore, titled "Of Politics and Style: Copland's Quartet for Piano and Strings," I first proposed that Copland's perceived need to distance himself from past political associations provided impetus for his twelve-tone composition experiments in the 1950s and '60s. My dissertation, "Copland in the Fifties: Music and Ideology in the McCarthy Era," completed in June 1997, was recognized the next year with the Society for American Music's dissertation prize. Since then, Richard Taruskin, Nadine Hubbs, and Elizabeth Bergman [Crist] are the most prominent of many subsequent scholars who have further developed this line of thought.

5. Copland to US Passport Office, November 2, 1953, ACCLC box 427/4.

6. Nadine Hubbs discusses the relationship between sexual identity, Copland's professional circles, and his compositional approach in *The Queer Composition of America's Sound*, 154–159 and 175; see also her earlier article, "French Connection."

7. Copland's vulnerability to anticommunist attacks on account of his sexuality, Jewishness, and past political associations are more fully treated in my article "Aaron Copland and the Politics of Twelve-Tone Composition in the Early Cold War United States." On Copland's Jewish identity, see also Pollack, "Copland and the Prophetic Voice," in *Copland and His World*, 1–14; Botstein, "Copland Reconfigured"; Pollack, *Aaron Copland*, 25–29 and 518–24. On anticommunism and anti-Semitism, see Joel Kovel, *Red Hunting*, and Crist, *Music for the Common Man*, 209–27.

8. Thomson, "Music in Review." Letter published in Thomson, "Music in Review," *New York Herald Tribune*, September 25, 1949; the exchange is described in Copland and Perlis, *Copland: Since 1943*, 152–54.

9. Copland issued a statement to the press disclaiming responsibility for that part of the score. Joseph Keeley to Mort Nathanson, March 6, 1950, ACCLC box 427/5.

On scandal over the title music to *The Heiress* see Copland and Perlis, *Copland: Since 1943*, 98–106, and Pollack, *Aaron Copland*, 433–37.

10. D'Emilio, *Sexual Politics*, 42.

11. *Red Channels*, 39–41.

12. Many of the connections among these supposedly separate organizations would come to light only after Copland's lifetime. See DeLapp-Birkett, "Twelve-Tone Composition," 45–46, and DeLapp-Birkett, "Government Censorship."

13. Since Stravinsky was commonly named as Schoenberg's stylistic opponent, Copland's substitution of Shostakovich, a Soviet citizen, underscored the political aspects of his comparison. That "Communism vs. the Profit System" had parallels in the composers' world would have been reinforced by his acquaintance Nicolas Nabokov, who was about to produce two anticommunist concerts in Europe with covert funding from the CIA; see Saunders, *Cultural Cold War*, Wellens, *Music on the Frontline*, and DeLapp-Birkett, "Twelve-Tone Composition," 52–55, 60–61.

14. Copland and Perlis, *Copland: Since 1943*, 151.

15. Copland's terminology is imprecise by most standards. Here and in other published writings, he follows contemporaneous popular usage when he uses "the atonal system," "atonality," "twelve-tone music," "dodecaphonic music," and even "serial techniques" or "serialism" interchangeably; see, for example, Thomson's use of "the atonal method" in "Atonality Today: I" and "Atonality Today: II."

16. Copland, *Our New Music*, 56.

17. Two well-known examples of Copland's emphasis on "purely musical" reasons for turning to serial techniques in 1950 date from 1967 and the late 1980s. In 1967 he told Edward T. Cone, "In the early years, in my own mind, [Schoenberg] and Berg and Webern were under something of a cloud for the reason that they were still writing German music, and German music was the thing we were trying to get out from under. . . . It was only later, at the end of the Second World War, the younger fellows, Boulez and such made it clear that you could keep the [serial] method while throwing away the esthetic." "Conversation with Aaron Copland" in *Perspectives on American Composers*, edited by Benjamin Boretz and Edward T. Cone (New York: Norton, 1971), 140–41. His autobiography states: "Composing with all twelve notes of the chromatic scale can give one a feeling of *freedom* in the formulation of melodic and harmonic ideas." Copland and Perlis, *Copland: Since 1943*, 151. For an excellent musicological discussion of the Cold War catchword *freedom* and its relationship to serial techniques at midcentury, see Shreffler, "Ideologies of Serialism," 217–45.

18. On Copland's post-1950 reinterpretation of his earlier involvement in popular-front ideology, see DeLapp, "Copland in the Fifties," 48–55, 68–93, and 112–13; Pollack, *Aaron Copland*, 296–97, 274–81, and 338; DeLapp-Birkett, "Twelve-Tone Composition," 59–61; Elizabeth Bergman Crist, "Copland and the Politics of Americanism," in Oja and Tick, *Aaron Copland and His World*, 299, 302; and Crist, *Music for the Common Man*, 200 (*Music for the Common Man* is a book-length treatment of political and ideological links between Copland's "accessible" music and radical and liberal politics). Copland's Depression-era politics were earlier addressed in Pollack, *Aaron Copland*, 270–87, and Bick, *Composers on the Cultural Front*, 59–61 and 152–57.

19. Copland, *Our New Music*, 56–57.

20. One basic principle of twelve-tone composition is that rather than using the traditional major or minor scale to structure pitch relationships, the composer creates a "tone row," usually specific to that piece, which has certain traits he or she wants to emphasize in the piece.

21. The row as he sketched it contains twelve pitches, yet it contains only eleven different ones. As Arthur Berger points out, Schoenberg's Serenade, Op. 24, does use an eleven-tone row. Berger, *Aaron Copland*, 84. Copland saw a tone row from the standpoint of a compositional realization, with a specific contour—that is, a series of rising and falling intervals. On properties of Copland's tone row, his familiarity with Schoenbergian compositional techniques, and the serial methods employed in all three movements of the Piano Quartet, see DeLapp, "Copland in the Fifties," 191–204. Richard Taruskin later presented many of the same ideas, using the Piano Quartet as his case study, in "The Apex," chap. 3 of *Music in the Late Twentieth Century*; see especially the chapter section titled "'Mainstream' Dodecaphony."

22. For additional analyses of the work, see Conte, "Aaron Copland's Piano Quartet"; McGowan, "Harmonic Organization"; and Taruskin, *Music in the Late Twentieth Century*, chap. 3.

23. The possibility that the lack of sharps and flats indicated C major in earlier movements is not borne out by the pitch material; no cadences on C or related pitch centers appear at important structural points. If movement 1begins in a key, it is E-flat minor, and it occurs without a key signature. Furthermore, measures 24 to 28 of the first movement establish D-flat temporarily, without any accompanying key signature. That Copland wrote diatonic passages without a key signature earlier in the work makes the appearance of one at the start of the third movement seem particularly striking.

24. This is particularly evident in the last minutes of act 1.

25. Evans, "Thematic Technique," 5. The key is really B-flat major, since the D is consistently naturalized when a B-flat triad occurs at structural points, but it is significant that Copland chooses five flats to set this poignant, restful text.

26. The opening chord, for example, is composed of three pitches a whole tone apart, which correspond to any of the whole-tone segments in the row.

27. Berger, *Aaron Copland*, 85; Peter Evans, "Thematic Technique," 6.

28. All twelve pitches occur in the piano from the double measure through the second beat of measure 28; if that second beat of measure 28 is also grouped with what follows, the piano presents all twelve chromatic pitches a second time in measures 28 through 33.

29. It must be noted that a "glassy" sonority was not unique to Copland's dodecaphonic compositions. However, Schoenberg was likely its inspiration. In *Our New Music*, he commented on certain aspects of Schoenberg's orchestral style: "Characteristic of one small corner of his orchestration is the love of a magical, bell-like sonority that is somehow extracted from harp, celesta, glockenspiel, mandolin, and so forth. Alban Berg took full advantage of that hint in his last orchestral works." Copland, *Our New Music*, 63n. Possibly related is the "crystalline" marking in the Piano Sonata's third movement.

30. McGowan, "Harmonic Organization," 59.

31. Ibid., 58.

32. Copland and Perlis, *Copland: Since 1943*, 151.

33. Taruskin, *Oxford History of Western Music*, chap. 3.

34. Copland, *Our New Music*, 56–57.

35. Hubbs, *Queer Composition of America's Sound*, 166. To acknowledge the fluidity of Copland's views is not to imply any sense of opportunism or insincerity but to make us wary of absolute statements ("Copland thought x") and to encourage us to situate his expressed opinions with as much historical specificity as possible.

36. Hubbs, *Queer Composition of America's Sound*, 144. The terms used for the poles of these binarisms, Hubbs cautions, are admittedly imprecise, even "reductive," leading to a "diminishment of semantic specificity." Yet the terms have definite "historical meanings and [do] cultural work." Hubbs, *Queer Composition of America's Sound*, 144. They are not denotative but connotative; they serve as cultural "shorthand" for complex and powerful forces within culture. Far from being prescriptive categories that logically follow from the individual's traits or choices, they arise as communities grapple with the meaning and significance of the artwork to their own time and place.

37. Gamble, "Framing Interval," 133–36. "[W]e should not be disappointed when the various strands of the musical fabric cannot be subsumed within a single over-arching interpretation. For twentieth-century works of art, this may be the norm, and not the exception." His perceptive analyses suggest that searching for a single interpretive or analytical scheme for much post-tonal music, including Copland's, may deny one of such works' most fundamental assumptions: the impossibility of unity.

References

Anderson, Paul. "'To Become as Human as Possible': The Influence of André Gide on Aaron Copland." In Oja and Tick, *Copland and His World*, 47–79.

Beal, Amy. "The Army, The Airwaves, and the Avant-Garde: American Classical Music in Postwar West Germany." *American Music* 21 (2003): 474–513.

Berger, Arthur. *Aaron Copland*. New York: Oxford University Press, 1953. Reprint, New York: Da Capo, 1990.

———. *Reflections of an American Composer*. Berkeley: University of California Press, 2002.

Bick, Sally M. A. *Composers on the Cultural Front: Aaron Copland and Hanns Eisler in Hollywood*. New Haven, Conn.: Yale University Press, 2001.

Botstein, Leon. "Copland Reconfigured." In Oja and Tick, *Copland and His World*, 454–71. Princeton, N.J.: Princeton University Press, 2005.

———. "Preserving Memory." *Musical Quarterly* 83 (1999): 298–302.

Brody, Martin. "'Music for the Masses': Milton Babbitt's Cold War Music Theory." *Musical Quarterly* 77 (1993): 161–92.

Carroll, Mark. *Music and Ideology in Cold War Europe*. Cambridge: Cambridge University Press, 2003.

Cazden, Norman. "What's Happening in Soviet Music?" *Masses and Mainstream* 1 (April 1948): 11–24.

Cone, Edward T., and Aaron Copland. "Conversation with Aaron Copland." in *Perspectives on American Composers*, edited by Benjamin Boretz and Edward T. Cone, 131–146. New York: Norton, 1971.

Conte, David Joseph. "Aaron Copland's Piano Quartet: An Analysis." MA thesis, Cornell University, 1982.

Copland, Aaron. *Copland on Music*. Garden City, N.Y.: Doubleday, 1960.

———. "The Effect of the Cold War on the Artist in the U.S." In Kostelanetz, *Aaron Copland*, 128–131.

———. "Gabriel Fauré, A Neglected Master." *Musical Quarterly* 10, no. 4 (October 1924): 573–86.

———. Letter to the editor. Published in Virgil Thomson, "Music in Review." *New York Herald Tribune*, September 25, 1949.

———. *Music and Imagination*. Cambridge, Mass.: Harvard University Press, 1952.

———. *The New Music: 1900–1960*. Rev. ed. New York: Norton, 1968.

———. "The New 'School' of American Composers." *New York Times*, March 14, 1948. Reprinted in Copland, *Copland on Music*, 164–174.

———. *Our New Music: Leading Composers in Europe and America*. New York: McGraw-Hill, 1941.

———. "The World of A-Tonality." *New York Times Book Review*, November 27, 1949, 5.

Copland, Aaron, and Vivian Perlis. *The Complete Copland*. Hillsdale, N.Y: Pendragon, 2013.

———. *Copland 1900–1942*. New York: St. Martin's/Marek, 1984.

———. *Copland: Since 1943*. New York: St. Martin's, 1989.

Crist, Elizabeth Bergman. "Aaron Copland and the Popular Front." *Journal of the American Musicological Society* 56, no. 2 (2003): 409–65.

———. "Critical Politics: The Reception History of Aaron Copland's Third Symphony." *Musical Quarterly* 85, no. 2 (2001): 232–63.

———. *Music for the Common Man: Aaron Copland during the Depression and War*. New York: Oxford University Press, 2005.

DeLapp, Jennifer. "Copland in the Fifties: Music and Ideology in the McCarthy Era." PhD diss., University of Michigan, 1997.

———. "Government Censorship and Aaron Copland's *Lincoln Portrait* during the Second Red Scare." In *The Oxford Handbook of Music Censorship*, edited by Patricia Hall, 511–34. New York: Oxford University Press, 2018.

———. "Speaking to Whom? Modernism, Middlebrow, and Copland's *Short Symphony*." In *Copland Connotations: Studies and Interviews*, edited by Peter Dickinson (Rochester, N.Y.: Boydell and Brewer, 2002), 96–97. DeLapp-Birkett, Jennifer. "Aaron Copland and the Politics of Twelve-Tone Composition in the Early Cold War United States." *Journal of Musicological Research* 27 (2008): 31–62.

D'Emilio, John. *Sexual Politics, Sexual Communities*. Chicago: University of Chicago Press, 1998.

Dietz, Betty A. "Aaron Copland Tops U.S. Composers with Hearings." *Daily News*, October 12, 1947.

Doss, Erica. *Benton, Pollock, and the Politics of Modernism: From Regionalism to Abstract Expressionism*. Chicago: University of Chicago Press, 1991.

Evans, Peter. "Compromises with Serialism." *Proceedings of the Royal Musical Association*, 88th Sess. (1961): 1–15.

———. "The Thematic Technique of Copland's Recent Works." *Tempo* 51 (Spring–Summer 1959): 2–13.

Gamble, Charles W. "The Framing Interval and Its Role in the Integration of Melody and Form in Four Early Works by Aaron Copland." PhD diss., City University of New York, 2001.

Gentry, Philip. "Leonard Bernstein's *The Age of Anxiety*: A Great American Symphony during McCarthyism." *American Music* 29, no. 3 (2011): 308–10.

Guilbaut, Serge. *How New York Stole the Idea of Modern Art: Abstract Expressionism, Freedom, and the Cold War*. Chicago: University of Chicago Press, 1983.

Hubbs, Nadine. "A French Connection: Modernist Codes in the Musical Closet." *GLQ: A Journal of Lesbian and Gay Studies* 6 (2000): 389–412.

———. *The Queer Composition of America's Sound: Gay Modernists, American Music, and National Identity*. Berkeley: University of California Press, 2004.

Jumonville, Neil. *Critical Crossings: The New York Intellectuals in Postwar America*. Berkeley: University of California Press, 1991.

Kostelanetz, Richard, ed. With Steve Silverstein. *Aaron Copland: A Reader; Selected Writings 1923–1972*. New York: Routledge, 2003.

Kovel, Joel. *Red Hunting in the Promised Land: Anti-Communism and the Making of America*. New York: Basic, 1994.

Lieberman, Robbie. *The Strangest Dream: Communism, Anticommunism, and the U.S. Peace Movement, 1945–1963*. Syracuse: Syracuse University Press, 2000.

Luce, Betsy. "Rival Rallies Debate Peace Policies: Pickets Mass for Keynote Session." *New York Post*, March 27, 1949.

McGowan, James. "Harmonic Organization in Aaron Copland's Piano Quartet." MM thesis, University of North Texas, 1995.

Nabokov, Nicolas. "Changing Styles in Soviet Music." *Listener*, October 11, 1951: 598–99.

———. "Festivals and the Twelve-Tone Row." *Saturday Review of Literature*, January 13, 1951, 36, 58, 83–84.

———. "Music in the Soviet Union: A View of the Shifting Battlefront." *Musical America*, February 1951: 12+.

Oja, Carol J., and Judith Tick, eds. *Copland and His World*. Princeton, N.J.: Princeton University Press, 2005.

O'Neil, James F. "How You Can Fight Communism." *America Legion Magazine* (1948): 15–17, 42–44.

Pollack, Howard. *Aaron Copland: The Life and Work of an Uncommon Man*. Urbana: University of Illinois Press, 2000.

Ramey, Phillip. Program notes to *Aaron Copland, Quartet for Piano and Strings*. Columbia LP M30376.

Red Channels: A Report on Communist Influence in Radio and Television. New York: American Business Consultants, 1950.

"Red Visitors Cause Rumpus." *Life* 26, no. 14 (April 4, 1949): 40–43.

Santa, Matthew. "Studies in Post-Tonal Diatonicism: A MOD7 Perspective." PhD diss., 1999.

Saunders, Frances Stonor. *The Cultural Cold War: The CIA and the World of Arts and Letters.* New York: New Press, 2000.

Schrecker, Ellen. *The Age of McCarthyism: A Brief History with Documents.* 2nd. ed. Boston: Bedford / St. Martin's, 2002.

"Schuman Requests Freedom of Artists." *New York Times,* October 12, 1950.

Schuman, William. "A Birthday Salute to Aaron Copland." *New York Herald Tribune,* October 30, 1960.

Shreffler, Anne C. "Ideologies of Serialism: Stravinsky's *Threni* and the Congress for Cultural Freedom." In *Music and the Aesthetics of Modernity,* edited by Karol Berger and Anthony Newcomb, 217–45. Cambridge, Mass.: Harvard University Department of Music, 2005.

———. "The Myth of Empirical Historiography: A Response to Joseph N. Straus." *Musical Quarterly* 84 (2000): 28–44.

Speaking of Peace: An Edited Report of the Cultural and Scientific Conference for World Peace, New York, March 25, 26 and 27, 1949, under the Auspices of National Council of the Arts, Sciences and Professions. Edited by Daniel S. Gillmor. New York: National Council of the Arts, Sciences and Professions, 1949.

Starr, Larry. "Copland's Style." *Perspectives of New Music* 19 (1980–81): 68–89.

Straus, Joseph N. "The Myth of Serial 'Tyranny' in the 1950s and 1960s." *Musical Quarterly* 83 (1999): 301–43.

———. *Remaking the Past: Musical Modernism and the Influence of the Tonal Tradition.* Cambridge, Mass.: Harvard University Press, 1990.

Taruskin, Richard. *Music in the Late Twentieth Century.* New York: Oxford University Press, 2009.

Thomson, Virgil. "Atonality Today: I" and "Atonality Today: II." In *Music, Right and Left,* 180–83, 184–86. New York: Holt, 1951.

———. "Composers in Trouble." *New York Herald Tribune,* February 22, 1948.

———. "Music in Review: Schoenberg Celebrates Seventy-Fifth Birthday with Attack on Conductors." *New York Herald Tribune,* September 11, 1949.

———. "Russians Recover." *New York Herald Tribune,* February 27, 1949.

———. "Soviet Aesthetics." *New York Herald Tribune,* May 2, 1948.

———. *The State of Music.* New York: Morrow, 1939.

Watkins, Glenn. *Soundings: Music in the Twentieth Century.* New York: Schirmer, 1988.

Wellens, Ian. *Music on the Frontline: Nicolas Nabokov's Struggle against Communism and Middlebrow Culture.* Burlington, Vt.: Ashgate, 2002.

ARCHIVAL SOURCES AND GOVERNMENT DOCUMENTS

Copland, Aaron. Interview with Pearson Underwood, October 30, 1950. Library of Congress, Recorded Sound Collection.

Copland, Aaron. "Speech to be delivered by Aaron Copland, composer, at the Fine Arts Panel of the Cultural and Scientific Conference for World Peace . . . March 27."

Press release, March 27, [1949], Aaron Copland Collection, Music Division, Library of Congress. [Reprinted in *Speaking of Peace* and *Aaron Copland: A Reader*]

Jelinek, Hanns. *Anleitung zur Zwolftonkomposition, nebst allerlei Paralipomena* (Vienna: Universal-Edition, 1952); Copland's personal copy with margin notes, ACCLC.

Keeley, Joseph. Letter to Mort Nathanson, March 6, 1950. Aaron Copland Collection, box 427/5, Music Division, Library of Congress.

US Congress. House. *The Communist "Peace" Offensive.* 82d Cong., 1st sess., 1951. H. Rept. 378.

———. "Report on the Communist 'Peace' Offensive, a Campaign to Disarm and Defeat the U.S." April 1, 1951. Washington, DC: GPO, 1951.

———. *A Review of the Scientific and Cultural Conference for World Peace Arranged by the National Council of the Arts, Sciences, and Professions and Held in New York City on March 25, 26, and 27 1949.* 81st Cong., 2d sess., 1950. H. Rept. 1954.

———. *Testimony of Walter S. Steele Regarding Communist Activity in the United States.* 80th Cong., 1st sess., July 21, 1947, 1–173.

US Congress. Senate. "Employment of Homosexuals and Other Sex Perverts in Government." 81st Cong, 2nd Sess. Washington, DC: GPO, Senate Document No. 241, 1950. Reprinted in *Major Problems in the History of Sexuality*, edited by Kathy Peiss, 376–77. Boston: Houghton Mifflin, 2002.

PART IV

Ethnography

For scholars of American music, ethnography and field-based work and research methods are far less commonly practiced than text-based styles of research, such as archival work and score analysis. While firmly established with studies of American Indian music by such luminaries as Alice Fletcher and Frances Densmore, the practice of fieldwork is today generally associated with the discipline of ethnomusicology, which is theoretically grounded in anthropology and, to a lesser extent, culture studies. As a rule, Americanists are not as tightly bound to these disciplines but rather are trained through programs emphasizing historical musicology as a scholarly model with an emphasis on score studies and text-based analysis. And while ethnomusicologists can indeed be Americanists by geographic area of study, they tend to not think of themselves in those terms but instead as scholars of the world whose piece of the world includes North America.

The four studies included in this section all utilize ethnographic work as the central focus of their research method, but they do it in different ways. Chapter 12, by Tara Browner, is a reexamination of ethnographic field research by Natalie Curtis Burlin and the intersection of her life with that of composer Ferruccio Busoni. Burlin, an amateur musical ethnographer, published *The Indian's Book* as Natalie Curtis in 1907. The contents were based on her travels around North America interacting with various tribal peoples, and because of a number of reprints—most recently by Dover in 1968—without a doubt, this book is the most common source information on Native music available. It is, in fact, ubiquitous, and in 2013 became available as an e-book. Given how influential this text was and is, a new look at Curtis Burlin's approach to research and how Busoni interpreted her transcriptions in his *Indianisches Tagebuch* (BV 267) is a kind of ethnographic reversal of the usual practice of starting with the score and working down through it in an analytical fashion. Instead, an approach through the lens of ethnography starts with the culture where the tune originated and then works upward through the "collection" process, and finally through the layers of European musical styles imposed upon it.

Chapter 13, by Joshua Duchan, reveals the nuts and bolts of just how empirical work in the form of ethnographic participant/observation can be done literally in the researcher's backyard, on a college campus. Drawn from his experiences while researching his dissertation, Duchan reveals to those unfamiliar with the mechanics of contemporary field research that it not only involves working with informants in often personally familiar settings but also consists of endless trials and difficulties involved in planning projects in a way that will pass the dreaded Institutional Review Boards (IRBs) and receive the coveted certification of Human Subjects exemption. Because ethnographic methods are so embedded in the minds of musicologists as constituting work on the non-Western "Other," Duchan reminds us that fieldwork is indeed a method and one not constrained by the location of its subject.

Mark Katz conducts ethnographic research in a twenty-first-century style, combining data from live interviews and contest attendance with observations drawn from postings and responses on internet forums. In chapter 14 he deals with two seemingly closely related but aesthetically different compositional practices, those of turntablists and mashup artists. While turntablism is a public form of instrumental performance with known celebrities whom Katz can interview and contests he can attend, the culture of mashup artists is primarily—but not exclusively—internet based and often subversive, in that practitioners are constantly skirting the boundaries of copyright statutes. For the most part, Katz's study is introductory inasmuch as he defines, compares, and contrasts turntablism and mash-up practices, and he also deftly tackles a key issue with these new popular styles, which is how to define the concept of "composer" in genres that do not easily conform to our ideas of composed or even improvised music.

In Tara Browner's 2009 essay "The Role of Musical Transcription in the Work of Ethnography" (*Songs from "A New Circle of*

Voices:" The 16th Annual Pow-wow at UCLA, 2009), she argues that in fundamental ways, transcribing music is a form of ethnographic practice. In this case, the transcriptions were of field recordings she had made herself. But for many music scholars, the transcription of live recordings is as close as they can get to the moment when the sounds first came to life. In the case of Mark Tucker (chapter 15), transcribing the Thelonius Monk Quartet's 1948 performance of *Misterioso* would have been a kind of practical ethnography, in that Tucker created a score from a performance that occurred six years before his birth and undoubtedly used it the way most musicians use their transcriptions: as a means for better understanding nonfigurative compositional practices. With no score to study, Tucker created his own visual text and, in doing so, reinscribed a moment of improvisation that had been originally fixed through the process of recording. The differences between analyzing a written score from a composer's pen and one that you have, for the lack of a better term, thrashed out yourself are profound in their levels of musical engagement and ethnographic understanding, as transcription pulls its practitioner into the musical performance, note by note and moment by moment.

In the ever-expanding field of American music scholarship, ethnographic work in all of its complex variations is increasingly taking its place next to archival studies and score analysis as a fundamental research technique, well suited to a world where the boundaries between composers, performers, and audience members are increasingly unfixed and permeable.

12 Ferruccio Busoni and *The Indians' Book*

TARA BROWNER

From 1913 through 1915, Italian virtuoso pianist and composer Ferruccio Busoni (1866–1924) wrote three works based on transcriptions of Native American songs that he had received from Natalie Curtis, an ethnographer who was also his former theory pupil. These pieces were *Indianische Fantasie* (op. 44, for piano and orchestra, 1913), *Indianisches Tagebuch: Erstes Buch* (BV 267, for piano, 1915), and *Gesang vom Reigen der Geister* (op. 45, for small orchestra, 1915). Busoni's use of American Indian melodies as a basis for European art music was unusual. Although Antonín Dvořák (1841–1904) used what could be Native songs in his Symphony no. 9 (*The New World*) and definitely adapted authentic melodies in smaller works, such as *Indian Canzonetta* and *Indian Lament*, in a general sense the notion of Indian music as a source material never caught on with European composers the way it did with a number of American composers—known colloquially as "Indianists"—during the same era. Busoni's works themselves, one of which is for solo piano, one for piano and orchestra, and one for small orchestra, are carefully crafted and sonically attractive yet not particularly well known. A number of questions arise from Busoni's unusual use of indigenous American themes, including his relationship with Curtis, his choices and usage of Native melodies, and why he decided to utilize them not just once but a number of times. Arguably the most significant issue is whether or not Busoni's "Indian" works fit into the American "Indianist" musical matrix or, instead, the larger European Primitivist movement emerging at that time.

Unlike Americans, who found the use of Indian melodies a popular way to give music an "American" flavor, European nations already possessed their own long-standing folk music traditions, with composers drawing upon them as needed to create music invoking national pride and identity. Still, the almost complete absence of Indian music or themes in European art music at the turn of the century is puzzling, since the intellectual climate in Europe of the fin de siècle was characterized by looking outward to other, non-European cultures, especially those of the Orient.[1] Searching their own past for ancient and often imagined traditions as source material, and adding ingredients from exotic locales, some European composers attempted a kind of musical rejuvenation by annexing these elements into their personal musical language. But although by the turn of the century Indians and Europeans had been in contact for four hundred years, Native American songs never really had an impact upon Europeans the way African American (most specifically jazz), African, or some Southeast Asian repertories did, perhaps understandably, considering the monophonic nature of most Native musical expression, at least as communicated through transcriptions. While Busoni had little or no experience with indigenous American musical expression prior to his meeting Natalie Curtis, that does not mean he had not encountered Indian cultures—at least in literary form—prior to their initial interactions, or that these encounters did not influence his compositional style.

European stereotypes of Indians were of a different sort than those held by Euro-Americans. In a letter to Hugo Leichtentritt in 1914, Busoni describes his *Indian Fantasy* as having "no program[, b]ut poetic simulations, such as the melancholy of the race."[2] As a rule, "melancholy" was not an attribute assigned to Indians by American settler colonialists; it had a uniquely European origin. According to historian Hugh Honour, "The melancholy Indian made his bow on the European scene in the very first year of the nineteenth century in Chateaubriand's *Atala*."[3] In 1791, French author François-René de Chateaubriand sailed to America, traveled through the new American Federation for five months, and ten years later upon his return to France published a novel, *Les amours de deux sauvages dans le desert* (1801), based on his American adventures. The hero and heroine of this purportedly factual tale are members of the Natchez Nation, a tribe located along the lower Mississippi River who were almost totally exterminated by the French in 1730.[4] In the narrative, Chactas, a Christian Indian, is rescued from the heathen Natchez by Atala, another Christian Indian, and together they flee to Florida. Unfortunately, Atala has taken a vow of perpetual chastity, and rather than be tempted into breaking it by Chactas, she commits suicide, leaving Chactas to spend the rest of his life in mourning. It is doubtful whether any elements of this tale are actually of Natchez origin, and even the names may be invented, for Chactas sounds suspiciously similar to Chahta, the proper pronunciation for the tribal name of the then Mississippi-based Choctaws. Nor are vows of chastity a common element in Native culture, although perhaps Atala, as a Christian, might conceivably have made one. Nevertheless, a lack of authenticity was not a barrier to popularity, and Chactas became the symbol all over Western Europe for the melancholy, grief-stricken Indian, inspiring paintings, engravings, and sculptures for decades after his first appearance.[5]

As the recipient of the imagery arising from his own culture, Busoni's reasons for writing pieces based on Native themes arguably differed from those of the American "Indianist" composers, as "melancholy Indians" were not identical to the "vanishing" variety American composers were commonly memorializing at the time. Moreover, through his association with Curtis, an advocate for Native music preservation and Euro-American education about indigenous peoples, Busoni also saw his "Indianist" works as having the potential to generate broader public exposure to Native cultures in the United States and Europe, and to do so in a positive manner.

Natalie Curtis first met Busoni in Vienna around 1890 when she was in her teens, and she studied harmony with him briefly. Two decades later, when Busoni was touring North America, she sought him out to renew their relationship. Busoni describes her in a letter to his wife as "a fine, cultivated, rich girl. . . . She has devoted the whole of this year to the study of Red Indian songs and has brought out a beautiful book."[6] Curtis had taken on Indians as her personal cause in 1903, when, during a tour of the United States, she had run across the Hopi people in Arizona. Fascinated by their music and ceremonies, she discovered the Bureau of Indian Affairs was suppressing their music and religious beliefs as part of a larger assimilationist agenda.[7] Curtis then decided to travel around North America, transcribing Indian songs along the way; when she finished, she created a book from these songs, *The Indians' Book* (1907), a sincere effort on Curtis's part to present the American public with a slice of Native culture in a positive way and to show the value of what was being lost during a time when traditional Indian ways of life were under attack from the federal government. Members of many Native communities, from Pawnee and Lakota to Pima and Pueblo, cooperated enthusiastically with Curtis, allowing her entrance into their homes and even contributing specially drawn artwork for each chapter.[8]

Curtis presented *The Indians' Book* as an offering to America from its Native peoples, over whom Americans had custodial responsibility. According to Curtis:

> This book reflects the soul of one of the noblest types of primitive man—the North American Indian. . . . The red man dictated and the white friend [Curtis] recorded. . . . All [has] been purposely contributed by Indians in a volume that should be their own. . . . This book reveals the inner life of a primitive race. The Indian looks out with reverence upon the world of nature, to him the only world.[9]

Although she expresses her affection for Indians with a language that is painful to contemporary ears, her work was considered progressive at the time. In the process, she also defines what Indian People mean to her: "primitive races" serving as a living connection between technological peoples and their own pretechnological ancestors, thus justifying the preservation of their cultures.

> The child-race of a by-gone age has left no written record of its thoughts. Silent through the ages has passed barbaric man. The voices that greeted the sunrise have died away without an echo. . . . Here we may look into the mind of a race unlike any other in the world. From the heart of the nature-world speaks the voice of man proclaiming deity. The Indian's religious thought, uttered with the simplicity of childhood, is born of his recognition of spirit in every form of life.[10]

Curtis reinforces this perspective in the conclusion of the book with an appendix full of quotations from popular historian John Fiske's *The Discovery of America* (1892). According to Fiske:

> Aboriginal America is the richest field in the world for the study of barbarisim. But among the red men of America the social life of the ages more remote than the lake villages of Switzerland is in many particulars preserved for us today, and as we study it we realize as never before the continuity of human development.[11]

Fiske is placing the indigenous peoples of the Americas into the framework of a popular theoretical paradigm of the era, known as Cultural Evolutionary Stages (CES). This theory of social evolution, originally developed by Lewis Henry Morgan and first published in his *Ancient Society* (1877), posits that all human cultures travel through a series of stages from savagery to barbarism, and then on up the ladder to civilization. By quoting Fiske, Curtis is imparting value to Native musical expression by virtue of its imagined relationship to early forms of European music, and value as a kind of laboratory for the study of the European past. This is one way she marketed Indian melodies to Busoni, which fits with the Primitivist aesthetic movement that became popular in Europe in the decade before World War I, except that Native Americans, through the universality of CES, can stand in for ancestral European cultures.

The story of how *The Indians' Book* came into Busoni's hands depends upon who is telling it. According to Busoni, Curtis presented it to him in New York at a concert as a remembrance of the first American performance of his opera *Turandot*.[12] Curtis, however, gives the events in a different order:

> A few years ago, out of a clear blue sky, I received a letter from Busoni, the great pianist then touring this country from the Atlantic to the Pacific coast. "Will you write out for me," he wrote, "a few Indian melodies, perhaps more—choosing those which you think capable of greater development and expansion. I have a wish to try an experiment with them—a rhapsody or fantasy for piano and orchestra."[13]

Whatever the order of events, Busoni ended up with a copy of *The Indians' Book*, and he used parts of thirteen melodies from eight Indian Nations in the three works he based on Indian themes. But just whose melodies did Busoni actually borrow?

It hard to judge Curtis's proficiency as a transcriber, because soon after she began her project, she abandoned the use of her cylinder recorder. Her explanation suggests that the more Native music she heard, the easier it became to transcribe it:

> The Indians sang the songs directly to the recording pencil. . . . At first the noting of the music was, to the recorder, though a musician, a task of no small difficulty. In the beginning the songs were first taken upon a phonograph, but the machine soon was abandoned as inadequate and unnecessary, and note-book, and pencil, a camera, and a color box for the use of the Indians made the sole equipment carried into camp or village. The songs were written down by the light of the tipi fire or under the glare of the desert sun; in adobe houses while the women ground the corn, or in open camp where after some festival or ceremonial gathering of the people a leader resang for the book a characteristic song.[14]

Post-Curtis Native actions, however, hint at a slightly different explanation. The Hopi were the first Indians Curtis had ever met, and the first and only she recorded. In 1979, anthropologist John Bierhorst confessed puzzlement that the Hopi *Flute Song* included in Curtis's book is the only example of its kind *ever* recorded.[15] Given that seventy-five years had passed since Curtis's recording and Bierhorst's comments, one possible explanation is that the Hopi simply never allowed another recording to be made, even by Hopi expert Jesse Walter Fewkes.[16] Arguably, one scenario is that Curtis was initially privileged within the culture, and then the Hopi found a reason to forbid her use of recording technology, so she abandoned it altogether. Considering that Curtis made her recordings in 1903, when the technology was still quite new, and the Hopi had not encountered it before, they may have objected to the machine's presence only after they realized what it could do. Not understanding exactly what Curtis was doing the first few times she had them sing into the funnel-shaped microphone, they left her with the only recorded example of sacred *Flute Song*.

Examining Curtis's rendering of a Hopi "Butterfly-Dance Song" (*Poli Tiwa Tawi*) highlights both her strengths and weaknesses as a transcriber. In 1992 David Leedom Shaul compared Curtis's transcription from *The Indians' Book* with one he made himself, taken down directly from the original cylinder recording.[17] Contrasting the two, Curtis is shown as accurate in matters of pitch but less so with rhythms, consistently changing from 2/4 to 3/4 meter rather than notating quarter-triplets. Since the gourd-rattle part should have served as a rhythmic metronome and marker during transcription, slowing down during the quarter-triplet passages, the reasons for Curtis's error are difficult to fathom. Moreover, this song accompanied a carefully choreographed dance, with performers hopping twice on one leg for the quarter triplets. Although the difference between changing 2/4 to 3/4 meters and moving in and out of straight quarter note and triplet figures may seem musically small, for a dancer the footwork shifts needed are crucial in order to stay within the rhythmic framework. Sitting there with her cylinder recorder, Curtis *saw* the dance but did not entirely perceive its careful marriage to the music. Oddly enough, in some of her other Hopi transcriptions, such as "He-Hea Katzina Tawi," which Busoni used as the basis for one of the movements of *Indian Diary* (1915), Curtis *did* notate quarter triplets using an approach that would work correctly for Hopi and Pueblo dance songs and dancers, but there is no way to know with certainty whether this transcription is an accurate rendering of the performance she heard, because by this time she had stopped making recordings.

Curtis's transcriptions were not unique in their lack of accuracy. Francis Densmore, a pioneer in the field of ethnomusicology who began her research in the decade following Curtis, articulated the general practices of transcription during the era (and also in later times) in a 1915 article for *The Musical Quarterly*:

> The other method [of transcription], which is the one I use, may be compared to a painting, in which outline and mass take precedence over detail. . . . The statement has been made that Indians use intervals of a quarter tone, or even smaller divisions of a tone. Such graduations of sound frequently occur in their singing, but to hear them is one thing and to believe that they are consciously sung or can accurately be repeated is another matter. . . . To believe this would imply that they, who are so far behind us on general development, have a musical proficiency far in advance of our own. . . . In these instances it was an evidence of lack of musical development rather that a sign of a high degree of culture . . . that same is true of the rhythmic combinations which characterize the musical performances not only of the Indians but of uncultured peoples of distant lands.[18]

Densmore often cued the Natives she recorded by sounding the "correct" starting pitch for their song on a pitch-pipe before they began, in part because it gave her a starting point for her transcriptions, which were in standard Western notation.[19] Assuming Curtis held beliefs about the competency of Native musicians similar to those of Densmore (and ethnologist Alice Fletcher), it may be that Curtis *did* hear the triplet patterns in the Hopi *Butterfly Song*, decided they were mistakes, and "fixed" them in spite of what she saw the dancers doing. How much she altered in her non-Hopi transcriptions can never be known, since there are no recordings to accompany them. By the standards of her time—as articulated by Densmore—Curtis's transcriptions may have been adequate. But as a gift to Hopi posterity, which demands absolute musical accuracy in the ceremonial repertoire, these transcriptions are poorer for their mistakes. Busoni, however, had no reason to suspect either Curtis's Indian transcriptions or her cultural knowledge. Even if he had, the impact on his decision to make use of her transcriptions probably would have been negligible, for the point of his project was to bring pianistic life to Europe's imagined Indian music with its melancholy voice, and not living Indians with their day-to-day struggles to maintain cultural integrity.

Not long after Busoni received *The Indians' Book* from Curtis, he had a chance encounter with a Native woman in Ohio. Afterward, he wrote to his wife that "the Red Indians are the only cultured people who will have nothing to do with money, and who dress the most everyday things in beautiful words."[20] As a result of this meeting, Busoni resolved to do "a great deal of study to get inside Indian life," so he could more properly use the Indian melodies.[21] In spite of this study, however, he still made use of the era's common pejorative vocabulary when referring to Natives, writing in a letter to Egon Petri, "Five times I had already come to the end of the slow movement of the Redskins; four times I had to scalp it."[22] Perhaps Busoni's frustration came from attempting to create a work that takes its melodic basis from not just one but four distinct tribal musical systems, all alien to his own.

Of Busoni's three "Red Indian" works, the only one still performed with any frequency is *Indian Diary* (*Indianisches Tagebuch: Erstes Buch*, 1915, no opus number, and no further volumes). The others, according to his biographer, Anthony Beaumont, are neglected not because they are unworthy but rather because they are not well known.[23] Availability of orchestral parts may also play a role.[24] For his *Indian Diary*, Busoni used songs that Curtis titled "He-Hea Katzina Tawi" (Hopi, no. 1); "Cheyenne Victory Song" (no. 2); "Blue-Bird Song" (Pima, no. 3); and "Passamaquoddy Dance Song" (no. 4).[25] In some cases he fit his accompaniment around the melodies, altering very little of what Curtis had given him. In these, most of his changes were expansions of phrases, usually either by repetition or development of melodic fragments into motives, although notes were occasionally altered. In other movements, however, Busoni uses bits and pieces of the Indian melodies, reassembling them according to his musical needs.

Example 1 shows the first line of Curtis's "He-Hea Katzina" transcription, and example 2 reveals Busoni's realization (no. 1). The original melody is transposed up one step. After a two-bar introduction, Busoni brings in the Hopi melody, changing it by repeating the first bar twice, and leaving out the third bar, which in the original is a repeat of the second. Even with the substitutions, he does retain the overall length of the phrase. The second entrance signals the beginning of greater variations, with a repetition in bars 10 and 11 of the dotted-eighth-to-sixteenth-note rhythm first found in bar six. This treatment is similar to that in American composer Arthur Farwell's (1872–1952) settings: minimal to small changes, with melodic phrases presented relatively intact so they are recognizable. But Busoni takes only the first phrase from the much longer original melody, which is both repetitive and limited in range, something characteristic of traditional Hopi and Pueblo music, where repetition enhances a song's spiritual power.

Example 1. Natalie Curtis Burlin's transcription of the Hopi
song "He-Hea Katzina," from *The Indians' Book* (1907)

Example 2. Ferruccio Busoni, *Indianisches Tagebuch, Erstes Buch, Nr.1*

Example 3 is closer to the spirit of Edward MacDowell (1860–1908) with the original song used for its value as musical material rather than any distinctly Indian cultural flavor.[26] The fourth setting in the collection, of the "Passama-quoddy Dance Song," bears only a faint resemblance to Curtis's transcription (example 4). Busoni has taken a quick multi-meter dance song (mm. 168, marked "rather fast") and recast it in a pastoral triple-meter setting, marked as *Maestoso ma andando*. The melody has been extracted in fragments from the original and reassembled so that the phrasing falls smoothly into a consistent triple meter. In doing so, Busoni has completely lost the character of the Passamaquoddy social dance original, which was predominantly duple-meter with shuffle-style footwork, with the added beats of the triple-meter measure signaling the dancers to jump.[27]

Example 3. Ferruccio Busoni, *Indianisches Tagebuch, Erstes Buch, Nr.4*

Example 4. Natalie Curtis Burlin's transcription of the "Passamaquoddy Dance Song," from *The Indians' Book* (1907)

In spite of Busoni's study of North American Natives, and the determination he expressed to use their melodies within a proper context, the results of his efforts at musical authenticity were mixed. Although he did not view the songs he used as abstract musical materials in the manner that MacDowell did, his sensitivities to Native cultures did not extend as far as keeping the melodies whole or the meters unbroken. As entries in a "diary," the four movements represent Busoni's poetic interpretations of each melody, snapshots of an Indian life he had only fleetingly encountered.

Participating in Curtis's venture to prove that Indian songs were adaptable and amenable to Western art repertoires, Busoni briefly added the prestige of a European composer to the "Indianist" mix. His works occupy a middle ground between the practices of MacDowell and nationalistic impulses of Arthur Farwell: personally sympathetic to Indians but unwilling to adapt his compositional style to better fit the Native melodies he "borrowed." While Busoni's interest in the Hopi and other American Indians was short term at best, their reaction to the recording and dissemination of their sacred music repertory has been much farther reaching: They close the roads to their mesas with barricades every summer, excluding outsiders and banning all recording equipment and photography.

Notes

1. For a detailed study of European perceptions of the Oriental "Other," see Said, *Orientalism*. For a discussion of European enthusiasm for touring "Indian" shows, see Watkins, *Pyramids at the Louvre*.

2. Beaumont, *Busoni the Composer*, 177.

3. Honour, *New Golden Land*, 220. Bloechl gives a detailed overview of European perceptions of Native music in the early modern era in *Native American Song*.

4. Cantor, *North American Indian Landmarks*, 78. The Natchez were the last of the pre-Columbian Mississippian cultures and the only one to survive intact long enough to be written about by Europeans from contemporary encounters. They styled their principal chief "The Sun King" and had a series of hostile encounters with the French of Louis XV's era. In 1729 the Natchez attacked a French fort and drew upon themselves a genocidal counterattack from French military, who enslaved most of the survivors. Two small communities survive today.

5. Honour, *New Golden Land*, 220–23.

6. Ley, *Ferruccio Busoni*, 163.

7. The period between the 1887 Dawes Act and the Indian Reorganization Act of 1934 was highlighted by constant assaults upon Native Religions, central to which was the ceremonial musical repertoire. These attempts culminated with the 1921 special circular on Indian dances, issued by Bureau of Indian Affairs commissioner Charles Burke, which outlawed religious dances. An account of these events can be found in Prucha, *Great Father*, 263–79.

8. Michelle Wick Patterson has recently published an extensive biography: *Natalie*

Curtis Burlin: A Life in Native and African American Music. She does not, however, discuss the Busoni/Curtis relationship at any length.

9. Curtis, *Indians' Book,* xxxiii.

10. Ibid., xxix.

11. Ibid., 533. The complete title of Fiske's work is *The Discovery of America: With Some Account of Ancient America and the Spanish Conquest.*

12. Ley, *Ferruccio Busoni,* 163.

13. Curtis, "Busoni's Indian Fantasy," 540.

14. Curtis, *Indians' Book,* xxi.

15. Bierhorst, *Cry from the Earth.*

16. Fewkes, generally considered the premier early ethnologist working with the Hopi, had a rather mixed relationship with them. There is a Hopi tradition that Fewkes was driven out of the village of Walpi by the Earth God Masauwu in 1898, never to return. Fewkes did make later recordings of nonrestricted Hopi ceremonial songs, such as Katchina songs, in villages. Curtis is the only non-Hopi ever allowed to record restricted material. See Nabokov, *Native American Testimony,* 227–29, for a Hopi account of Fewkes and Masauwu.

17. Shaul, "Hopi Song-Poem."

18. Densmore, "Study of Indian Music."

19. A striking example of this can be found preceding "Kimiwun's Dream Song," in the recorded collection *Ojibwe Music from Minnesota: A Century of Song for Voice and Drum* (St. Paul: Minnesota Historical Society, 1989). Thomas Vennum, who compiled this collection, left in Densmore's playing a tone on her pitch-pipe before Kimiwun began to sing. These interludes are absent from any of the collected recordings of tribal songs whose issuance was supervised by Densmore.

20. Ley, *Ferruccio Busoni,* 163.

21. Ibid., 186.

22. Beaumont, *Busoni the Composer,* 177.

23. Since Beaumont's study in 1985, this situation has begun to change. American pianist Jeffrey Swann made the premier recording of the *Indianische Fantasie für Klavier mit Orchester* (op.44) in 1993 with the Orchestre Philharmonique de Montpellier (Arkadia Records) on an Italian label commercially available only in Europe.

24. Much of Busoni's orchestral music can only be rented or is unavailable in the United States. However, with all copyrights having expired in 1999, Busoni's works are now beginning to enter the public domain. In 1993 Kalmus Bros. released a miniature-score version of *Indianische Fantasie für Klavier mit Orchester* (op.44), but as yet does not have the individual orchestral parts for sale.

25. All songs from Curtis, *Indians' Book.* There is no pagination in the sections containing song transcriptions. Pagination in the second table of contents (Songs) lists the songs Busoni used respectively on pages 517 (nr.1), 176 (nr.2), 319 (nr.3), and 25 (nr.4).

26. See Browner, "Breathing the Indian Spirit," for a discussion of Edward MacDowell's practices of using Indian melodies in his works.

27. Examples of this dance style can be seen in the American Indian Dance Theater's video *Dances for the New Generation* (*Great Performances,* PBS, 1992).

References

Beaumont, Anthony. *Busoni the Composer*. London: Faber and Faber, 1985.

Bierhorst, John. *A Cry from the Earth*. New York: Folkways Records, 1979.

Bloechl, Olivia A. *Native American Song at the Frontiers of Early Modern Music*. Cambridge: Cambridge University Press, 2008.

Browner, Tara. "'Breathing the Indian Spirit': Thoughts on Musical Borrowing and the 'Indianist' Movement." *American Music* 15, no. 3: 265–84.

Busoni, Ferruccio. *Indianisches Tagebuch, Erstes Buch: Vier Klavierstudien über Motive der Rothäute Amerikas*. 1915. Wiesbaden: Breitkopf and Härtel, 1944.

Cantor, George. *North American Indian Landmarks: A Traveler's Guide*. Detroit: Visible Ink, 1993.

Curtis [Burlin], Natalie. "Busoni's Indian Fantasy." *Southern Workman* 44 (1915): 538–44.

———. *The Indians' Book*. New York: Harper and Brothers, 1907.

Densmore, Francis. "The Study of Indian Music." *Musical Quarterly* 1 (1915): 187–97.

Fiske, John. *The Discovery of America: With Some Account of Ancient America and the Spanish Conquest*. Boston: Houghton-Mifflin, 1892.

Honour, Hugh. *The New Golden Land*. New York: Pantheon, 1975.

Ley, Rosamund. *Ferruccio Busoni: Letters to His Wife*. London: Arnold, 1938.

Nabokov, Peter. *Native American Testimony: A Chronicle of Indian-White Relations from Prophecy to the Present 1492–1992*. New York: Viking, 1991.

Patterson, Michelle Wick. *Natalie Curtis Burlin: A Life in Native and African American Music*. Lincoln: University of Nebraska Press, 2010.

Prucha, Francis Paul. *The Great Father: The United States Government and the American Indians*. Abridged edition. Lincoln: University of Nebraska Press, 1986.

Said, Edward. *Orientalism*. New York: Random House, 1978.

Shaul, David Leedom. "A Hopi Song-Poem in 'Context,'" In *On the Translation of Native American Literatures*, edited by Brian Swann, 228–41. Washington, DC: Smithsonian Institution Press, 1992.

Vennum, Thomas. *The Ojibwe Dance Drum: Its History and Construction*. Washington, DC: Smithsonian Institution Press, 1982.

Watkins, Glenn. *Pyramids at the Louvre: Music, Culture, and Collage from Stravinsky to the Postmodernists*. Cambridge, Mass.: Harvard University Press, 1994.

13 Fieldwork on the American Campus

JOSHUA S. DUCHAN

In the past, field research in music was generally done "somewhere else." As a matter of course, one who was doing the fieldwork would leave his or her institutional home, travel to the field site, and collect the all-important data to bring back for analysis. Whether the destination was an archive of scores or a remote village, one always went somewhere. The list of examples is plentiful, including some scholars who may not have called themselves ethnomusicologists but nonetheless provided a foundation on which ethnomusicological fieldwork rests: Franz Boas (who conducted fieldwork in, for example, the Pacific Northwest and circumpolar regions), George Herzog (a wide range of North Amerindian locales), Mantle Hood (Indonesia), and Alan Merriam (Montana, the Democratic Republic of Congo, and Burundi). Some of the seminal texts, often used in graduate courses teaching the next generation of ethnomusicologists about their disciplinary roots, offer definitions of "the field" that, perhaps unsurprisingly, reflect both their times and disciplinary ideologies. In *Ethnomusicology: An Introduction* (1992), for example, Helen Myers draws on E. C. Hughes's 1960 definition, which emphasizes the movement of the ethnographer to those he or she studies: "The observation of people *in situ*, finding them where they are, staying with them in some role which, while acceptable to them, will allow both intimate observation of certain parts of their behavior, and reporting it in ways useful to social science but not harmful to those observed."[1] More recently, in *Tales of the Field* (2011), John Van Maanen observes, "Whether or not the fieldworker ever really does 'get away' in a conceptual sense is becoming increasingly problematic, but physical displacement is a requirement." Contrasting ethnography in anthropology and sociology, he concludes, "The most fundamental distinction is that anthropologists go elsewhere to practice their trade while sociologists stay home."[2]

For musical ethnography, it has become increasingly accepted for the distance between home and field to be collapsed. Urban ethnography, such as Charles Keil's work on urban blues, was perhaps an early harbinger of this change.[3] "The classic model of the mid-twentieth century was a minimum of twelve months 'away' in some remote locale—the more 'exotic' the better," explain Gregory F. Barz and Timothy J. Cooley. "In the first decade of the twenty-first century we find a much broader spectrum of fieldwork situations," including those in which "ethnomusicologists stay at home and study their own community or travel within their own country to research other communities in our increasingly multicultural society."[4] Indeed, Jonathan P. J. Stock and Chou Chiener suggest that "doing fieldwork at home contributes to a more rounded ethnomusicology where all music making is treated as genuinely worthy of study, not just the far distant."[5] With the advent of the internet toward the end of the twentieth century have come ethnographic projects that require no travel at all, at least in the physical sense. Studies employing virtual fieldwork remind us not only that diverse musical communities may be accessed electronically but also that "new technologies offer new modes of communication, at once reflecting and shaping how culture is produced, performed, transmitted, consumed, and understood," technologies that "benefit our work and magnify our reflexive anxieties about the impact of our data collection methods on our ethnographic integrity."[6]

This chapter examines a form of fieldwork that is neither as distant as the more traditional sort nor as virtual as that which is done solely on the internet: I seek to consider the American college or university campus as a fieldwork site. The campus is usually the place to which the ethnographer returns; however, it can also be a rich source of musical data. Most music scholars are probably aware of the official musical ensembles in their midst—the campus choir, orchestra, and band, among other departmental or athletic ensembles—but may be less cognizant or appreciative of the potentially deep and vast sea of less "official" musical organizations. Students usually direct those groups with little faculty guidance beyond perhaps a signature on a form indicating a professor's willingness to serve as an "advisor." My research into one facet of student musical life has revealed a complex, interconnected world of activity serving both musical and social purposes.

Students are probably more aware of this musical world than are their professors. After all, the bulletin boards in dormitories are often covered with announcements advertising auditions and performances. There are a few articles and monographs that consider campus ensembles—Ted Solís's *Performing Ethnomusicology* (2004) comes to mind—but they are few and far between and still tend to focus mostly on "official" campus groups.[7] While admirably considering world music ensembles, world performance programs, and their implications for students and ethnomusicology, *Performing Ethnomusicology* emphasizes departmental ensembles led by professional musicians and scholars over the world of unofficial, student-led ventures.

Those of us who teach general education courses in "world music" may be steering our students toward this musical world. One of the popular world music textbooks, Jeff Todd Titon's *Worlds of Music* (2008), includes an entire chapter devoted to planning and conducting an ethnographic project on campus or in the local community.[8] Bruno Nettl observes that "the concept of doing fieldwork at home . . . has become a fairly standard technique in seminars," offering the investigation of "rehearsals of the university symphony orchestra"—again, an "official" ensemble—as an example.[9] Projects focusing on unofficial student ensembles are probably more successful on certain campuses than others: in my experience, residential colleges and those with students of the traditional college age, eighteen to twenty-two, were more likely to boast a greater variety of student musical groups than commuter campuses or those with more age-diverse student populations. My perspective on this topic comes from my study of collegiate a cappella, in which student-led singing groups on college and university campuses take popular songs and arrange, perform, and record them without instrumental accompaniment. This research has taken me to a variety of American campuses, including large universities in cities big and small (for example, Penn in Philadelphia and Michigan in Ann Arbor), as well as regional state universities (Bowling Green in Ohio) and small liberal arts colleges (Bowdoin in Maine). Collegiate a cappella, as a genre and practice, can trace its roots, in part, to college campuses in the colonial and early federal United States but were also strongly influenced by other American genres that were popular on campus in the nineteenth and twentieth centuries, including barbershop and doo-wop.[10]

Introducing the American Campus

Taking a long view of the history of higher education, the very concept of a world of activities created, managed, and experienced by students without much faculty direction is a fairly recent development. In the seventeenth and eighteenth centuries, the daily routine of the typical American college student left little time unaccounted for. A chapel service began the day, followed by class and breakfast. Classes then resumed until lunch, after which additional classes and recitations occupied students until dinner. Study and tutoring then kept them busy until bedtime. What little time was left over was commonly spent on religious, philosophical, literary, or debating clubs.[11]

As curricula began to change during the nineteenth century, musical activities were slowly added. At Harvard, a music club called the Pierian Sodality was founded in 1808. There were attempts to establish a glee club in 1833 and 1841, but that goal was achieved only in March 1858.[12] Other clubs, such as the University of Michigan Men's Glee Club, began shortly thereafter.[13] At Yale University, singing groups formed within academic classes and eventually led to the establishment of several clubs, some direct offshoots of student-led glee clubs, of which anecdotal evidence remains. "Back in the eighteen-sixties and seventies," writes Yale student Carl Lohmann, "there were the Midnight Caterwaulers, the Beethoven Bummers, the Four Sharps, the Theologians, the Owls, and probably others."[14] And these are just the choral examples—the fact that the Pierian Sodality was primarily an instrumental ensemble suggests that student-directed instrumental music was a growing force as well. For instance, banjo clubs were particularly popular in the late nineteenth century and often joined forces with glee clubs.[15]

Helen Lefkowitz Horowitz uses the term "college life" to refer to this expanding world of extracurricular activities.[16] Other historians of higher education have adopted the term as well. "For many undergraduates," explains John Thelin, "compliance with the formal curriculum was merely the price of admission into 'college life,'" participation in which was clearly becoming desirable.[17] The notion of "college life" became increasingly widespread as the turn of the twentieth century approached and is easy to observe today on many campuses, not just in music clubs and those listed above but also in theater and drama groups, disciplinary clubs, political associations, community-service organizations, amateur athletic teams, and so on.

In many cases, college life provides not only an opportunity for extracurricular activity on campus but also the chance to travel to other campuses for collaborative or competitive events as well as social activities. Many collegiate a cappella groups routinely go on tour during their school's spring break, venturing to other colleges and universities to perform and socialize with groups there. While some groups drive only a few hundred miles, others travel much greater distances. For example, when I conducted fieldwork with VoiceMale, a men's a cappella group at Brandeis University (Waltham, Massachusetts), the ensemble flew to California for its spring-break tour. In addition, many groups compete in the annual International Championship of Collegiate A Cappella, which hosts competitions across the United States and has grown to include competitors from Europe and Africa.[18]

Although it is clear from Lohmann's recollection that collegiate singing groups existed during the nineteenth century, the oldest collegiate a cappella group still singing today is the one Lohmann helped establish at Yale in 1909, the Whiffenpoofs. Other groups slowly appeared in the years that followed as college life, too, expanded in its offerings and to new campuses. For example, the all-male Spizzwinks(?) began at Yale in 1914 (the question mark is part of the name); the Smiffenpoofs (a play on the Whiffenpoofs), a women's group at Smith

College, was founded in 1936; and the University of Virginia Gentlemen was established in 1953. But the movement really exploded later in the century. The 1980s saw the total number of groups nationwide double, from approximately 110 to 225, while co-ed groups made significant gains. The 1990s saw 318 new groups established, with mixed groups outnumbering men's and women's by 1994. This rapid growth was built on a foundation of decades of music education in American public schools and the advent of coeducational institutions. In addition, a string of successful a cappella recordings from musicians such as Billy Joel (1983), Bobby McFerrin (1988), and Boyz II Men (1991) built stylistically on barbershop, doo-wop, and R&B vocal trends. Finally, stylistic innovations within the musical practice itself, and the establishment of organized competitions, societies, and websites helped sustain the movement and its growing network of student musicians.[19] What follows are some of my observations and thoughts based on my fieldwork on several campuses in the Midwest and the Northeast between 2001 and 2010, focusing in particular on my year in Boston (2004–05), which I have grouped into two sections covering, first, social and cultural challenges, and then bureaucratic, legal, and ethical ones. Appreciating these challenges can help us see both the similarities and differences between campus ethnography and ethnography in other settings.

Identity and Distinction

College constitutes a time of tremendous change, a transition from adolescence to adulthood. As the support structures students once held close—family and friends from home—are made distant, new networks of sociability must be forged.[20] It makes sense, then, that many a cappella singers I interviewed discussed their groups in terms of family, fraternity, and sorority. In this process of identity (re)formation, it may seem helpful to fall back on established identity fault lines. In other words, it may seem natural for students to delineate for themselves what they are and, sometimes as important, what they are *not*, who is like them and who is *not*. Distinction is, in fact, a common goal of a cappella groups, who often strive to separate themselves from official campus music ensembles and other student-led groups through musical and social differences alike.[21] That being said, I would like to explore two social and cultural challenges that come with campus ethnography: the student-professor relationship and social structures that exist among students themselves.

Friendly though they sometimes are, faculty members and students are typically not friends; their relationship may be close in some instances, but most of the time it is one of a certain distance. (As is often the case, strong personal ties are not usually forged between those subject to judgment—the grades that affix value to the quality of one's work, which may affect one's future—and those pronouncing it in this hierarchical social organization.) And although many students may not realize it, that sense of distance is, in fact, historically situated. In the late nineteenth and early twentieth centuries it was common to portray college life in terms of war between students and faculty.[22] One can imagine, then, how the camaraderie built through participation in a peer-led activity can lend a sense of security and comfort to an undergraduate student.

This student-professor relationship may therefore pose a challenge to adult ethnographers entering campus and seeking to establish some kind of relationship with members of student groups, as the ethnographers may be viewed (at least at first) as similar to professors, whether or not they hold such a title. While conducting my dissertation fieldwork, I benefited from the fact that I was still, in some sense, a student. Many undergraduate singers seemed to recognize an unspoken kinship because I shared their student status and was still being judged by faculty. At other times, however, it was clear that the singers with whom I worked were well aware of how I was different. Once they became comfortable with my presence, some groups actively sought my feedback on both their musical performance and their relationships to various official campus entities with which they had to interact, including funding sources, administration officials, and the like. I occasionally got the feeling that my (slightly) more advanced age was seen as providing insight into the world of adult diplomacy.

Second, campus ethnographers should be aware of and sensitive to the social structures that exist within a student body. After all, most American students have grown up in a highly delineated system of class and rank from grade school through high school, which naturally extends through the college years.[23] While freshmen may be unusually quiet and reserved simply because they are living in a new place and surrounded by new faces, they may also be acutely aware of those whose time at their institution and in their group renders them (seemingly) inherently more powerful.

For example, it became clear to me that certain members of the Fallen Angels, a women's a cappella group at Harvard University, wielded more power than others. Sometimes these women held official, elected positions within the group, and sometimes they did not, but they were almost always juniors or seniors. This power enabled them to have an impact on the very sound of the group. One singer, a junior, offered verbal suggestions to the other women while they warmed up at the beginning of rehearsals. "Listen to each other," she said one evening, "and match vowel shapes." I noticed how the other members glanced intently around the room, calibrating the shapes of their mouths and lips to match those of their peers in an effort to create a well-rounded, unified sound. Younger members often looked toward older members, whose singing served as a sort of model to follow. On one hand, this junior had recently served as the group's music director, a position that entails a measure of authority. On the other hand, she might not have been elected to that position in the first place had she not achieved a certain rank and status.

Of course, social hierarchies exist in myriad cultures; that we find them on American college campuses should come as no surprise. What is important here, then, is that the ethnographer appreciates how deeply embedded such hierarchies can be and how they can affect and be evident in musical behavior in the collegiate context. For example, answers to interview questions, which constitute some of the ethnomusicologist's data, may be shaped by the student interviewee's place within the social structure of his or her group. This is not in itself problematic, as long as the interviewer is aware of the circumstances and social forces at play.

Another social structure might revolve around other aspects of students' lives. For example, student musicians may distinguish each other by major or degree program, one of the primary labels affixed to individuals in the vast system of American higher education. In some instances, I saw members of a cappella groups defer to music majors or those enrolled in their institution's School of Music when crucial musical decisions had to be made. But the op- posite also occurs: in order to emphasize how highly developed technical skills and years of music lessons are *not* essential for membership, participation, or leadership—in other words, to realize a group's egalitarian ideal—I witnessed some groups promote members who were not music students as evidence of such inclusivity.[24]

In other instances, rather than distinguishing between individuals within a group, some a cappella groups, as a whole, are specifically and explicitly oriented toward particular kinds of identities. Religious identities are the most common: Shir Appeal, a mixed group at Tufts University, promotes itself as a Jewish a cappella group and has been especially successful with its Hebrew-language songs,[25] while the University of Delaware's campus in Newark includes Vision, a Christian a cappella group, to name only two examples. Other kinds of iden- tities are also promoted in these student-run ensembles. At the University of Pennsylvania, a group called The Inspiration bills itself as a "musical outlet for individuals with a desire to celebrate the legacy of Black music."[26] And 58 Greene, at the University of Michigan, designates itself a "multicultural" a cap- pella group.[27] These kinds of groups are in the minority; generally speaking, most a cappella groups carry no such affiliation, at least not explicitly.

Identity-based social structures—be they ethnic, religious, racial, or oth- erwise—may be less official or, in some cases, even contested. For example, members of a "mainstream" group once complained to me about what they perceived as a quasi-religious mission being promoted by two of their group's leaders. Aside from the stories the leaders told during a group-bonding exercise (which allegedly carried strong religious undertones), one of the songs in the group's repertory was drawn from the genre of contemporary Christian music—an unusual choice in light of the ensemble's many years of strictly secular jazz and pop choices. As in other fieldwork settings, establishing trusting relationships with musicians can lead to the kinds of conversations where distinctions are revealed, regardless of whether they occur in a specifically musical context, such as a rehearsal or concert performance. Western ethnographers working within Western institutions like college and university campuses may benefit from the extra effort to look out for these revelations, lest they be overlooked in such a familiar setting.

The "Lone Ethnographer" Gives Back

In addition to the social and cultural challenges highlighted above, I would like to briefly mention three of a more practical nature. The first, a bureaucratic challenge, caught me by surprise when I conducted fieldwork on several campuses other than my own institution's. Any time a researcher works with human subjects, he or she must seek approval from the appropriate supervisory body. At the University of Michigan, this was the Institutional Review Board (IRB), although it goes by other names at other schools. I secured approval for my ethnographic research before beginning my fieldwork but did not consider that the IRBs from the campuses on which I would be conducting my work would also want approval. Complicating things was the fact that my study was multi-sited, involving a cappella groups on several different university campuses. Imagine my surprise when multiple IRBs made their approvals contingent upon each other's approvals! In many fieldwork contexts, ethnographers need permission from a local agency—in addition to one from "home"—before beginning their work; as it turned out, the campus was no exception. Although this situation was straightened out after a few days of phone calls, it added an additional bureaucratic wrinkle to the research process before it even began.

Another issue that arises has to do with ownership: To whom does the ethnographer's data belong? Do student musicians have a claim on their representation within the data or the resulting ethnography? On one level, these questions bring us to well-trodden territory. Ethnographers of many stripes have debated if and how much credit should be given to research participants when writing and publishing articles and books, a debate that certainly applies to campus ethnography. In fact, this debate constitutes just one part of the larger discussion of ways to challenge what Bruce Horner calls "the myth of the Lone Ethnographer," a metaphor for traditional understandings of the professional academic researcher employing ethnographic methods. (Those understandings include four defining assumptions: that all the work results from the researcher's own "genius"; that practical issues such as funding, informants, clerical assistants, and the like are necessary to the ethnographic process but irrelevant to the actual work; that the field and its inhabitants are unaffected by the ethnographer's presence; and that the value of the resulting work is derived from the "features of the text itself as a commodity.") Methodological approaches such as collaboration in the field between the researcher and those being researched, multivocality in ethnographic texts, and self-reflexivity in both field method and ethnographic writing have been proposed as solutions to the ethical dilemmas posed by this Lone Ethnographer.[28]

Ethnomusicology has certainly included calls for these three approaches.[29] Nicole Beaudry discusses how interpreters, assistants, and interviewees become more than the titles we give them, enriching the ethnographic work: "Human relationships not only influence the quality of my work but are what makes fieldwork a meaningful experience."[30] Michelle Kisliuk points to "dialogue" between "the field researcher and the people among whom she works" as one of the important "conversations" comprising the process of ethnographic fieldwork and writing.[31] Nettl observes how "by the 1990s . . . the world's musicians now rather uniformly expect to be treated as individuals and to get credit for their contributions to our literature."[32] And Barz and Cooley remark that reflexivity was once merely a trend but "is now an expectation."[33]

Steven Feld's concept of "dialogic editing" perhaps best sums up ethnomusicology's efforts at collaboration, multivocality, and reflexivity.[34] Yet other writings about ethnography acknowledge that, however much one might strive for the inclusion of others and self-awareness in one's ethnography, the ethnographic text is, in the end, the ethnographer's: "While the give-and-take of relations in the field continue to shape the ethnographer's understanding, the finished ethnography is the ethnographer's version of those happenings and events. Most ethnographic conventions allow the writer to represent others (and her experience with them) as she sees best. In this sense, the ethnographer openly assumes and exercises authorial privilege."[35]

On another level, however, the question of *institutional* ownership arises: Does the work of an institutionally based ethnographer "belong" to his or her home institution, the funding source (which need not be his or her home institution), or the institutions whose campuses are serving as the field? Here, ethnomusicology begins to brush against legal issues. According to American copyright law, facts and figures cannot themselves be copyrighted or owned.[36] But it can be argued that the data generated during ethnographic fieldwork go beyond just facts and figures. Especially in cases where ethnomusicologists record not only conversations and interviews but also rehearsals and performances (which themselves may consist of copyrighted material), the "data" that result are in fact fixed forms of creative and artistic expression. Once a creative work is "fixed in a copy or phonorecord for the first time," it is considered under copyright, and if it can be copyrighted, it can be owned.[37] If an ethnographer is employed by a college or university, his or her work may be considered "work for hire," in which case the data belong, legally, to the college or university.[38] While I can find no major precedent of a university suing for ownership of data collected on its campus by an ethnographer employed by another university, just the fact that data can be owned by one university raises the specter of individuals' voices being "owned" not by the ethnographer with whom they worked and forged a trusting relationship but instead by a seemingly more distant institution. (Issues of representation certainly figure here as well.) The fact that collegiate a cappella is a genre consisting mostly of covers of copyrighted works merely adds another layer of complexity to this legal onion.

One of the reasons that mechanisms of oversight, such as the IRB, exist is to ensure the safety of research participants. From a legal standpoint, men and women who are adults and fully informed of a study's risks can offer their consent to participate. A problem that arises when conducting campus ethnography is that not all students are, legally, adults: some first-year students may arrive at college before their eighteenth birthday, complicating any effort to get informed consent. Even if they turn eighteen during their first year, it may be too late for the ethnographer. A cappella groups often spend a lot of time and energy—including insightful conversations about their identities as individuals and groups—recruiting new students at the beginning of the academic year. When recruiting student musicians as research participants, an ethnographer must therefore take care that they are legally able to give such permission.

Finally, the ethical challenge has to do with the ethnographer's responsibility for reciprocity. In other words, how does the ethnographer "give back" to student ensembles? Sharing expertise may be one method, as many music scholars themselves bear considerable musical training. In my case, singers occasionally looked to me for musical feedback during rehearsals. I specifically recall one night when the Boston University Treblemakers were deciding who should sing the lead solo on one of the new songs in their repertory. Two members had auditioned and then left the room as their peers debated. Observing this process, the "right" choice seemed clear to me, but I did my best to restrain myself, quietly listen to the arguments the other members made about the auditions, and let the conversation unfold naturally. Well, my efforts at self-restraint were insufficient, as one of the members noticed what must have been a look on my face and specifically asked for my thoughts. I panicked: Would my opinion change the direction of the conversation? Should I attempt to demur? Yet I could already feel the crippling pangs of guilt if I flat-out refused to answer the question. After all, the singers in this group had shared their time, music, thoughts, and lives with me for months and rarely asked for anything in return. Moments like this are indicative of great trust but also fraught with the possibility of directly and significantly influencing the decisions made by, and artistic directions of, the very musicians we study. Here, once again, Horner's Lone Ethnographer and the ideas of critical ethnography and self-reflexivity reappear.[39] Of course, it would be impossible *not* to have some influence: "Clearly," reads one recent fieldwork guide, "ethnographic immersion precludes conducting field research as a detached, passive observer . . . the fieldworker cannot and should not attempt to be a fly on the wall."[40]

In other instances, the singers invited me to join them in a performance, a gesture of trust that presented another opportunity to contribute to the group's musical efforts while gathering vital experiential data. "Cultural barriers evaporate when musicologist meets musician," Myers writes. "There is no substitute in ethnomusicological fieldwork for intimacy born of shared musical experiences."[41] If the invitation is issued because one member is unable to attend a gig, then one's ability to step into the empty place onstage preserves the group's capacity to carry on its usual activities. If the invitation is issued because the group wants the ethnographer to perform *in addition* to the regular members, it signals a different kind of inclusion. Such participation is no doubt useful for its experiential aspects, but it bears saying that it changes the ethnographer's perspective, drawing him or her out of the realm of the observer and fully into that of the participant; out of the world of the audience and fully onto the stage with the performers—two groups who, in Western cultures, are often deliberately, if implicitly, separated.[42] In my fieldwork, I settled into a somewhat happy medium, singing in rehearsal, when invited, but joining the audience at most performances.

These ways of "giving back" take place while the ethnographer is still regularly conducting fieldwork and are certainly not the only possibilities. But the pace of academic research and publication can be slow. What about when the ethnographer wants to "give back" years later? Keeping in touch with contacts from one's fieldwork would seem a basic modus operandi for ethnographers and may work well in cases where populations are largely geographically stable. Yet the case of campus ethnography complicates this picture a bit. After all, when studying student music culture, one must recognize that, above all, the musicians are students—they will eventually graduate and leave. Traditional modes of correspondence, whether postal mail, e-mail, or telephone, may become useless as addresses and numbers change with new jobs, new homes, new lives.

One advantage of campus ethnography is that, since the musicians the ethnographer studies are, principally, students, they may better understand and appreciate the value attached to scholarship, making its material manifestations gifts of certain significance. My book on collegiate a cappella, *Powerful Voices* (2012), was published seven years after I completed my year of fieldwork in Boston, a gap in time that saw all of my Boston-based musicians graduate and leave their a cappella groups. Although I was still in touch with a few, most had moved away, and I had not been in contact with the vast majority in a rather long time. Those who are meticulously organized can perhaps keep up with the changing lives and locales of many student musicians. But if not, one tool I found useful for keeping some line of communication open was social media. Today, many students are members of online social networks, such as Facebook, during and after college, and can easily be reached there. Another method was through alumni networks, which some (though unfortunately not all) student groups maintain for their graduated members. By sending an e-mail message to the current group, word of the book's publication could be passed along to interested alumni, who themselves were featured in its pages, perhaps a sort of academically enabled immortality.

There is much work to be done with student musicians, especially with regard to their musicking outside the auspices of their degree programs; as a whole, music scholarship seems much closer to the beginning of this conversation than its end. It should be clear that ethnography on American college and university campuses can be both challenging and fruitful. It has much in common with fieldwork in general, but it also bears some distinctive features that arise from its historical, social, and cultural contexts. And, as I hope to have illustrated, the particular challenges of campus ethnography are not insurmountable. In fact, in my experience, student musicians were especially forthcoming and easy to talk to, eager to have their voices heard, and enthusiastic about contributing to the ethnographic project and the scholarly enterprise—just the kind of partners ethnographers would be lucky to work with.

Notes

I must thank the many collegiate a cappella groups with whom I have had the pleasure of working, including the Boston University Treblemakers, the Brandeis University VoiceMale, the Harvard University Fallen Angels, and the University of Michigan Amazin' Blue. Thank you, as well, to Fiona Linn and Katherine Meizel for their input and comments on earlier drafts of this essay. Finally, I owe thanks to Judith Becker, Richard Crawford, Mark Clague, and the editors of this volume for their insight and guidance.

1. E. C. Hughes, "Introduction: The Place of Fieldwork in Social Science," in *Fieldwork: An Introduction to the Social Sciences*, 6th ed., edited by Buford Junker (Chicago: University of Chicago Press, 1960), v., qtd. in Meyers, "Fieldwork," 23.

2. Van Maanen, *Tales of the Field*, 3, 21.

3. Keil, *Urban Blues*. It is revealing that this monograph was based not on Keil's doctoral work but on his master's thesis, "Urban Blues" (University of Chicago, 1964). For his PhD Keil followed a more traditional path, conducting fieldwork in Nigeria from 1965 to 1967. Nettl, in *Study of Ethnomusicology*, also links the rise of "doing ethnomusicology 'at home'" after 1985 "with the study of urban culture" (186).

4. Barz and Cooley, "Casting Shadows," 13.

5. Stock and Chiener, "Fieldwork at Home," 123.

6. Cooley, Meizel, and Syed, "Virtual Fieldwork," 106–7.

7. Solís, *Performing Ethnomusicology*. Other examples include Kingsbury, *Music, Talent, and Performance*; Koskoff, "Cognitive Strategies in Rehearsal"; and Montgomery, *Brothers, Sing On!* Although not dealing with musical groups, a notable study of student culture is Moffatt, *Coming of Age*.

8. Titon, *Worlds of Music*. Campus ethnography features in chapter 11, "Discovering and Documenting a World of Music." In another example, Bonnie Wade offers a thorough, step-by-step guide to student ethnographic research, including reference to campus music, in *Thinking Musically*, 195–204.

9. Nettl, *Study of Ethnomusicology*, 192.

10. Duchan, *Powerful Voices*, 11–44.

11. Lucas, *American Higher Education*, 127–30. Lucas also draws on Brubacher and Rudy, *Higher Education in Transition*, 85–86, and Cowley and Williams, *International and Historical Roots*, 104–9.

12. Weber, "Universities"; Broyles, *"Music of the Highest Class"*, 128–38. H. Wiley Hitchcock, in *Music of the United States*, 3rd ed. (Englewood Cliffs, NJ: Prentice Hall, 1988), 77, locates the founding of the Harvard Glee Club in 1828, but other sources do not confirm this claim. According to Spalding in *Music at Harvard*, the earliest record of the Pierian Sodality to reflect "actual singing by the Pierian Glee Club" is dated April 29, 1834, although earlier efforts at organizing such an ensemble occurred on November 12, 1833, and again in 1841 (52, 120).

13. According to *The History of the University of Michigan Men's Glee Club*, the club was founded in 1859.

14. Qtd. in Bartholomew, "Short History."

15. See Linn, *That Half-Barbaric Twang*, 18, 24–27.

16. Horowitz, *Campus Life*.

17. Thelin, *History*, 65. See also Lucas, *American Higher Education*, 200–201.

18. The International Championship of Collegiate A Cappella was founded in 1996 as the National Championship of Collegiate A Cappella. Competitors were organized into several geographic regions, with the winner of each advancing to the final round in New York City. The name was soon changed to "International," as groups from Canadian universities were included in the competition. Groups from the United Kingdom joined the competition in 2006, and the 2012 season included competitors from South Africa.

19. Duchan, *Powerful Voices*, 45–63.

20. Karp, Holmstrong, and Gray, "Leaving Home for College."

21. See Duchan, *Powerful Voices*, 72–73, 181.

22. Horowitz, *Campus Life*, 12–13, 150.

23. Educational settings have been well studied for the ways they impose or reproduce structures in their students' lives. Perhaps the classic study of this kind is Bourdieu and Passeron, *Reproduction*.

24. Liz Garnett also finds egalitarianism in her study of barbershop quartets, whose

"musical practices become a vehicle, as well as a metaphor, for social harmony" (*British Barbershopper*, 35).

25. Shir Appeal has had several tracks selected for the annual *Best of College A Cappella* compilation album (for example, in 2000, 2003, 2005, and 2008), three of which featured Hebrew-language songs. "Shir" means "song" in Hebrew.

26. University of Pennsylvania, The Inspiration (blog).

27. University of Michigan 58 Greene.

28. Horner, "Critical Ethnography."

29. Horner's critique is that those solutions don't go far enough to acknowledge the materiality of ethnography—as both process and product—and its reception: "Given the inevitably asymmetrical relations of power between these different parties [involved in ethnographic research], researchers are now expected to ask themselves what would constitute ethically responsible ways of defining, initiating, carrying out, and reporting on their research. Those asking themselves such questions have produced myriad recommendations, but I'll focus on the three that have garnered the most attention and that are most germane to questions of materiality: an emphasis on collaboration, on multivocality, and on self-reflexivity. While all three challenge the traditional model of academic work . . . they are not materialist enough in the framework by which they understand that model, so the recommendations they present remain insufficient" ("Critical Ethnography," 562–63).

30. Beaudry, "Challenges of Human Relations."

31. Kisliuk, "(Un)Doing Fieldwork," 202.

32. Nettl, *Study of Ethnomusicology*, 200.

33. Barz and Cooley, "Casting Shadows," 13. They point specifically to Barbara Myerhoff and Jay Ruby, eds., *A Crack in the Mirror: Reflexive Perspectives in Anthropology* (Philadelphia: University of Pennsylvania Press, 1982) as a particularly eloquent discussion of the issue of reflexivity.

34. Steven Feld, "Dialogic Editing," 190–210.

35. Emerson, Fretz, and Shaw, *Writing Ethnographic Fieldnotes*, 209.

36. US Copyright Office, Circular 1: "Copyright Basics" (Washington, DC: Library of Congress, 2012), 3, lists examples of materials "generally not eligible for copyright protection," including "mere listings of ingredients of contents," "ideas, procedures, methods, systems, processes, concepts, principles, discoveries, or devices, as distinguished from a description, explanation, or illustration," and "works consisting entirely of information that is common property and containing no original authorship" (see also http://www.copyright.gov/circs).

37. Ibid.

38. Many institutions then reassign license or ownership back to the faculty, but the details differ from institution to institution.

39. Horner, "Critical Ethnography." The subject of ethnographic reflexivity is beyond the scope of this chapter. See, for example, Clifford and Marcus, *Writing Culture*; Bourdieu and Wacquant, *Invitation to Reflexive Sociology*; and Myerhoff and Ruby, *A Crack in the Mirror*.

40. Emerson, Fretz, and Shaw, *Writing Ethnographic Fieldnotes*, 2–3.

41. Myers, "Fieldwork," 31.

42. Small, *Musicking*, 27, 64–65.

References

Bartholomew, Marshall. "A Short History of the Yale Glee Club." Unpublished manuscript. Marshall Bartholomew Papers, mss 24, box, folder 1, Irving S. Gilmore Music Library, Yale University.

Barz, Gregory F., and Timothy J. Cooley, "Casting Shadows: Fieldwork is Dead! Long Live Fieldwork!" In Barz and Cooley, *Shadows in the Field*, 3–24.

———, eds. *Shadows in the Field: New Perspectives for Fieldwork in Ethnomusicology*. 2nd ed. New York: Oxford University Press, 2008.

Beaudry, Nicole. "The Challenges of Human Relations in Ethnographic Enquiry: Examples from Arctic and Subarctic Fieldwork." In Barz and Cooley, *Shadows in the Field*, 224–45.

Bourdieu, Pierre, and Jean-Claude Passeron. *Reproduction in Education, Society, and Culture*. Translated by Richard Nice. Beverly Hills, Calif.: Sage, 1977.

Bourdieu, Pierre, and Loïc Wacquant. *An Invitation to Reflexive Sociology*. Chicago: University of Chicago Press, 1992.

Broyles, Michael. *"Music of the Highest Class": Elitism and Populism in Antebellum Boston*. New Haven, Conn.: Yale University Press, 1992.

Brubacher, John S., and Willis Rudy. *Higher Education in Transition: A History of American Colleges and Universities, 1736–1976*. 3rd ed. rev. New York: Harper and Row, 1976.

Clifford, James, and George E. Marcus, eds. *Writing Culture: The Poetics and Politics of Ethnography*. Berkley: University of California Press, 1986.

Cooley, Timothy J., Katherine Meizel, and Nasir Syed. "Virtual Fieldwork: Three Case Studies." In Barz and Cooley, *Shadows in the Field*, 90–107.

Cowley, W. H., and Don Williams. *International and Historical Roots of American Higher Education*. New York: Garland, 1991.

Duchan, Joshua S. *Powerful Voices: The Musical and Social World of Collegiate A Cappella*. Ann Arbor: University of Michigan Press, 2012.

Emerson, Robert M., Rachel I. Fretz, and Linda L. Shaw. *Writing Ethnographic Fieldnotes*. Chicago: University of Chicago Press, 1995.

Feld, Steven. "Dialogic Editing: Interpreting How Kaluli Read *Sound and Sentiment*." *Cultural Anthropology* 2, no. 2 (1987): 190–210.

Garnett, Liz. *The British Barbershopper: A Study in Socio-Musical Values*. Burlington, Vt.: Ashgate, 2005.

The History of the University of Michigan Men's Glee Club. http://www.umich.edu/~ummgc. N.p., 2003.

Horner, Bruce. "Critical Ethnography, Ethics, and Work: Rearticulating Labor." *JAC: A Journal of Composition Theory* 22, no. 3 (2002): 561–84.

Horowitz, Helen Lefkowitz. *Campus Life: Undergraduate Cultures from the End of the Eighteenth Century to the Present*. New York: Knopf, 1987.

Karp, David A., Lynda Lytle Holmstrom, and Paul S. Gray. "Leaving Home for College: Expectations for Selective Reconstruction of Self." *Symbolic Interaction* 21, no. 3 (1998): 253–76.

Keil, Charles. *Urban Blues*. Chicago: University of Chicago Press 1966.

Kingsbury, Henry. *Music, Talent, and Performance: A Conservatory Cultural System.* Philadelphia: Temple University Press, 1988.

Kisliuk, Michelle. "(Un)Doing Fieldwork: Sharing Songs, Sharing Lives." In Barz and Cooley, *Shadows in the Field*, 183–205.

Koskoff, Ellen. "Cognitive Strategies in Rehearsal." In *Selected Reports in Ethnomusicology*, 7:59–68. Los Angeles: Department of Ethnomusicology, University of California, Los Angeles, 1988.

Linn, Karen. *That Half-Barbaric Twang: The Banjo in American Popular Culture*. Urbana: University of Illinois Press, 1991.

Lucas, Christopher J. *American Higher Education: A History*. New York: St. Martin's, 1994.

Moffatt, Michael. *Coming of Age in New Jersey: College and American Culture*. New Brunswick, N.J.: Rutgers University Press, 1989.

Montgomery, Bruce. *Brothers, Sing On! My Half-Century around the World with the Penn Glee Club*. Philadelphia: University of Pennsylvania Press, 2005.

Myers, Helen. "Fieldwork." In *Ethnomusicology: An Introduction*, edited by Helen Myers, 21–49. New York: Norton, 1992.

Nettl, Bruno. *The Study of Ethnomusicology: Thirty-One Issues and Concepts*. 2nd ed. Urbana: University of Illinois Press, 2005.

Small, Christopher. *Musicking: The Meanings of Performing and Listening*. Middletown, Conn.: Wesleyan University Press, 1998.

Solís, Ted, ed. *Performing Ethnomusicology: Teaching and Representation in World Music Ensembles*. Berkeley: University of California Press, 2004.

Spalding, Walter Raymond. *Music at Harvard: A Historical Review of Men and Events*. New York: Coward-McCann, 1935.

Stock, Jonathan P. J., and Chou Chiener. "Fieldwork at Home: European and Asian Perspectives." In Barz and Cooley, *Shadows in the Field*, 108–24.

Thelin, John R. *A History of American Higher Education*. Baltimore, Md.: Johns Hopkins University Press, 2004.

Titon, Jeff Todd, ed. *Worlds of Music: An Introduction to the Music of the World's Peoples*. 6th ed. Belmont, Calif.: Cengage, 2017.

University of Michigan 58 Green. Website. "History: Our Roots." http://www.umich.edu/~corundum/History.html.

University of Pennsylvania. The Inspiration (blog). "About Us." (No longer available.)

Van Maanen, John. *Tales of the Field: On Writing Ethnography*. 2nd ed. Chicago: University of Chicago Press, 2011.

Various artists. *Best of College A Cappella 2K*. Varsity Vocals compact disc MAC1801, 2000.

Various artists. *Best of College A Cappella 2003*. Varsity Vocals compact disc VV1807, 2003.

Various artists. *Best of College A Cappella 2005*. Varsity Vocals compact disc 1809, 2005.

Various artists. *Best of College A Cappella 2008*. Varsity Vocals compact disc VV1813, 2008.

Wade, Bonnie. *Thinking Musically: Experiencing Music, Expressing Culture*. 2nd ed. New York: Oxford University Press, 2009.

Weber, William. "Universities." *The New Grove Dictionary of Music and Musicians*. §II.2. http://www.grovemusic.com.

14   Authorship in the Age of Configurable Music

MARK KATZ

Consider two twenty-first-century musicians. Both create music by mixing fragments of preexisting works into sound collages. One, a type of hip-hop DJ known as a turntablist, performs in front of an audience using phonographs as musical instruments. The other, what I will call a mashup artist, uses digital sound files and a personal computer, constructing collages in solitude before distributing them anonymously over the internet. Both create what can be called configurable music, in which electronic technologies are used to fashion works that are recognizable as permutations of "found" sounds and compositions.[1]

Despite their similarities, these two artists have very different views about the authorship of their creations.[2] In general, turntablists strongly assert authorship over their creations, and within turntablist culture this authority is inviolate. By contrast, mashup artists tend to reject the notion that they are authors (or composers) of anything, characterizing their practice as one of arranging, remixing, or juxtaposing. What might account for such radically different attitudes toward authorship, given that both communities of artists create music by manipulating preexisting works? The differences are not strongly tied to musical practice or content. Rather, it is the values, ideals, and histories of the turntablist and mashup communities that shape their notions of authorship. Applying this point more broadly, I argue here that musical authorship is best understood not as an objectively measurable phenomenon but as a cultural construct.

A turntablist is a type of disc jockey, or DJ.[3] Although there are many types of DJs, turntablists are what I call *performative* DJs who treat their equipment as a musical instrument. (The typical turntablist's "instrument" consists of two record players, vinyl records, and an audio mixer that controls the sound of the turntables.) Turntablists, therefore, not only select recordings but also manipulate them in real time for audiences. This manipulation can consist of repeating short passages from a recording (known as looping), mixing fragments of sound from multiple records in counterpoint (called beat juggling), or distorting recorded sounds by pushing a record quickly back and forth underneath the stylus (scratching).

Turntablism traces its history to the birth of hip-hop in 1970s New York. Hip-hop arose when a small group of African American and Latino DJs in the New York borough of the Bronx started playing records at dance parties in an unusual way. Instead of playing whole records, they isolated and repeated brief percussion solos known as breaks. These DJs had noticed that crowds always danced more exuberantly during these breaks, so they sought to cater to the dancers by repeating these short passages. A new, solo form of dancing called b-boying or b-girling—popularly known as breakdancing—arose in response. Hip-hop, therefore, arose out of the DJ's reconfiguration of previously recorded music. In fact, it was only later that rapping (which at first required DJs to provide instrumental accompaniment in the form of looped breaks) came to be common.[4]

Over the course of the 1980s the art of the hip-hop DJ became more complex and virtuosic, and a subset of DJs started describing themselves as *turntablists*. The California-based DJ known as Babu, who is credited with popularizing this term, explained: "You know, we can't even really call ourselves DJs anymore. There's guitarists, there's pianists, why not turntablists?"[5] Turntablists, as Babu suggests, are performers, but they can also be thought of as composers or, more accurately, performer-composers. Although turntablists often improvise, many also create fixed (and almost always un-notated) works that maintain a stable sound and structure over repeated performances. These compositions are called routines and are typically heard in live performance, often in competitions known as battles.

Turntablist routines are usually brief, lasting anywhere from one to ten minutes, and all are created from the manipulation of prerecorded—and usually commercially released—discs. Yet, as I will explain, authorship is almost always unambiguously assigned to the DJ rather than to the composers of the works being manipulated. Consider an example of a highly respected routine. The performer is Rob Swift, and the routine was originally created in 1992 for a battle, though he performed it on many later occasions and released a version of it for the 1995 album *Return of the DJ*.[6] The routine, as mandated by the rules of the battle, is about six minutes long. Swift opens with the beginning of the 1973 song, "Blow Your Head," by Fred Wesley and the J.B.'s, in which he creates a stepwise melody out of a long synthesizer note by making small changes to the speed (and therefore pitch) of the record. He moves quickly to another sample, this time "The Bridge" (1985) by MC Shan and Marley Marl, which itself manipulates the drum break from the Honeydrippers' "Impeach the President" (1973). Swift's choice of "The Bridge" is no accident, for the song celebrates the New York borough of Queens, Swift's birthplace; the video shows Swift nodding vigorously as a voice introduces MC Shan and Marley Marl, intoning, "They want to tell you a little story about where they come from." These two samples constitute only the introductory thirty seconds of the routine. Much of the rest of the routine draws on a single work: Biz Markie's "Nobody Beats the Biz" (1988). ("Nobody Beats the Biz," in turn, samples the keyboard part of "Fly Like an Eagle" [1976] by the Steve Miller Band and the drumbeat of "Hihache," by the Lafayette Afro Rock Band [1973].) Swift isolates just a few notes from "Nobody Beats the Biz," and over the next few minutes he executes a series of variations, reconfiguring the pitch, tempo, rhythm, and timbre of the source material. Nearly four minutes into the routine, Swift switches records again, moving now to Public Enemy's "Welcome to the Terrordome," which itself incorporates a dozen or more samples. Swift juggles the phrase (as spoken by rapper Chuck D), "I got so much trouble on my mind" and a few other fragments, transforming each to the edge of recognizability and back again. To further demonstrate his skill, Swift ends his routine with what are known as body tricks; he spins around while he performs, occasionally stopping and releasing the record with his back before walking offstage to the applause and cheers of the audience.

A scholar might be excused for hearing Rob Swift's routine as a postmodern pastiche and—because of its dense web of allusions, borrowings, and second-order borrowings—deeming it a virtuosic dismantling of the very notion of authorship. In the world of turntablism, however, the authorship of this routine, and of routines in general, is never in question. No insider would describe Swift's routine as an anti-authorial pastiche or as an interpretation or even arrangement of a Biz Markie song, despite the fact that much of the routine is generated from "Nobody Beats the Biz" and that the source material is easily recognized. Turntablists and fans typically refer to this routine as "Rob Swift's Nobody Beats the Biz Routine," and when a version was released on the *Return of the D.J.* CD, it was called "Rob Get's Busy." The *only* name attached to this music is Rob Swift. Swift himself refers to the routine as one of his "turntable compositions."[7] "I definitely consider myself a composer," Swift explained to me. "I just happen to use a non-conventional instrument."[8]

All turntablists start with prerecorded material; that is simply the nature of the art. Thus creativity—and by extension, authorship—is judged not so much by the material that is used but by the originality and skill of the DJ's manipulation of prerecorded sounds. Swift's routine is admired because he mixes the records in ways that most DJs would never have considered. In a short video documentary made after the 1992 battle, Swift makes a telling statement after demonstrating part of the routine. "Another DJ who wasn't pushing himself," he explains, "would have probably just kept backspinning [repeating] this part. He would have ended like that, real normal, you know what I'm saying? But that's not the goal. The goal is to, you know, be as different and creative as possible."[9]

It is this type of novel treatment that has led fans and other turntablists to praise Swift's routine as "genius," a word that comes up multiple times in the viewer comments on YouTube, where this video was posted. But more than generating praise, Swift's creative manipulation of music by Biz Markie, Public Enemy, and others is why the turntablist community considers this routine to be a work by Rob Swift and no one else. Another DJ could well use the same records in a routine, but if the routine were not deemed sufficiently original, the DJ might well be called a "biter." In hip-hop parlance, to bite is to steal, and DJs who bite the work of other DJs are considered beneath contempt.

Battle rules, in fact, often expressly forbid using the same records as another competitor. Consider, for instance, the rules for the 2010 Gong Battle held in New York City:

> 4. BITING, REPEATING ROUTINES AND OUTRIGHT WACKNESS [poor musicianship]: A DJ will be gonged [eliminated] if the judges think that he/she is biting or wack. It's OK to show influence but outright use of the same records and doing the same routine will be grounds for being eliminated by way of the gong.[10]

This sense of authorship, of ownership, is so strong that many turntablists are nervous about recreating another DJ's routine, even if solely for study purposes. DJ X2K, for example, posted a video on his website called "DJ Babu's Blind Alley Juggle Explained." X2K went to great pains to give due credit to Babu and repeatedly insisted that he was in no way trying to bite Babu's routine. As he explained in a text preceding and following the demonstration:

> This video . . . is for education purposes only! Do not try to learn this and perform it or try to claim it as your own!!! Remember BITING IS A CRIME. DISCLAIMER: I hope that should DJ Babu find out about this that he'll see it as a mark of respect rather that an act of theft, and should he request for me to remove this video then I would without question.[11]

There is one exception to the biting rule in battles. A DJ may use sounds or records closely associated with a rival for the purpose of parody or one-upmanship. For example, in a now-legendary 1996 battle between Rob Swift and Mix Master Mike, Mike performed a routine based on the long synthesizer tone that Swift had manipulated in the beginning of his "Nobody Beats the Biz" routine.[12] It was a bold move, and in his reworking of a sound associated with Swift, he was clearly trying to beat Swift at his own game. This act—sometimes known as flipping—only had meaning insofar as listeners recognized the reference to Rob Swift's routine; in other words, insiders recognized that Mix Master

Mike was playing *Swift's* routine. Both biting and flipping, therefore, reinforce the strong sense of authorship in turntablism.

The turntablist view of authorship is much like the Romantic view of authorship. Both value originality, creativity, and a combination of hard work and inspiration; both accord the composer a privileged status, exalting certain among them as geniuses. The turntablist ideal, however, goes further. Authorship in hip-hop turntablism is so valuable that the composer of a routine is deemed to have such control over his or her work that, with rare exceptions, it cannot even be performed by others.

The contrast between turntablists and what I call mashup artists could hardly be starker. In its current and common form, the mashup dates to about 2000, coinciding with the rise of cheap software programs for the manipulation of digital files and the emergence of file-sharing networks (such as Napster) that greatly increased the ease and speed with which recorded music could be acquired and disseminated over the internet.[13] Most mashups are created by digitally combining recognizable elements of two or more commercially recorded pop songs. In its most common form—what is called an A+B mashup—the instrumental part of one song accompanies the vocals of another song. For example, a mashup might consist of the synthesizer line of Eurythmics' "Sweet Dreams (Are Made of This)" (1982) accompanying Eminem's rapid-fire rapping from "Without Me" (2002); or Ben E. King's vocal line from "Stand by Me" floating atop the arpeggiated guitar line from "Every Breath You Take" (1983) by The Police. More complex mashups might combine large sections of three or more songs or fragments of a dozen or more pieces.

Regardless of the number of songs or the extent to which they are reconfigured, however, mashup artists largely eschew authorial credit. The extent to which mashup artists avoid claims of authorship was made clear to me when in 2009 I posted a query on a website where mashup artists share and critique their work.[14] I posed the following question: As someone who creates mashups, do you consider yourself a composer? Nearly all who responded rejected that term. Among the alternate labels were: assembler, audio hacker, bootlegger, burglar, charlatan, manipulator, re-arranger, recomposer, tickler of tunage, and wanker. My favorite was "composter" a rich mashup of the words composer, imposter, and perhaps compost. As some of the more self-deprecating terms suggest, many thought that it would be presumptuous to call themselves composers. One wrote, "I think you would have to be pretty deluded to consider constructing mashups 'composition.'"

What might explain this anti-authorial attitude? For one thing, most mashups are illegal, often violating copyright, so there is good reason for mashup artists to avoid any claim of authorship. One could also point to the practice itself. In mashups the combination of songs is typically intended to sound seamless, drawing little attention to the masher's manipulations or even presence. Mashups thus tend not to proclaim authorial agency. By contrast, in a turntablist routine the hand of the composer is literally meant to be noticed, for the DJ's hands are the center of attention, and the manipulation of prerecorded sound is visible and obvious.

Yet these observations are not sufficient to explain the mashup view of authorship. Given that most mashups are never sold, their creators are rarely sued. Moreover, the seeming erasure of the artist in mashups does not diminish the agency of their creators. The seamlessness of the best mashups is the result of painstaking work selecting, manipulating, and juxtaposing fragments of sound, all of which requires creativity and a keen ear. "The best mashup producers," a practitioner named Adrian told me, "are people who understand songcraft. You need to understand what a verse and a chorus and a bridge are, you need to understand keys. You also have to understand audio engineering to take two or more completely different songs and mash them up into something listenable."[15] Internet forums are devoted to the discussion of the craft of mashing songs, and a specialized jargon has arisen as part of the discourse. Consider, for example, the terms OOT and OOK. These are used when the songs that form a mashup are either out of time (that is, the tempos do not match) or out of key and clash harmonically with each other. These terms further indicate the care with which mashup artists approach their work. Given the attention that many mashup artists devote to their craft, one could plausibly argue that mashups are compositions in their own right and that their creators might justifiably think of themselves as composers. Yet when I posted my query about mashup artists as composers, some of the respondents were clearly offended, responding as if I had been trying to foist an unwanted label on them.

We can now return to the question posed at the beginning of this chapter: how do we explain two such different perspectives on authorship? Answering this question requires a closer look at the histories and values of the turntablist and mashup communities.

When the term *turntablism* came into use in the 1990s, it was not simply a way to identify a particular approach to DJing. The "ism" in *turntablism* is more than a suffix—it is a crucial signifier that lends a sense of seriousness to the art. There is a common perception among outsiders that DJs simply play records, reproducing rather than creating music. Yet turntablists, as they often assert, are musicians, instrumentalists in their own right. In addition to being dismissed by the general public, turntablism has also been marginalized within hip-hop itself. Starting in the 1980s, DJs came to be overshadowed by rappers and excluded from hip-hop recording sessions and concert tours, their analog art replaced by the digital technologies of drum machines, samplers, and the digital audiotape (DAT). The battles and turntablist concerts that flourished in

the 1990s, therefore, created a space in which the art of the DJ was again a fo-
cal point. We can thus understand the emergence of turntablism as a reaction
against this marginalization, an attempt to assert the independence and artistry
of DJs. Furthermore, turntablists often seek legitimacy outside of hip-hop altogether, comparing themselves to jazz musicians and creating DJ academies
that draw upon the model of the university. In this context, it is not difficult to
see why turntablists claim authorship over their routines and why some even
identify themselves as composers. Such moves confer the legitimacy so often
denied them by the public and even by their hip-hop colleagues.[16]

Mashups, by contrast, have never been about legitimacy. Subversiveness has
long been part of the mashup ethos, and many mashup artists take pride in the
fact that they occupy a musical underground. As Adrian explains, "Part of the
mashup mystique is their illegality."[17] More broadly—and of particular relevance
here—the subversiveness of the mashup seems aimed at resisting or denying
authorial intention. Consider the well-known mashup of Nirvana's "Smells Like
Teen Spirit" (1991) with TLC's "Bootylicious" (2001): it seems aimed at mocking
both the nihilistic self-seriousness of the former and the mindless carnality of
the latter. As one scholar suggests, this mashup (but also mashups in general)
"undermines author intent and erases originally coded meanings and readings."[18]

Mashups may be seen as oppositional in another way as well. In the 1990s
the most popular dance music DJs were accorded rock star status, respect,
and fees; the rise of the mashup should be seen in the context of the "DJ God-
star phenomenon," as Simon Reynolds called it.[19] "The emergence of mash-up
culture is," John Shiga writes, "a backlash against the cultural authority of professional DJs."[20] This notion of authority is closely tied to authorship, as these
star DJs came to be presented as the primary or sole creators of the music—all
of it in various ways reconfigurations of previously existing recordings—they
performed in clubs or released on recordings. Referring to the figure of the star
DJ as "a musical author-god," Bill D. Herman argues that "the DJ's authorship
comes not from what he or she does but how these practices get represented in
the capitalist system," and that "the industry instilled the DJ with authorship
to fill a vacuum left by the increasing anonymity of dance music producers."[21]
Put another way, the "musical author-god" was in part a construction intended
to generate revenue from electronic dance music, which was deemed more
marketable if associated with easily identifiable authors. In downplaying their
own authorship, the first generation of mashup artists can be seen as protest-
ing the perceived artificiality of the star DJ and, at the same time, retraining
attention on the music rather than on the DJ or remixer. Avoiding authorship
can thus be motivated by ideology (or perhaps jealousy or resentment).[22] The
larger point, however—and this is true for turntablists and mashup artists—is

that the motivation for embracing or rejecting authorship, whatever it may be, is largely extramusical in nature.

We academics often say that we want to "complicate" an issue. This is not my goal here. I actually have something simple to say. I want to say that authorship is a cultural construct, or more precisely that it is a subcultural construct. In other words, views of authorship are shaped, even generated, by the values of small communities of artists and listeners. To make this point I have focused on two communities that create configurable music. Their technological reconfiguration of recorded music is similar in many ways, and we might well expect turntablists and mashup artists to have a comparable view of authorship. That their attitudes about authorship are so different, I argue, is a function of how these relatively small groups see themselves in relation both to the musical spheres in which they operate (hip-hop, electronic dance music) and in relation to mainstream culture. Turntablists reacted to their marginalization by celebrating virtuosity and authorship; mashup artists, by contrast, essentially marginalized themselves, working in near anonymity and obscurity as a way of celebrating subversiveness and rejecting the figure of the star DJ.

The differences between these two views of authorship raise two broader points with which I will conclude. Many scholars proclaim a strong exceptionalism for the products and practices of those who create configurable art. For example, in his 2010 book *Mashed Up*, Aram Sinnreich plainly asserts, "I must disagree with any claims of continuity between past and current practices."[23] And in *Bytes and Backbeats* (2011) Steve Savage claims that "music making in the digital environment represents not just a change in degree, but a fundamental change in 'kind'—a change that strikes at the very heart of music creation."[24] I must disagree with both Savage and Sinnreich, however, for I see a great deal of continuity, past and present. Turntablists can be understood as a modern instantiation of the virtuosic composer-performer of the nineteenth-century; they can also be compared to the figure of the bebop musician, an independent-minded artist on the margins of the broader jazz community. By contrast, the music of mashup artists seems to demonstrate a family resemblance to the postmodernism of twentieth-century works by Andy Warhol, George Crumb, or Luciano Berio. We might even study mashups alongside the works of Charles Ives or the parody masses of the sixteenth century. My point is not that turntablist routines or mashups grew out of these older practices, but that they raise similar questions about authorship and that their comparative study would be mutually illuminating. Broadly speaking, I have to agree with Henry Jenkins, who offers a valuable perspective that accounts for both the novelty of digital remix practices and their little-acknowledged historical precedents. "The digital era," he points out, "has refocused our attention on the expressive potential of borrowing and remixing, expanding who gets to be an author and what counts as authorship." Yet, as he explains, "this new model of authorship is not that radical when read against a larger backdrop of human history, though it flies in the face of some of the most persistent myths about creative genius and intellectual property that have held sway since the Romantic era."[25] In other words, if we understand the Romantic notion of the author as a historical anomaly rather than as the norm, we can see both the mashup artist and the turntablist as continuing ancient traditions of borrowing from and reconfiguring existing works in the creation of new ones. Or, to borrow from the language of theology, authorship itself is best understood not as *creatio ex nihilo* but as *creatio ex materia*.[26]

My second point is that scholars have much to gain by taking an ethnographic approach to the study of authorship. It is certainly important to understand musical processes, practices, and forms when investigating issues of authorship. I would suggest, however, that studying "the music itself"—to the extent that this is a meaningful phrase—cannot tell us everything that is important about the authorship of the music. To put this more boldly, I do not believe that there can be a purely objective measure of authorship. If we study musical practices without regard to the communities in which they arose, we risk misunderstanding them, offering distorted views, or imposing foreign values. I once felt the need to describe mashup artists as composers. I believed they deserved greater respect, so I bestowed an unwanted title upon these self-identified assemblers, bootleggers, and composters. But after seeking their opinions on the matter, I realized that I was doing them no favors and had even offended some with my presumption. I came away from the experience with a deeper understanding of this music and a newfound respect for the agency of the artists. My interactions with turntablists have been just as enlightening. Had I simply studied turntablist performances, I might have interpreted their radical reconfiguration of other composers' works as a violent rejection of traditional notions of authorship. Yet, as I discovered in talking with the artists, this could hardly be further from the truth. The lesson here is simple: we can learn so much more when we listen to what musicians are saying and not simply to what they are playing.[27]

Notes

The publisher gratefully acknowledges the Paul Sacher Stiftung for permission to publish the English language version of this chapter, which first appeared in German in the 2017 volume *Wesier Klänge? Über Autoschaft in neue Musik*, edited by Hermann Danuser and Matthias Kassel.

1. I take the term *configurable music* from Sinnreich, *Mashed Up*.

2. By *authorship* I mean the source or origin of an artistic work and the identification of (in most cases) a single individual as the creator of that work. In this chapter I use the term *composer* to signify a type of author.

3. What follows is a brief overview of turntablism. I explore turntablism in greater length in *Groove Music*.

4. Although the term *hip-hop* is often used synonymously with *rap*, hip-hop is best understood as the broader culture in which the practices of DJing, rapping (also known as MCing), b-boying and b-girling, and graffiti art arose. These artistic practices are typically referred to as the four "elements" of hip-hop. For an excellent history of hip-hop see Chang, *Can't Stop*.

5. DJ Babu, qtd. in Chonin, "An Itch to Scratch," 60.

6. "Rob Swift DMC 1992." The CD version was released as "Rob Get's Busy," on *Return of the D.J. Vol. 1*, Bomb Hip-Hop compact disc BOMB 2002 (1995).

7. Swift, "X-Ecutioner Style."

8. Rob Swift, e-mail message to the author, November 28, 2011.

9. "DJ Rob Swift—The Biz Routine," http://www.youtube.com/watch?v=kd7Zp YnC1Cs.

10. "Gong DJ Battle."

11. "DJ Babu's."

12. This routine can be seen on the Rob Swift documentary film *As the Tables Turn*, Red Line Music DVD, no label number, 2007.

13. I explore mashups in more depth in *Capturing Sound*, 165–74. For more on mashups, see also Sinnreich, *Mashed Up*.

14. This discussion was initiated on May 24, 2009. All quotations from this discussion were originally from http://www.gybo5.com/index.php?option=com_kunena &Itemid=3&func=view&catid=17&id=55675. This link is no longer active.

15. DJ Adrian, interview with the author, San Francisco, California, November 1, 2006.

16. For more on the issue of legitimacy in the turntablist world, see Katz, *Groove Music*, chap. 7.

17. DJ Adrian, interview with the author.

18. Serazio, "Apolitical Irony," 83.

19. Simon Reynolds, qtd. in Shiga, "Copy-and-Persist," 104. Note that this term refers to a subset of dance music DJs and not to the turntablists discussed in these pages.

20. Shiga, "Copy-and-Persist," 104.

21. Herman, "Scratching Out Authorship: Representations of the Electronic Music DJ at the Turn of the 21st Century," *Popular Communication* 4 (2006): 21.

22. To say this does not mean that all mashup artists are so motivated. Moreover, the oppositional nature of mashups was likely more pronounced in the early years of the practice. A decade on, the practice has developed a community and set of distinctive practices around it and may no longer be characterized as strongly oppositional.

23. Sinnreich, *Mashed Up*, 74.

24. Savage, *Bytes and Backbeats*, 9. I should point out that, despite my disagreement with their claims of digital exceptionalism, I find both books by Sinnreich and Savage compelling and useful.

25. Jenkins, "Multiculturalism," 109.

26. As many scholars have pointed out, the meaning of the word *author* has changed over time, and they have noted that its root initially suggested augmentation rather

than creation. See, for example, Donovan, Fjellestad, and Lundén, *Authority Matters*, 1–19.

27. I am certainly not the first scholar to emphasize the importance of drawing on insider perspectives in the study of performance and compositional practices. Ingrid Monson has made this point even more strongly, arguing that "the only ethical point of departure for work in jazz studies and ethnomusicology remains the documentation and interpretation of vernacular perspectives." Monson, *Saying Something*, 6. For exemplars of this approach to "vernacular perspectives" in popular music, I would also point to Berliner, *Thinking in Jazz*, and Schloss, *Making Beats*.

References

As the Tables Turn. DVD. Red Line Music, no label number, 2007.

Berliner, Paul. *Thinking in Jazz: The Infinite Art of Improvisation*. Chicago: University of Chicago Press, 1994.

Chang, Jeff. *Can't Stop, Won't Stop: A History of the Hip-Hop Generation*. New York: Picador, 2005.

Chonin, Neva. "An Itch to Scratch: The New School Turntablists." *Option* 77 (November–December 1997): 56–61.

"DJ Babu's Blind Alley Juggle Explained." http://www.youtube.com/watch?v=9kGie T8UQ-8.

DJ Quest. Telephone interview with the author, August 10, 2010.

Donovan, Stephen, Danuta Fjellestad, and Rolf Lundén, eds. *Authority Matters: Rethinking the Theory and Practice of Authorship*. Amsterdam: Rodopi, 2008.

"Gong DJ Battle Info and Rules." http://www.myspace.com/thegongdjbattle/blog/242145843.

Herman, Bill D. "Scratching Out Authorship: Representations of the Electronic Music DJ at the Turn of the 21st Century." *Popular Communication* 4 (2006): 21–38.

Jaszi, Peter. "Toward a Theory of Copyright: The Metamorphoses of 'Authorship.'" *Duke Law Journal* 1991 (April 1991): 455–502.

Jenkins, Henry. "Multiculturalism, Appropriation, and the New Media Literacies: Remixing Moby Dick." In *Mashup Cultures*, ed. Stefan Sonvilla-Weiss, 98–119. Vienna: Springer, 2010.

Katz, Mark. *Capturing Sound: How Technology Has Changed Music*. Rev. ed. Berkeley: University of California Press, 2010.

———. *Groove Music: The Art and Culture of the Hip-Hop DJ*. New York: Oxford University Press, 2012.

Monson, Ingrid. *Saying Something: Jazz Improvisation and Interaction*. Chicago: University of Chicago Press, 1996.

Return of the D.J. Vol. 1. Bomb Hip-Hop compact disc BOMB 2002 (1995).

"Rob Swift DMC 1992." http://www.youtube.com/watch?v=GGT-r8qrjOw.

Savage, Steve. *Bytes and Backbeats: Repurposing Music in the Digital Age*. Ann Arbor: University of Michigan Press, 2011.

Schloss, Joseph G. *Making Beats: The Art of Sample-Based Hip-Hop.* Middletown, Conn.: Wesleyan University Press, 2004.

Serazio, Michael. "The Apolitical Irony of Generation Mash-Up: A Cultural Case Study in Popular Music," *Popular Music and Society* 31 (February 2008): 79–94.

Shiga, John. "Copy-and-Persist: The Logic of Mash-Up Culture." *Critical Studies in Media Communication* 24 (June 2007): 93–114.

Sinnreich, Aram. *Mashed Up: Music, Technology and the Rise of Configurable Culture.* Amherst: University of Massachusetts Press, 2010.

Swift, Rob. "X-Ecutioner Style," October 14, 2011. http://www.djrobswift.com/2011/10/14/x-ecutioner-style.

15 Mark Tucker, Thelonious Monk, and "Misterioso"

INTRODUCTION BY JEFFREY TAYLOR

TRANSCRIPTION BY MARK TUCKER

On April 18, 2000, as part of the spring lecture series by Columbia University's Center for Jazz Studies, jazz historian and musicologist Mark Tucker delivered a talk titled "Monk's Technique." The event, which took place less than eight months before Tucker's untimely passing at age forty-six, is still discussed with awe by those in attendance. At the time, Tucker was at work on a book about Thelonious Monk, and his talk provided a tantalizing glimpse at a major work of scholarship that, sadly, was never to be completed.[1]

A master teacher as well as scholar, Tucker began his remarks by sharing his difficulties in introducing Monk to a college class, a challenge familiar to most professors who teach jazz history courses:

> For all the years I've taught a college-level jazz history course I'm still not sure how best to prepare my students for an encounter with Thelonious Monk. Not that they actively resist or dislike his music (those reactions come when they hear Ornette Coleman's *Free Jazz* for the first time). Rather, they just don't know what to make of Monk. He's like no other character they meet during the semester: watching him perform on film as he wears his unusual hats, spins in circles, and attacks the piano with right hooks and jabs, they are baffled, amused, and intrigued.
>
> Some students have trouble with Monk's harsh-sounding intervals and chords. When I point out that he derived much of his dissonant vocabulary from the blues—translating its slides, smears, and wails to a percussive instrument of hammers and strings—I sense they don't fully buy it. By this point in the course they know something about instrumental blues and they've heard Bessie Smith, Robert Johnson, and Billie Holiday; getting from this expressive territory to the land of Monk, though, requires not just listening experience but a long jump of the imagination.[2]

Moving beyond his own classroom experience, Tucker acknowledged the wide range of reactions to Monk from both jazz enthusiasts and proponents of Western art music—from outright hostility to bewilderment and fascination. However, his main goal was to "put aside the critical debate and focus on the specific methods Monk used to construct his sonic universe."[3] Tucker explored this unique soundscape with a deft combination of prose, film clips, pointed listening to recorded examples, reference to transcriptions, and elegant demonstrations at the piano. In this way, he showed Monk's distinctive physical presence at the piano: Monk performs with arms angled down toward the keyboard; he uses a hammering, percussive technique and a vertical drop (and release) in his attack of keys; his fingers are not curved and in close position (as in traditional piano technique) but flat and splayed; and he throws his entire body into playing, using not just arm weight but his back and shoulders as well. With regard to this last point, he recalls the many stories of Monk dancing around the piano when particularly moved by the performance and maintains this occurred at the keyboard as well: "There's also a strong element of dance when Monk was playing—from his right foot swinging back and forth in time, to his arms working in varied rhythmic patterns, outlining shapes in space, to the involvement of his upper body in the performance, turning side to side, angling elbows, sometimes using his right elbow on the keys. There's something almost stylized about it that reminds me of martial arts, or a synthesis of dance and fighting, like Brazilian capoeira."[4]

After discussing specific gestures associated with Monk—a fondness for seconds, the use of hand crossing, and so on—Tucker turned to what he considered the most important, and most elusive, element of Monk's style: his sound. As he put it, "One thing that registers immediately when we listen to a Monk recording is that he was fascinated, even obsessed by 'sound' as an expressive element of music."[5] Using Monk's 1964 solo performance of "I Should Care," Tucker encouraged the audience to "note especially the way each sound event is carefully sculpted—treated with different weight, intensity, dynamic control, pedaling, and so on. The slow, rubato tempo allows Monk to make the most of each gesture and moment."[6] Then, after playing the recording in its entirety, he closed by maintaining that "Monk's technique can set a[n] . . . example for aspiring musicians and our students, reminding them that no school or method or teacher can supply the stubborn and audacious self-confidence required of all artists seeking to liberate the imagination."[7]

Tucker's 2000 talk showed not only a deeply engaged and thoughtful researcher and scholar but also a consummate musician with remarkably perceptive ears. These traits shine through in his complete transcription of "Misterioso," which Monk recorded on July 2, 1948, with vibraphonist Milt Jackson, bassist John Simmons, and drummer Rossiere "Shadow" Wilson.[8] As anyone who has tried it knows all too well that transcription is not only a slow and arduous process but one that raises ideological issues. As I myself wrote some years ago in an edition of transcriptions of piano solos by Earl Hines:

> To commit improvised music to paper . . . raises complex ideological questions. Over the past twenty years the issues surrounding transcription have been widely discussed among musicians and scholars. Perhaps composer and popular music scholar Peter Winkler has addressed the topic most provocatively in "Writing Ghost Notes: The Poetics and Politics of Transcription." [In David Schwarz, Anahid Kassabian, and Lawrence Siegel, eds., *Keeping Score: Music, Disciplinarity, Culture* (Charlottesville: University Press of Virginia, 1997)]. Beyond the valid criticism that Western music notation can never adequately represent the rhythmic and timbral subtleties of jazz, Winkler brings in troubling issues of appropriation and ownership. Scholars, as he sees it, seek both to legitimize an improvised music by adapting it to Eurocentric concepts of a musical score and to maintain control over a recorded event by capturing it on the page.
>
> Winkler argues that the primary benefits of transcription are for the transcriber: it is the "process" rather than the "product" that holds the greatest rewards, for there is no better way to enter a musician's inner world. But if transcription allows one to engage deeply with the creative process of an artistic genius, then the finished score seeks to capture—at least to some extent—the essence of that experience. To borrow Winkler's insightful simile, a transcription then becomes something like a "translation" of a recording; it conveys a personal conception of the original, shaped by the scholar's background, training, taste, and artistic experience. A parallel might be the many translations of the Koran. None would claim to substitute for the highly referential, intricately layered complexity of the original Arabic, but each seeks to capture and to honor the source's animating spirit.[9]

I believe this document can be best appreciated this way: as a guide to the performance, used with the actual recording never far from reach. The harmonic and rhythmic eccentricities of Monk's idiom (along with Jackson's complex improvised lines) can be closely studied, as can the interactions between all four musicians. Yet, what is perhaps most significant about Monk—his sound—can be grasped only by listening. It is an essential shortcoming of transcription that Tucker undoubtedly fully understood.

"Misterioso" was Monk's first blues recording, and though it did not fare well with critics after its 1949 release (Mike Levin of *Down Beat* cited the record as proof of the pianist's "technical inadequacies"[10]), it has become an iconic performance, included in *The Smithsonian Collection of Classic Jazz* (both the original and revised editions) as well as 2010's *Jazz: The Smithsonian Anthology*. Monk's melody—what seems like an intentionally stilted study in parallel sixths—gives way to powerful, blues-infused solos by Jackson and Monk. And as Robin Kelley has observed, the inclusion of Simmons and Wilson—both non-beboppers firmly entrenched in the Swing tradition—results in a performance that integrated modern jazz language with a rhythm that "begins like a slow-moving locomotive, but, once we are past the melody . . . takes off and swings so hard you might forget your destination."[11] Hearing this recording, following along with the score, and perhaps visualizing Monk's idiosyncratic technique and keyboard "dance" deeply immerses the listener in Monk's vivid musical imagination.

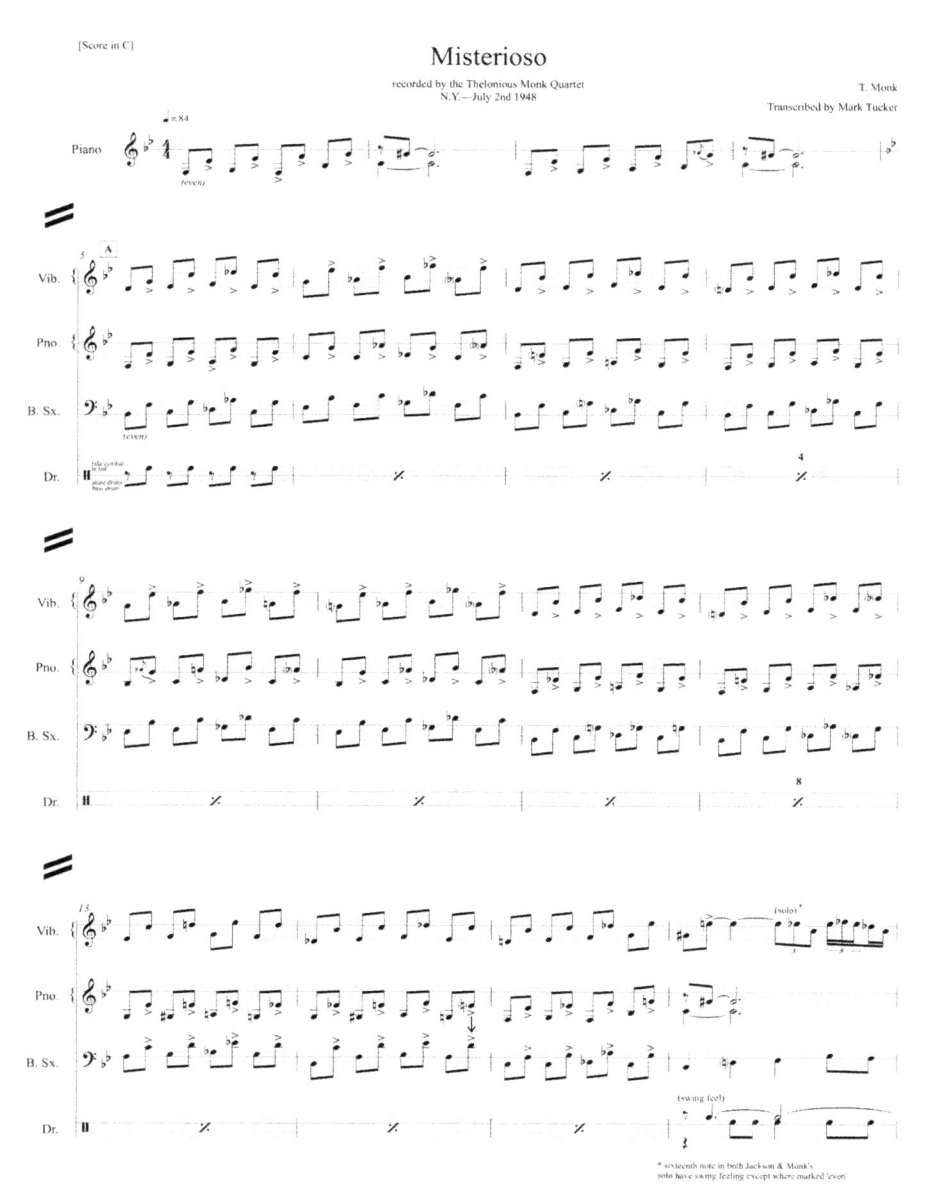

Transcription of Thelonious Monk's "Misterioso"

Transcription of Thelonious Monk's "Misterioso" (continued)

Transcription of Thelonious Monk's "Misterioso" (continued)

Transcription of Thelonious Monk's "Misterioso" (continued)

Transcription of Thelonious Monk's "Misterioso" (continued)

Notes

1. My thanks to Carol J. Oja for making available the script of Tucker's paper, as well as a manuscript version of the transcription included here.

2. Tucker, "Monk's Technique."

3. Ibid.

4. Ibid.

5. Ibid.

6. Ibid.

7. Ibid.

8. Though undocumented, Tucker's transcription was likely part of a plan by Martin Williams, editor of *The Smithsonian Collection of Classic Jazz*, to produce a volume of transcriptions to accompany the recording set. The volume was never completed.

9. Taylor, *Earl "Fatha" Hines.*

10. Qtd. by Robin D. G. Kelley, booklet for *Jazz: The Smithsonian Anthology* (Smithsonian Folkways Recordings SFW CD 40820, 2010), 87.

11. Kelley, *Jazz: The Smithsonian Anthology,* 87.

References

Kelley, Robin D. G., annotator. *Jazz: The Smithsonian Anthology*. Smithsonian Folkways Recordings. Washington, DC: Smithsonian Institution, 2010.

Schwarz, David, Anahid Kassabian, and Lawrence Siegel, eds. *Keeping Score: Music, Disciplinarity, Culture*. Charlottesville: University Press of Virginia, 1997.

Taylor, Jeffrey, ed. *Earl "Fatha" Hines: Selected Piano Solos, 1928–41*. Middleton, Wisc.: A-R, 2006.

Tucker, Mark. "Monk's Technique." Paper presented at Columbia University, April 18, 2000.

Williams, Martin, annotator. *The Smithsonian Collection of Classic Jazz*. 2nd rev. ed. Washington, DC: Smithsonian Institution, 1987.

Contributors

KAREN AHLQUIST is associate professor emerita of music at The George Washington University. She writes on European musical traditions and institutions in nineteenth-century United States, music and immigration, musicians' education, music in cities, and music historiography. She is author of *Democracy at the Opera: Music, Theater, and Culture in New York City, 1815–1860* (University of Illinois Press, 1997), and author-editor of *Chorus and Community* (University of Illinois Press, 2006). She was a founding editor of *Women and Music* and has curated prizewinning articles as editor of the *Journal of the Society of American Music*. Her scholarship has been supported and/or honored by George Washington, the University of Michigan, National Endowment for the Humanities, German Academic Exchange Service, and Choice.

AMY C. BEAL is professor of music at the University of California, Santa Cruz. She is the author of *New Music, New Allies: American Experimental Music in West Germany from the Zero Hour to Reeducation* (University of California Press, 2006), and *Carla Bley* (2011) and *Johanna Beyer* (2016), both at the University of Illinois Press, as well as many articles and book contributions on the history of twentieth-century American music. She remains active as a performer of classical, contemporary, and improvised music.

TARA BROWNER is professor of ethnomusicology at the University of California, Los Angeles. She is the author of *Heartbeat of the People: Music and Dance of the Northern Pow-Wow* (University of Illinois Press, 2002), editor of *Music of the First Nations: Tradition and Innovation in Native North American Music* (University of Illinois Press, 2009), and editor of *Songs from "A New Circle of Voices": The Sixteenth Annual Pow-wow at UCLA* (MUSA, 2009), and has published in several major journals, including *Ethnomusicology*, *The Journal of Musicological Research*, and *American Music*.

MARK CLAGUE served as the executive editor of the Music in the United States of America (MUSA) critical edition series under Richard Crawford from 1997 to 2003, when he joined the musicology faculty at the University of Michigan School of Music, Theatre and Dance. Now associate dean of student and academic affairs, his research addresses African American composers, arts business, historiography, urban soundscapes, orchestras, *Sacred Harp*, and "The Star-Spangled Banner." He serves as editor-in-chief of the George and Ira Gershwin Critical Edition, for which he edited *An American in Paris*, and as editor-in-chief of MUSA.

ESTHER R. CROOKSHANK has served on the Southern Baptist Theological Seminary faculty since 1994 and as Ollie Hale Chiles Professor of Church Music since 2004, teaching hymnology, musicology, applied ethnomusicology, and musical aesthetics. Since 2009 she has served as director of the Academy of Sacred Music, the seminary's guest artist and lecture forum. She has published articles and essays in *Grove Dictionary of American Music*, 2nd ed. (Oxford, 2013); *Canterbury Dictionary of Hymnology Online* (2013); *Die Religion in Geschichte und Gegenwart* (1998); *Wonderful Words of Life: Hymns in American Protestant History and Theology* (2004); and *Minds and Hearts in Praise of God: Hymns and Essays in Church Music in Honor of Hugh T. McElrath* (2006).

TODD DECKER is professor and chair of the Department of Music at Washington University in St. Louis and author of *Music Makes Me: Fred Astaire and Jazz* (University of California Press, 2011), *Show Boat: Race and the Making and Remaking of an American Musical* (Oxford University Press, 2013), *Who Should Sing "Ol' Man River"?* (Oxford University Press, 2015), and *Hymns for the Fallen* (University of California Press, 2017).

JENNIFER DeLAPP-BIRKETT is an independent scholar living in Ithaca, New York. She is presently a consulting musicologist for the Aaron Copland Fund for Music. Her publications include the "Shaker Music" entry for the *Grove Dictionary of American Music*, 2nd ed., and a 2008 article on Aaron Copland and Cold War politics for the *Journal of Musicological Research*. Her long-standing pedagogical interests were developed while earning her PhD at the University of Michigan and put into practice over almost nine years as a full-time university professor. For many years she taught Introduction to Music Research to first-year graduate students at the University of Maryland, where she also advised theses and dissertations.

JOSHUA S. DUCHAN is associate professor of music and director of graduate studies in the Department of Music at Wayne State University, where he teaches courses in music history and world music. His research focuses on American popular music, particularly the music and practice of collegiate a cappella groups. He has authored two books, *Powerful Voices: The Musical and Social World of Collegiate A Cappella* (University of Michigan Press, 2012), and *Billy Joel: America's Piano Man* (Rowman and Littlefield, 2017), as well as essays in *American Music, American Music Research Center Journal, Cambridge Companion to the Singer-Songwriter*, and several other journals.

MARK KATZ is Ruel W. Tyson Jr. Distinguished Professor of Humanities at the University of North Carolina, Chapel Hill. His research and teaching focus on music and technology, popular music, and performance practice. He has written three books, *Groove Music: The Art and Culture of the Hip Hop DJ* (Oxford University Press, 2012), *Capturing Sound: How Technology Has Changed Music* (University of California Press, 2004, rev. ed. 2010), and *The Violin: A Research and Information Guide* (Routledge, 2006). He is editor (with Timothy Taylor and Anthony Grajeda) of *Music, Sound, and Technology in America: A Documentary History of Early Phonograph, Cinema, and Radio* (Duke University Press, 2012).

JEFFREY MAGEE is professor and Director of the School of Music at the University of Illinois. He is the author of *The Uncrowned King of Swing: Fletcher Henderson and Big Band Jazz* (New York: Oxford University Press, 2005); and his book *Irving Berlin's American Musical Theater* (New York: Oxford University Press, 2012) was supported as a We the People Project of the National Endowment for the Humanities and was runner-up for the Lowens Award. His book-in-progress, Gypsy *and the American Dream*, is under contract with Oxford University Press. He has published articles in the *Journal of the American Musicological Society, American Music, Black Music Research Journal, Current Musicology, Studies in Musical Theatre*, and *Musical Quarterly*.

STERLING E. MURRAY retired in 2007 as professor of music history from the faculty of the School of Music at West Chester University in West Chester, Pennsylvania. He taught there for thirty-five years and served as interim dean and chair of the Music History Department. His research has concentrated on the instrumental music of the late eighteenth century on both sides of the Atlantic. He is the author of *The Music of Antonio Rosetti, ca. 1750–1792: A Thematic Catalog* (Harmonie Park Press, 1976) and *The Career of an Eighteenth-Century Kapellmeister: The Life and Music of Antonio Rosetti* (University of Rochester Press, 2014). He is the founding president of the Society for Eighteenth-Century Music, and currently is involved in a study of music and theater in Philadelphia during the early years of the Republic.

GUTHRIE P. RAMSEY JR. is the Edmund J. and Louise W. Kahn Term Professor of Music at the University of Pennsylvania. A widely published author, pianist, and composer, he is the author of *Race Music: Black Cultures from Bebop to Hip-Hop* (University of California Press, 2003), *The Amazing Bud Powell:*

Black Genius, Jazz History and the Challenge of Bebop (University of California Press, 2013), and *American Music: Grove Music Essentials*. His documentary film *Amazing: The Tests and Triumphs of Bud Powell* was a selection at the BlackStar Film Festival in 2015.

THOMAS L. RIIS is the Joseph Negler professor of music emeritus and director of the American Music Research Center at the University of Colorado, Boulder (1992–2018). His book *Just Before Jazz* (Smithsonian Institution Press, 1989, 1995) received an ASCAP-Deems Taylor Award. He is the author of *Frank Loesser* (2008), published by the Yale University Press in its Broadway Masters series. He has been a Fulbright Senior Scholar at the University of Lueneburg, now Leuphana University, Germany, and was president of the Society for American Music (2009–11).

DAVID WARREN STEEL is professor emeritus of music and Southern culture at the University of Mississippi and has been singing in the *Sacred Harp* since 1972. A graduate of Harvard College and the University of Michigan, he published the collected works of early American composers Stephen Jenks and Daniel Belknap. He provided liner notes for several recordings of Sacred Harp music; his book *The Makers of the Sacred Harp* (with Richard H. Hulan) was published in 2010 by the University of Illinois Press. He has taught at Camp Fasola, a residential singing school, and appears in the documentary film *Awake My Soul*.

JEFFREY TAYLOR is professor of music and director of the H. Wiley Hitchcock Institute for Studies in American Music at Brooklyn College. He serves on the faculty of the CUNY Graduate Center. His scholarly work has focused primarily on pre-1940s jazz, the work of early jazz pianists Jelly Roll Morton, Fats Waller, and James P. Johnson. His writing has appeared in *Musical Quarterly*, *Black Music Research Journal*, *American Music*, and *American Music Review*. His volume in the MUSA (Music of the United States) series, *Earl "Fatha" Hines: Collected Piano Solos, 1928–41*, won the Claude Palisca Award from the American Musicological Society in 2007.

MARK TUCKER (1954–2000), a professor at Columbia University from 1987 to 1997 and the College of William and Mary until 2000, was a master teacher, scholar, and performer of classic jazz. Besides his books on Duke Ellington (*Ellington: The Early Years* [University of Illinois Press, 1991] and *The Duke Ellington Reader* [Oxford University Press, 1993]), Tucker contributed critiques and articles to the *New York Times*, *Black Music Research Journal*, *American Music*, and the *New Grove Dictionary of Music and Musicians*. As a pianist, he played programs at the Kennedy Center for the Performing Arts and the Smithsonian Institution, and as a soloist with the Chicago Jazz Ensemble. A book focusing on the music of Thelonious Monk was in progress at the time of his death.

Index

Melford, Myra, 139
memorization of hymns by children, 116–17
Mendelssohn, Felix, 24–25, 232
Merriam, Alan, 295
Messenger, The (journal), 222
Metropolitan Opera (New York), 15, 20, 222
Michigan, University of, 298, 301, 302
middle class values, 13–14, 22–23, 25, 27n21, 35, 44, 116
Midwest (American) in late 19th century, 201, 207–8, 209, 217n22, 217n26
Mielziner, Jo, 236
Miller and Lyles (black act), 223
Mingus, Charles, 140
minstrelsy, blackface: 19th century attitudes on, 186; "authentic," 204–5, 209, 210, 215; consequences of 21st century attitudes on, 183, 200–201, 211–12, 215–16; descriptions of, 203, 206–7; as opportunity for African Americans in 19th century, 183, 186, 203–5, 206–7, 209, 210, 211; origins of, 4, 58, 203; popularity of, 186, 203–4; stereotypes in, 39, 44, 203, 230
Mirageas, Evans, 168
Miseducation of Lauren Hill, The (Hill), 132–33
Missouri Harmony (patent-note collection), 54, 59
"Misterioso" (Monk), 281, 325–27, *327–31,* 331n8
Mitchell, Abbie, 209
Mitchell, Roscoe, 139
Mix Master Mike, 315–16, 321n12
"Moanin' Low" (Dietz/Rainger), 236–37, 238, 240
Moiret and Fredi, *227,* 231
Monahan, Gordon, 148
Monarchs of Minstrelsy (Rice), 210
Monk, Meredith, 149
Monk, Thelonious, 281, 324–32; dancing of, 325, 327; listener reactions to, 324–25; techniques and sound of, 325; and Tucker's transcription of "Misterioso," 281, 325–27, *327–31,* 331n8
Moody, Dwight L., 120–21
morality in shape-note music, 53, 55, 56–57, 57–58
Morgan, Helen, *227,* 230, 234, 239–40, 242
Morgan, Lewis Henry, 286
Morrison, Toni, 194

"Mount Zion" (Brown), *121,* 127–28
"Moving Mosaic or N.A.A.C.P. Dance, 1929" (Imes), 238
Mozart, Wolfgang Amadeus, 158
Mumma, Gordon, 147, 148
Mungo (ballad opera character), 201–2
Murphy, Joseph M., 191
Murray, Albert, 201
Murray, Sterling, 71–72, 77–102
Music, David, 109, 111, 112, 114, 129
Musical Primer and Juvenile Instructor (pamphlet), 58–59, 66–67
Musical Quarterly, The, 288
musical theater. *See* Broadway musicals; cozy-cottage trope in musical theater; *Love in a Village* (Arne/Bickerstaff)
music as art and social hierarchy in late 19th century, 5, 7–33; in audience behavior and experience, 18–21; contemporary directions for research on, 25–26; elite control and, 7–8, 11–14, 15, 17–18, 20–21, 25, 26, 28n45, 211; in events and performance spaces, 15–17; German influence on, 14–15; in highbrow/lowbrow division, 5, 7–9, 12; philanthropic and progressive support for, 21–23; in theoretical discussions, 8, 9–14, 24–25
Music Box Theatre (Broadway), 236
Music in America (Ritter), 159–60
Music Study in Germany (Fay), 16
Mycall, John, 110
Myers, Helen, 295, 305
"My heart's my own" (Arne), *90,* 93
My Own Song Book (songster), 57–58, 66

NAACP (National Association for the Advancement of Colored People): origins and goals of, 222, 225, 242, 243n6; White's leadership of, 221, 222, 235, 239, 242–43; Women's Auxiliary of, 225, 234, 243
NAACP benefit concert (1929), 183, 221–46; audience for, 223–24, 225, 231, 238–39, 241–43; audience reaction to, 234–35, 237, 240, 243; closing acts of, 240–41; controversial programming in, 233–35; earnings from, 226, 241, 242; as "Follies," 232; initial planning of, 222–23; as interracial model, 223, 226, 231, 233, 242; master of ceremonies for, 228–30; opening acts of, 230–32; overview of performers, 223, *227,* 242; press coverage of, 225–26, 239; ques-

Music in American Life

The University of Illinois Press
is a founding member of the
Association of University Presses.

_____

University of Illinois Press
1325 South Oak Street
Champaign, IL 61820-6903
www.press.uillinois.edu

Printed by Printforce, United Kingdom